Popular Culture:
Past and Present

Edited by Bernard Waites,
Tony Bennett and Graham Martin

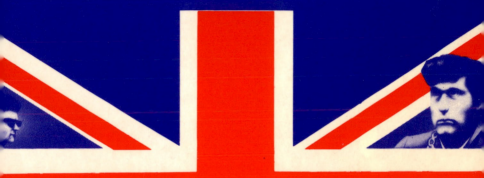

OPEN UNIVERSITY
SET BOOK

The Open University Press

Popular Culture: Past and Present

A Reader Edited by
BERNARD WAITES, TONY BENNETT AND
GRAHAM MARTIN
at the Open University

ROUTLEDGE
London and New York
in association with
THE OPEN UNIVERSITY PRESS

First published 1982
by Croom Helm Ltd

Reprinted 1983 and 1986

Selection and editorial material copyright © The Open University 1982

Reprinted 1989, 1993
by Routledge
11 New Fetter Lane, London EC4P 4EE
29 West 35th Street, New York, NY 10001

This reader is one part of an Open University Integrated teaching system and the selection is therefore related to other material available to students. It is designed to evoke the critical understanding of students. Opinions expressed in it are not necessarily those of the course team or of the University.

Printed and bound in Great Britain by
Biddles Ltd, Guildford and King's Lynn

British Library Cataloguing in Publication Data

Popular culture.
  1. Culture
  I. Waites, Bernard   II. Bennett, Tony
  III. Martin, Graham, 1927–
  306   HM101

  ISBN 0–415–04033–7

CONTENTS

Acknowledgements

Course Team List

Preface

Part One

Part Two

ACKNOWLEDGEMENTS

This book is largely the result of the collective effort of a number of people involved in preparing the Open University course *Popular Culture*. The editors would therefore like to thank all members of the course team for the part they played in the discussions which gave birth to the shape of this Reader. In particular, our thanks to John Golby, Bill Purdue, James Donald, Tony Aldgate, John Muncie and Ruth Finnegan for their help both in suggesting articles for inclusion in the Reader and indicating how best they might be edited. Thanks also to Jane Bailey, whose assistance in co-ordinating the activities of the editors has been invaluable, and to Deirdre Smith — a secretary valued as much for her unfailing good humour as for her remarkable efficiency. We are also indebted to John Taylor of the Publishing Division at the Open University for the assistance he has rendered the course team in all stages of the production of this Reader. Finally, we are grateful to all of the contributors to this volume for allowing us to publish their work in an abbreviated form.

THE COURSE TEAM

Authors

Tony Bennett, Course Team
  Chairman
Tony Aldgate
Geoffrey Bourne
David Cardiff
Alan Clark
Noel Coley
James Donald
Dave Elliott
Ruth Finnegan
Francis Frascina
John Golby
Stuart Hall
Graham Martin

Colin Mercer
Richard Middleton
Dave Morley
John Muncie
Gill Perry
Bill Purdue
Carrie Roberts
Paddy Scannell
Grahame Thompson
Ken Thompson
Bernard Waites
Paul Willis
Janet Woollacott

Other Members

Jane Bailey	Course Manager
Susan Boyd-Bowman	BBC Producer
Kate Clements	Editor
Tony Coulson	Liaison Librarian
Liz Lane	Editor
Vic Lockwood	BBC Producer
Robert Nicodemus	Representative from the Institute of Educational Technology, the Open University
Lesley Passey	Designer
Mike Philps	BBC Producer
Sarah Shepherd	Editor

PREFACE

This collection of readings is intended primarily to support the Open University interdisciplinary course on Popular Culture, U203. The social and historical span of the course is Britain since the early nineteenth century. We hope, however, that the Reader will be of interest to teachers and students in other institutions of higher education where the study of popular culture has, in recent years, attracted growing interest. This introduction is addressed to OU students and other interested parties alike.

Briefly defining the field of study is by no means easy. The cultural forms and practices which are — or have been — in a descriptive sense 'popular' are legion: the music hall, the cinema, football, science fiction, motor-cycle gangs — all are in some way 'popular culture', but there is no consistent patterning to their social definition as popular. The difficulty of defining the field is amplified by the number of academic specialisms which touch on the study of popular culture without making it their exclusive domain: the history and sociology of leisure, 'media' and communications studies, literary criticism, semiology and so on. The body of social, psychoanalytic and semiotic theory which these specialisms now bring into play is daunting.

In preparing this course, the course team found it valueless to think of popular culture as an aggregate of forms and practices or as a historically continuous entity. Rather, we have come to think of it as a shifting region within a historical and cultural totality where cultural domination, negotiation and exchange take place. Popular culture is defined relationally and the social definition has changed in the conjunctures of history. We have tried to turn the interdisciplinary 'mix' to good account by forming a matrix of skills on which the student can draw to 'read' critically cultural forms and understand cultural change. The readings in this collection are all substantive in character and the theoretical range of the course is represented by a complementary volume of readings: *Culture, Ideology and Social Process* (Batsford, 1981).

PART ONE

INTRODUCTION

The readings collected in the first section of the Reader are intended as a guide to current debates in the historical study of popular culture. They are not, of course, totally comprehensive. One striking absence is the neglect of those historical studies which have sought to reconstruct the popular culture of pre-industrial, early modern Europe. The intellectual richness of recent research into magic, witchcraft and popular mentalities, pursued by historians like Keith Thomas, Peter Burke and Carlo Ginzburg, makes this neglect very regrettable.[1] However, we have used the term 'popular culture' in a historically privileged sense. For us, it is specific to societies where the market economy has penetrated most forms of cultural production and consumption. Popular culture entails a system of production, although that is not all it entails and pin-pointing its historical origins in Britain is not easy. Until recently, many historians would have accepted the idea of a 'Bleak Age' for the common people separating the popular pursuits of eighteenth-century, largely rural, society from the new pattern of working-class leisure of urban, mid-Victorian Britain. Such an idea fitted the pessimistic interpretation of the social consequences of early industrialisation. Yet Hugh Cunningham describes a thriving popular culture dating from the 1820s, based on fairs, shows and travelling theatrical troupes, supplied by thrusting cultural entrepreneurs and common to rural and urban society (Reading 3). To his own surprise, he finds himself amongst the 'optimist' school of historians.[2] Cunningham's and others' work emphasises the many continuities between the plebeian culture of the late eighteenth century and the culture provided by the market for the new working class of the nineteenth.

Our historically privileged use of the term does not, we hope, result from wilful indifference to all the evidence for historical continuity. None the less, we would argue that cultural relationships were fundamentally transformed with the working out of capitalist industrialisation during the second and third quarters of the nineteenth century. There was an inner disparity between the demotic culture of a largely rural world and the new urban popular culture which the experience of particular social and ethnic groups clarifies with some sharpness. Lynn Lees, in her excellent study of Irish immigrants in London, writes: 'The comparison of nineteenth century rural Irish religion and folk beliefs with the popular Catholicism of Irish migrants in London reveals two very different worlds of imagination and action.'[3] The rituals and symbols of belief were transformed in the city, a process which can be

15

illustrated by the contrast between the rural St Brigit of the Irish land-less peasantry and the urban St Briget of the immigrant working class: the latter lost all links with agriculture and the provision of food and changed from the patroness of cattle to a symbol of female virtue and chastity.

Whereas migrant groups, like the Irish, experienced cultural change as part of a physical dislocation of a whole way of life, local communities did so as part of a new pattern of conflict engendered by the transition from a society of ranks and orders to class society. The first reading, from Robert Malcolmson's *Popular Recreations in English Society 1700-1850* (1973) documents cultural change through conflict as the local magistracy, employers and the newly formed police of the 1830s attempted to suppress and control the often turbulent customary recreations of pre-industrial rural and urban society. It is scarcely an accident that Malcolmson should have been supervised in his research in this field by Edward Thompson, whose *The Making of the English Working Class* (1963) has had an influence on the understanding of the early nineteenth century, and on historical scholarship more generally, which can scarcely be exaggerated. His own work is represented by Reading 2, which discusses the relationship between literacy, political consciousness and artisan culture during the 1820s. The presence of this extract makes clear how wide we take the historical field to be, for Thompson attempted no less than the reconstruction of a popular culture as a whole way of life. Cunningham explicitly,[4] and Gareth Stedman Jones in Reading 4 implicitly, are indebted to Thompson's project. Stedman Jones traces the relationships between working-class politics and working-class culture in later-nineteenth-century London, provocatively concluding that the Labour Party was the apotheosis and not a rejection of the defensive, enclosed culture articulated in the working-class music hall.

So strong has Thompson's influence been that it is worth pausing to reflect on the making of *The Making* and on the trajectory of socialist humanist history since 1963. The book was composed when the reverberations of Khrushchev's denunciation of Stalin and the Soviet suppression of the Hungarian uprising were still palpable. Thompson took part in the massive exodus from the British Communist Party. (He, John Saville — a fellow historian — and others, were expelled for circulating a party discussion journal.) In concrete historical detail, *The Making* challenged a number of orthodoxies of both the left and the right. Thompson insisted that class was as much a cultural as an economic formation and that the class consciousness found in real history could not (in the idealist fashion of George Lukács) be typified as 'the appropriate and rational reactions "imputed" to a particular position in the process of production'.[5] To think thus led to a facile dismissal of the real traditions, value systems and ideas in which men and women had embodied class experience as 'false'. It was one facet of that 'enormous condescension of posterity' which assumed that the repressed had no understanding of their own struggle, and it opened the way to the elite party as the 'true' bearer of proletarian consciousness. Thompson insisted on freeing the historical process from determinism and teleology and restoring human agency to it. He rebuked the prevailing right-wing orthodoxies of economic history for their shallow and propagandist preoccupation with economic growth and their incomprehension of the exploitation and conflict which lay behind aggregate accounts of economic change. 'Process', 'experience' and 'culture' were the key terms in Thompson's conceptual framework, which he had developed partly out of an engagement with Raymond Williams's *Culture and Society* (1958) and *The Long Revolution* (1961).

The liberalisation, during the late 1960s and 1970s, of social history from the narrow confines of economic and 'Labour' history, clearly owed much to Thompson's initiative. Typically, the new social history sought to bring the boundaries of history closer to people's lives by reconstructing the fundamental elements of work, family and class relations in working-class experience. Its most vigorous forum was the History Workshops begun in 1967 by teachers and worker-students from Ruskin College; some of its most striking achievements are to be found in the *History Workshop* journal and in the series edited by Raphael Samuel.[6]

Recently, some of the presuppositions and methods of socialist humanist history have themselves been called into question. Richard Johnson, in a stimulating critique, has argued that the tendency in this history to reduce class 'upwards' to culture actually obscures the determining roles of the mode of production. Johnson has called for a use, in historians' practice, of the critical categories of the structuralist Marxist, Louis Althusser.[7] Should this take place, it would help break down the strong division in the study of popular culture between 'culturalists', primarily interested in the analysis of 'lived' cultures and experience, and 'structuralists', primarily interested in the analysis of texts. Whether such a *rapprochement* between two profoundly different modes of apprehension will occur, it is too early to say. At present, the history of popular culture is strongly biased towards 'culturalism'.

It is also biased towards the nineteenth century. Historians have now written fairly extensively on such popular cultural forms as the music hall,[8] the nineteenth-century pub,[9] the melodrama theatre[10] and the seaside holiday (the last represented here by Reading 6). Unfortunately, twentieth-century popular culture has been much less well served. The general historical survey of the growth of leisure by James Walvin[11] gives only a very compressed treatment of the post-1914 years. For the inter-war period, the student is heavily reliant on the contemporary documentation by Mass Observation of the 'lived' cultures of the pub and the seaside holiday;[12] there is really a dearth of systematic accounts of popular cultural change through time. The mass media of communications have been more closely scrutinised — notably in Asa Briggs's multi-volume history of British broadcasting[13] — and it is from this field of study that we have taken George Perry's account of the inter-war film industry and Paddy Scannell's and David Cardiff's essay on the social foundations of British broadcasting (Readings 7 and 8). Scannell and Cardiff emphasise the influence of a conception of culture derived from Matthew Arnold and the late-nineteenth-century liberal intelligentsia on the definition of the BBC's social role. Arnold conceived of 'culture' as a unifying force in a society wracked by the dissensions of social class. The ambiguity of the BBC's role, originally seen as serving a 'national culture' but increasingly responsive to the tastes of a popular audience, illustrates the shifting and negotiated character of a major form of twentieth-century popular culture.

The historical section of this Reader ends with the Second World War. By this we do not wish to imply that, since 1945, there has been a continuous present. However, the post-war period has not yet been a subject of serious historical interest. Contemporary cultural studies — whose origins are briefly discussed in the introduction to Part Two — have been emphatically 'contemporary'; Chas Critcher's essay on 'Football since the War' (Part Two, Reading 10) is exceptional in being socio-historical in character. It is much to be hoped that twentieth-century popular culture will soon become as fruitful an area of historical enquiry as nineteenth-century.

B.A. Waites
Tony Bennett
Graham Martin

The Open University
Milton Keynes

Notes

1. K. Thomas, *Religion and the Decline of Magic* (1971); P. Burke, *Popular Culture in Early Modern Europe* (1978); C. Ginzburg, *The Cheese and the Worms* (1980).

2. H. Cunningham, *Leisure and the Industrial Revolution* (1980), p. 9.

3. L. Lees, *Exiles of Erin* (1979), p. 185.

4. Cunningham, *Leisure*, p. 192 and elsewhere.

5. G. Lukács, *History and Class Consciousness* (1971), p. 51.

6. See *Village Life and Labour* (1976) and *Miners, Quarrymen and Saltworkers* (1976), both edited by R. Samuel.

7. R. Johnson, 'Thompson, Genovese and Socialist-Humanist History', *History Workshop*, vol. 6 (Autumn 1978), pp. 79-100.

8. See Martha Vicinus, *The Industrial Muse* (1974), Chapter 6; Peter Bailey, *Leisure and Class in Victorian England* (1979), Chapter 7; Laurence Senelick, 'Politics as Entertainment: Victorian Music Hall Songs', *Victorian Studies*, vol. xix, no. 2 (Dec. 1975).

9. B. Harrison, *Drink and the Victorians* (London, 1971).

10. M.R. Booth, *English Melodrama* (1965).

11. J. Walvin, *Leisure and Society 1830-1950* (1978).

12. See Mass Observation, *The Pub and the People* (London, 1943) and T. Harrisson, *Britain Re-visited* (London, 1961).

13. *A History of Broadcasting in the United Kingdom*: vol. i (1961); vol. ii (1965); vol. iii (1971).

1 POPULAR RECREATIONS UNDER ATTACK

Robert Malcolmson

Source: *Popular Recreations in English Society 1700-1850*
(Cambridge University Press, 1973), Ch. 7. © R. Malcolmson.

From around the middle of the eighteenth century there are many signs
of an increasing willingness among people of authority to intervene
against the customary practices of popular recreation. Recreational
customs were subjected to a multitude of direct attacks, many of
which were initiated and organized at the local level, though they were
usually related to some of the more general changes in attitudes and
circumstances [. . .]. Attacks of this kind were always intended to
achieve the outright suppression of some particular practice, and
their objectives, at least in the long run, were normally fulfilled. Efforts
to eliminate some long-standing custom − a blood sport in one place,
a fair, a wake, or a football match in another − were taking place in all
parts of the country, and some of the campaigns for reform resulted
in passionate controversy, and occasionally even physical confrontations.

The traditional blood sports, along with most of the common
people's pastimes, had been sometimes condemned and vigorously
attacked during the Tudor and Stuart periods, but it was not until the
eighteenth and early nineteenth centuries that they were subjected to a
systematic and sustained attack. Prior to the mid-eighteenth century
they still retained a degree of favour, or at least sufferance, from the
governing class, and many gentlemen, as we have seen, actively patronized cock-fighting and sometimes even bull-baiting. Blood sports had not
yet come to be widely regarded as cruel or disreputable. When Prince
Lewis of Baden was being entertained by William III in January 1694 it
was reported that 'there was bear's baiting, bulls' sport, and cock
fighting instituted for his diversion and recreation'.[1] With time, however, the mood of public opinion altered. One of the early statements
of dissatisfaction with such amusements appeared in the *Craftsman* of
1 July 1738:

> I am a profess'd Enemy to Persecution of all Kinds, whether against
> Man or Beast; though I am not so much a Pythagorean as to extend
> my Philosophy to those Creatures, which are manifestly design'd for
> our Food and Nourishment; but We ought to make the Manner of
> their Deaths as easy to Them as possible, and not destroy or torment

Them out of Wantonness. Upon this principle I abhor Cock-fighting, and throwing at Cocks, as well as Bull-baiting, Bear-baiting, Ass-baiting, and all the other butcherly Diversions of Hockley in the Hole.

In later years criticisms of this sort were voiced with greater warmth, and by the early nineteenth century the opposition to blood sports was vehement and intense. [. . .] The movement against popular blood sports was at its peak during the first forty years of the nineteenth century; by the 1840s most of them had been almost entirely eliminated.

Throwing at cocks was the first of the blood sports to be seriously attacked and the first to be generally suppressed. Periodic attempts may have been made to curtail the sport during the Stuart period, but it was not until the middle of the eighteenth century that a sustained and widespread campaign was directed against the custom. [. . .]

Throwing at cocks was not immediately suppressed. Like many of the people's diversions, its long history and deeply-rooted practice armed it with a certain short-run resilience, and in many cases it was only put down after repeated exertions. Orders against the sport were sometimes reissued several times by local authorities. The *Northampton Mercury* of 1 March 1762 reported that on Shrove Tuesday 'our Mayor and Justices, attended by their proper Officers, perambulated the Precincts of this Town, to prevent the scandalous and inhuman Practice of Throwing at Cocks,' adding that 'we hope the same will be no more used'; but as late as 1788 a warning against the practice was still felt to be necessary: 'We cannot but express our Wishes,' the paper observed, 'that Persons in Power, as well as Parents and Masters of Families, would exert their authority in suppressing a Practice too common at this Season – throwing at Cocks.' In the same breath, however, it was acknowledged that the pastime, 'to the Credit of a civilized People, is annually declining'.[2] Indeed, towards the end of the century it was generally agreed that the custom was very much on the wane, if not already completely eliminated. In 1777 John Brand reported that in Newcastle-upon-Tyne the pastime 'is now laid aside'; by the last quarter of the century it was seldom found in East Sussex, and in the early 1780s James Spershott of Chichester claimed that 'this cruel practice is almost over in these parts'.[3] In 1781 a contributor to the *Gentleman's Magazine* was of the opinion that throwing at cocks 'is in many places abolished', and a letter in the *Monthly Magazine* of 1797 suggested that 'cock-throwing is . . . nearly extinct'.[4] 'The magistrates,' wrote Joseph Strutt, 'greatly to their credit, have for some years past put a stop to this wicked custom, and at present it is nearly, if not entirely, discontinued in every part of the kingdom.'[5] A few residues managed to survive into the nineteenth century. The magistrates in Warwickshire were taking steps to suppress the sport in 1814, and a decade later the mayor of Warwick was obliged to issue a request that 'so disgraceful a Practice', a custom which was thought to have been completely abandoned, would not be revived by any of the inhabitants.[6] In 1825 William Hone said that the diversion 'is still conspicuous in several parts of the kingdom', and at Quainton in Buckinghamshire it was said to have continued until as late as 1844.[7] However, it would appear that these were only the last remnants of the amusement. For most of the common people in most parts of the country throwing at cocks was a forbidden and neglected recreation by the end of the eighteenth century.

The relatively early demise of throwing at cocks seems to have stemmed from a number of circumstances. For one thing, it was widely regarded as exceptionally unsporting; it was thought to be lacking even the elementary features of fair competition. 'What a Noble Entertainment is it', wrote one critic, 'for a Rational Soul, to fasten an innocent weak defenceless Animal to ye ground, and then dash his bones to pieces with a Club? I can compare it to nothing but the behaviour of that silly Fellow, who boasted of his Activity, because he had tripp'd up a Beggar who had a pair of Wooden Leggs!'[8] Throwing at cocks, argued the *Warwick and Warwickshire Advertiser* of 6 March 1824, 'is far more barbarous than . . . cock-fighting; the poor sufferer has no rival bird to inflame his jealousy, and call forth his powers, but, fastened to a stake, he is compelled to endure the battering of stocks and other missiles'. This fact of unfairness, the fact that the cock was put in such a weak competitive position, was mentioned by many of the critics, and it probably served to draw the attention of people with doubts about animal sports in general to cock-throwing first, and to the other sports, those with one or two extenuating features, not until later. In addition, since cock-throwing was more a game for small groups than a major community activity, it lacked the underlying strength of a broadly-based social support (the more a community was united en masse behind a festive event, the more difficult it was to suppress the event); consequently, it was relatively vulnerable to any organized attacks. Moreover, the suppression of cock-throwing did not imply a really drastic curtailment of the people's recreational life, for its elimination involved not the complete loss of a holiday, but only one of the holiday's diversions. Finally, it was of some importance that throwing at cocks was almost exclusively a plebeian sport, for it was always easier to suppress a recreation when there was little risk of encroaching on the interests of gentlemen. Several critics condemned with equal fervour both of the Shrovetide blood sports, cock-fighting as well as cock-throwing, but in almost all cases it was only the distinctly popular pastime which was actually prohibited.

Bull-baiting, which drew more controversial attention than any of other blood sports, may have already been in decline by around 1800, at least in certain parts of the country. 'This custom of baiting the bull,' claimed the *Sporting Magazine* in 1793, 'has of late years been almost laid aside in the north of England'; at Lincoln it was said in 1789 to be 'in a dwindling state'.[9] In 1797 a contributor to the *Monthly Magazine* referred to the sport as 'greatly diminished', and Joseph Strutt was of the same opinion.[10] In Nottingham and at Hornsea in the East Riding bull-baiting seems to have died out by the beginning of the nineteenth century.[11] The reasons for this apparent decline are not at all clear. There is little evidence of outright suppressions of bull-baiting during the eighteenth century. Perhaps the growing hostility of genteel opinion discouraged its survival in areas where the authority of such views could not be easily ignored. The sport was particularly dependent on some form of outside assistance — patronage, sponsorship, or promotion — and it is likely that such assistance was increasingly difficult to obtain. By the late eighteenth century butchers were no longer providing bulls for baiting, as they had often done in the past; gentlemen had in almost all cases given up their patronage of the sport; and many publicans must have become increasingly reluctant to act as promoters, especially when such involvement might put their licences in jeopardy.

But whatever the reasons may have been for this eighteenth-century decline (and some contemporaries may have overstated their case), it is clear that bull-baiting was still being practised in many places during the first forty years of the nineteenth century. It continued to be a popular 5th of November diversion at Lincoln, Bury St Edmunds, and at Axbridge, Somerset.[12] At Norwich it survived through at least the first two decades of the century and at Bristol until the 1830s.[13] It persisted in many Derbyshire towns (for instance, Chesterfield, Wirksworth, Chapel en le Frith, Bakewell, Ashbourne) and in parts of Buckinghamshire and Oxfordshire (Oakley, Thame, Wheatley).[14] It was a customary practice at Wokingham, Berkshire (on 21st December), until at least 1823 and at Beverley (on the annual swearing-in of the mayor) it continued during the first two decades of the century.[15] Bull-baiting remained widespread in south Lancashire, and it was particularly prevalent in Shropshire, Staffordshire, and the Birmingham area.[16]

The persistence of bull-baiting (along with other blood sports) was a cause for considerable concern in respectable society, especially among the increasingly influential evangelicals, and this concern was frequently voiced during the first third of the century in the political arena. The legal standing of blood sports remained ambiguous: cruelty to animals could be dealt with under the common law (usually as a common nuisance), but the lack of any statute on the subject tended to militate against prosecutions. Reformers were well aware of the limitations of the law and attempted to rectify the situation: between 1800 and 1835 Parliament considered eleven bills on cruelty to animals, most of which were explicitly or indirectly concerned with blood sports. Bills against bull-baiting were introduced in 1800 and 1802; both were lost by narrow margins, principally because of the vigorous opposition and eloquence of William Windham.[17] Bills generally dealing with cruelty to animals were debated in 1809 and 1810, and again both efforts failed.[18] An Act of 1822 to 'Prevent the Cruel Treatment of Cattle' was interpreted by some magistrates to apply to bull-baiting, though this had probably not been Parliament's intention (in fact, in a decision of 1827 the King's Bench declared that the bull, which was not referred to in the Act, was not included in the genus of 'cattle').[19] Efforts to outlaw blood sports were continued after 1822; bills to this purpose were introduced in 1823, 1824, 1825, 1826, and 1829, on each occasion without success.[20] Finally, in 1835, a Cruelty to Animals Act unequivocally established the illegality of all blood sports which involved the baiting of animals.[21]

There were other indications of the growing revulsion against blood sports. A large number of essays dealing in part or entirely with blood sports (all of them critically) were published during the later eighteenth century and the first half of the next century. In 1800-2 at least three tracts appeared which were specifically directed against bull-baiting.[22] Sermons on the theme of humanity to animals were often delivered, sometimes as a result of special endowments. Newspapers and journals periodically included condemnations of some blood sport, commonly in the form of a letter to the editor. By the second quarter of the century genteel concern was substantial enough to support the formation of several reform societies, all of which drew some of their strength from the sentiments against blood sports: the Society for the Prevention of Cruelty to Animals (established in 1824); the Association for Promoting Rational Humanity Towards the Animal Creation (1830-3); the Animals' Friend Society (1832-c.1852); the Ladies' Society for the Suppression of Cruelty to Animals (the 1830s); and in a region where blood sports were especially prevalent, the South Staffordshire Association for the Suppression of Bull-baiting (established in 1824). Some of these societies sponsored tracts and periodicals (for instance, the *Voice of Humanity* and the *Animals' Friend*), and during the 1830s they were active in investigating and carrying to court many cases of animal sports.

As the nineteenth century advanced bull-baiting was gradually overpowered. Clergymen were especially active in preaching and informing against bull-baiting and in organizing practical efforts of resistance. In early July 1796, for instance, the vicar of St Gluvias, Cornwall, noted in his diary: 'Wrote a few pages in the morning, and snatched some moments in the evening and on Sunday before prayers, of a Sermon respecting inhumanity to animals, induced by a Bull-baiting in the parish: a brutal amusement.'[23] Aside from a small body of Tories, genteel opinion had become almost solidly hostile. At Tutbury the sport was 'at length suppressed by the humane interference of the surrounding gentry', and at Stone, also in Staffordshire, it was eliminated in 1838.[24] It was suppressed at Aylesbury in 1821-2, at Beverley in 1822-3, and at Wheatley by 1837.[25] At Lincoln bull-baiting had been put down by the mid-1820s, and it was reported that on the 5th of November 1826 'the bullwards, notwithstanding much threats and boasting, did not venture to revive their barbarous diversion, which has been happily declining in public favor for some years past'.[26] In 1837 it was said that 'Thame is no longer the scene of that brutality which once cast a blemish over its inhabitants; the bull-baiting is now done away with, and in its place we had a really good and efficient band of music parading the town'.[27] By the early 1840s bull-baiting had been eliminated in Ashbourne, Derbyshire, during the wakes week and some of the residents were thinking of introducing steeplechase races as a substitute.[28]

Such suppressions were often only effected after years of opposition and numerous failures, for in many places the people were keen in their resistance and capitulated only under persistent and determined pressure. In the Birmingham-Black Country area a vigorous campaign against bull-baiting was continued through the first third of the century – there were prosecutions, convictions, sermons, journalistic attacks, personal interventions by clergymen and magistrates; and during the 1830s, especially after a strong legal leverage was provided through the Cruelty to Animals Act of 1835, there was a final wave of charges (and normally convictions) against bull-baiters, many of which were actively supported or initiated by the Animals' Friend Society.[29] [. . .]

The demise of bull-baiting was complete by the early years of Victoria's reign. 'Happily', reported a tract of 1838 on bull-baiting and running, 'they are now nearly every where abandoned.' 'After many a hard contest,' said William Howitt, bull-baiting '[has] been virtually put down'. 'The appeal of good sense and of humanity has been listened to in almost every part of the United Kingdom', rejoiced a reformer in 1839, 'and this useful animal is no longer tortured amidst the exulting yells of those who are a disgrace to our common form and nature.'[30] [. . .]

The other blood sports retreated more gradually and their decline was accompanied by considerably less controversy and social conflict. Badger-baiting and dog-fighting, both of which were secondary amusements, were under attack during the same period as bull-baiting; during the later 1830s the Animals' Friend Society was in the habit of investigating dog-fighting (and sometimes badger-baiting) as well as bull-baiting on the occasions of its annual missions into the Birmingham area. Neither sport, however, prompted much public outcry or heated discussion. They were both substantially reduced by the 1840s, probably to negligible proportions in the country as a whole. In a few areas, however, they survived into the later nineteenth century, mostly because of the difficulties of tracking them down; they could be more easily conducted in secrecy, in confined places away from the public gaze (such concealment was not possible with bull-baiting), and this also meant that their offensiveness was less immediately disturbing. It is likely that they are not unknown today.[31] Cock-fighting was even more resilient, partly for the same reasons, partly because of its considerable genteel following. Advertisements for gentlemen's cock-fights continued to appear in the provincial press during the first quarter of the nineteenth century, and though its support among all classes was certainly falling off in this period, it was not until the beginning of Victoria's reign, when the great majority of gentlemen had abandoned the sport, leaving it for the most part in the hands of lesser men, that an active campaign against the sport was actually mobilized. The R.S.P.C.A. began its attack in the late 1830s, and between 1838 and 1841 it prosecuted at least thirteen cases against cock-fighting, almost all of which were against men of little social standing. The sport still retains a small following today.

What were the main grounds for the complaints against blood sports? Why had they come to be so poorly regarded? Many of the criticisms arose from moral and religious considerations which can be easily appreciated: such diversions were 'barbarous', 'inhuman', 'uncivilized', and generally at odds with enlightened morality. They involved 'such scenes as degrade mankind beneath the barbarity of a savage, and which are totally inconsistent with the laws of nature, the laws of religion, and the laws of a civilized nation'.[32] 'Such a custom might comport with the barbarism and darkness of past ages,' conceded a critic of the Stamford bull-running, 'might suit the genius of an uncivilized and warlike race; but surely, must be regarded as an indelible stain upon the history of an enlightened and professedly christian people.'[33] This was a familiar line of argument: the 'march of intellect' should be overpowering such primitive practices. Many of the common people regarded combat with animals as an inherent part of the 'natural' processes of life; the reformers, of course, had a quite different view of man's place in the order of nature. For them, the general framework of man's moral duties was to be found in the great chain of being: man had been granted the power to govern the animal world, but just as God benevolently oversaw the lives of humans, so man should not misuse his authority over subordinate creatures. There was a hierarchy of rights and duties, and man's obligations towards the dumb creation were not to be lightly neglected. As a clergyman put it in 1830: 'man was appointed the terrestrial sovereign of the brute creation. But did God, in entrusting the brute creation to the care of man, and in giving him the power of awing their brute force into submission and obedience, at the same time give him the power to put them to unnecessary torture, and to destroy them in mere wantonness?'[34] 'Clemency to Brutes is a Natural Duty,' argued another reformer, 'and Natural Duties are of eternal and universal Obligation.'[35] [. . .]

It was also argued that blood sports served to undermine social morality. 'Every act that sanctions cruelty to animals', observed the *Manchester Mercury* of 15 April 1800, 'must tend to destroy the morals of a people, and consequently every social duty.' [. . .]

It was thought that 'all such trainings of the mind of a people to delight in scenes of cruelty, are as dangerous in their tendency to the public peace and order, as they are corruptive of the young and uninstructed, whose most natural principles, (benevolence and compassion) they extinguish, and pervert their hearts to the contrary'.[36] The logical consequence of indulgence in such sports could be crime of the highest order: 'Whatever is morally bad cannot be politically right. The monster, who can wilfully persevere to torture the dumb creation, would feel little or no compunction, to serve a purpose, in aiming his bludgeon at the head, or ingulfing the murderous blade within the warm vitals of his fellow creature.'[37] One writer felt that 'much of the misery and crime of the English rural districts, is to be ascribed to the influence' of cock-fighting, 'which has trained many a victim for the gallows, and reduced many a family to want and beggary'.[38]

Blood sports, then, involved special dangers, but they also shared with other popular diversions a general tendency to undermine social discipline. They tempted men from productive labour; they disrupted the orderly routine of everyday life; they encouraged idleness, improvidence, and gambling; and sometimes they resulted in boisterous and tumultuous assemblies. Speaking in favour of the bull-baiting bill in 1800, Sir William Pulteney declared that the sport 'was cruel and inhuman; it drew together idle and disorderly persons; it drew also from their occupations many who ought to be earning subsistence for themselves and families; it created many disorderly and mischievous proceedings, and furnished examples of profligacy and cruelty'.[39] Similarly, Sir Richard Hill pointed out that 'men neglected their work and their families, and in great crowds spent whole days in witnessing those barbarous exhibitions. From the baiting-field they retired to the alehouse, and wasted the whole night in debauchery, as they had done the day in idleness.[40] In short, the concern for cruelty and its consequences was strongly reinforced by the solicitude for public order and for labour discipline.

Many traditional football matches, especially the major holiday events, were increasingly condemned during this period, and some of them were successfully put down. Football, of course, had never enjoyed full approval from people of affluence. From the fourteenth to the sixteenth century it had been frequently prohibited on the grounds that it distracted public attention from the much more useful recreation of archery. Thereafter other arguments began to be directed against the sport, in particular the inconvenience of its exercise in public thoroughfares. [. . .]

Public thoroughfares had always been regarded as legitimate playing places by the common people, but as the pace of urbanization accelerated, and as the means of social control became increasingly sophisticated, the clash between this popular point of view and the growing concern for orderliness and property rights was very much accentuated. The sort of conflict which must have been very common is illustrated by an incident of 1818 in Hull: elaborating on a report concerning a man who had recently been fined 40s. for playing football in the streets, a local newspaper pointed out that 'the police of Sculcoates have strict orders to prevent any person from playing at any games in the streets troublesome to the inhabitants of the said parish, which have of late been so prevalent, to the great annoyance and personal danger of the public'.[41] In 1829 and 1836 the vestry of Barnes, Surrey, complained of the nuisance of street football and recommended its suppression to the officers of the peace.[42] The Highways Act of 1835 made explicit reference to the sport (5 & 6 William IV c. 50, clause 72): it provided for a fine of up to 40s. for playing 'at Football or any other Game on any Part of the said Highways, to the Annoyance of any Passenger', and thereby afforded solid grounds for future prosecutions. In later years football in the streets was forcibly terminated at a number of towns in Surrey: at Richmond (1840), at East Mousley and Hampton Wick (1857), at Hampton (1864), and at Kingston-upon-Thames (1867).[43]

Shrovetide football in Derby was only put down after considerable controversy. During the early decades of the nineteenth century its practice had been periodically deplored, but no direct action was taken until 1845. [. . .]

Many [. . .] holiday football matches were particularly resilient, for they were fortified by a festival context, long-standing traditions, and large numbers of followers. The Nuneaton game was still extant in the late nineteenth century, and the Dorking and Workington matches survived into the twentieth century. Several games were able to continue by shifting their ground to more open spaces (though in so doing they sometimes lost much of their peculiar appeal). When steps were taken at Alnwick in 1827-8 to bar the Shrovetide game from the streets, the Duke of Northumberland provided a convenient meadow for its refuge.[44] At Twickenham in 1840 the magistrates prevented the Shrovetide football from 'taking place in the town, but it was most spiritedly carried on in a meadow belonging to Mr Cole, the brewer of that parish, under the superintendence of a man named Kirby, who has been "master of the sports" for the last 50 years'; 'formerly . . . the sport had been extended throughout every avenue of the place; but of late years, and more particularly since the passing of the new Highway Act, by which it has altogether been prohibited in any public thoroughfare . . . it has been confined to' the meadow of 'Mr. Cole, who kindly offered it for the purpose'.[45] There was periodic talk of putting down the annual football at Kingston-upon-Thames, but nothing came of it until 1867 when the corporation directed the players off the streets and onto a new playing field, an order which sparked off some angry protests and a little rioting but was generally accepted the following year.[46] The Ashbourne game, after weathering an attack in 1860-1, removed itself to the outskirts of town[47] and survived into the twentieth century to be condoned and patronized, not only by the common people, but by civic officials, the Church, and on one occasion (in 1927) by the Prince of Wales.

The main objections against popular football stemmed from the concern for public order. 'The Game of Football as practised in this Town on Shrove Tuesday', it was claimed in a motion introduced at the Kingston Town Council on 29 February 1840, 'is an obstruction to the passengers, a great annoyance to the peaceable Inhabitants, subversive of good order and prejudicial to the morality of the Town.'[48] Football in the streets obviously disturbed the normal routine of business, and such disruptions were no longer as readily tolerated.

> It is not so much with a wish to deprive the lovers of this sport of their enjoyment, that I advocate its abolition [wrote a Derby critic in 1832], but more particularly to condemn the fitness of the place of its competition for such a purpose; instead of emanating from the centre of the town, let them assemble in the Siddals, or some such place, so as not to interfere with the avocation of the industrious part of the community; it is not a trifling consideration that a suspension of business for nearly two days should be created to the inhabitants for the mere gratification of a sport at once so useless and barbarous.[49]

During a discussion of the Kingston game in 1857 one of the Town Councillors claimed that 'he knew what loss he sustained on that day by the diminution of trade, and no doubt his friend Mr. Jones knew too, and so did every grocer and draper'.[50] In 1845 Derby's Mayor was suggesting that

> In former times, when the town contained but few inhabitants, the
> game was not attended with its present evils, but it was now a well
> ascertained fact that many of the inhabitants suffered considerable
> injury, in person as well as property, from this annual exhibition;
> and he himself knew of instances where persons having an interest in
> houses, especially the larger ones, had experienced losses from want
> of occupiers, at adequate rents; parties who would otherwise have
> expended many thousands a year on the trade of the town, having
> left it, or declined to reside in it, because they did not like to bring
> up their families here, under the idea that Derby was one of the
> lowest and wickedest places in the kingdom.[51]

[. . .]

Although there was a definite element of moral opposition to the
holiday matches (at Derby the game was variously spoken of as 'brutal-
izing', 'disgraceful', 'inhuman', 'filthy and disgusting'), it is clear that
moral outrage was a much less prominent theme in the opposition to
football than it was in the attacks against blood sports, or perhaps even
pleasure fairs. There were fewer objective grounds for passionate denun-
ciations: while many football games were undoubtedly rough and
unregulated, serious injuries during the major holiday matches seem to
have been uncommon; for the most part the crowds were relatively
orderly, and the games were pursued in a reasonably sporting manner.[52]
'During these boisterous *Saturnalia*,' remarked one observer of the
Kingston game, 'the inhabitants are reduced to the necessity of barrica-
ding their windows; and the trade of the town is somewhat impeded;
yet the general good-humour with which the sport is carried on pre-
vents any serious complaints; and the majority of the corporation are
favourable to its continuance.'[53] Football was regarded by some gentlemen as a 'manly sport', rugged but character-building, and there was
some feeling that it helped to sustain the Englishman's 'bull-dog courage'. Several matches enjoyed a considerable genteel following, a feature which was often remarked on. One writer, for instance, spoke of
how at Derby 'the crowd is encouraged by respectable persons attached
to each party . . . who take a surprising interest in the result of the
day's "sport", urging on the players with shouts, and even handing to
those who are exhausted, oranges and other refreshment.'[54] The circumstances at Kingston were much the same: many gentlemen were
known to be favourably disposed towards the custom. An attempt to
suppress the practice in 1840 was blocked by the Town Council, and
at the same time a petition from the inhabitants was sent to the Com-
missioners of the Metropolitan Police requesting that they not interfere
with the sport.[55] In 1860-1, when efforts were made to put down the
Ashbourne game, its supporters included some of 'the most respectable

citizens of the town'.[56] Indeed, the resilience of some of the holiday matches is partly explained by the fact that they received a reasonable degree of backing from respectable opinion, and when popular and genteel conservatism joined hands the attacks of the reformers were much less likely to succeed.

The only other athletic sport to be frequently criticized was boxing. From the later eighteenth century magistrates became increasingly prepared to prohibit the staging of prize-fights and to prosecute their principals whenever possible. In 1791, for instance, the Bedfordshire justices, 'being convinced of the ill Tendency of Stage fighting or Boxing Matches have resolved that publick notice be given that they are determined not to suffer them to take Place'.[57] Prize-fighting could be readily restrained under the law, either as a breach of the peace or an unlawful assembly, and though many matches were winked at – some were partly protected by their influential patrons, and others were accompanied by crowds too large for the resources of local constables – successful interventions against intended prize-fights were often reported in the newspapers of the first half of the nineteenth century. Boxing was not infrequently the cause of accidental deaths and serious maulings, a circumstance which incurred for it much public disfavour. 'These dreadful catastrophes', suggested one paper, 'bespeak it the duty of every magistrate, as well as every man, to use their utmost endeavours to repress so disgraceful, so dangerous, and so increasing an evil.'[58] More significantly, a prize-fight was attended by considerable problems of public order. A crowd of thousands, some of them persons of dubious employments, seriously threatened the tranquillity of an unprepared locality – 'the established order, and good decorum of society,' complained one writer, 'have been, of late, much disturbed, and nearly set at defiance' by the prevalence of boxing matches;[59] moreover, such gatherings tended to undermine the assurance and reputation of the local guardians of the peace. Cat-and-mouse contests between the promoters and magistrates were common; matches were often staged near county borders in the hope that, should the magistrates appear, jurisdictional divisions could be more readily exploited. [. . .]

There was no systematic and sustained campaign which was intent on undermining the essential fabric of the traditional holiday calendar. The legitimacy of some sort of festivity, or at least relaxation, at Christmas, Easter, and Whitsuntide was only infrequently brought into question, for the most part they were accepted as justifiable occasions of leisure – they were celebrated in some form by almost everyone, and they were associated with the customary practices of various established institutions (the Church, annual fairs, clubs and friendly societies). Most of the discontent with the traditional holidays was directed at wakes and pleasure fairs, which were open to criticism on a number of grounds: they involved large (sometimes very large) public assemblies and consequently could be difficult for the authorities to control; they were often boisterous and 'licentious', many of them were exclusively plebeian and only marginally associated with 'respectable' institutions; they were thought by many observers to be thoroughly committed in the crudest of ways to the pursuit of sensual pleasures. One writer suggested that 'few persons are ever to be intrusted to feast. And fewer are to be allowed to meet in numbers together. There is a contagious viciousness in crowds. Though each individual of them, alone and by himself, would act with a religious propriety; yet all together they act with irreligion and folly.'[60] William Somerville claimed that at country wakes 'We see nothing but broken Heads, Bottles flying about, Tables overturn'd, outrageous Drunkenness, and eternal Squabble.'[61] [. . .]

The concern for public order and morality was the major source of the opposition to wakes. A Bedfordshire magistrate, for instance, complained that during the feast night at Sharnbrook there was 'an almost riotous assembly of men and women dancing and walking about on the road, clasping each other in a loving manner, all along the turnpike road. He thought this was not conducive to the morals of the public, which was the chief object he should have in view.'[62] This was the sort of complaint which was registered time and time again about many kinds of popular diversion. But there were also several criticisms which were more peculiar to wakes. It was often argued that wakes had seriously degenerated from their original institution as religious occasions, and that as almost exclusively profane assemblies their continuance could not be justified. Since they no longer served any significant religious purpose, it would be best (thought some) if their practice were terminated. 'When a thing not only fails to answer the end proposed,' suggested one writer in 1783, 'but operates commonly on the contrary, the sooner it is laid aside or changed the better.'[63] A religious commemoration had become a gathering for licentiousness: 'the Feasting and Sporting got the ascendant of Religion,' complained Henry Bourne, 'and so this Feast of Dedication, degenerated into Drunkenness and Luxury'.[64] Moreover, since wakes normally began on a Sunday, they were liable to disapproval on Sabbatarian grounds. Public sensuality was bad enough, but sensuality on the Lord's Day was completely intolerable. Various efforts were made to restrain these impieties, especially the setting up of booths and the sale of drink. In July 1825, for example, the vicar of Bucklebury, Berkshire, noted that he 'Gave instructions to my brother in law to provide that no beer should be sold in private houses nor Booths be erected on the Revel-Sunday, July 31st.'[65] And finally, wakes were thought to involve the common people in financial extravagance, in an improvident expenditure of time and money. A sympathetic commentator was of the opinion that 'the excitement lasts too long, and the enjoyment, whatever it may be, is purchased at the sacrifice of too great expense. It is a well-known fact, that many of the poor who have exerted every effort to make this profuse, but short-lived display, have scarcely bread to eat for weeks after. But there is no alternative, if they expect to be received with the same spirit of hospitality by their friends.'[66] Amusement had to be tailored to suit a family's financial capabilities, and the wake, it was thought, was too frequently an occasion when the working man's expenditure became grossly over-extended.

The attacks on other popular holidays were directed mostly against hiring fairs and outright pleasure fairs. In Essex, where pleasure fairs abounded, their suppression was ordered on numerous occasions after the mid-eighteenth century. In 1761-2 two standing orders from Quarter Sessions prohibited a total of twenty-four fairs; during the 1780s and early 1790s several more orders were published against fairs in other parishes.[67] None (or virtually none) of these fairs was a chartered event, and consequently they were regarded by the authorities as 'pretended fairs . . . not warranted by Law'; they were unofficial assemblies, organized only for pleasure and petty business, and they were objected to on the usual grounds — for their 'riots and tumults', their drunkenness, their 'unlawful games and plays', their 'debauching of Servants Apprentices and other unwary people'.[68] (These and other vices were subjected to detailed poetic scrutiny in 1789 by William Sheldrake in his *Picturesque Description of Turton Fair, and its Pernicious Consequences*.) Orders against fairs similar to those in Essex were issued by the Surrey Quarter Sessions in the late 1780s.[69] Although fairs continued to be attacked and sometimes prohibited in particular localities during the first half of the nineteenth century, it seems that their numbers did not significantly decline until later in the century: an Act of 1871 (34 Victoria c.12) provided efficient machinery for the abolition of 'unnecessary' fairs, and during the period 1871-8 its provisions were used to suppress more than 150 fairs.[70]

There appears to have been little active and articulated opposition to hiring fairs prior to the Victorian period. Many of them continued to provide useful service as labour exchanges, and they were still supported by a large number of farmers. It was only in the second half of the century that they came under frequent attack and noticeably declined in importance: several essays were published against them and attempts were made to regulate them more effectively or to substitute other procedures for hiring labour.[71] They were condemned for the same reasons as pleasure fairs, and particular stress was placed on the mingling of young, inexperienced servants with the older, hardened, and profligate followers of statute meetings (thieves, prostitutes, seducers, adventurers of all sorts) in circumstances which greatly encouraged drunkenness, uproar, and sexual promiscuity. Reformers were particularly concerned about their consequences for innocent maid-servants.

It should be emphasized that in comparison with some of the traditional recreations (such as blood sports), many fairs and parish feasts displayed a considerable staying power. If the area around Stamford was at all representative, it appears that wakes were still being widely celebrated as late as the 1840s; some may already have been suppressed but many certainly survived.[72] There was still a large number of fairs all through the country during the second half of the nineteenth century. Northamptonshire, for instance, had more fairs in the 1850s than it had had a century before.[73] In the countryside fairs continued to serve important marketing functions, and most of them were able to survive as long as they retained some significant economic rationale. This was a point of considerable importance: those fairs, especially the smaller ones, which blended pleasure with business were usually much more resilient than those which were strictly for pleasure; when a fair became economically redundant (and many did during the Victorian period) it was much more liable to attack. The Society for the Suppression of Vice had suggested in 1803 that it would 'be expedient to suppress all Fairs whatever, unless when they are really wanted for the purpose of useful traffic. Such an Act would be extremely beneficial to the morals of the community, without being productive of the smallest inconvenience to the public'.[74] This was a distinction which was widely acknowledged. Unofficial, unchartered fairs, such as those which were suppressed in Essex during the late eighteenth century, could not be defended on any acceptable criteria of economic usefulness. Statute fairs very much fell out of favour after the mid-nineteenth century, partly because by this time, as their hiring services were in many places of depreciating value (at least for employers), they were functioning almost entirely as pleasure fairs. A petition of 1875 against the two annual fairs in Sawbridgeworth, Hertfordshire, focused clearly on the central kinds of issues:

> In former, and very different times, the holding of these Fairs might have, as a matter of expediency, been defended on alleged commercial grounds, and for the convenience of the Residents; but now the old order of things has entirely passed away. Even the last lingering shadow of pretence for these Fairs — the Sale of Stock — is rapidly passing away; for, in the opinion of competent judges, the supply of stock is yearly becoming more limited in extent and inferior in quality . . .
> But whilst these Fairs are of the smallest possible conceivable

worth in a commercial point of view, indefensibly and indisputably they are the prolific seed plots and occasions of the most hideous forms of moral and social evil — drunkenness — whoredom — robbery — idleness and neglect of work . . . [75]

We can see, then, that gatherings which were largely plebeian, and unabashedly devoted to pleasure, enjoyed considerably less security than those in which substantial economic interests were involved — and with time most of these popular events disappeared. However, it should be emphasized that their decline was gradual and relatively gentle; by the mid-nineteenth century it was only moderately advanced. In the long run, in fact, this decline was probably more a consequence of the diminishing role of the countryside in the overall life of the nation, and the rise of a predominantly urban culture, than of the organized attacks of influential opinion. Many changes in rural recreations were a result of a whole set of larger transformations in the nature of rural society. Thomas Hardy, for instance, pointed to the increasing mobility in the countryside as the major reason for the disappearance of many popular traditions: the main change, he thought,

has been the recent supplanting of the class of stationary cottagers, who carried on the local traditions and humours, by a population of more or less migratory labourers, which has led to a break of continuity in local history, more fatal than any other thing to the preservation of legend, folk-lore, close inter-social relations, and eccentric individualities. For these the indispensable conditions of existence are attachment to the soil of one particular spot by generation after generation. [76]

Moreover, as urban diversions became more accessible to country dwellers, as alternative entertainments became available, the attractiveness and strength of the rural traditions was correspondingly weakened. It was only when the society which supported many of the traditional festivities was fundamentally altered — when the numbers of labouring people in the countryside were declining, when faster communications were breaking down rural insularity, when the countryside was becoming subordinate to the cities, and when the rural proletariat was increasingly assimilating many of the urban manners and pastimes — that those diversions which were intrinsically rooted in a country parish, or the environs of a market town, were finally and irreparably dissolved.

It is worth noting, in conclusion, the extent to which many of the attacks on traditional recreations betrayed a pronounced class bias. The reformers' energies were mobilized largely against popular amusements; few were so indelicate as to storm the citadels of genteel pleasure. The critics were able to discriminate nicely between the fashionable diversions of the rich and the less fashionable of the poor – and to act accordingly. Such discrimination was especially noticeable in the movement against animal sports. The R.S.P.C.A., despite disclaimers to the contrary, discreetly disregarded the pleasures of the fashionable world and almost always prosecuted only plebeian sportsmen.[77] The Act of 1835 against cruelty to animals conveniently confined its attention to cattle and domestic animals; it was at pains to exclude from its frame of reference such 'wildlife' as rabbits, deer, and foxes. Henry Alken's *National Sports of Great Britain*, which condemned the baiting of bulls, found it expedient to eulogize field sports and (more remarkably) even to defend cock-fighting and badger-baiting, both of which still retained a select genteel following (the defence here was partly on grounds which were rejected as a justification for bull-baiting – that is, the natural ferocity of the combatants). Fighting cocks, it was ingeniously argued, 'die of that which they love, for it is impossible to make a Cock fight against his will; and as they are in no case, or seldom, permitted to die a natural death, it matters little, in reality of rhyme or reason, at what period, early or late, they may be accommodated with an artificial one'.[78] Richard Martin, a persistent sponsor of bills for the protection of animals during the 1820s, countered the charge of discrimination with the argument that 'Hunting and shooting, in his opinion, were amusements of a totally different character. Many gentlemen who indulged in those recreations had been the foremost to support his bill for preventing cruelty to animals.' 'Those who sported on their own manors, or fished in their own streams,' he suggested, 'were a very different sort of men. He had known men as humane as men could be who followed the sports of the field.'[79]

The flaws in such arguments did not go unnoticed by some contemporaries, especially those who were unimpressed by the general tenor of the evangelical movement. Indeed, there was a considerable awareness of the prejudices and partiality which were involved in the programmes for recreational reform. At the beginning of the century this objection was advanced with particular vigour by William Windham, a vocal opponent of the various legislative attempts to restrain cruelty to animals. His case, which was to be frequently repeated both in and out of Parliament during the next several decades, was given public currency through the debate on the Bull-baiting bill of 1800:

> The advocates of this bill . . . proposed to abolish bull-baiting on the score of cruelty. It is strange enough that such an argument should be employed by a set of persons who have a most vexatious code of laws for the protection of their own amusements . . . When gentlemen talk of cruelty, I must remind them, that it belongs as much to

shooting, as to the sport of bull-baiting; nay more so, as it frequently happens, that where one bird is shot, a great many others go off much wounded . . . And do not gentlemen, for the empty fame of being in at the death, frequently goad and spur their horses to exertions greatly beyond their strength? . . . The common people may ask with justice, why abolish bull-baiting, and protect hunting and shooting? What appearance must we make, if we, who have every source of amusement open to us, and yet follow these cruel sports, become rigid censors of the sports of the poor, and abolish them on account of their cruelty, when they are not more cruel than our own?[80]

[. . .]

The one-sidedness of the reformers' concerns was widely recognized, at least by a substantial body of respectable opinion. 'The *privileged* orders can be as cruel as they please,' complained a Stamford journal in 1819, 'and few are the mortals who dare say wrong they do; while every evil action of the lowly is trumpeted forth: the perpetrator is even *named*, that he may be shunned and despised.'[81] John Drakard's *Stamford News* was at pains to defend the town's bull-running against the outrage of genteel sensibilities (especially as expressed in the *Stamford Mercury*): 'Away, then with this spurious feeling and bastard humanity! which froths and foams at one yearly indulgence of the lower orders, and sympathizes with the daily and destructive enjoyments of the high and the wealthy, or leaves them sanctified and untouched.'[82] Even one of the reform bodies, the Animals' Friend Society (which was much less fashionably supported than the R.S.P.C.A.), showed some awareness of the partiality of the movement which it helped to sustain:

The lower classes have, as they deserve, been unsparingly censured by every one having the least claim to humanity who has treated on the subject, for bull-baiting, dog-fighting, etc., and even by stag-hunters themselves – while their own equally savage sports are held by them as virtues, and their heartless outrages and treachery to defenceless animals are related by them with all the glee that belongs to brave and generous deeds, with bravado added to their crimes.[83]

Sometimes these objections were simply brushed aside as unworthy of consideration. Another reply was to accept and sanction such discriminations, more or less openly, as an inherent aspect of a hierarchical society. Henry Alken's *National Sports of Great Britain*, for instance, was a candid apologia for the sports of the landed elite. Objections to coursing on the grounds of cruelty were not to be seriously considered:

'The arguments for its high gratification to those who possess leisure and wealth, more especially in land, and for its undisputed conduciveness to health and hilarity, will ever prove decisive.'[84] There was some distress at the general meeting of the R.S.P.C.A. in 1840 when a person stood up and asked 'the noblemen and gentlemen on the platform, who declaimed upon the subject of cruelty to animals, how many hunters had they in their stables, and how many had been ridden to death for their amusement? (Cries of no, no.)'; but the Society's supporters were quick to defend themselves. 'I, for one,' admitted Lord Dudley C. Stuart, 'keep several hunters, and love the pleasures of the chase as sincerely as any man':

> At the same time, my notion is, that as all animals were made for the use of man, there can be no possible harm in making them conducive to our rational enjoyments, as well as employing them for our profit and convenience; but at the same time, I trust, that I never in my life ill-used any animal to promote my pleasure or amusement; (Hear, hear,) and I believe, generally speaking, that in pursuing the sport of hunting, little or no cruelty is practised. No doubt the stern advocate for humanity may object both to hunting and steeple-chasing as unnecessary, and shooting and fishing would of course come within the same rule; but I think these objections to our national sports may be carried too far, and, so long as unnecessary cruelty is avoided, I see no reason to cry them down on the score of inhumanity; and I believe it is generally admitted, that the sports of the field, if unavoidably attended with a certain degree of suffering on the one hand, produce, on the other hand, many advantages which might fairly be brought forward as a set-off against the alleged cruelty of such practices. (Hear, hear.)[85]

Popular blood sports, however, could not be discovered to offer any such compensating features. Bull-baiting, for instance, was thought to admit of '*no one* palliation that may be urged in excuse of some recreations, which though on principles of humanity, cannot be altogether justified; yet not being marked with any of the *peculiar atrocities* of the other, must not be brought into comparison'.[86] Rationalizations for field sports, however, were not always easily sustained, and some writers found it useful to call upon the will of Providence:

> though having no partiality or fondness for the chase in any form, [we are] yet constrained to believe that there is such a provision made for it by an all-wise Providence in the constitution of man, the instinct of hounds, and even in the strategems of fleetness of the hare herself, who may often have a gratification in eluding or out-

stripping her pursuers, as to afford some justification of the practice. It has been strongly argued that the great propensity to field sports, which operates on many like an uncontrolled instinct, is a sure indication of the intention of the Deity, not only to permit, but to stimulate to those pursuits. And here, as in all things else, we may discern wisdom and goodness.[87]

'How shall we account for' the fact, queries another advocate of humanity to animals, 'that in every country and every age of the world, the love of the chase has been the distinguishing characteristic of a considerable portion, and far from being the worst portion, of the community?' It must, he concluded, be a legitimate pastime, not to be compared with the atrocities of plebeian diversions.[88]

Other reasons were sometimes advanced in support of a careful differentiation between popular and genteel recreations. It was argued that protection should be given to animals whenever politically possible, that reform should be pursued with due regard for the limits of public tolerance, and that it was not to be expected that everything could be accomplished at once.[89] Some writers allowed that the elegance, excitement, and refinement of certain genteel amusements compensated in part for the cruelty involved.[90] Unlike the popular sports, genteel diversions had been incorporated into a code of sensibility and refined manners. Moreover, while fashionable pleasures were typically private, enjoyed within the confines of a personal estate, the amusements of the people were normally on public display, open to the view of delicate tastes, and consequently they were much more likely to violate the increasingly severe standards of public decorum. 'Open sin' was the principal concern; private vices were not as socially dangerous.[91] The degree of a diversion's publicness significantly conditioned the extent to which there might be a concern for its regulation. 'The Legislature ought to interfere for the protection of animals, wherever public control can be extended,' suggested one writer, 'although it may be deemed impossible to regulate the conduct of individuals in regard to their own property.'[92] Property, as always, was a substantial deterrent to incautious public meddling.

There was as well a pronounced and appreciating general bias against recreations which were public and in favour of domestic pleasures, and such a view was bound to accentuate any established animosities towards popular traditions. The amusements of Christians 'should be rather of a private, than a public and gregarious, kind', opined a contributor to the *Christian Observer* in 1805.[93] 'That the human mind requires recreation, experience proves', admitted an essay of 1827; 'but where the taste is not vitiated, the necessary recreation is more easily and satisfactorily found in domestic privacy, than in the haunts

of dissipation and vice, or even in large assemblies of a better character.'[94] Here, then, was a basis for another direct clash of sentiment:
while respectability increasingly favoured family relaxation, the traditional pastimes were mostly of a public character, conditioned by their
involvement in crowded settings, and hence were out of tune with the
newer tastes. The home was a sanctuary and its 'fireside comforts'
were the highest rewards. And since these satisfactions were imagined
to be accessible to all — 'these best pleasures of our nature the Almighty
has put within the reach of the poor no less than the rich', thought
Wilberforce[95] — there was no reason to encourage the continuance of
more primitive recreational habits. The older usages were incapable of
providing genuine pleasure. Happiness, argued William Howitt, 'does
not consist in booths and garlands, drums and horns, or in capering
around a May-pole. Happiness is a fireside thing. It is a thing of grave
and earnest tone; and the deeper and truer it is, the more is it removed
from the riot of mere merriment.'[96]

Perhaps the most important basis for the discriminating treatment
of recreational practices was the accepted, long-standing distinction
between a life of leisure, which was a perquisite of gentility, and a life
of onerous and involuntary labour, which was a mark of a plebeian
existence. For gentlemen recreation was a natural and legitimate part
of their culture; for labouring men it was (or could easily become) a
dangerous temptation, a distraction from their primary concerns. 'To
be born for no other Purpose than to consume the Fruits of the Earth',
wrote Henry Fielding, 'is the Privilege (if it may be really called a
Privilege) of very few. The greater Part of Mankind must sweat hard to
produce them, or Society will no longer answer the Purposes for which
it was ordained.'[97] Diversion (indeed, often diversion in abundance)
was an indulgence which the affluent could readily afford, but the
common people had to guard themselves, or be protected, from such
potentially destructive practices. This was a distinction which was
widely acknowledged. For the working people, said Fielding, 'Time
and Money are almost synonymous; and as they have very little of each
to spare, it becomes the Legislature, as much as possible, to suppress
all Temptations whereby they may be induced too profusely to squan-
der either the one or the other; since all such Profusion must be
repaired at the Cost of the Public.'[98] It was entirely proper, then, to
treat recreation with due regard for the status of its participants — 'In
Diversion, as in many other Particulars, the upper Part of Life is distinguished from the Lower' — and to apply the sort of restraints on
popular indulgence which would be quite unnecessary for the upper
classes.[99] Labour discipline was not to be directed towards men of
property; indeed, for them it was socially meaningless. Social regulations dealt only with the lower classes, and among these classes recreation

was found to be especially in need of control from above: 'while these classes ought to be protected and encouraged in the enjoyment of their *innocent* amusements,' reported the Society for the Suppression of Vice, 'surely a greater benefit cannot be conferred upon them, than to deprive them of such amusements as tend to impair their health, to injure their circumstances, to distress their families, and to involve them in vice and misery'.[100] Just as the Game Laws discriminated in favour of the sport of gentlemen, and did so with the approval, or at least general acquiescence, of 'public opinion' — 'Rural diversions certainly constitute a very pleasing and proper amusement for all ranks above the lowest', remarked one essayist[101] — so the attacks on traditional recreation accommodated themselves to the circumstances of social and political power, concentrated their attention on the culture of the multitude, and fashioned their moral protest in a manner which was consistent with the requirements of social discipline.

Notes

1. Abraham de la Pryme, *The Diary of Abraham de la Pryme*, ed. Charles Jackson (Surtees Society, LIV, 1870).

2. *Northampton Mercury*, 2 February 1788.

3. John Brand, *Observations on Popular Antiquities* (Newcastle-upon-Tyne, 1777), revised edn by Henry Ellis (2 vols., London, 1813), p. 234 (cf. p. 377n); F.E. Sawyer, 'Sussex Folk-Lore and Customs Connected with the Seasons', *Sussex Archaeological Collections*, vol. XXXIII (1883), p. 239; and James Spershott, *The Memoirs of James Spershott*, ed. Francis W. Steer, Chichester Papers No. 30 (1962), p. 14.

4. *Gentleman's Magazine*, vol. LI (1781), p. 72; *Monthly Magazine*, vol. IV (1797), p. 198.

5. Joseph Strutt, *Glig-Gamena Angel-Deod; or, the Sports and Pastimes of the People of England* (London, 1801), p. 212; cf. *Gentleman's Magazine*, vol. LXXII (1802), Part II, p. 998.

6. *Warwick and Warwickshire General Advertiser*, 19 February 1814 and 6 March 1824.

7. William Hone, *The Every-Day Book* (2 vols.; London, 1825-7), vol. I, col. 252; Robert Gibbs, *A History of Aylesbury* (Aylesbury, 1885), pp. 554-5.

8. Joseph Greene, *Correspondence of the Reverend Joseph Green 1712-1790*, ed. Levi Fox (London, 1965), pp. 42-3; cf. Josiah Tucker, *An Earnest and Affectionate Address to the Common People of England, Concerning their Usual Recreations on Shrove Tuesday* (London, n.d.; probably published *c.* 1752-3), p. 4.

9. *Sporting Magazine*, vol. III (1793), p. 77; *Stamford Mercury*, 13 November 1789.

10. *Monthly Magazine*, vol. IV (1797), p. 198; Strutt, *Sports and Pastimes*, p. 193.

11. Roy A. Church, *Economic and Social Change in a Midland Town: Victorian Nottingham 1815-1900* (London, 1966), p. 15; E.W. Bedell, *An Account of Hornsea, in Holderness, in the East-Riding of Yorkshire* (Hull, 1848), p. 88.

12. *Stamford Mercury*, 9 November 1821; *Bury and Norwich Post*, 18 November 1801 and 10 November 1802, and *Monthly Magazine*, vol. XII (1801), p. 464; *Gentleman's Magazine*, vol. LXXV (1805), Part I, pp. 203-4.

13. *Norfolk Chronicle*, 14 March 1807, 21 January 1815, and 23 May 1818; John Latimer, *The Annals of Bristol in the Nineteenth Century* (Bristol, 1887), p. 68; K. Backhouse, *Memoir of Samuel Capper* (London, 1855), p. 31; *Animal's Friend*, no. 5 (1837), p. 18.

14. *Victoria County History of Derbyshire*, vol. II, p. 304; *The History and Topography of Ashbourn* (Ashbourn, 1839), pp. 94-5; *Derby Mercury*, 2 September 1829; Gibbs, *Aylesbury*, pp. 559-60; Oxfordshire RO, Quarter Sessions, Rolls, 1827, Epiphany no. 5, and 1828, Epiphany nos. 1-4; W.O. Hassall (ed.), *Wheatley Records 956-1956* (Oxfordshire Record Society, vol. XXXVII, 1956), pp. 90-1.

15. H. Edwards, *A Collection of Old English Customs* (London, 1842), pp. 63-4; Arthur T. Heelas, 'The Old Workhouse at Wokingham', *Berks. Bucks and Oxon Archaeological Journal*, vol. XXXI (1927), pp. 170-1; *Hull Advertiser*, 11 October 1817 and 13 October 1820.

16. On Lancashire: *Parliamentary History*, vol. XXXVI, p. 840 (a remark of William Windham in a debate of 1802); *Northampton Mercury*, 18 November 1820 (on Rochdale); and *Voice of Humanity*, vol. I (1830-1), pp. 50-1; on the West Midlands: Charlotte S. Burne (ed.), *Shropshire Folk-lore: a Sheaf of Gleanings* (London, 1883), p. 447; B.S. Trinder, 'The Memoir of William Smith', *Shropshire Archaeological Society Transactions*, vol. LVIII, Part II (1966), pp. 181-2; *Voice of Humanity*, vol. I (1830-1), pp. 49-52; *Animals' Friend*, no. 3 (1835), p. 6; *Christian Advocate*, 22 November 1830; and Abraham Smith, *A Scriptural and Moral Catechism, Designed Chiefly to Lead the Minds of the Rising Generation to the Love and Practice of Mercy, and to Expose the Horrid Nature and Exceeding Sinfulness of Cruelty to the Dumb Creation* (Birmingham, 1833), Part II, pp. 5-6.

17. *Parliamentary History*, vol. XXXV, pp. 202-14, and vol. XXXVI, pp. 829-54.

18. *Cobbett's Parliamentary Debates*, vol. XIV, pp. 851-3, 989-90, 1,029-41 and 1,071; and vol. XVI, pp. 726 and 845-6.

19. 3 George IV c. 71; *Parliamentary Debates*, New Series, vol. XIX, pp. 1,121-2 (6 June 1828); F.A. Carrington and J. Payne, *Reports of Cases Argued and Ruled at Nisi Prius* (9 vols.; London, 1823-41), vol. III, pp. 225-8; and *Voice of Humanity*, vol. I (1830-1), p. 49. The one unequivocal statute on the subject was the 121st section of 3 George IV c. 126, which made illegal bull-baiting on the public highways.

20. *Parliamentary Debates*, New Series, vol. IX, pp. 433-5; vol. X, pp. 130-4, 368-9 and 486-96; vol. XII, pp. 657-61 and 1,002-13; vol. XIV, pp. 647-52; and vol. XXI, pp. 1,319-20.

21. 5 & 6 William IV c. 59. An Act of 1849 'for the more effectual Prevention of Cruelty to Animals', 12 & 13 Victoria c. 92, was similar to the Act of 1835, though it was more explicit about the illegality of cock-fighting (the earlier Act had only outlawed the keeping of cockpits).

22. [Sir Richard Hill], *A Letter to the Right Hon. William Windham, on his Late Opposition to the Bill to Prevent Bull-Baiting* (London, 2nd edn, n.d.), first published in 1800; Percival Stockdale, *A Remonstrance Against Inhumanity to Animals; and Particularly Against the Savage Practice of Bull-Baiting* (Alnwick, 1802); Edward Barry, *Bull-Baiting! A Sermon on Barbarity to God's Dumb Creation* (Reading, 1802).

23. Lewis Bettany (ed.), *Diaries of William Johnston Temple 1780-1796* (Oxford, 1929), p. 187.

24. Sir Oswald Mosley, *History of the Castle, Priory, and Town of Tutbury* (London, 1832), p. 90; RSPCA, MS Minute Book no. 3, pp. 14 and 24-6.

25. Gibbs, *Aylesbury*, p. 559; George Oliver, *The History and Antiquities of the Town and Minster of Beverley, in the County of York* (Beverley, 1829), p. 422; RSPCA, MS Minute Book no. 2, pp. 93-4 and 202-4, and *Twelfth Annual Report of the SPCA* (1838), pp. 81-2.

26. *Stamford Mercury*, 10 November 1826.

27. *Derby Mercury*, 10 August 1842.

28. *Jackson's Oxford Journal*, 21 October 1837.

29. *Animals' Friend*, no. 4 (1836), pp. 4-5; no. 5 (1837), pp. 16-18; no. 6 (1838), pp. 31-2; no. 7 (1839), p. 27; and *Aris's Birmingham Gazette*, 20 November 1837.

30. William H. Drummond, *The Rights of Animals, and Man's Obligation to Treat them with Humanity* (London, 1838), p. 104; William Howitt, *The Rural Life of England* (2 vols.; London, 1838; 2nd edn (1 vol.) London, 1840), p. 525; and William Youatt, *The Obligation and Extent of Humanity to Brutes* (London, 1839), p. 159.

31. For evidence concerning the practice of modified forms of badger-baiting, see the *Guardian*, 25 October 1967, p. 6.

32. *Stamford Mercury*, 13 November 1789.

33. Ibid., 12 November 1814.

34. *Voice of Humanity*, vol. I (1830-1), pp. 68-9. Cf. ibid., p. 20; Nehemiah Curnock (ed.), *The Journal of the Rev. John Wesley* (8 vols.; London, 1909-16), vol. IV, pp. 175-6; Stockdale, *Inhumanity to Animals*, p. 4; and J.F. Winks, *The Bull Running at Stamford, a Transgression of the Divine Laws, and a Subject of Christian Grief; Being the Substance of a Sermon Delivered in the General Baptist Meeting-House, Stamford, on Lord's Day Evening, Nov. 15, 1829* (London, n.d.), p. 4.

35. *Clemency to Brutes: The Substance of Two Sermons preached on a Shrove-Sunday, With a particular View to dissuade from that Species of Cruelty annually practised in England, The Throwing at Cocks* (London, 1761), p. 6.

36. *Bury and Norwich Post*, 18 November 1801.

37. Barry, *Bull-Baiting*, p. 12.

38. James Macaulay, *Essay on Cruelty to Animals* (Edinburgh, 1839), p. 124; cf. Abraham Smith, *Scriptural and Moral Catechism*, Part II, p. 19.

39. *Parliamentary History*, vol. XXXV, p. 202.

40. *Annual Register* (1800), p. 148.

41. *Hull Advertiser*, 25 April 1818.

42. Surrey RO, P 6/3/5, vestry meetings of 5 March 1829 and 10 February 1836.

43. Richmond Borough Library, Richmond Vestry Minute Book for 1829-42, pp. 466 and 468, and *Surrey Standard*, 6 March 1840; *Surrey Comet*, 28 February 1857, 13 February 1864 and 9 March 1867.

44. Morris Marples, *A History of Football* (London, 1954), pp. 101-2; Francis P. Magoun, *History of Football from the Beginnings to 1871* (Bochum-Langendreer, 1938), p. 126.

45. *The Times*, 2 and 6 March 1840.

46. *Surrey Comet*, 2 and 9 March 1867, 29 February 1868.

47. *Derby Mercury*, 15, 22 and 29 February and 7 March 1860, 20 February and 6 March 1861; 12 March 1862; *Derbyshire Advertiser*, 20 February 1863; cf. Magoun, *History of Football*, pp. 109-10 and Marples, *History of Football*, pp. 102-4.

48. Kingston-upon-Thames Guildhall, Kingston Court of Assembly Book 1834-1859, D.I.4.5.

49. *Derby and Chesterfield Reporter*, 23 February 1832.
50. *Surrey Comet*, 7 February 1857.
51. *Derby and Chesterfield Reporter*, 7 February 1845.
52. For evidence in support of these points, see the *Derby Mercury*, 9 February 1815 and 29 January 1845; *Penny Magazine*, 6 April 1839; *Surrey Standard*, 20 February 1836 and 13 March 1840; *Surrey Comet*, 9 February 1856, 7 February 1857 and 13 February 1858.
53. E.W. Brayley, *A Topographical History of Surrey* (5 vols.; London, 1841-8), vol. III, pp. 51-2.
54. Stephen Glover, *The History and Gazetteer of the County of Derby* (2 vols.; Derby, 1831), vol. I, p. 262. The newspapers often alluded to the genteel followers of the match.
55. Kingston-upon-Thames Guildhall, Court of Assembly Book 1834-59, D.I.4.5., meetings of 29 February and 6 May 1840; *The Times*, 6 March 1840.
56. *Derby Mercury*, 7 March 1860.
57. Bedfordshire RO, QSR 17, 3 (Epiphany Sessions, 1791).
58. *Northampton Mercury*, 11 June 1791.
59. Edward Barry, *A Letter on the Practice of Boxing* (London, 1789), p. 7; cf. a letter of 2 September 1790 from Charles Dundas to Lord Kenyon in *Historical Manuscripts Commission, 14th Report, Appendix, Part IV. The Manuscripts of Lord Kenyon* (London, 1894), pp. 531-2.
60. John Whitaker, *The History of Manchester* (London, 1775), Book II, pp. 443-4.
61. William Somerville, *Hobbinol, or the Rural Games. A Burlesque Poem in Blank Verse* (London, 1740), p. ii.
62. *Bedfordshire Mercury*, 7 January 1861.
63. *Gentleman's Magazine*, vol. LIII (1783), Part II, p. 1,004. See also Aulay Macaulay, *The History and Antiquities of Claybrook, in the County of Leicester* (London, 1791), p. 128; George Cope, *The Origin, Excellence, and Perversion of Wakes or Parish Feasts* (Hereford, 1816), which was drawn to my attention by Mr Jolyon Hall; William J. Kidd, *Village Wakes; Their Origin, Design and Abuse. A Sermon Preached in the Parochial Chapel of Didsbury, on Sunday Afternoon, August 1, 1841* (Manchester, 1841); and John Bowstead, *The Village Wake, or the Feast of the Dedication* (London, 1846).
64. Henry Bourne, *Antiquitates Vulgares; or, the Antiquities of the Common People* (Newcastle, 1725), p. 228.
65. Arthur L. Humphreys, *Bucklebury: a Berkshire Parish* (Reading, 1932), p. 369. Cf. *Leeds Intelligencer*, 20 June 1786; *Hull Advertiser*, 4 June and 23 July 1808; *Stamford Mercury*, 20 October 1837; *Derby Mercury*, 1 July 1840; and *Bedfordshire Mercury*, 7 January 1861.
66. Hone, *Every-Day Book*, vol. II, col. 55; cf. *Gentleman's Magazine*, vol. LIII (1783), Part II, p. 1,005; and James Pilkington, *A View of the Present State of Derbyshire* (2 vols.; London, 1789), vol. II, p. 55.
67. Essex RO, Q/SBb 225/16 and Q/SO 10, pp. 337-8; Q/SBb 323/52; Q/SO 14, pp. 292-4; Q/SBb 343/26; and Chelmsford Chronicle, 26 May 1786 and 8 July 1791.
68. Essex RO, Q/SBb 225/16.
69. Surrey RO, Acc. 450 (1788); William Godschall, *A General Plan of Parochial and Provincial Police* (London, 1787), p. 111; and Leon Radzinowicz, *A History of English Criminal Law and its Administration from 1750* (4 vols.; London, 1948-69), vol. III, pp. 491-3.
70. *Quarterly Review*, vol. XXIV (October 1820), p. 258; Essex RO, D/P 263/28/6; *Norfolk Chronicle and Norwich Gazette*, 22 July 1826; Hertfordshire RO, D/P 121/8/1; and PRO, 'Subject Index and Box List to Home Office Papers

1871/1878 (HO 45)', pp. 70-7.

71. See in particular Greville J. Chester, *Statute Fairs: Their Evils and Their Remedy* (York and London, 1856), and the same author's *Statute Fairs*, a sermon preached in 1858; Nash Stephenson, 'On Statute Fairs: Their Evils and Their Remedy', *Transactions of the National Association for the Promotion of Social Science* (1858), pp. 624-31; J. Skinner, *Facts and Opinions Concerning Statute Hirings, Respectfully addressed to the Landowners, Clergy, Farmers and Tradesmen of the East Riding of Yorkshire* (London, 1861); T.E. Kebbel, *The Agricultural Labourer* (London, 1870), pp. 118-22 and 131-3; and article on 'Mops' in the *Illustrated London News*, 26 October 1878, p. 398; and Francis G. Heath, *Peasant Life in the West of England* (London, 1880), pp. 68-9.

72. See the *Penny Magazine*, 12 August 1837, pp. 311-12.

73. William Owen, *An Authentic Account . . . of All the Fairs in England and Wales* (London, 1756 and numerous later editions), 1756 and 1859 edns.

74. *An Address to the Public from the Society for the Suppression of Vice* (London, 1803), Part II, p. 61n. Those pleasure fairs which did in fact prosper during the Victorian period were often the very large events, such as the Nottingham Goose Fair and St Giles's Fair in Oxford. See Sally Alexander, *St Giles's Fair, 1830-1914: Popular Culture and the Industrial Revolution in the 19th Century* (Ruskin College History Workshop, pamphlet no. 2, 1970).

75. Hertfordshire RO, D/P 98/29/6; cf. Brian Harrison, *Drink and the Victorians: the Temperance Question in England 1815-1872* (London, 1971), pp. 328-9.

76. From the preface to *Far From the Madding Crowd*.

77. Brian Harrison, 'Religion and Recreation in Nineteenth-Century England', *Past & Present*, no. 38 (December 1967), pp. 116-18.

78. Henry Alken, *The National Sports of Great Britain* (London, 1821), captions for plate i on cock-fighting, plate ii on bull-baiting, and the plate 'Drawing the Badger'.

79. *Parliamentary Debates*, New Series, vol. X, pp. 133 and 487 (11 and 26 February 1824).

80. *Parliamentary History*, vol. XXXV, p. 207 (18 April 1800); cf. *Cobbett's Parliamentary Debates*, vol. XIV, p. 990 (12 June 1809).

81. *Fireside Magazine*, vol. I (1819), p. 48.

82. *Stamford News*, 19 November 1819.

83. *Animals' Friend*, no. 6 (1838), p. 16.

84. Alken, *National Sports*, caption for the plate 'Coursing-Death of the Hare'.

85. *Fourteenth Annual Report of the RSPCA* (1840), pp. 40-1 and 45-6.

86. Barry, *Bull-Baiting*, pp. 8-9.

87. Drummond, *Rights of Animals*, p. 37; cf. pp. 41 and 44.

88. Youatt, *Humanity to Brutes*, pp. 109-11.

89. *Parliamentary Debates*, New Series, vol. IX, p. 433 (21 May 1823), and vol. X, p. 133 (11 February 1824); Macaulay, *Cruelty to Animals*, pp. 55-7.

90. Howitt, *Rural Life* (1838 edn), vol. I, pp. 41-2 and 45; Stockdale, *Inhumanity to Animals*, p. 10n.

91. Ford K. Brown, *Fathers of the Victorians: the Age of Wilberforce* (Cambridge, 1961), p. 435; Radzinowicz, *English Criminal Law*, vol. III, p. 182.

92. Macaulay, *Cruelty to Animals*, p. 42.

93. *Christian Observer*, vol. V (1805), p. 13.

94. *Observations on Some of the Popular Amusements of this Country, Addressed to the Higher Classes of Society* (London, 1827), p. 21.

95. Robert Isaac Wilberforce and Samuel Wilberforce, *The Life of William Wilberforce* (5 vols.; London, 1838), vol. II, p. 449.

96. Howitt, *Rural Life* (1840 edn), p. 420.

97. Henry Fielding, *An Enquiry into the Causes of the Late Increase of Robbers* (London, 1751), p. 7.

98. Ibid., pp. 11-12; cf. *Life of Wilberforce*, vol. II, pp. 448-9.

99. Fielding, *Increase of Robbers*, pp. 10-11 and 22-3.

100. *Address from the Society for the Suppression of Vice*, Part II, p. 61n.

101. Vicesimus Knox, *Essays Moral and Literary* (2 vols.; London, 1791), vol. II, pp. 153-4.

2 CLASS CONSCIOUSNESS: THE RADI⟨ CULTURE

Edward Thompson

Source: *The Making of the English Working Class* (Penguin, Harmondsworth, 1968), Ch. 16. © E.P. Thompson.

When contrasted with the Radical years which preceded and the Chartist years which succeeded it, the decade of the 1820s seems strangely quiet — a mildly prosperous plateau of social peace. But many years later a London costermonger warned Mayhew:

> People fancy that when all's quiet that all's stagnating. Propagandism is going on for all that. It's when all's quiet that the seed's-a-growing, Republicans and Socialists are pressing their doctrines.

These quiet years were the years of Richard Carlile's contest for the liberty of the press; of growing trade union strength and the repeal of the Combination Acts; of the growth of free thought, cooperative experiment, and Owenite theory. They are years in which individuals and groups sought to render into theory the twin experiences which we have described — the experience of the Industrial Revolution, and the experience of popular Radicalism insurgent and in defeat. And at the end of the decade, when there came the climactic contest between Old Corruption and Reform, it is possible to speak in a new way of the working people's consciousness of their interests and of their predicament as a class.

There is a sense in which we may describe popular Radicalism in these years as an intellectual culture. The articulate consciousness of the self-taught was above all a political consciousness. For the first half of the nineteenth century, when the formal education of a great part of the people entailed little more than instruction in the Three R's, was by no means a period of intellectual atrophy. The towns, and even the villages, hummed with the energy of the autodidact. Given the elementary techniques of literacy, labourers, artisans, shopkeepers and clerks and schoolmasters, proceeded to instruct themselves, severally or in groups. And the books or instructors were very often those sanctioned by reforming opinion. A shoemaker, who had been taught his letters in the Old Testament, would labour through the *Age of Reason*; a schoolmaster, whose education had taken him little further than worthy

47

ᵤious homilies, would attempt Voltaire, Gibbon, Ricardo; here and ᵤnere local Radical leaders, weavers, booksellers, tailors, would amass shelves of Radical periodicals and learn how to use parliamentary Blue Books; illiterate labourers would, nevertheless, go each week to a pub where Cobbett's editorial letter was read aloud and discussed.

Thus working men formed a picture of the organization of society, out of their own experience and with the help of their hard-won and erratic education, which was above all a political picture. They learned to see their own lives as part of a general history of conflict between the loosely defined 'industrious classes' on the one hand, and the unreformed House of Commons on the other. From 1830 onwards a more clearly defined class consciousness, in the customary Marxist sense, was maturing, in which working people were aware of continuing both old and new battles on their own.

It is difficult to generalize as to the diffusion of literacy in the early years of the century. The 'industrious classes' touched, at one pole, the million or more who were illiterate, or whose literacy amounted to little more than the ability to spell out a few words or write their names. At the other pole there were men of considerable intellectual attainment. Illiteracy (we should remember) by no means excluded men from political discourse. In Mayhew's England the ballad-singers and 'patterers' still had a thriving occupation, with their pavement farces and street-corner parodies, following the popular mood and giving a Radical or anti-Papal twist to their satirical monologues or chaunts, according to the state of the market. The illiterate worker might tramp miles to hear a Radical orator, just as the same man (or another) might tramp to taste a sermon. In times of political ferment the illiterate would get their workmates to read aloud from the periodicals; while at Houses of Call the news was read, and at political meetings a prodigious time was spent in reading addresses and passing long strings of resolutions. The earnest Radical might even attach a talismanic virtue to the possession of favoured works which he was unable, by his own efforts, to read. A Cheltenham shoemaker who called punctually each Sunday on W.E. Adams to have 'Feargus's letter' read to him, nevertheless was the proud owner of several of Cobbett's books, carefully preserved in wash leather cases.[1]

Recent studies have thrown much light on the predicament of the working-class reader in these years. To simplify a difficult discussion, we may say that something like two out of every three working men were able to read after some fashion in the early part of the century, although rather fewer could write. As the effect of the Sunday schools and day schools increasingly became felt, as well as the drive for self-improvement among working people themselves, so the number of the illiterate fell, although in the worst child labour areas the fall was delayed. But the ability to read was only the elementary technique. The ability to handle abstract and consecutive argument was by no means inborn; it had to be discovered against almost overwhelming difficulties – the lack of leisure, the cost of candles (or of spectacles), as well as educational deprivation. Ideas and terms were sometimes employed in the early Radical movement which, it is evident, had for some ardent followers a fetishistic rather than rational value. Some of the Pentridge rebels thought that a 'Provisional Government' would ensure a more plentiful supply of 'provisions'; while, in one account of the pitmen of the north-east in 1819, 'Universal Suffrage is understood by many of them to mean universal suffering . . . "if one member suffers, all must suffer".'[2]

Such evidence as survives as to the literary accomplishment of working men in the first two decades of the century serves only to illustrate the folly of generalization. In the Luddite times (when few but working men would have supported their actions) anonymous messages vary from self-conscious apostrophes to 'Liberty with her Smiling Attributes' to scarcely decipherable chalking on walls. We may take examples of both kinds. In 1812 the Salford Coroner, who had returned a verdict of 'Justifiable Homicide' upon the body of a man shot while attacking Burton's mill was warned:

> . . . know thou cursed insinuater, if Burton's infamous action was 'justifiable', the Laws of Tyrants are Reasons Dictates. – Beware, Beware! A month's bathing in the Stygian Lake would not wash this sanguinary deed from our minds, it but augments the heritable cause, that stirs us up in indignation.

The letter concludes, 'Ludd finis est' – a reminder that Manchester boasted a grammar school (which Bamford himself for a short time attended) as well as private schools where the sons of artisans might obtain Latin enough for this. The other paper was found in Chesterfield Market. It is much to the same purpose but (despite the educational disadvantages of the writer) it somehow carries a greater conviction:

> I Ham going to inform you that there is Six Thousand men coming to you in Apral and when We Will go and Blow Parlement house up and Blow up all afour hus/labring Peple Cant Stand it No Longer/ dam all Such Roges as England governes but Never mind Ned hud when general nody and his harmey Comes We Will soon bring about the greate Revelution then all these great mens heads gose of.

Others of the promised benefits of 'general nody' were: 'We Will Nock doon the Prisions and the Judge we Will murde whan he is aslepe.'

The difference (the critics will tell us) is not only a matter of style: it is also one of sensibility. The first we might suppose to be written by a bespectacled, greying, artisan — a cobbler (or hatter or instrument-maker) with Voltaire, Volney and Paine on his shelf, and a taste for the great tragedians. Among the State prisoners of 1817 there were other men of this order from Lancashire: the seventy-year-old William Ogden, a letter-press printer, who wrote to his wife from prison: 'though I am in Irons, I will face my enemies like the Great Caractacus when in the same situation'; Joseph Mitchell, another printing worker, whose daughters were called Mirtilla, Carolina and Cordelia, and who — when another daughter was born while he was in prison — wrote in haste to his wife proposing that the baby be called Portia; or Samuel Bamford himself, whose instructions to his wife were more specific: 'a Reformers Wife ought to be an heroine'. The second letter (we can be almost sure) is the work of a collier or a village stockinger. [. . .]

'If the Bible Societies, and the Sunday School societies have been attended by no other good,' Sherwin noted, 'they have at least produced one beneficial effect; — they have been the means of teaching many thousands of children to read.'[3] The letters of Brandreth and his wife, of Cato Street conspirators, and of other State prisoners, give us some insight into that great area between the attainments of the skilled artisan and those of the barely literate. Somewhere in the middle we may place Mrs Johnston, addressing her husband ('My Dear Johnston'), who was a journeyman tailor, in prison:

> . . . believe me my Dear if there is not a day nor a hour in the day but what my mind is less or more engage about you. I can appeal to the almighty that it is true and when I retire to rest I pray God to forgive all my enimies and change thare heart . . .

Beside this we may set the letter of the Sheffield joiner, Wolstenholme, to his wife:

> Our Minaster hath lent me four vollams of the Missionary Register witch give me grat satisfaction to se ou the Lord is carin on is work of grais in distant contres.

The writing of this letter was attended with difficulties, since 'Have broke my spettacles'. Such letters were written in unaccustomed leisure. We can almost see Wolstenholme laboriously spelling out his words, and stopping to consult a more 'well-lettered' prisoner when he came to the hurdle of 'satisfaction'. Mrs Johnston may have consulted (but probably did not) one of the 'professional' letter-writers to be found in most towns and villages, who wrote the appropriate form of letter at 1*d*. a time. For, even among the literate, letter-writing was an unusual pursuit. The cost of postage alone prohibited it except at infrequent intervals. For a letter to pass between the north and London might cost 1*s*. 10*d*., and we know that both Mrs Johnston and Mrs Wolstenholme were suffering privations in the absence of their husbands — Mrs Johnston's shoes were full of water and she had been able to buy no more since her husband was taken up.

All the Cato Street prisoners, it seems, could write after some fashion. Brunt, the shoemaker, salted some sardonic verses with French, while James Wilson wrote:

> the Cause wich nerved a Brutus arm
> to strike a Tirant with alarm
> the cause for wich brave Hamden died
> for wich the Galant Tell defied
> a Tirants insolence and pride.

Richard Tidd, another shoemaker, on the other hand, could only muster: 'Sir I Ham a very Bad Hand at Righting'. We cannot, of course, take such men as a 'sample', since their involvement in political activity indicates that they belonged to the more conscious minority who followed the Radical press. But they may serve to warn us against *under*stating the diffusion of effective literacy. The artisans are a special case — the intellectual *élite* of the class. But there were, scattered throughout all parts of England, an abundance of educational institutions for working people, even if 'institution' is too formal a word for the dame school, the penny-a-week evening school run by a factory cripple or injured pitman, or the Sunday school itself. In the Pennine valleys, where the weavers' children were too poor to pay for slates or paper, they were taught their letters by drawing them with their fingers in a sand-table. If thousands lost these elementary attainments when they reached adult life, on the other hand the work of the Nonconformist Churches, of friendly societies and trade unions, and the needs of industry itself, all demanded that such learning be consolidated and advanced. 'I have found,' Alexander Galloway, the master-engineer, reported in 1824,

> from the mode of managing my business, by drawings and written descriptions, a man is not of much use to me unless he can read and write; if a man applies for work, and says he cannot read and write, he is asked no more questions . . .

In most artisan trades the journeyman and petty masters found some reading and work with figures an occupational necessity.

Not only the ballad-singer but also the 'number man' or 'calendar man' went round the working-class districts, hawking chap-books, almanacs, dying speeches and (between 1816 and 1820, and at intervals thereafter) Radical periodicals. (One such 'calendar man', who travelled for Cowdrey and Black, the 'seditious [i.e. Whig] printers in Manchester', was taken up by the magistrates in 1812 because it was found that on his catalogues was written: 'No blind king – Ned Ludd for ever.') One of the most impressive features of post-war Radicalism was its sustained effort to extend these attainments and to raise the level of political awareness. At Barnsley as early as January 1816 a penny-a-month club of weavers was formed, for the purpose of buying Radical newspapers and periodicals. The Hampden Clubs and Political Unions took great pains to build up 'Reading Societies' and in the larger centres they opened permanent newsrooms or reading-rooms, such as that at Hanley in the Potteries. This room was open from 8 a.m. till 10 p.m. There were penalties for swearing, for the use of indecent language and for drunkenness. Each evening the London papers were to be 'publicly read'. At the rooms of the Stockport Union in 1818, according to Joseph Mitchell, there was a meeting of class leaders on Monday nights; on Tuesday, 'moral and political readings'; on Wednesdays, 'a conversation or debate'; on Thursdays, 'Grammar, Arithmetic, &C' was taught; Saturday was a social evening; while Sunday was school day for adults and children alike. In Blackburn the members of the Female Reform Society pledged themselves 'to use our utmost endeavour to instil into the minds of our children a deep and rooted hatred of our corrupt and tyrannical rulers.' One means was the use of 'The Bad Alphabet for the use of the Children of Female Reformers': B was for Bible, Bishop, and Bigotry; K for King, King's evil, Knave and Kidnapper; W for Whig, Weakness, Wavering, and Wicked.

Despite the repression after 1819, the tradition of providing such newsrooms (sometimes attached to the shop of a Radical bookseller) continued through the 1820s. In London after the war there was a boom in coffee-houses, many of which served this double function. By 1833, at John Doherty's famous 'Coffee and Newsroom' attached to his Manchester bookshop, no fewer than ninety-six newspapers were taken every week, including the illegal 'unstamped'. In the smaller towns and villages the reading-groups were less formal but no less important. Sometimes they met at inns, 'hush-shops', or private houses; sometimes the periodical was read and discussed in the workshop. The high cost of periodicals during the time of the heaviest 'taxes on knowledge' led to thousands of *ad hoc* arrangements by which small groups clubbed together to buy their chosen paper. During the Reform Bill agitation Thomas Dunning, a Nantwich shoemaker, joined with his shopmates and 'our Unitarian minister . . . in subscribing to the *Weekly Dispatch*, price 8½*d*., the stamp duty being 4*d*. It was too expensive for *one* ill-paid crispin . . .'

The circulation of the Radical press fluctuated violently. Cobbett's 2*d. Register* at its meridian, between October 1816 and February 1817, was running at something between 40,000 and 60,000 each week, a figure many times in excess of any competitor of any sort.[4] The *Black Dwarf* ran at about 12,000 in 1819, although this figure was probably exceeded after Peterloo. Thereafter the stamp tax (and the recession of the movement) severely curtailed circulation, although Carlile's periodicals ran in the thousands through much of the Twenties. With the Reform Bill agitation, the Radical press broke through to a larger circulation once more: Doherty's *Voice of the People*, and *The Pioneer* all had circulations above ten thousand, Carlile's *Gauntlet*, Hetherington's *Poor Man's Guardian*, while a dozen smaller periodicals, like the *Destructive*, ran to some thousands. The slump in the sale of costly weekly periodicals (at anything from 7*d*. to 1*s*.) during the stamp tax decade was to great degree made up by the growth in the sales of cheap books and individual pamphlets, ranging from *The Political House that Jack Built* (100,000) to Cobbett's *Cottage Economy* (50,000, 1822-8), *History of the Protestant 'Reformation'*, and *Sermons* (211,000, 1821-8). In the same period, in most of the great centres there were one or more (and in London a dozen) dailies or weeklies which, while not being avowedly 'Radical', nevertheless catered for this large Radical public. And the growth in this very large *petit-bourgeois* and working-class reading public was recognized by those influential agencies — notably the Society for the Promotion of Christian Knowledge and the Society for the Diffusion of Useful Knowledge — which made prodigious and lavishly subsidized efforts to divert the readers to more wholesome and improving matter.

This was the culture — with its eager disputations around the book-sellers' stalls, in the taverns, workshops, and coffee-houses — which Shelley saluted in his 'Song to the Men of England' and within which the genius of Dickens matured. But it is a mistake to see it as a single, undifferentiated 'reading public'. We may say that there were several different 'publics' impinging upon and overlapping each other, but nevertheless organized according to different principles. Among the more important were the commercial public, pure and simple, which might be exploited at times of Radical excitement (the trials of Brandreth or of Thistlewood were as marketable as other 'dying confessions'), but which was followed according to the simple criteria of profitability; the various more or less organized publics, around the Churches or the Mechanics' Institutes; the passive public which the improving societies sought to get at and redeem; and the active, Radical public, which organized itself in the face of the Six Acts and the taxes on knowledge. [. . .]

There is perhaps no country in the world in which the contest for the rights of the press was so sharp, so emphatically victorious, and so peculiarly identified with the cause of the artisans and labourers. If Peterloo established (by a paradox of feeling) the right of public demonstration, the rights of a 'free press' were won in a campaign extending over fifteen or more years which has no comparison for its pig-headed, bloody-minded, and indomitable audacity. Carlile (a tin-smith who had nevertheless received a year or two of grammar school education at Ashburton in Devon) rightly saw that the repression of 1819 made the rights of the press the fulcrum of the Radical move-ment. But, unlike Cobbett and Wooler, who modified their tone to meet the Six Acts in the hope of living to fight another day (and who lost circulation accordingly), Carlile hoisted the black ensign of unquali-fied defiance and, like a pirate cock-boat, sailed straight into the middle of the combined fleets of the State and Church. As, in the aftermath of Peterloo, he came up for trial (for publishing the Works of Paine), the entire Radical press saluted his courage, but gave him up for lost. When he finally emerged, after years of imprisonment, the combined fleets were scattered beyond the horizon in disarray. He had exhausted the ammunition of the Government, and turned its *ex officio* informa-tions and special juries into laughing-stocks. He had plainly sunk the private prosecuting societies, the Constitutional Association (or 'Bridge-Street Gang') and the Vice Society, which were supported by the patronage and the subscriptions of the nobility, bishops and Wilber-force.

Carlile did not, of course, achieve this triumph on his own. The first round of the battle was fought in 1817, when there were twenty-six prosecutions for seditious and blasphemous libel and sixteen *ex officio* informations filed by the law officers of the Crown. The laurels of victory, in this year, went to Wooler and Hone, and to the London juries which refused to convict. Wooler conducted his own defence; he was a capable speaker, with some experience of the courts, and defen-ded himself with ability in the grandiloquent libertarian manner. The result of his two trials (5 June 1817) was one verdict of 'Not Guilty' and one muddled verdict of 'Guilty' (from which three jurymen demur-red) which was later upset in the Court of King's Bench. The three trials of William Hone in December 1817 are some of the most hilarious legal proceedings on record. Hone, a poor bookseller and former member of the L.C.S., was indicted for publishing blasphemous libels, in the form of parodies upon the Catechism, Litany, and Creed. Hone, in fact, was only a particularly witty exponent of a form of political squib long established among the news vendors and patterers, and practised in more sophisticated form by men of all parties, from Wilkes to the writers in the *Anti-Jacobin*. Hone, indeed, had not thought his parodies worth risking liberty for. When the repression of February 1817 commenced, he had sought to withdraw them; and it was Carlile, by republishing them, who had forced the Government's hand. Here is a sample:

> Our Lord who art in the Treasury, whatsoever be thy name, thy power be prolonged, thy will be done throughout the empire, as it is in each session. Give us our usual sops, and forgive us our occasional absences on divisions; as we promise not to forgive those that divide against thee. Turn us not out of our places; but keep us in the House of Commons, the land of Pensions and Plenty; and deliver us from the People. Amen.

Hone was held in prison, in poor health, from May until December, because he was unable to find £1,000 bail. Not much was expected when it was learned that he intended to conduct his own defence. But Hone had been improving the time in prison by collecting examples, from the past and present, of other parodists; and in his first trial before Justice Abbott he secured an acquittal. In the next two days the old, ill and testy Lord Chief Justice Ellenborough himself presided over the trials. Page after page of the record is filled with Ellenborough's interruptions, Hone's unruffled reproofs to the Chief Justice on his conduct, the reading of ludicrous parodies culled from various sources, and threats by the Sheriff to arrest 'the first man I see laugh'. Despite Ellenborough's unqualified charge ('. . . in obedience to his conscience and his God, he pronounced this to be a most impious and profane libel') the jury returned two further verdicts of 'Not Guilty', with the consequence (it is said) that Ellenborough retired to his sick-room never to return. From that time forward — even in 1819 and 1820 — all parodies and squibs were immune from prosecution.[5]

Persecution cannot easily stand up in the face of ridicule. Indeed, there are two things that strike one about the press battles of these years. The first is, not the solemnity but the delight with which Hone, Cruikshank, Carlile, Davison, Benbow and others baited authority. (This tradition was continued by Hetherington, who for weeks passed under the noses of the constables, in his business as editor of the unstamped *Poor Man's Guardian*, in the highly unlikely disguise of a Quaker.) Imprisonment as a Radical publisher brought, not odium, but honour. Once the publishers had decided that they were ready to go to prison, they outdid each other with new expedients to exhibit their opponents in the most ludicrous light. Radical England was delighted (and no one more than Hazlitt) at the resurrection by Sherwin of *Wat Tyler* — the republican indiscretion of Southey's youth. Southey, now

Poet Laureate, was foremost in the clamour to curb the seditious licence of the press, and sought an injunction against Sherwin for infringement of copyright. Lord Eldon refused the injunction: the Court could not take notice of property in the 'unhallowed profits of libellous publications'. 'Is it not a little strange,' Hazlitt inquired, 'that while this gentleman is getting an injunction against himself as the author of *Wat Tyler*, he is recommending gagging bills against us, and thus making up by force for his deficiency in argument?'[6] On the other hand, Carlile (who had taken over Sherwin's business) was more than pleased that the injunction was refused — for the sales of the poem were a staple source of profit in his difficult period at the start of business. 'Glory be to thee, O Southey!', he wrote six years later: '*Wat Tyler* continued to be a source of profit when every other political publication failed. The world does not know what it may yet owe to Southey.'[7]

The incidents of the pirating of *Queen Mab* and the *Vision of Judgement* were part of the same ebullient strategy. No British monarch has ever been portrayed in more ridiculous postures nor in more odious terms than George IV during the Queen Caroline agitation, and notably in Hone and Cruikshank's *Right Divine of Kings to Govern Wrong, The Queen's Matrimonial Ladder, Non Mi Ricordo*, and *The Man in the Moon*. The same authors' *Slap at Slop and the Bridge-Street Gang* (1822) appeared in the format of the Government-subsidized *New Times*, complete with a mock newspaper-stamp with the design of a cat's paw and the motto: 'On Every Thing He Claps His Claw', and with mock advertisements and mock lists of births and deaths:

Marriage

His Imperial Majesty Prince Despotism, in a consumption, to Her Supreme Antiquity, The *ignorance* of Eighteen Centuries, in a decline. The bridal dresses were most superb.

While Carlile fought on from prison, the satirists raked his prosecutors with fire.

The second point is the real toughness of the libertarian and constitutional tradition, notwithstanding the Government's assault. It is not only a question of support in unexpected places — Hone's subscription list was headed by donations from a Whig duke, a marquis, and two earls — which indicates an uneasiness in the ruling class itself. What is apparent from the reports of the law officers of the Crown, in all political trials, is the caution with which they proceeded. In particular they were aware of the unreliability (for their purposes) of the jury system. By Fox's Libel Act of 1792 the jury were judges of the libel as well as of the fact of publishing; and however judges might seek to set this aside, this meant in effect that twelve Englishmen had to decide whether they thought the 'libel' dangerous enough to merit imprisonment or not. One State prosecution which failed was a blow at the morale of authority which could only be repaired by three which succeeded. Even in 1819-21 when the Government and the prosecuting societies carried almost every case[8] (in part as a result of their better deployment of legal resources and their influence upon juries, in part because Carlile was at his most provocative and had shifted the battlefield from sedition to blasphemy), it still is not possible to speak of 'totalitarian' or 'Asiatic' despotism. Reports of the trials were widely circulated, containing the very passages — sometimes, indeed, whole books read by the defendants in court — for which the accused were sentenced. Carlile continued imperturbably to edit the *Republican* from gaol; some of his shopmen, indeed, undertook in prison the editing of another journal, as a means of self-improvement. If Wooler's *Black Dwarf* failed in 1824, Cobbett remained in the field. He was, it is true, much subdued in the early Twenties. He did not like Carlile's Republicanism and Deism, nor their hold on the artisans of the great centres; and he turned increasingly back to the countryside and distanced himself from the working-class movement. (In 1821 he undertook the first of his *Rural Rides*, in which his genius seems at last to have found its inevitable form and matter.) But, even at this distance, the *Political Register* was always there, with its columns — like those of the *Republican* — open to expose any case of persecution, from Bodmin to Berwick.

The honours of this contest did not belong to a single class. John Hunt and Thelwall (now firmly among the middle-class moderates) were among those pestered by the 'Bridge-Street Gang'; Sir Charles Wolseley, Burdett, the Reverend Joseph Harrison, were among those imprisoned for sedition. But Carlile and his shopmen were those who pressed defiance to its furthest point. The main battle was over by 1823, although there were renewed prosecutions in the late Twenties and early Thirties, and blasphemy cases trickled on into Victorian times. Carlile's greatest offence was to proceed with the unabashed publication of the *Political Works*, and then the *Theological Works*, of Tom Paine — works which, while circulating surreptitiously in the enclaves of 'old Jacks' in the cities, had been banned ever since Paine's trial *in absentia* in 1792, and Daniel Isaac Eaton's successive trials during the Wars. To this he added many further offences as the struggle wore on, and as he himself moved from Deism to Atheism, and as he threw in provocations — such as the advocacy of assassination — which in any view of the case were incitements to prosecution. He was an indomitable man, but he was scarcely loveable, and his years of imprisonment did not improve him. His strength lay in two things.

First, he would not even admit of the possibility of defeat. And second, he had at his back the culture of the artisans.

The first point is not as evident as it appears. Determined men have often (as in the 1790s) been silenced or defeated. It is true that Carlile's brand of determination (*'The shop in Fleet Street will not be closed as a matter of course'*) was peculiarly difficult for the authorities to meet. No matter how much law they had on their side, they must always incur odium by prosecutions. But they had provided themselves, under the Six Acts, with the power to *banish* the authors of sedition for offences far less than those which Carlile both committed and proudly admitted. It is testimony to the delicate equilibrium of the time, and to the limits imposed upon power by the consensus of constitutional opinion, that even in 1820 this provision of the Act was not employed. Banishment apart, Carlile could not be silenced, unless he were to be beheaded, or, more possibly, placed in solitary confinement. But there are two reasons why the Government did not proceed to extreme measures: first, already by 1821 it seemed to them less necessary, for the increased stamp duties were taking effect. Second, it was apparent after the first encounters that if Carlile were to be silenced, half a dozen new Carliles would step into his place. The first two who did so *were*, in fact, Carliles: his wife and his sister. Thereafter the 'shopmen' came forward. By one count, before the battle had ended Carlile had received the help of 150 volunteers, who — shopmen, printers, newsvendors — had between them served 200 years of imprisonment. The volunteers were advertised for in the *Republican* — men 'who were free, able, and willing to serve in General Carlile's Corps':

> it is most distinctly to be understood that a love of propagating the principles, and a sacrifice of liberty to that end . . . *and not gain*, must be the motive to call forth such volunteers; for — though R. Carlile pledges himself to . . . give such men the best support in his power — should any great number be imprisoned, he is not so situated as to property or prospects as to be able to promise any particular sum weekly . . .

From that time forward the 'Temple of Reason' off Fleet Street was scarcely left untenanted for more than a day. The men and women who came forward were, in nearly every case, entirely unknown to Carlile. They simply came out of London; or arrived on the coach from Lincolnshire, Dorset, Liverpool and Leeds. They came out of a culture.

It was not the 'working-class' culture of the weavers or Tyneside pitmen. The people most prominent in the fight included clerks, shop assistants, a farmer's son; Benbow, the shoemaker turned bookseller; James Watson, the Leeds warehouseman who 'had the charge of a

saddlehorse' at a dry-salter's; James Mann, the cropper turned bookseller (also of Leeds). The intellectual tradition was in part derived from
the Jacobin years, the circle which had once moved around Godwin
and Mary Wollstonecraft, or the members of the L.C.S., the last authentic spokesman of which — John Gale Jones — was one of Carlile's most
constant supporters. In part it was a new tradition, owing something to
Bentham's growing influence and something to the 'free-thinking
Christians' and Unitarians, such as Benjamin Flower and W.J. Fox. It
touched that vigorous sub-culture of the 'editors of Sunday newspapers
and lecturers at the Surrey Institute' which *Blackwood*'s and the
literary Establishment so scorned — schoolmasters, poor medical students, or civil servants who read Byron and Shelley and the *Examiner*,
and among whom, not Whig or Tory, but 'right and wrong considered
by each man abstractedly, is the fashion'.[9]

It is scarcely helpful to label this culture *bourgeois* or *petit-bourgeois*,
although Carlile had more than his share of the individualism which (it
is generally supposed) characterizes the latter. It would seem to be
closer to the truth that the impulse of rational enlightenment which (in
the years of the wars) had been largely confined to the Radical intelligentsia was now seized upon by the artisans and some of the skilled
workers (such as many cotton-spinners) with an evangelistic zeal to
carry it to 'numbers unlimited' — a propagandist zeal scarcely to be
found in Bentham, James Mill or Keats. The subscription lists for
Carlile's campaign drew heavily upon London; and, next, upon Manchester and Leeds. The artisan culture was, above all, that of the self-
taught. 'During this twelve-month,' Watson recalled of his imprisonment, 'I read with deep interest and much profit Gibbon's *Decline and
Fall of the Roman Empire*, Hume's *History of England*, and . . .
Mosheim's *Ecclesiastical History*.'[10] The artisans, who formed the
nuclei of Carlile's supporting 'Zetetic Societies' (as well as of the later
Rotunda) were profoundly suspicious of an established culture which
had excluded them from power and knowledge and which had
answered their protests with homilies and tracts. The works of the
Enlightenment came to them with the force of revelation.

In this way a reading public which was increasingly working class in
character was forced to *organize itself*. The war and immediate post-war
years had seen a 'kept' press, on the one hand, and a Radical press on
the other. In the Twenties much of the middle-class press freed itself
from direct Government influence, and made some use of the advantages which Cobbett and Carlile had gained. *The Times* and Lord
Brougham, who disliked the 'pauper press' perhaps as much as Lord
Eldon (although for different reasons), gave to the term 'Radicalism' a
quite different meaning — free trade, cheap government, and utilitarian
reform. To some degree (although by no means entirely) they carried

the Radical middle-class with them — the schoolmasters, surgeons, and shopkeepers, some of whom had once supported Cobbett and Wooler — so that by 1832 there were two Radical publics: the middle-class, which looked forward to the Anti-Corn Law League, and the working-class whose journalists (Hetherington, Watson, Cleave, Lovett, Benbow, O'Brien) were already maturing the Chartist movement. Throughout the Twenties the working-class press struggled under the crushing weight of the stamp duties,[11] while Cobbett remained loosely and temperamentally affiliated to the plebeian rather than to the middle-class movement. The dividing-line came to be, increasingly, not alternative 'reform' strategies (for middle-class reformers could on occasion be as revolutionary in their tone as their working-class counterparts) but alternative notions of political economy. The touchstone can be seen during the field labourer's 'revolt' in 1830, when *The Times* (Cobbett's 'bloody old Times') led the demand for salutary examples to be made of the rioters, while both Cobbett and Carlile were prosecuted once again on charges of inflammatory writing.

In 1830 and 1831 the black ensign of defiance was hoisted once again. Cobbett found a loophole in the law, and recommenced his *Twopenny Trash*. But this time it was Hetherington, a printing worker, who led the frontal attack. His *Poor Man's Guardian* carried the emblem of a hand-press, the motto 'Knowledge is Power', and the heading: 'Published contrary to "Law" to try the power of "Might" against "Right".' His opening address, quoted clause by clause the laws he intended to defy:

> . . . the *Poor Man's Guardian* . . . will contain '*news, intelligence and occurrences,*' and '*remarks and observations thereon,*' and '*upon matters of Church and State tending,*' decidedly, '*to excite hatred and contempt of the Government and Constitution of . . . this country, as* by law *established*', and also, '*to vilify the* abuses *of Religion*' . . .

It would also defy every clause of the stamp tax legislation,

> or any other acts whatsoever and despite the 'laws' or the will and pleasure of *any tyrant* or *body of tyrants* whatsoever, any thing herein-before, or any-where-else . . . to the contrary notwithstanding.

His fourth number carried the advertisement, '*Wanted*': 'Some hundreds of *poor men* out of employ who have *nothing to risk* . . . to sell to the poor and ignorant' this paper. Not only were the volunteers found, but a score of other unstamped papers sprang up, notably Carlile's *Gauntlet*, and Joshua Hobson's *Voice of the West Riding*. By

1836 the struggle was substantially over, and the way had been opened for the Chartist press.

But the 'great unstamped' was emphatically a working-class press. The *Poor Man's Guardian* and the *Working Man's Friend* were in effect, organs of the National Union of the Working Classes; Doherty's *Poor Man's Advocate* was an organ of the Factory Movement; Joshua Hobson was a former hand-loom weaver, who had built a wooden hand-press by his own labour; Bronterre O'Brien's *Destructive* consciously sought to develop working-class Radical theory. These small, closely printed, weeklies carried news of the great struggle for General Union-ism in these years, the lock-outs of 1834 and the protests at the Tol-puddle case, or searching debate and exposition of Socialist and trade union theory. An examination of this period would take us beyond the limits of this study, to a time when the working class was no longer in the making but (in its Chartist form) already made. The point we must note is the degree to which the fight for press liberties was a central formative influence upon the shaping movement. Perhaps 500 people were prosecuted for the production and sale of the 'unstamped'.[12] From 1816 (indeed, from 1792) until 1836 the contest involved, not only the editors, booksellers, and printers, but also many hundreds of newsvendors, hawkers, and voluntary agents. [. . .]

A whole pattern of distribution, with its own folklore, grew up around the militant press. Hawkers (Mayhew was told), in order to avoid 'selling' the *Republican*, sold straws instead, and then *gave* the paper to their customers. In the Spen Valley, in the days of the 'un-stamped', a penny was dropped through a grating and the paper would 'appear'. In other parts, men would slip down alleys or across fields at night to the known rendezvous. More than once the 'unstamped' were transported under the noses of the authorities in a coffin and with a godly cortège of free-thinkers.

We may take two examples of the shopmen and vendors. The first, a shop*woman*, serves to remind us that, in these rationalist and Owenite circles, the claim for women's rights (almost silent since the 1790s) was once again being made, and was slowly extending from the intelligentsia to the artisans. Carlile's womenfolk, who underwent trial and imprison-ment, did so more out of loyalty than out of conviction. Very different was Mrs Wright, a Nottingham lace-mender, who was one of Carlile's volunteers and who was prosecuted for selling one of his *Addresses* containing opinions in his characteristic manner:

A Representative System of Government would soon see the pro-priety of turning our Churches and Chapels into Temples of Science and . . . cherishing the Philosopher instead of the Priest. Kingcraft and Priestcraft I hold to be the bane of Society. . . . Those two evils operate jointly against the welfare both of the body and mind, and to palliate our miseries in this life, the latter endeavour to bamboozle us with a hope of eternal happiness.

She conducted her long defence herself[13] and was rarely interrupted. Towards the end of her defence,

Mrs Wright requested permission to retire and suckle her infant child that was crying. This was granted, and she was absent from the Court twenty minutes. In passing to and fro, to the Castle Coffee House, she was applauded and loudly cheered by assembled thousands, all encouraging her to be of good cheer and to persevere.

Some time later she was thrown into Newgate, on a November night, with her six-months' baby and nothing to lie on but a mat. Such women as Mrs Wright (and Mrs Mann of Leeds) had to meet not only the customary prosecutions, but also the abuse and insinuations of an outraged loyalist press. 'This wretched and shameless woman,' wrote the *New Times*, was attended by '*several females*. Are not these circumstances enough to shock every reflecting mind?' She was an 'abandoned creature' (the conventional epithet for prostitutes) 'who has cast off all the distinctive shame and fear and decency of her sex'. By her 'horrid example' she had depraved the minds of other mothers: 'these monsters in female form stand forward, with hardened visages, in the face of day, to give their public countenance and support — *for the first time in the history of the Christian world* — to gross, vulgar, horrid blasphemy'. She was a woman, wrote Carlile, 'of very delicate health, and truly all spirit and no matter'.

The longest sentences endured by a newsvendor were probably those served by Joseph Swann, a hat-maker of Macclesfield. He was arrested in 1819 for selling pamphlets and a seditious poem:

Off with your fetters; spurn the slavish yoke;
Now, now, or never, can your chain be broke;
Swift then rise and give the fatal stroke.

Shunted from gaol to gaol, and chained with felons, he was eventually sentenced to two years imprisonment for seditious conspiracy, two years for blasphemous libel, and a further six months for seditious libel to run consecutively. When these monstrous sentences had been passed, Swann held up his white hat and enquired of the magistrate: 'Han ye done? Is that all? Why I thowt ye'd got a bit of hemp for me, and hung me.' His wife also was briefly arrested (for continuing the sale of pamphlets); she and her four children survived on a parish allowance of 9s. a week, with some help from Carlile and Cobbett. Cobbett, indeed, interested himself particularly in the case of Swann, and when Castlereagh committed suicide it was to Swann that Cobbett addressed his triumphant obituary obloquies: '*Castlereagh has cut his own throat and is dead*! Let that sound reach you in the depth of your dungeon . . . and carry consolation to your suffering soul.' After serving his four and a half years, Swann 'passed the gate of Chester Castle . . . in mind as stubborn as ever', and resumed his trade as a hatter. But he had not yet been discharged from service. In November 1831 the *Poor Man's Guardian* reported proceedings at the Stockport magistrate's court, where Joseph Swann was charged with selling the 'unstamped'. The Chairman of the Bench, Captain Clarke, asked him what he had to say in his defence:

Defendant. — Well, Sir, I have been out of employment for some time; neither can I obtain work; my family are all starving . . . And for another reason, the weightiest of all; I sell them for the good of my fellow countrymen; to let them see how they are misrepresented in Parliament . . . I wish to let the people know how they are humbugged . . .
Bench. — Hold your tongue a moment.
Defendant. — I shall not! for I wish every man to read these publications . . .
Bench. — You are very insolent, therefore you are committed to three months' imprisonment in Knutsford House of Correction, to hard labour.
Defendant. — I've nothing to thank you for; and whenever I come out, I'll hawk them again. And *mind you* [looking at Captain Clark] the first that I hawk shall be to your house . . .

Joseph Swann was then forcibly removed from the dock.

In the twentieth-century rhetoric of democracy most of these men and women have been forgotten, because they were impudent, vulgar, over-earnest, or 'fanatical'. In their wake the subsidized vehicles of 'improvement', the *Penny Magazine* and the *Saturday Magazine* (whose vendors no one prosecuted) moved in; and afterwards the commercial press, with its much larger resources, although it did not really begin to capture the Radical reading public until the Forties and the Fifties. (Even then the popular press — the publications of Cleave, Howitt, Chambers, Reynolds, and Lloyd — came from this Radical background.) Two consequences of the contest may be particularly noticed. The first (and most obvious) is that the working-class ideology which matured in the Thirties (and which has endured, through various translations, ever since) put an exceptionally high value upon the rights of the press, of speech, of meeting and of personal liberty. The tradition of the 'free-born Englishman' is of course far older. But the notion to be found in some late 'Marxist' interpretations, by which these claims appear as a heritage of 'bourgeois individualism' will scarcely do. In the contest between 1792 and 1836 the artisans and workers made this tradition peculiarly their own, adding to the claim for free speech and thought their own claim for the untrammelled propagation, in the cheapest possible form, of the products of this thought.

In this, it is true, they shared a characteristic illusion of the epoch, applying it with force to the context of working-class struggle. All the enlighteners and improvers of the time thought that the only limit imposed to the diffusion of reason and knowledge was that imposed by the inadequacy of the means. The analogies which were drawn were frequently mechanical. The educational method of Lancaster and Bell, with its attempt at the cheap multiplication of learning by child monitors, was called (by Bell) the *'steam engine* of the *moral world'*. Peacock aimed with deadly accuracy when he called Brougham's Society for the Diffusion of Useful Knowledge the 'Steam Intellect Society'. Carlile was supremely confident that 'pamphlet-reading is destined to work the great necessary moral and political changes among mankind':

> The Printing-press may be strictly denominated a Multiplication Table as applicable to the mind of man. The art of Printing is a multiplication of mind. . . . Pamphlet-vendors are the most important springs in the machinery of Reform.

Owen contemplated the institution, by means of propaganda, of the *new moral world* with messianic, but mechanical, optimism.

But if this was, in part, the rationalist illusion, we must remember the second — and more immediate — consequence: between 1816 and 1836 this 'multiplication' seemed to *work*. For the Radical and un-stamped journalists were seizing the multiplying-machine on behalf of the working class; and in every part of the country the experiences of the previous quarter-century had prepared men's minds for what they now could read. The importance of the propaganda can be seen in the steady extension of Radical organization from the great towns and manufacturing areas into the small boroughs and market towns. One of the Six Acts of 1819 (that authorizing the search for weapons) was specifically confined only to designated 'disturbed districts' of the Midlands and the north.[14] By 1832 — and on into Chartist times — there is a Radical nucleus to be found in every county, in the smallest market towns and even in the larger rural villages, and in nearly every case it is based on the local artisans. In such centres as Croydon,

Colchester and Ipswich, Tiverton and Taunton, Nantwich or Cheltenham, there were hardy any militant Radical or Chartist bodies. In Ipswich we find weavers, saddlers, harness-makers, tailors, shoemakers; in Cheltenham shoemakers, tailors, stonemasons, cabinet-makers, gardeners, a plasterer and a blacksmith — 'earnest and reputable people — much above the average in intelligence'. These are the people whom Cobbett, Carlile, Hetherington and their newsvendors had 'multiplied'.

'Earnest and reputable people . . .' — this autodidact culture has never been adequately analysed. The majority of these people had received some elementary education, although its inadequacy is testified from many sources.

Notes

1. W.E. Adams, *Memoirs of a Social Atom* (1903), I, p. 164.
2. *Political Observer*, 19 December 1819.
3. Sherwin's *Political Register*, 17 May 1817.
4. In 1822 the circulation of the leading daily, *The Times*, was 5,730; the *Observer* (weekly), 6,860.
5. An old patterer told Mayhew (I, p. 252) that despite the acquittals, it remained difficult to 'work' Hone's parodies in the streets: 'there was plenty of officers and constables ready to pull the fellows up, and . . . a beak that wanted to please the high dons, would find some way of stopping them . . .'
6. *The Complete Works of William Hazlitt*, ed. P.P. Howe after the edition of A.R. Waller and A. Glover (J.M. Dent and Sons Ltd, London and Toronto, 21 vols., 1930-4), vol. VII, pp. 176 ff. 'Instead of applying for an injunction against *Wat Tyler*,' Hazlitt opined, 'Mr Southey would do well to apply for an injunction against Mr Coleridge, who has undertaken his defence in *The Courier*.'
7. Sherin's *Republican*, 29 March 1817; Carlile's *Republican*, 30 May 1823.
8. In these three years there were 115 prosecutions and 45 *ex officio* informations.
9. Keats to his brother George, 17 September 1819, *Works* (1901), V, p. 108. The letter continues: 'This makes the business of Carlile the bookseller of great moment in my mind. He has been selling deistical pamphlets, republished Tom Paine, and many other works held in superstitious horror . . . After all, they are afraid to prosecute. They are 'afraid of his defence; it would be published in all the papers all over the empire. They shudder at this. The trials would light a flame they could not extinguish. Do you not think this of great import?'
10. W.J. Linton, *James Watson* (Manchester, 1880), p. 19.
11. In 1830 these taxes amounted to a 4*d*. stamp on each newspaper or weekly periodical, a duty of 3*s*. 6*d*. on each advertisement, a small paper duty, and a large surety against action for libel.
12. Abel Heywood, the Manchester bookseller, claimed the figure to be 750.
13. Most of Carlile's shopmen were provided with long written defences by Carlile, and this was probably so in her case.
14. The counties of Lancaster, Chester, the West Riding, Warwick, Stafford, Derby, Leicester, Nottingham, Cumberland, Westmorland, Northumberland, Durham, the city of Coventry, and the country boroughs of Newcastle-upon-Tyne and Nottingham.

3 CLASS AND LEISURE IN MID-VICTORIAN ENGLAND

Hugh Cunningham

Source: *Leisure in the Industrial Revolution* (Croom Helm, London, 1980). © H. Cunningham.

[. . .]

Historians with an apparently insatiable compulsion to compartmentalise have seen [the] different forms of entertainment [that flourished during the 1820s and 1830s] in isolation one from the other — there are histories of sport, of drama, of the pantomime, and of the circus. Yet what is most striking is the connections between these different forms of entertainment, connections so strong that one can speak of this world of entertainment as part of one close-knit popular culture. All these forms of entertainment were frankly commercial in nature, all aimed to attract spectators, all employed professionals. And beyond this there were personal and institutional connections: people like Billy Purvis, familiar with different forms of entertainment, and buildings which could play host to pantomime or circus, sport or drama. It was no accident that wrestling could be seen at the Eagle Tavern, soon to become the Grecian Saloon, and not simply coincidence that Pierce Egan was at home in both the theatre and the prize-ring, nor that so many of these forms of entertainment could be witnessed at the horse-race or fair. One man could straddle this whole world: for example, David Prince Miller was at various times publicist for Richardson, impersonator of a black giantess, prize-fighting sparrer, conjuror, equestrian, fortune-teller, employee of Wombwell, magician, manager of the Royal Adelphi Theatre, Glasgow, lessee of the Queen's Theatre, Manchester, and interviewer for Henry Mayhew.[1]

The different components of this culture were further drawn together by the political necessity of defending it. On the receiving end of a barrage of hostile comment and legal manoeuvrings, the culture retaliated in its own way: by puncturing the pretensions of politicians, and portraying them as showmen;[2] by fighting for a freer stage and an end to theatrical monopoly;[3] and, as we shall see, by elaborating at every opportunity on the claim that their culture promoted patriotism and class harmony and prevented effeminacy. On occasions there could be embarrassing conflicts within the culture, as when, to Pierce Egan's horror, prize-fighters allowed themselves to be brought in to try to control the Old Price riots at Covent Garden.[4] But more generally there was a consistent radical cutting edge to the culture, and it is again no accident that much of our information about it comes from two radicals, William Hone in the 1820s, and the Chartist Thomas Frost, recalling his youth in the 1870s; the latter indeed being one of the few people to perceive the unity of the culture.[5]

It is customary to think of this as a cultural world on the wane — yet another doomed survival from pre-industrial times. This is a serious misinterpretation, and for four reasons. First, it was not a *survival*: so much in this culture was new, an invention of the Industrial Revolution era. Secondly, the culture was as at home in the big city as in the village, and could move easily back and forth from one to the other: it was not a victim, as we too easily assume so many things to be, of 'urbanisation'. On the contrary many of the entrepreneurs of the culture flourished precisely because they were alert to the new opportunities open in the big towns. Thirdly, the culture had a remarkable and (to opponents) alarming ability to diffuse itself upwards. Time and again entertainers who had started in the humblest circumstances, touring the fairs and races, received the supreme accolade of a royal command performance; and did so while still working the traditional circuits. Wombwell gave no less than five performances before royalty at Windsor; Van Amburgh not only displayed his talents and his lions before royalty, but was also the subject of a famous painting by Landseer. Ducrow [. . .] won royal patronage for the circus, and it was while travelling in dire poverty with Richardson that the young Edmund Kean received a summons to recite at Windsor.[6]

In part this is simply to say that entertainment was a career open to talent. But it is more than this. Not only were individual performers rising to fame, but whole types of performance, popular in origin, were having a marked impact on high culture. The most obvious sign of this is in the appearance of animals on the legitimate stage. It was with an eye to profit but with a sense of betrayal of high culture that the managers of Covent Garden and Drury Lane admitted horses, lions and elephants to their stages. And having done it once it was hard to stop. As late as the 1850s when Charles Kean was supposedly inaugurating a revival of legitimate drama at the Princess's Theatre, he followed the example of William Cooke, who was equestrianising Shakespeare at Astley's, and once more brought horses on to the stage; an example which reminds us that influence did not flow in one direction alone, for since very early days circus proprietors had built stages alongside their rings, and had made popular that curious hybrid, hippodrama.[7]

But what I think one can assert is that there was an upsurge of influence from below which left the defenders of high culture in sorry straits: none more so than the painter Benjamin Haydon whose exhibition at the Egyptian Hall was ignored by a public who streamed to see the American Barnum's display of Tom Thumb in the very same building and at the same time, a conjunction of events which resulted in Haydon's suicide.[8]

This then is a culture diffusing itself upwards. And finally it is a culture which does not peter out into those sorry street showmen interviewed by Mayhew, but leads us directly to the music-hall. For the moment one can nod in assent when Louis James comments that theatre programmes of the first half of the nineteenth century show 'the promiscuity of a music-hall bill', or when Ronald Pearsall writes of the saloon theatres that they were 'already music halls'. If leisure for the middle class became commercialised in the eighteenth century, as Plumb has argued, for the mass of the people it was being commercialised from the very early nineteenth century, and in a form which gave rise to a vigorous popular culture of entertainment.[9]

The term 'popular' to describe this culture is one which, unless carefully defined, might in the present context be described as evasive. By 'popular' I mean 'of the people', as opposed to the culture of those in positions of power and authority who, since early modern times, had developed their own high culture in isolation, so far as possible, from popular culture: and had been so successful in this that in the late eighteenth and early nineteenth century, under the impetus of romanticism, they had to rediscover popular culture. But the popular culture of the Industrial Revolution that I have described did not consist solely of the traditional customs which began to be so lovingly described by antiquarians.[10] It was [. . .] essentially an innovatory culture. And, in contrast to the culture of the leisure class, it was inclusive, welcoming into its ambit the huge human and occupational variety covered by the words 'labourers, artisans, shopkeepers and tradesmen'. From its petty capitalist base it reached up and down the social scale, and penetrated to remote hamlets and to the heart of big cities. It cannot by any stretch of the historical imagination be described as 'a working-class culture', but at the same time it was imbued with a sense of popular rights. Its politics were the politics of instant reaction to threats to what it perceived as its customary and legitimate independence.

As such, in the conditions of the early Industrial Revolution, it was necessarily radical. But it had no long-term goals for the people, no vision of improvement; and in its live-and-let-live hedonism it was opposed by other cultures, not only that of the leisure class but also two minority cultures which, like the popular culture, drew their impetus from the people. These were a secular radical and a religious culture, both of which had visions of a new destiny and role for the people, whom the former in particular now began to think of as 'the working class'. These two cultures opposed the popular culture not because they lacked class consciousness but precisely because of their growing sense of it. The popular culture, as they perceived it, had too many ties with paternalism and 'Old Corruption', too little sense of the dignity of the people. In proposing their programmes of political and religious reform they were recognising the coming of a society in which class was experienced much more directly and constantly than in the past; from within the people they were making a claim for the leadership of the people. [. . .]

Charles Kingsley's hopes that leisure might serve the social function of bringing the classes together seemed to receive some confirmation as the Great Exhibition of 1851 ushered in a period of relative social harmony. Historians have affirmed the same theory, arguing that there was an alliance of the respectable within all classes against the joining together in unrespectable leisure of the aristocracy and the poor. Certainly, there was a colossal investment of time and effort in the attempt to bring the classes together in leisure, an investment of such an extent that it constituted the dominant ideology of leisure in the mid-Victorian years; an investment, too, whose chances of success were all the greater because the sponsors were now willing and anxious to include physical recreation amongst the respectable leisure activities. Nevertheless, for a number of reasons, the return on that investment was minimal or non-existent. Class and not the divisions within classes continued to be of prime importance for an understanding of leisure. [Here I] will explore the ideology of class conciliation in leisure, and seek to explain its failure.

Historically at mid-century the hope that the classes might be brought together in leisure had two distinct roots. On the one hand were those who had opposed the attack on popular leisure in the later eighteenth and early nineteenth centuries, arguing instead for a paternalist patronage of the people's customs and sports. These, they claimed, brought the classes together, prevented effeminacy and promoted patriotism. The attack on popular leisure seemed to them motivated by class interest. The Cruelty to Animals Bill of 1809, said Windham, was 'A Bill for harrassing and oppressing certain Classes among the lower Orders of His Majesty's Subjects'.[11] And this kind of argument appealed not only to Tory traditionalists but also to middle-class people with a social conscience and radical disposition. On the other hand there was rational recreation which was a first if hardly explicit admission on the side of reformers that there was something to Windham's accusations. The remedy they proposed of course was quite different. They advocated not the preservation of the past but the creation of new institutions and activities. Within these, they argued, the respectable of all classes could meet in harmony. Thus it was a commonplace in the

1840s to argue that mechanics' institutes, or Sunday School excursions, or music, or art, or any improving rational recreation would amongst other things bring the classes together.

These two traditions, distinct and opposed to each other as they were, carried on a kind of dialogue in which each tried to appropriate the strong points of the other's argument and language. Sportsmen made claims for the rationality of their pastimes. 'Intellectual pursuits may gain the ascendancy', wrote the *Sporting Magazine*, 'but they will never exclude other means of rational enjoyment.' Shooting, claimed Blaine in 1840, once 'constituted the healthful and rational recreation of thousands'. Popular entertainment, too, made the claim to be 'rational', as in mid-century advertisements in Hartlepool for Smith's Royal Music Saloon and the Royal Casino, Dock Hotel.[12] On the other side the process of appropriation demanded nothing less than a turnabout. The hostility to physical recreation, the notion that there was a split between mind and reason on the one hand and body and animality on the other, remained strong at mid-century. [. . .]

[An] instinctive distaste for physical recreation owed much to the history and associations of sport. The drink-seller and the book-maker were its organisers and inspirers. Many popular sports, such as pugilism and cock-fighting, involved not only drinking and gambling, but also excited the worst lusts of mankind — violence, and cruelty to fellowmen and to animals. Moreover sportsmen inhabited a peculiar world of their own, the world of 'the Fancy' with its own language, its own literature, and its own meeting-places. Even the more liberal sections of the middle class found this a totally alien world. In Dickens's journal, *Household Words*, G.A. Sala described 'The Sporting World' in 1852, and did so by outlining to his readers the contents of *Bell's Life*, a journal dominated by horse-racing and prize-fighting. Yet these sports, Sala insisted, however distasteful, 'are bound up with us . . . they are bone of our bone, and flesh of our flesh — they are crackling cinders at almost every Englishman's fireside'. Clearly, though, not at the firesides of his readers. These were sports which the respectable could not countenance. But Sala in 1852 did not reject all sport: he was hopeful for the future, and had glimpses of a world in which sport might be the pride and property of *his* world. [. . .] Apply the traditional nostrums of the middle class, it is suggested, and sport can render real service to the nation; it will produce a breed of 'yeomen' — the process of appropriation has begun.[13]

That process is most clearly evident in the history of cricket. In the early nineteenth century cricket was morally suspect. We can see why if we look at Miss Mitford's famous description of a country cricket match in the 1820s. She carefully distinguishes the type of cricket she is writing about from others:

> I doubt if there be any scene in the world more animating or delightful than a cricket-match — I do not mean a set match at Lord's Ground for money, hard money, between a certain number of gentlemen and players, as they are called — people who make a trade of that noble sport, and degrade it into an affair of bettings, and hedgings, and cheatings, it may be, like boxing or horse-racing; nor do I mean a pretty *fête* in a gentleman's park, where one club of cricketing dandies encounter another such club, and where they show off in graceful costume to a gay marquee of admiring belles. . . . No! The cricket that I mean is a real solid old-fashioned match between neighbouring parishes, where each attacks the other for honour and a supper, glory and half-a-crown a man. If there be any gentlemen amongst them, it is well — if not, it is so much the better.

Cricket, like so many other sports, was 'noble', but liable to be degraded. And even in this idealised village cricket match the morally sensitive would note that money is passing hands, and that for lack of gentry patronage, it was the publicans who organised the game. In less idealised form, and at much the same period, cricket at Pudsey was unknown

> except as played mostly in the lanes or small openings in the village — with a tub leg for a bat, made smaller at one end for a handle, a wall cape, or some large stone, set on end for a stump (called a 'hob'), and a pot taw or some hard substance covered with listing and sometimes sewed on the top with twine or band. They were all one-ball overs if double cricket was played; no umpires, and often those who cheated the hardest won.[14]

It was from these suspect origins, much more than from the gentry-sponsored games of the south, that cricket emerged as a popular spectator sport in the first half of the century. In 1824 there were 17,000 spectators at a match in Sheffield, and in 1835 20,000 working-class men, women and children watched the Nottingham versus Sussex match. These and other less notable games were reported in that journal of the Fancy, *Bell's Life in London*, and there was only pardonable exaggeration in its editor's claim in 1844:

> I attribute the Extension of the Game of Cricket very much to the Paper of which I am the Editor. Having been the Editor Twenty Years, I can recollect when the Game of Cricket was not so popular as it is at the present Moment; but the Moment the Cricketers found themselves the Object of Attention almost every Village had its Cricket Green. The Record of their Prowess in Print created a Desire

still more to extend their Exertions and their Fame. Cricket has become almost universal . . .[15]

Indeed, but under auspices which must make the respectable shudder. And probably more important than the journals of the Fancy was something equally worrisome, the role of the professional. As Mandle has written, 'In England, cricket, hitherto a game for gentry and their servants or a knock-about recreation for self-employed Midland weavers, entered national life through the itinerant efforts of William Clarke's All-England Eleven from 1846 on.' Clarke was a Nottingham man, a bricklayer by trade, a fine bowler, and an astute manager: he paid each of his men £4 a match, and took the balance of takings for himself. He soon had rivals. In 1852 John Wisden formed the breakaway 'United England Eleven', in 1858 Sherman and Chadband organised a 'New All England Eleven', in 1862 Fred Caesar was responsible for 'Another New All England Eleven' and in 1865 for the United South of England Eleven. These were touring professional teams, and as Altham and Swanston acknowledge, 'were truly missionaries of cricket, winning to knowledge and appreciation of the game whole districts where hitherto it had been primitive and undeveloped'. In 1859 there occurred the first overseas tour, all professional, to America and Canada, and in 1861 the first, again all professional, to Australia. In the light of these developments there can be no dissent from the conclusion of C.L.R. James that in the development of cricket 'The class of the population that seems to have contributed least was the class destined to appropriate the game and convert it into a national institution. This was the solid Victorian middle class.'[16]

The process of appropriation owed something to a change in the rules in 1864, legalising over-arm bowling, but much more to the achievements of one man, W.G. Grace. In the early 1860s county cricket, the key to upper- and middle-class control, was in a most rudimentary state. It was only in that decade that the county cricket clubs of Hampshire, Lancashire, Middlesex and Yorkshire came into being. Grace, entering the first-class scene in 1864, was an immediate and spectacular success. His achievement, helped by the legalisation of over-arm bowling, was to reverse the trend whereby the professionals dominated the game, and he did it by outplaying them; of 40 matches between the Gentlemen and the Players between 1865 and 1881 the Gentlemen won 27 and lost only 5. Through these victories the amateurs could reassert their control over the game, and reduce the professionals to a subordinate position. As James writes, 'It is not possible that cricket would have reached and held the position it did among the upper classes if the Gentlemen, that is to say the products of the public schools and the universities, had been as consistently and cruelly beaten as they had been by the professionals before W.G. began.'[17]

By the late 1860s the Eton versus Harrow match had become an important part of the London season. By 1870 the counties were ranked according to performance, and in the course of that decade the last book-makers were removed from Lord's. The MCC after a period in the doldrums began to revive. Upper and middle-class control was being asserted, and on the basis of it the moral qualities of cricket could safely be preached. Christians now exalted in their prowess at the game, rather than denied it. And in Pudsey those primitive beginnings were but a dim memory from the past; in the 1880s Joseph Lawson could write that cricket

> has had a most wonderful influence for good on the young men of Pudsey — not only on the players, but on the spectators as well. By cricket, players are taught self-respect and gentlemanly conduct in bowing to the decision of the umpires, and derive physical benefit as well. The discipline taught by the game of cricket is great and invaluable . . .

With such a comment, we may safely say, the process of appropriation was complete.[18]

The appropriation of sport was all the more urgent because of its traditional importance in the public schools. Now, with the foundation of new middle-class-oriented public schools — Cheltenham, Marlborough, Rossall and Radley all in the 1840s — the problems posed by sport had to be faced. Some of the older schools, Harrow in particular, and then Winchester in the mid-1830s through the influence of the old Harrovian Charles Wordsworth, had given a serious purpose to games-playing in the first half of the century, but equally common was the attitude of Butler, Headmaster of Shrewsbury 1798-1836, who saw football as 'only fit for butcher boys'. And traditionally it was in games above all that the boys asserted their independence of authority.

It was no part of Thomas Arnold's plans for the reform of Rugby that organised games should become as important as in time they did. But since they embodied that antagonism between masters and boys which he wished to overcome, he could not simply ignore them. He himself favoured individualistic sports, like gymnastics and throwing the spear, but the traditional games flourished. As McIntosh has written, 'the growth of athleticism at Rugby may be regarded . . . as the price paid by Arnold for the cooperation of the boys in maintaining discipline and effecting the reforms which he desired'.[19]

It was Arnold's disciples who began to see organised sport as a key means of asserting control and moulding character, while at the same time allowing boys some measure of self-government. Between 1845 and 1862 the seven main public schools committed their football rules to written form. Headmasters became advocates of organised sports. At Marlborough G.E.L. Cotton sent a circular letter to parents in 1853 extolling the 'healthy and manly' games of cricket and football as against

> other amusements, often of a questionable character in themselves, or at least liable to considerable abuse, and which have no effect in providing constant and wholesome recreation for the boys. Many do not spend their half-holidays in the playground, but in wandering about the country, some in bird's nesting, or in damaging property of the neighbours, or other undesirable occupations.

The element of social control in the fostering of organised games could hardly be more openly stated. In the following year Thring became Headmaster at Uppingham, and not only preached the gospel of organised games but also participated in them. In the 1850s and 1860s Clifton, Haileybury, Wellington and King Edward VI, Birmingham, all had headmasters who had been pupils or masters under Arnold, and all adopted the Rugby game. Official support for games-playing came with the 1864 Clarendon Commission on the older public schools which concluded that 'the importance which boys themselves attach to games is somewhat greater, perhaps, than might reasonably be desired; but within moderate limits it is highly useful'.[20]

'Useful': that is certainly one reason why games-playing spread in the mid-century period, for it became an essential part of the organisation and structure of the public schools. But it was not simply utility which encouraged the growth, nor was that growth confined to the public schools. There were other reasons, which take us back to the process of appropriation, and which may best be appreciated by looking at Thomas Hughes's *Tom Brown's School-Days*, first published in 1857, and selling 11,000 copies within a year. In its celebration of public schools and games, the book is at the same time a criticism of industrial, commercial and urban life. As Hughes put it, 'The ideas and habits which those who have most profited by them bring away from our public schools do not fit them to become successful traders.' Rather it was the life-style of the gentry which was held up for admiration, a life-style which could reconcile the middle class's urge for social acceptance and its wish not simply to ape the aristocracy. In the public school boys could acquire the new-model gentry values: unintellectual, combative, manly, Christian and patriotic. As Tom says to Arthur: 'I want to be A1 at cricket and football and all the other games, and to make my hands keep my head against any fellow, lout or gentleman. I want to get into the sixth before I leave, and to please the Doctor; and I want to carry away just as much Latin and Greek as will take me through Oxford respectably.' These values, it is suggested, not only now, but throughout English history have been at the heart of the nation's achievement. 'Talbots and Stanleys, St Maurs, and such-like folk, have led armies and made laws time out of mind; but those noble families would be somewhat astounded − if the account ever came to be fairly taken − to find how small their work for England has been by the side of that of the Browns.' For Hughes, it seems, the process of appropriation must be facilitated by the rewriting of history so that the star roles are played by the Browns; and it was easy for the mid-nineteenth-century middle class to identify with the new-model gentry values of the Browns.

The appeal of *Tom Brown's School-Days* was enhanced by the fact that it was written in the aftermath of the aristocratic mismanagement of the Crimean War, a war which also had the effect of bringing Englishmen face to face with the role of force and of fighting in industrial and urban communities. The war created the myth of the Christian hero, and Tom Brown was that same hero in fiction. Both were living proof that 'old English' virtues could survive in an industrial and urban civilisation, and that their social location now lay within the gentry, not the aristocracy. War, and its nearest approximation, sport, also served as a bulwark against two other insidious and connected threats: tractarianism and effeminacy. Puseyism, as David Newsome has commented, was the greatest stimulus to muscular Christianity. Games-playing was English, Protestant and masculine. 'Fighting with fists', wrote Hughes, 'is the natural and English way for English boys to settle their quarrels.'[21] How often had Pierce Egan and others said the same in the heyday of prize-fighting? Now the argument, and the sport, were being taken away from the Fancy and appropriated for the benefit of the public schools and the respectable middle class.

The implications of the book and of its popularity seem inescapable. Sport, said Veblen at the end of the century, was an atavistic survival of the old barbarian virtue of prowess. 'The ground of an addiction to sports', he wrote, 'is an archaic spiritual constitution − the possession of the predatory emulative propensity in a relatively high potency.'[22] And however modernised the sports became − defined space and time, set rules and so on − they retained something of the characteristic noted by Veblen. In its attempt to appropriate sport the middle class was seeking an escape from its own world, and an escape not into the future but into the past; the model which it held up before itself was that of the gentry − of what one might call a purposeful leisure class. In view of this it is hardly surprising that with the sports that they appropriated the middle class should also take over the ideological lumber with which they were encrusted. That included not only the arguments that sport promoted patriotism and prevented effeminacy, but also, and most important of all, that it effected a union of classes.

With this new acceptance of physical recreation and of sport the argument for class conciliation through leisure could be broadened from the rather restricting recreations of the 1840s. And in the 1850s, in the aftermath of Chartism, and in the rosy glow shed by the Great Exhibition, the moment seemed appropriate for a new initiative. [. . .]

The task was obvious: the upper class must once again take an interest in the pastimes of the lower class. What could not be predicted was the extent to which recourse would be had both to the sports and pastimes and to the language of those early-nineteenth-century traditionalists, whose landscape was inhabited by the peer and the peasant.

The first sign that this language and its implications were meeting with some acceptance outside the ranks of their more obvious advocates may be seen in the 1844 House of Lords Select Committee on Gaming which, called to enquire into 'the extensive Frauds which have of late been perpetrated on the Turf' resisted the temptation to clamp down on racing, thinking it 'desirable that this Amusement should be upheld, because it is in accordance with a long-established National Taste; because it serves to bring together, for a common Object, vast Bodies of People in different Parts of the Country, and to promote intercourse between Classes of Society.' Nothing very remarkable here, it may be said, considering the aristocratic source of the comment; but it was an indication that these kinds of argument about the social function of leisure were beginning to be thought sufficiently weighty to be worth the consideration of government. Move ahead a quarter of a century, moreover, and we will find the same arguments, this time in defence of Derby Day, being put by a very different figure, the journalist Blanchard Jerrold:

> All classes are intermingled for a few hours on the happiest terms . . . It cannot be pretended by the keenest lover of the course and the hunting-field that racing promotes any of the virtues. On the other hand it fosters a general love of gambling. But this Derby-day has its bright — even its useful side. It gives all London an airing, an 'outing'; makes a break in our over-worked lives; and effects a beneficial commingling of classes.[23]

In the intervening quarter of a century every form of leisure was assessed and weighed in terms of the contribution it could make to an improvement in class relations. Small events became pregnant with larger consequences. The annual flower show evoked this comment from the *Banbury Guardian* in 1866:

> Floriculture and horticulture while being a health giving is also a pure and harmless recreation, which may be engaged in by individuals of either sex and of all stations of life — the peasant as well as the peer, the overtoiled man of business and the industrious artisan, on every imaginable scale from a single flower pot to the princely conservatory.[24]

Cricket was a more obvious example, and, once safely appropriated, its potential seemed vast. The local press had this to say on an 1869 match between Lord Monson's Burton Park Club and the Gentlemen's Servants Club:

> This match strikingly shows that cricket recognizes no distinctions of class; that it is, and ever has been, one of the principal agents in bringing the different grades of society into contact, and showing that God's mental and moral as well as His natural gifts, are bestowed alike upon the peasant and the peer. Some thirty, or even twenty years ago, this match would have been a social impossibility.

[. . .]

The tone and language of these comments are significant. It was not simply that mid-Victorians were hoping that the classes could meet in leisure; it was that they were doing so in the language of 'peer' and 'peasant'. In an urban and industrial society, and one in many ways dominated by middle-class values, the advocates of class conciliation in leisure use a language which bears no relation to social reality; England in the second half of the nineteenth century is not peopled by peers and peasants. How can we explain this language? What is happening, I suggest, is an attempt by the middle class to appropriate to itself the values of a refined gentry. And this in itself is symptomatic of a profound rejection of urban and industrial civilisation, and of a wish to escape back into a simpler patron-client kind of society. [. . .]

Indeed it was a sense of the difficulty of achieving any kind of understanding between the classes in work which drove people to look for it in leisure. The more intensive use of labour which seems to begin in mid-century required more labour discipline not less, and hence made difficult any relaxation of class relationships at the workplace. Even optimists, even those creating working conditions most favourable to class co-operation, found themselves looking to leisure for its achievement. [. . .] Ludlow, instigator of many of the co-operative workshops, believed that it was easier to achieve class conciliation in leisure than in work. The students of the London Working Men's College, he said, went on many expeditions, 'bringing back with them, with invigorated health, a store of new memories and new ideas, and a power of assimilation to other classes which could never have been acquired within the four walls of the workshop'.[25] If it could not be acquired within the workshop, however, it was unlikely to be achieved elsewhere, for work is of primary importance in determining class relationships. The failure of mid-Victorians to recognise this was another reason why the aim of achieving class conciliation in leisure was not fulfilled.

Closely related to it was a further reason, the fact that when the classes did meet in leisure they often interpreted the meaning of the meeting in different ways. The middle class hoped that the working class in leisure would accept and assimilate middle-class norms and values. Even someone like Ludlow, sensitive to working-class objectives, could write of them having 'a power of assimilation to other classes'. Others, less sensitive, hoped to achieve this in ways both patronising and authoritarian. It would be quite wrong to pretend that just because class conciliation was a new and dominant ideology of leisure, the older wish simply to suppress and control the leisure of the working class had evaporated. More interestingly, however, where the meeting of the classes was apparently on more equal terms and where the ideology was openly stated, the meanings attached to the experience were very different. And those meetings were likely in the nature of the case to be with the upper working class, with the aristocracy of labour. Until recently it might have been argued that the emergence of an aristocracy of labour at mid-century suggests a convergence of middle and upper working-class values; or more crudely that the aristocracy of labour accepted bourgeois values. The closely related and convincing work of Gray, Crossick and Tholfsen, however, has shown that a simple assimilationist model does less than justice to the complexity of the value system of the labour aristocracy, or, it may be added, of other sections of the working class. Their argument is that although the stated values of the labour aristocrats — respectability, thrift and so on — look bourgeois in content they were in fact invested with different meanings; in particular that they express the aspirations of a group rather than of an individual. Gray thus argues that, for the labour aristocracy, respectability 'is properly interpreted as a claim to status recognition and citizenship on behalf of skilled workers as a corporate group'.[26]

Armed with these insights we may see how the class-conciliatory objectives embedded in many of the recreational institutions of mid-Victorian England failed to be realised. [. . .] The classes met, but no new understanding, far less camaraderie, resulted.

The history of football follows much the same pattern. In the conventional history of the game the public schools and Oxbridge are the dominant force from the moment the public schools begin to write down their rules, through the foundation of the Football Association in 1863 and up to that symbolic defeat of the Old Etonians by Blackburn Olympic in the Cup Final of 1883, and the legalisation of professionalism in 1885. There is a period of amateur dominance, almost exactly paralleling that in cricket. And during that period the middle class are seen as missionaries, using football as, amongst other things, a forum for class conciliation, and founding many of the clubs that dominate the professional leagues today. Aston Villa, Bolton Wanderers, Wolverhampton Wanderers, Everton, all foundations of the 1870s, have their origins, we learn, in religious organisations. Preston North End were financed by their employers, Peel Hall Mill, and the committee of the first Sheffield Football Club included the later chairman of the Sheffield Forge Company and the future head of Vickers Engineering.[27]

This history is inadequate on two grounds. First, seeing things through public school spectacles, it ignores the continuous history of football as a popular sport. It is true that those local, traditional, annual matches ranging over huge spaces and involving whole populations had for the most part been abolished during the first half of the century. But it seems highly likely that the more casual practice of kicking a ball around, a practice much closer to the modern game of football, survived. Irishmen, for example, were reported by Hone to play football on Sunday afternoons in open fields near Islington. And in the West Riding coalfield, football as well as cricket and nor-&-spell were played on wasteland by young miners in their relatively plentiful spare time.[28] This kind of football, precisely because it was so casual, was unlikely to leave behind it many records; that however is no indication that it was rare. At this stage of historical research one can do no more than speculate that the middle-class missionaries found it unnecessary to spend time converting the working-class natives; the latter were already enthusiastic lovers of the game.

This brings us to our second criticism of the conventional history. Listing the ultra-respectable origins of the leading clubs implies that middle-class ideology permeated the game and all its players. What seems more plausible is that football as developed by the amateurs required a defined space and some capital investment, and that such access to land and money was beyond the working class. Hence they needed sponsors, and the middle-class amateurs were sponsors more than missionaries. As such, they might be little more than a respectable façade to be cast aside when necessary. Aston Villa, for example, although connected with the Bible Class of a Wesleyan Chapel, had playing fields provided by a local butcher, and a dressing room supplied

by a local publican. Working men, anxious to play football, were perhaps none too concerned about the means by which they could translate their aspirations into reality. The sponsorship and patronage of the
rich certainly did not imply a submission to their control and values.

Detailed examination of the development of the game, indeed,
suggests that the middle-class input was much less than one might
suppose. Geographically the 1860s and 1870s saw not only the
flowering of the southern public school tradition, but also the laying of
the foundations of the game in Sheffield, Nottingham, Birmingham, the
Black Country and Lancashire. Contemporaneously with horse-racing,
clubs started charging for admission, Aston Villa leading the way in the
early 1870s. County cups in Lancashire, Birmingham and Staffordshire
established forms of competition, and in the 1870s the number of spectators was already substantial. All these developments owed much more
to the greater availability and regularity of time for leisure amongst the
working class than they did to the impact on the game of the public
schools.[29] We may conclude indeed that middle-class claims for their
own impact on the game have had more influence on the historiography
of football than they have had on its practice.

The suggestion we are making here is that the working class, for lack
of any alternative, was prepared to accept for as long as necessary, the
fact of middle-class sponsorship, but not its ideology. The demand for
recreation was great, and in this mid-Victorian period the commercialisation of it was only partial. Hence middle-class rational recreationists
had an apparent opportunity to achieve in leisure their supreme objective — a better understanding between the classes. They failed to realise
that working-class people approached these recreational occasions without any such objective. They wanted simply to enjoy what was being
offered, and as soon as financial constraints allowed they shook off
what they perceived as heavy-handed patronage. Within the Working
Men's Clubs and in football this had been achieved by the mid-1880s.
[. . .]

These [. . .] forms of recreation, typical as they are of those espou-
sed by the middle class in the search for class conciliation, were all
exclusively male. And herein lies a fourth reason for the failure of the
hopes. Class conciliation was intended to bring middle-class men into
contact with working-class men, and to a lesser extent middle-class
women with working-class women, but scarcely at all to let down the
barriers of both class and sex. If the sexes were to meet in leisure it
must be within class boundaries. The more liberal rational recreationists
could be happy at the sight of working-class wives accompanying their
husbands to the music-hall, but would not invite their own wives to
observe such a scene. And on the other side of the class barrier, croquet
and archery could, as Jerrold put it, beguile 'the hours of sentiment',

but only because there was no danger of class mixing in them. Women began to hunt only in the 1850s when the social exclusivity of the sport had been firmly established.[30]

Leisure for women, it was assumed, posed little problem, for the solution to it lay in the home, and in the home, in the nature of the case, there could be no class-mixing. Although there was some unease that on the Saturday half-holiday the men might be free to enjoy themselves while the women scrubbed and cleaned, the answer was not that men should help, but that wives should not work. The proper task of women was that of home-making, one of particular importance among the working class. 'In no rank of society', wrote Thomas Wright, 'have home influences so great a power for good or evil, as among the working classes.' In any minutes spared from this almost unending task women might possibly engage in some self-improving occupation or join in a family excursion, but generally their leisure was confined within the bounds of home, family and class. This was the almost instinctive ideal of the middle-class rational recreationists, and as a result they gave little thought to the leisure of women. As Walter Besant wrote in 1884, 'As regards the women, I declare that I have never been able to find out anything at all concerning their amusements.' Almost exclusively they were men dealing with men.[31]

The sexual barriers could be crossed in class-conciliatory leisure only when the relationship was clearly one of authority, and the occasion therefore as far as possible asexual. Even in such circumstances there was a certain piquant novelty; in the mid-1860s the Working Men's College spawned a Working Women's College; A.J. Munby who taught there noted in his diary:

One has to remind oneself that these are girls, sitting in front of one, writing or repeating their latin; that this is for oneself a new relation of the sexes; and after all tis hard to realize that it *is* new; it seems so natural, so independent of sex.

In any more relaxed setting the crossing of the sexual as well as the class barrier was fraught with difficulty. The general rule was that any woman in a public place of leisure, and unaccompanied by husband or other suitable male, was a prostitute. And if there was any real commingling of classes in recreation it was, ironically enough, where prostitute met client. The prostitute was evidently easily recognisable, and as a result not only particular places of entertainment, but whole areas of towns were no-go areas, at least at night, for respectable women. In London the Haymarket was the principal area for higher class prostitution, and a gentleman could make a choice between Kate Hamilton's, Lizzie Davis's, Sam's, Sally's and other more or less select supper rooms.

No respectable woman would wish to be seen anywhere in the area, nor would she go near either of the two leading casinos, the Argyll Rooms and the Holborn, or Cremorne Gardens. Acton, who visited the latter in the course of duty, described it as frequented by some 700 men of the upper and middle classes, none of them looking as though they were enjoying themselves; and though decorum reigned, he 'could have little moral doubt' of the character of the female visitors.[32]

Music-hall, and to a lesser extent theatre, were also suspect because of the presence of prostitutes. Although in giving evidence before the 1866 Select Committee on Theatrical Licences and Regulations, the police and magistrates stressed the decorous behaviour of the prostitutes who frequented the halls, they would perhaps have agreed with the sentiments of Benjamin Webster, Proprietor and Manager of the Adelphi Theatre who when asked, 'Do you think that a person must lose caste by going to a music hall?' replied, 'Yes; even if my son went there I should not like it: and as to taking my wife and family there I should think I was a scandalous person if I did so.'[33] The awkward fact, however, remained that only in such places did middle-class men meet working-class women in leisure, a meeting which was vitiated by the fact that for women this was work.

In almost every society it is one of the functions of leisure to provide an opportunity for sexual encounters. An ideology of leisure which tries to prevent that is saddling itself with difficulties. The ideology of class conciliation through leisure did precisely that, and it did it, it may be argued, not because of some unrelated ideology of sex, but precisely because that ideology was bound up with compulsions of class. The perfect lady of the mid-Victorian years, removed not only from worldly concerns, but also from household ones, was a symbol of her husband's wealth and status. She was part of the leisure class, but in somewhat the same way as an unemployed man was – by compulsion. And while in the latter case the opportunities to be enjoyed in leisure were cruelly curtailed by lack of money, in the former they were restricted by a concern for the maintenance of status. Conspicuous leisure and conspicuous consumption were a mark of status, their utility for purposes of reputability lying in the element of waste common to both – waste of time and effort, or waste of goods. Dress for women, therefore, has to be both expensive and impractical for productive labour; designedly uncomfortable, it testified in a general way to woman's economic dependence on man, and specifically to the status of a particular man. These concerns with status led, as is well known (and was much deplored at the time), to late marriages, so that the husband, well set in his career, could keep his wife in the manner which she had been led to expect as daughter. And this in turn encouraged a boom in prostitution as young middle-class men, unable for financial reasons to marry, sought an outlet for their sexual urges.[34] [. . .] It is true that towards the end of the century women of all classes gained more autonomy in the pursuit of leisure, but in the mid-Victorian period, in the heyday of the ideology of class conciliation through leisure, it might be said that women of all classes, though in different ways, were confined in a world where they were more the objects than the subjects of leisure. As such neither they nor their men-folk could contemplate any lowering of both sex and class barriers except when the relationship was overtly authoritarian or patronising.

There was one further reason, and a most important one, for the failure of the attempt to achieve class conciliation in leisure: there was a thrust in the opposite direction, within the middle class, towards the creation of sports and other leisure activities from which the working class was excluded. This took three forms. First, middle-class infiltration into the previously exclusive leisure world of the aristocracy. Secondly, the appropriation and imposition of a middle-class ethos on sports and other leisure activities which might previously have been described as popular. And thirdly, the invention of new leisure activities which were designedly class-specific.

The infiltration of the leisure world of the aristocracy was part of a widespread emulation of aristocratic life-styles by the wealthier sections of the middle-class. From this encounter both sides gained. The middle class brought much-needed cash to the more exclusive pastimes and in return received a boost in status. The timing of this challenge to aristocratic exclusiveness varied. In concert life, for example, it was as early as the 1820s that the upper middle class began to show signs of dissatisfaction with a musical life centering on the aristocratic private salon. Seeing their hold threatened, the aristocracy responded by expanding the salons into large-scale private concerts, featuring the most popular musicians and emphasising the exclusiveness of the gatherings. These, however, proved too expensive, and the outcome was a compromise whereby the formal and public concert replaced the salon. By the 1840s this coming together in musical life of the aristocracy and the upper middle class was symbolised by the creation of the Musical Union which replaced both the aristocratic Concerts of Ancient Music and the upper-middle-class Philharmonic concerts. High-status classical music now had an institutional form suited to the needs of a new elite which was both aristocratic and upper middle class.[35]

In hunting the challenge came a little later. The first step was to dispel any lingering ideas that it was a sport for all classes. In the 1840s Surtees was attacking publicans who for their own profit got up hunts of bag foxes for what he called the 'riff raff of the countryside', and Scrutator in 1861 hoped 'not to see any revival of that state of things which existed in the latter part of the eighteenth century, when few manufacturing towns were without a subscription pack, kept up by a club of clerks and apprentices, to the great loss of their time, injury to the surrounding country, and general demoralisation of the neighbourhood'. The poor were now firmly excluded, not that they had ever played much part in the sport, but the middle class was accepted. What happened in the age of the railway was an influx of middle-class capital, and greater participation by middle-class and frequently urban people. [. . .]

The second way in which one can see a thrust towards the exclusion of the poor lay in the appropriation of sports which were previously popular. Rowing, for example, had been described by Strutt at the beginning of the century as 'exceedingly popular', attracting large crowds, and it remained so in 1844 when the editor of *Bell's Life in London* described rowing matches as 'among the most popular Sports we have in the Neighbourhood of London', a particular feature of them being that all classes participated.[36] Athletics was even lower in social tone, being associated with the pub and gambling. A young solicitor in the 1860s had to break off his engagement when his fiancée's mother discovered that he took part in athletics. Precisely at this time, however, there was a determined attempt at appropriation of both sports by the middle class. In 1866 rules were drawn up excluding not only those who made a profit or living from them, but also anyone who 'is a mechanic, artisan or labourer'. It was a ruling which lasted only some 15 years, and the middle-class ethos was never fully imposed on either sport. [. . .]

The third form taken by the thrust to exclude the working class was the invention of new, designedly class-specific leisure occasions. Once again this is most obvious in sport. It was in these years that mountaineering, tennis, cycling and golf were founded as elite recreations. Cycling, for example, in the 1870s was 'a middle-class male pastime with a sprinkling of aristocratic participants'. The class nature of the new sports was apparent too in the development of golf. The major period of growth in England came at the turn of the century, but in its Scottish homeland, and in England as it developed after the founding of the first specifically English club at Westward Ho! in 1864, it was marked by strong class distinctions. The clubs formed in the 1870s and 1880s in Lancashire, Kent and elsewhere were either on private land, charging high fees, or more contentiously on common land – in the London region on Clapham Common (1873), and on common land at Epsom, Epping Forest and Tooting Bec. Such courses led to disputes with other users of common land. As Cousins writes, 'in 1887 golf in England was played by only a few people, all belonging to the upper classes, and was regarded with indifference, if not with suspicion and aversion, by the uninitiated majority'.[37]

There can be little doubt that the desire for exclusivity was the most important reason for the failure of the hope that class conciliation might be achieved in leisure. Quite simply the Industrial Revolution had created what Trollope in 1868 described as 'the largest and wealthiest leisure class that any country, ancient or modern, ever boasted'. As a class which gained at least part of its identity from its possession of leisure, the spending of that leisure in exclusive and status-enhancing settings was of paramount importance. Not only in the three ways we have discussed but in others too the class showed considerable ingenuity in securing for itself the desired exclusivity. In the seaside resorts, for example, it appropriated to itself fashionable seasons within the year as well as whole areas of towns. In all this it behaved no differently from the leisure class of early modern times; indeed it was this very behaviour that confirmed that it was indeed a class.[38]

For centuries it had been traditional in European society to see an occasional recreational release for the populace as necessary in the interests of social control. In the mid-nineteenth century in Britain, the emphasis was different; it was not to maintain the social order by allowing the people a modicum of those 'violent delights' which Jerrold thought typical of Londoners as late as 1870.[39] It was, in consciousness of the growth of class feeling in the first half of the century, to halt and reverse the process; not to abandon authority, nor allow it on occasion to be mocked, but to reassert its legitimacy by the class-conciliatory nature of the leisure that was offered. Some middle-class Victorians strove earnestly, through co-operative workshops and the like, to reform the experience of work. Many more, accepting as given the nature and permanence of capitalism, strove to mitigate the hardships it entailed for the working class by organising their leisure for them, and doing it in such a way as to emphasise, they hoped, the spirit of community, not of class.

Their efforts were doomed to failure. Community can hardly be created when the wish for it comes almost exclusively from one side of the class barrier. It is even less likely to do so when some of the promoters of the ideal are concerned solely to assimilate, not to give and take. In the class conciliation projects of the mid-Victorian years, the concern to establish authority was as evident as the desire for reconciliation. The building of community through leisure also bore the marks of wishful thinking, of escapism, of retreat to an ideal, patriarchal, gentry-dominated society. For respectable liberal middle-class Victorians to whom revolution was anathema, and the cash nexus of capitalism socially and morally distasteful, the reform of leisure, and at the same time an emphasis on its importance, offered the best hope of a socially harmonious civilisation.

The debates on leisure in the mid-Victorian years, then, have a different tone from those of earlier decades. The aim set by the middle class for itself was more ambitious and positive. It reflected the deep concern about class division, and in seeing the solution to it in leisure, it both inflated the importance of leisure and helped in the process of delimiting it. Leisure had imposed upon it perhaps the supreme task confronting the ruling Victorian middle class, that of improving class relations, and there could be no greater testimony to its new stature. The task imposed upon it, however, was too great. If anything in the third quarter of the century and beyond, leisure became more rather than less confined by class boundaries as new class-specific entertainment flourished. And leisure itself proved to be something which could not simply be utilised to serve the immediate purposes of a hegemonic middle class. [. . .]

[Our understanding of change during the Industrial Revolution has, explicitly or implicitly, been shaped by a certain kind of thinking.] There was, it seemed, an old traditional, rural, pre-industrial society which yet had enough dynamism in it to generate the Industrial Revolution, and that in turn transformed every aspect of people's lives, and necessarily their leisure; hence 'the vacuum'. By the 1830s, this line of argument continued, despite some survivals, this older culture was effectively dead, wiped out by the pressures of industrialism, urbanisation, evangelicalism and a reactionary government.

Then came new initiative from above, whether in the form of rational recreation or in the provision of modern commercial entertainment. And in the context of a vacuum, rational recreation had sufficient attraction to appeal to members of the working class; hence that linking of the respectable of all classes against the rough, and the theory that the key divisions were within rather than between classes.

This hypothetical structure, I have argued, was misleading. The modes of thinking about cultural change were vitiated in two fundamental ways. First, because culture was seen as something passive, reflecting, but for odd survivals, an economic base; this is a kind of thinking, without the Marxist language, to be found very frequently in anti-Marxist writers. Indeed in recent years the crudest economic determinism has been voiced by those on the right. And secondly, and following from this, because human society was split up into various separate sections — 'culture', 'economic activity', 'politics', 'thought', and so on.

This brings us back to Thompson, for it was precisely these errors which he avoided. Yet these very emphases in Thompson's work were, one may suspect, directed as much against orthodox Marxists as against conservatives. For Marxism is of course very precisely concerned to establish the degree to which history is determined; and Thompson, it could be argued, seemed to want, in a romantic way, to escape that determination. In 1963 it was easier to show in empirical fact how people could be active in the shaping of their history than it was to explain this in theoretical terms. Since then Marxist theory has become a subject of hot and productive debate, and there is now, based on the work of Gramsci, a theory through which we can better understand the process of cultural change. For the purpose of what follows, Gramsci's theory and other Marxist approaches, including his own, have been most cogently argued by Raymond Williams in *Marxism and Literature.*[40]

The basic problem may be put in this way. Many, whether or not they call themselves Marxists, write or think in fundamental agreement with Marx's famous formulation of the relationship of base or infra-structure to superstructure in the 1859 Preface to *A Contribution to the Critique of Political Economy*:

In the social production of their life, men enter into definite rela-tions that are indispensable and independent of their will, relations of production which correspond to a definite stage of development of their material productive forces. The sum total of these relations of production constitutes the economic structure of society, the real foundation, on which rises a legal and political superstructure and to which correspond definite forms of social consciousness. The mode of production of material life conditions the social, political and intellectual life process in general. It is not the consciousness of men that determines their being, but, on the contrary, their social being that determines their consciousness . . . With the change of the economic foundation the entire immense superstructure is more or less rapidly transformed . . .

This kind of thinking, crudely interpreted, lies behind much of our interpretation of cultural change in the Industrial Revolution. The economic foundation changed, goes the argument, hence so did 'the entire immense superstructure' which is taken, without question, to include leisure. Now if we accept this crude interpretation of what Marx was saying, then, if the argument of this book has any validity, Marx was clearly wrong; the relationship of leisure to the economic structure was exceedingly complex, and not a simple one-way process of influence; leisure cannot be reduced to or explained in terms of something else. The problem we are left with, however, is to gain more understanding of the relationship between leisure and the economic structure, and to see in what ways leisure was 'determined'.

In the passage quoted above I deliberately omitted parts which modify the crude force of Marx's formulation. Marx in the remainder of the passage, and both he and Engels in their later lives, qualified the

1859 statement. It may be, as Williams suggests, that no amount of qualification will remove the difficulties of the formulation, and that we should abandon the language of base and superstructure, but that is more easily said than done. Whether or not we retain it we must be clear of two things. First, with regard to determination. Many Marxists, uncomfortable with the notion of strict economic determinism, have argued that the base does not strictly determine but merely sets limits to the form of the superstructure. This, Williams argues, is not enough: we must look not only for 'the negative determinations that are experienced as limits' but also for positive determinations which may be pressures either to maintain or otherwise 'a given social mode'. In any real social process, writes Williams, there is 'an active and conscious as well as, by default, a passive and objectified historical experience'. Secondly, we must think of 'productive forces' as more than particular kinds of agricultural or industrial production. Marx himself wrote that a maker of a piano was a productive worker whereas a pianist was not. Clearly though, as Williams argues, the production of music as well as of its instruments is an important branch of capitalist production. Music, and by extension culture generally, and in some of its meanings, leisure, must be seen as themselves productive and material practices, not as something abstracted and divorced from economic life. Leisure, therefore, if we retain the language, can function as part of the infrastructure during our period as more and more leisure was 'produced': not simply as commercialised leisure, but also in the non-profit-making but nevertheless very material form of parks, museums, libraries and so on.

Once we begin to think of leisure as a form of production with specific social relations of production (and for Marx, remember, it was the relations of production which constituted the economic structure), then our understanding of it is transformed. We can see not only the fact that it is something active and changing, not simply a resource, but also why that should be so.

But, and this is where Gramsci's thought becomes important, it is active and changing within a complex interlocking of economic, political, social and cultural forces in a total situation of dominance and subordination. In the nineteenth century, in the complicated and ongoing process whereby hegemony was established and maintained, leisure was important. At the outset it was perceived to pose a real threat. It was an economic problem, for its quantity and irregularity for the mass of the people were counterposed to the work ideals of the industrialists. And it was a political, social and moral problem for its practice, and the ideology bound up with that practice, could be threatening, disorderly and immoral. Its legitimacy for the people was denied: only 'the leisured' had leisure. By the end of our period, however, its legitimacy for all could be accepted; hegemony had been maintained, but not without meeting a series of challenges the outcome of which was the modern leisure we have described. Those challenges, alternative or counter-hegemonies, took the form both of an amoral and therefore uncivilising commercialism, and also, in Owenism and Primitive Methodism for example, of an outwardly respectable (but actually threatening, because consciously working-class) form of rational recreation. Both these threats were headed off, though not totally defeated.

The same could be said for what might be called the idealist expression of hegemony, the notion that leisure might be the instrument of class conciliation. The outcome was in one sense a compromise, but it was a compromise in which the hegemony was unthreatened. Leisure became legitimate for the mass of the people precisely because it was shorn of other associations, and in particular of economic and political (or rather radical political) associations. A part of people's lives – that not spent working – and areas of public space became isolated as 'leisure'. Over that leisure the dominant culture had acquired a degree of control which was sufficient to enable it to legitimise that leisure. What people did in their spare time was not always or often uplifting, it might be irritating or annoying, as at Bank Holidays, but it was no longer a threat to hegemony. The outcome of a century of battles over the problem of leisure was that for the dominant culture leisure was safely residual, unconnected with and possibly a counterweight to new and socialist challenges to hegemony. Publicists continued and continue to talk about a problem of leisure, but it occupies only a very minor part of the dominant culture's concern. For since the later nineteenth century both the provision and the control of leisure have, from the point of view of hegemony, been adequately dealt with by increasingly powerful leisure industries, and by a new but minor branch of bureaucracy, the leisure services. It has become too the subject of an equally minor branch of academic life in which scholars spend much time debating both the importance and the nature of what they are studying. That situation is very precisely the outcome of the ambiguous victory for hegemony whereby leisure in the century we have studied became both tamed and legitimate because separated from the other concerns of people's lives.

Notes

1. On Egan, J.C. Reid, *Bucks and Bruisers* (London, 1971); D.P. Miller, *The Life of a Showman* (London, n.d.).
2. J.M. Butwin, 'Seditious Laughter', *Radical History Review*, no. 18 (1978), pp. 17-34.

3. W. Nicholson, *The Struggle for a Free Stage in London* (Boston and New York, 1906); C. Barker, 'The Chartists, Theatre, Reform and Research', *Theatre Quarterly*, vol. I (1971), pp. 3-10, and his 'A Theatre for the People' in K. Richards and P. Thomson, *Essays on Nineteenth Century British Theatre* (London, 1971).

4. P. Egan, *Boxiana* (1st edn 1812, repr. Leicester, 1971), p. 333.

5. W. Hone, *The Every-Day Book*, 2 vols. (London, 1826, 1827); *Table Book* (London, 1827); *Year Book* (London, 1832); T. Frost, *The Old Showmen and the Old London Fairs* (1st edn 1874, London, 1881); *Circus Life and Circus Celebrities* (1st edn 1875, London, 1881); and *The Lives of the Conjurors* (London, 1876). On Frost, see B. Sharratt, 'Autobiography and Class Consciousness', unpublished Univ. of Cambridge PhD thesis, 1973.

6. E.H. Bostock, *Menageries, Circuses and Theatres* (New York, 1972), pp. 5-6; P. Egan, *The Life of an Actor* (1st edn 1825, repr. London, 1904), pp. 200-2.

7. Nicholson, *Struggle for a Free Stage*, pp. 240 ff; A.H. Saxon, *Enter Foot and Horse* (New Haven and London, 1968), pp. 89-93, 153-61, 168-70.

8. R.D. Altick, *The Shows of London* (Cambridge, Mass., and London, 1978), pp. 413-14.

9. L. James, *Print and the People 1819-1851* (London, 1976), p. 84; R. Pearsall, *Victorian Popular Music* (Newton Abbot, 1973), p. 28; J.H. Plumb, *The Commercialisation of Leisure in Eighteenth-century England* (Reading, 1973).

10. P. Burke, *Popular Culture in Early Modern Europe* (London, 1978), pp. 3-22, 270-86; R.M. Dorson, *The British Folklorists* (Chicago, 1968), pp. 1-43.

11. W. Windham, *Speeches in Parliament*, 3 vols. (London, 1812), vol. 3, p. 315.

12. *Sporting Magazine*, September 1832, p. 359; D.P. Blaine, *An Encyclopaedia of Rural Sports* (London, 1840), p. 718; R. Wood, *Victorian Delights* (London, 1967), pp. 35, 39.

13. G. Combe, *The Constitution of Man*, 8th edn (Edinburgh and London, 1847), p. 288; *Household Words*, vol. VI (1852), pp. 133-9; P. Egan, *Book of Sports* (London, 1847 edn), p. 56.

14. M.R. Mitford, *Our Village*, 5 vols. (London, 1824-32), p. 169; J. Lawson, *Letters to the Young on Progress in Pudsey During the Last Sixty Years* (Stanninglen, 1887, repr. Caliban Books, Firle, 1979), pp. 62-3.

15. J. Ford, *Cricket, a Social History 1700-1835* (Newton Abbot, 1972), p. 123; W. Howitt, *The Rural Life of England* (2 vols. 1838, repr., 1 vol. Shannon, 1971) vol. II, pp. 273-8; S.C. of the House of Lords to inquire into the Laws respecting Gaming, PP 1844 (604), vol. VI, q. 234.

16. W.F. Mandle, 'Games People Played: Cricket and Football in England and Victoria in the Late Nineteenth Century', *Historical Studies*, vol. 15 (1973), p. 511, and 'The Professional Cricketer in England in the Nineteenth Century', *Labour History*, no. 23 (1972), p. 2; H.S. Altham and E.W. Swanston, *A History of Cricket*, 4th edn (London, 1948), p. 88; C.L.R. James, *Beyond a Boundary* (London, 1976), p. 159.

17. R. Bowen, *Cricket* (London, 1970), pp. 106-19; James, *Beyond a Boundary*, pp. 157-84.

18. P.C. McIntosh, *Physical Education in England since 1800*, revised and enlarged edn (London, 1968), p. 55; Bowen, *Cricket*, pp. 113-14; P. Scott, 'Cricket and the Religious World in the Victorian Period', *Church Quarterly*, vol. III (1970), pp. 134-44; Lawson, *Progress in Pudsey*. p. 63.

19. D. Newsome, *Godliness and Good Learning* (London, 1961), pp. 80-1; McIntosh, *Physical Education*, pp. 20-33.

20. E. Dunning, 'The Development of Modern Football' in Dunning (ed.), *The Sociology of Sport* (London, 1971), p. 143; McIntosh, *Physical Education*, pp. 38-53.

21. T. Hughes, *Tom Brown's School-Days* (London, 1857). See also Hughes's *The Scouring of the White Horse* (London, 1858); Newsome, *Godliness*, pp. 207-8; O. Anderson, 'The Growth of Christian Militarism in mid-Victorian Britain', *English Historical Review*, vol. LXXXVI (1971), pp. 46-72.

22. T. Veblen, *The Theory of the Leisure Class* (New York, 1919), p. 255.

23. S.C. on Gaming, 3rd Report, PP 1844, vol. VI, p. v; G. Doré and B. Jerrold, *London, a Pilgrimage* (New York, 1970), pp. 73-80.

24. Quoted in B. Trinder, 'Conflict and Compromise: Evangelicals and Popular Culture in Banbury 1830-1870', Paper to Conference of the Society for the Study of Labour History, November 1975, p. 16.

25. H. Solly, *Working Men's Social Clubs and Educational Institutes*, 2nd edn (London, 1904), p. 87; J.M. Ludlow and Lloyd Jones. *Progress of the Working Class 1832-1867* (London, 1867), p. 196.

26. R.Q. Gray, *The Labour Aristocracy in Victorian Edinburgh* (Oxford, 1976), *passim*, esp. p. 139; G. Crossick, 'The Labour Aristocracy and its Values: a Study of Mid-Victorian Kentish London', *Victorian Studies*, vol. XIX (1976), pp. 301-28; T.R. Tholfsen, *Working Class Radicalism in Mid-Victorian England* (London, 1976).

27. Dunning, *Sociology of Sport*, pp. 133-51, 357-8; P.C. McIntosh, *Sport in Society* (London, 1963), pp. 72-3; J. Walvin, *The People's Game* (London, 1975), pp. 44-5, 57.

28. W. Hone, *The Every-Day Book* (2 vols. London, 1826-7), vol. II, p. 187; R.C. on Children in Mines and Manufactories, 1st Report, PP 1842, vol. XV, p. 123.

29. P.C. Bailey, *Leisure and Class in Victorian England: Rational Recreation and the Contest for Control, 1830-1885* (London, 1978), pp. 138-9; T. Mason, *Association Football and English Society 1863-1915* (Hassocks, 1980).

30. Doré and Jerrold, *London*, p. 174; P. Cunnington and A. Mansfield, *English Costume for Sports and Outdoor Recreation* (London, 1969), p. 62; D.C. Itzkowitz, *Peculiar Privilege: A Social History of English Fox-hunting 1753-1885* (Hassocks, 1977), pp. 55-7.

31. T. Wright, *Some Habits and Customs of the Working Classes* (London, 1867, repr. New York 1967), *The Great Unwashed*, 1st edn 1868 (London, 1970), pp. 31-41; M. Anderson, *Family Structure in Nineteenth-century Lancashire* (London, 1971), p. 77; W. Besant, 'The Amusements of the People' in *As We Are And As We May Be* (London, 1903), p. 279.

32. D. Hudson, *Munby, Man of Two Worlds* (London, 1972), p. 215; H. Mayhew, *London Labour and the London Poor* (4 vols., London, 1861-2), vol. IV, pp. 210-72; W. Acton, *Prostitution* (2nd edn 1870, repr. London, 1972), pp. 16-22.

33. S.C. on Theatrical Licences and Regulations, PP 1866 (373), vol. XI, q. 6882.

34. J.A. and O. Banks, *Feminism and Family Planning in Victorian England* (Liverpool, 1964), pp. 58-76; Veblen, *Theory of the Leisure Class*, pp. 57-187.

35. W. Weber, *Music and the Middle Class* (London, 1975), pp. 24-63.

36. J. Strutt, *The Sports and Pastimes of the People of England* (London, 1801, new edn 1830), p. 89; S.C. on Gaming, PP 1844, vol. VI, qq. 218-27.

37. D. Rubinstein, 'Cycling in the 1890s', *Victorian Studies*, vol. 21 (1977), p. 48; G. Cousins, *Golf in Britain* (London, 1975), pp. 16-23.

38. A. Trollope (ed.), *British Sports and Pastimes* (London, 1868), p. 18; J. Walton, 'Residential Amenity, Respectable Morality and the Rise of the Entertainment Industry: the case of Blackpool 1860-1914', *Literature and History*, no. 1 (1975), pp. 62-78.

39. Doré and Jerrold, *London*, pp. 161-2.

40. London, 1977, esp. Part II.

WORKING-CLASS CULTURE AND WORKING-CLASS POLITICS IN LONDON, 1870-1900: NOTES ON THE REMAKING OF A WORKING CLASS

Gareth Stedman Jones

Source: *Journal of Social History*, vol. 7 (Summer 1973-4) © Peter N. Stearns.

In the London of the 1880s, Charles Masterman recalled, the future that all had foretold had been one of class war and the formation of a workers' party. But that future had not materialized. For, 'a wave of imperialism has swept over the country, and all these efforts, hopes and visions have vanished as if wiped out by a sponge.'[1] Masterman was writing in 1900, the year of the Mafeking celebrations. No one who saw the crowds on Mafeking night ever forgot them. 'Mafficking' entered the English language, and the memory was still vivid in the twenties and thirties. [. . .] The celebration was not confined to the central pleasure area or the middle-class suburbs. According to the *Times* report of the events, 'the news was received with extraordinary enthusiasm in East London and Saturday was generally observed as a holiday.'[2] [. . .] It is not surprising that startled liberals, like Masterman, should have imagined that they were witnessing the emergence of a 'new race . . . the city type . . . voluble, excitable, with little ballast, stamina or endurance — seeking stimulus in drink, in betting, in any unaccustomed conflicts at home or abroad.'[3]

This picture painted by anxious liberals and complacent conservatives must be somewhat modified. The predominant feeling on Mafeking night was not aggression but relief after the disasters of the 'black week.' There was little hooliganism or violence. It has recently been established that not workers but students and clerks formed the loutish jingo mobs which broke up pro-Boer meetings and ransacked the property of 'little Englanders.'[4] Recent research also suggests that the Boer War was not the main concern of working-class voters in the 'khaki election' of 1900. The poll was below average and the decisive issues in poorer London constituencies were local and material — high rents, job opportunities, Jewish immigration, the protection of declining trades and the improvement of the water supply.[5] Finally, the recruitment figures show that workers did not volunteer to fight in the war in any significant numbers until the return of unemployment in 1901.[6]

These qualifications are important, but it is unlikely that they would have done much to assuage the anxiety felt by radicals and socialists at the time. For, if the working class did not actively promote the jingoism, there can be no doubt that it passively acquiesced to it. [. . .]

Modern historians have tended to belittle the anxieties of Masterman and the perplexity of radicals and socialists. Standard interpretations of the period, 1870-1914, have tended to concentrate on the great waves of trade union expansion, the growth of socialism, the foundation of the Labour party, the conversion of the working class from liberalism, the demand for social reform and the beginnings of the welfare state. Phenomena like Mafeking and the prevalence of conservatism among the working class in a large city like London, when discussed at all, have generally appeared as accidental or aberrant features of a period whose basic tendency was the rise of labour and the mounting pressure for social reform. When attempts have been made to explain such deviations in the Boer War period, they have concentrated almost exclusively upon short term causes and subjective factors: dissensions within the Liberal Party; the absence of a 'charismatic' figure like Gladstone. [. . .] In reality, weakness of platform, absence of effective leadership and feeble organization were symptoms rather than causes of the lack of vitality in London working-class politics. The failure of radicals and socialists to make any deep impression on the London working class in the late Victorian and Edwardian period had deeper roots than subjective deficiency. Underlying it were longer term structural changes in the character of London working-class life which made attempts at political mobilization increasingly difficult. What Mafeking and other imperial celebrations portended was not so much the predominance of the wrong politics among the mass of London workers, but rather their estrangement from political activity as such. There was general agreement that the politically active working man of the time was a radical or a socialist. Loyalism was a product of apathy.

One of the features of this period which has generally received little attention from historians was the emergence of a distinctively new pattern of working-class culture in the years between 1870 and 1900: a type of culture which literary critics like Hoggart were to label 'traditional' in the 1950s.[7] [. . .] It [is] impossible to explain the behaviour and attitudes of the working class during this epoch outside the context of this culture and the material situation which it represented.

In this paper, I shall attempt — very tentatively — to trace the conditions of emergence of a new working-class culture in London and to delineate its characteristic institutions and ideology. Given this task, however, it must be borne in mind that nineteenth-century London not only gave birth to a new working-class culture, but also to a new form of middle-class culture based upon an increasing convergence of outlook between the middle class and the aristocracy. Both these 'cultures' must be examined, for it is impossible to understand the one except in relation to the other. By juxtaposing the two, I hope to explain the emergence of a working-class culture which showed itself staunchly impervious to middle-class attempts to guide it, but yet whose prevailing tone was not one of political combativity, but of an enclosed and defensive conservatism. In this way, I hope to open up a different line of approach to the problem of London politics in the age of imperialism and to go a little way towards reconciling the cultural, economic and political history of the working class. [. . .]

It was only at the beginning of the twentieth century — in London at least — that middle-class observers began to realize that the working class was not simply *without* culture or morality, but in fact possessed a 'culture' of its own. Charles Booth's observation that the London working class was governed by 'strict rules of propriety,' but that these rules did not necessarily coincide with 'the ordinary lines of legal or religious morality,'[8] may appear bald and incurious when compared with the work of later connoisseurs like Orwell or Hoggart. Nevertheless, it signalled the beginnings of a new attitude towards the working class. Of course, there had been anticipations. Henry Mayhew, ahead of his time and class in so many respects, had gestured unsuccessfully towards this idea in his primitive anthropological distinctions between 'wandering' and 'civilized' tribes.[9] But Mayhew's approach found no echo in the slum life literature of the ensuing forty years. London workers were 'heathen.' 'Civilization' had not reached them. [. . .] When missionaries from 'civilisation' ventured into that 'Babylon,' they were confronted by 'terrible sights,' and if struck by guilt or fear, they recalled the stories of Dives and Lazarus or Jacob and Esau. The terms, 'working classes' or 'toiling masses' carried no positive cultural connotations, for they signified *ir*religion, *in*temperance, *im*providence or *im*morality. Indeed, it was often difficult for these strangers from the 'civilized' world to discover where the 'working classes' ended and where the 'dangerous classes' began. For crime, prostitution, disorder and sedition were also thought to lurk in these poor regions, hidden from the gaze of the well-to-do, and when left to fester in this 'nether world,' could suddenly break out and threaten the town.[10] [. . .]

The working class lacked 'civilization' because it was hidden away and removed from it: The imagery of this language and the situation which it represented was itself a novel product of the Victorian period. [. . .]

Eighteenth-century writers had often been perturbed by the 'insolence of the mob' but the mob was in no sense geographically isolated from the more prosperous districts of the town. [. . .] Masters, traders, journeymen and labourers not only inhabited the same areas, but often resided on different floors of the same houses. Distinctions between trades were more important than distinctions between masters and journeymen. [. . .] Social distinctions abounded at every level, but there was no great political, cultural or economic divide between the middle class and those beneath them. Despite the great turbulence of the London crowd, its political outlook was generally in accord with that of the City of London's Common Hall which tended to reflect the views of the less substantial merchants and masters.[11] It was only after the Gordon riots that the alliance began to break down. Culturally, there were certainly greater affinities between these groups than were to exist later. All classes shared in the passions for gambling, theatre, tea gardens, pugilism and animal sports.[12] All except the richest merchants lived within a short distance of their work, if not at the place of work itself.[13] The pub was a social and economic centre for all and heavy drinking was as common among employers as among the workmen.[14]

In the period 1790-1840, the distance between the London middle class and those beneath them increased dramatically. Political positions were polarized by the French Revolution. The propertied classes turned increasingly to Evangelicalism. The small masters and traders, after an initial flirtation with the London Corresponding Society, found Benthamite ideas of cheap government, franchise extension and political economy more congenial. [. . .] Artisans forged a political position of their own from the writings of Paine and the Jacobinism of the French Revolution. Their ideology was atheist, republican, democratic and fiercely anti-aristocratic. The alliance between middle-class radicalism and artisan democracy came under increasing strain after 1815. The incompatibility between the growth of trade unionism and the radicals' espousal of political economy announced the breach. After the 1832 Reform Bill, the alliance had no common basis. Owenism and the New Poor Law completed the rupture. The direct impact of the industrial revolution upon London was slight. The vast majority of firms remained small and factories rare. But the indirect impact was formidable. It can be detected in the decline of the Spitalfields weavers, the removal of legislative protection of apprenticeship, in the growth of the slop trades in clothing, furniture and footwear, in the huge expansion of commercial activity and in the growth of the port of London. Even in the absence of factories, middle-class consciousness developed just as surely. From the end of the 1820s, more and more of the middle class abandoned the city and the industrial quarters for the exclusiveness of the suburbs. The centre became the sphere of the counting house, the workshop, the warehouse and the workers' dwellings, while the periphery became a bourgeois and petit bourgeois elysium — a private world where business was not discussed and where each detached or semi-detached villa with its walled garden and obsession with privacy aspired in miniature to the illusion of a country estate.[15] Shilibeer's omnibus, the Metropolitan Police Act and the 1832 Reform Bill inaugurated a new pattern of class relations in London.

In the forty years after the Reform Bill, this process of segregation and differentiation completed itself. By the 1870s, it had become part of the natural order of things. [. . .] Only sixteen years after 1832, the middle classes were enrolling as special constables to aid the Duke of Wellington against the Chartists, and by the 1870s they were generally voting Conservative. Evangelicalism and Utilitarianism, originally distinct and to some extent opposed philosophies, increasingly coalesced. [. . .] By the time the Charity Organization Society was founded in 1869, the evangelical and utilitarian traditions were scarcely distinguishable. The social basis of this coalescence was the ever more insistent middle-class striving towards gentility. [. . .]

Moreover, this style of life, if not its material standards, was increasingly adopted by the growing army of clerks, teachers and new 'professional' men. Not to compete for these trophies, or at least the semblance of them, was to invite ostracism. [. . .]

In general, middle-class incomes were rising. Even so, gentility of this kind was expensive, especially for those whose incomes could not match their aspirations to status. Sacrifices were necessary. The age of marriage was postponed and from the 1870s the size of families began to be restricted. Subtle savings were made in that part of the household budget not on public display. Needlework, ostensibly for charity, often supplemented the family income.[16] In the mid-Victorian period, prudence and thrift [. . .] were not merely the battle cries of economists and politicians. They were integral necessities of middle-class domestic economy.

How then, did these new aspirants to gentility regard the 'unwashed' proletarians crammed together in the smoky regions which they had left behind? In times of prosperity and stability, they probably thought little about them at all, since their major concern was to create a life style as far as possible removed from them. [. . .]

But in times of political disturbance and economic depression, this complacent self-absorption gave way to fear and anxiety. [. . .] At these times of insecurity, fears for property were combined with a great emotive yearning to re-establish personal relations between the classes. The enormous popularity of the novels of Dickens in the late 1830s and 1840s, with their nostalgia for Christmas spirit and traditional personal benevolence, was an expression of this desire.[17] But this was only a phantasy solution, a wish fulfilment. In reality, relations of benevolence could only be re-established by proxy. So money was invested in missionary organizations designed to eradicate pernicious customs and dangerous class prejudices from the poor, and to promote acceptance of the moral and political code of their superiors. The policeman and the workhouse were not sufficient. The respectable and the well-to-do had to win the 'hearts and minds' of the masses to the new moral order and to assert their right to act as its priesthood. Propertied London had no need of the new industrial religion of Comte, its ascendancy was to be established through the implantation of self-help and evangelical Christianity.

In the Victorian period, there were three major waves of anxiety among the propertied classes about the behaviour and attitudes of the London working class.[18] The first was a response to the uncertain conditions of the 1840s and early 1850s. There was anxiety about cholera, about Chartism and the Revolutions of 1848, about the inrush of Irish immigrants and the deteriorating condition of artisans threatened by the expansion of the 'dishonourable' and sweated trades. [. . .]

The second peak of religious and philanthropic energy occurred between 1866 and 1872. Anxiety was less intense and certainly less widespread than it had been in the 1840s. Nevertheless, these were the years of the Second Reform Bill and the Paris Commune, of high bread prices coinciding with high unemployment in the East End, of another cholera epidemic and almost equally lethal outbreaks of scarlet fever and smallpox. The country as a whole was stable, but in London the number of paupers rose dramatically and the working class was suspected of republicanism. The spate of reforming concern which these uneasy years produced, is reflected in the foundation of the Charity Organization Society, the beginning of Octavia Hill's housing experiments, the promotion of church-run workmen's clubs, Edward Denison's residence in the East End, the foundation of Dr. Barnardo's East End Juvenile Mission, James Greenwood's journalistic investigations of the 'wilds' of London and Ruskin's *Fors Clavigera*. But despite the demonstrations, unemployed marches and over-filled stone yards, the problem of order was never acute. By 1873, the last traces of anxiety had passed away.

The third wave of insecurity reached its peak in the years between 1883 and 1888. It was a period of low profits, of high unemployment, of acute overcrowding, of another threatened visitation of cholera and of large scale Jewish immigration into the East End. Artisans were known to be secularist and to support Henry George's single tax proposals; unemployed and casual workers were suspected of harbouring violent solutions to their misery and appeared to be falling under the sway of socialist oratory. Forebodings were increased by the uncertainties of the Irish situation, by suspicions of police inefficiency and evidence of municipal corruption. The reaction to this situation can be seen in the sensational journalism of Andrew Mearns, G.R. Sims, Arnold

White and W.E. Stead, in the novels of Gissing and the first investigations of Charles Booth. Attempts to re-establish harmony ranged from Barnett's *Toynbee Hall* and Besant's *People's Palace* to the Salvation Army's *Darkest England* scheme and a rash of new missions promoted by churches, universities and public schools. But again, the crisis was not long-lived. Fear of disorder and insurrection began to fade as the depression lifted and virtually disappeared after the dock strike of 1889.

In each of these waves, the combination of high unemployment, social unrest abroad, threatened epidemics and doubts about the political loyalties of the masses, created varying degrees of uneasiness among the respectable and the well-to-do. [. . .] Those with property assumed an intimate link between begging, crime and political disorder. It is not surprising that some of them felt that they were sitting on a powder keg and that each wave of anxiety should leave behind it a new crop of social and religious organizations determined to hasten the work of christianizing and 'civilizing' the city.

Two major strategems can be detected in this christianizing and 'civilizing' activity. The first was to use legislation to create a physical and institutional environment in which undesirable working-class habits and attitudes would be deterred, while private philanthropy could undertake the active propagation of a new moral code. The material needs of the poor would then be used as a means towards their moral reformation. Thus, in the sphere of housing: street clearance acts, railway promotion, sanitary legislation, common lodging house inspection and Artisans' Dwellings Acts demolished rookeries and slums and dispersed their inhabitants, while model dwelling companies and philanthropic housing trusts provided what propertied London considered to be more appropriate working-class housing. Habits of order and regularity were enforced through the insistence upon regular payment of rent and through detailed regulatory codes governing the use of facilities. The presence of the caretaker was designed to ensure that the rules were observed. Even the architectural design of these buildings, as George Howell noted of the Peabody blocks, was intended to insure 'regulation without direct control.'[19]

A similar and even more calculated attempt to weight the worker's felicific calculus in favour of middle-class norms of conduct was apparent in the organizational ambitions of the Charity Organization Society. The aim of the Society (never remotely realized) was to act as a clearing house for all requiring charitable assistance in London: all applicants were to have their cases thoroughly investigated; if found 'deserving' (showing signs of thrift and temperance) they were to be directed to the appropriate specialized charity; if found 'undeserving' (drunken, improvident) they were instructed to apply to the workhouse. The C.O.S. was a logical complement to the reforms in London poor law administration which occurred at the end of the 1860s. The intention of these reforms was to make the workhouse effectively deterrent to the able-bodied pauper and to abolish outdoor relief. Control of charitable outlets allied to strict poor law administration would, it was hoped, effectively demonstrate to the poor that there could be no practicable alternative to 'incessant self-discipline'.

These attempts to reform the manners of the working class through the control of its physical and institutional environment were generally accompanied by a firm belief in the civilizing effects of personal relations between the classes. Evangelical in origin, the intensity of this belief grew virtually as a reflex reaction to the growing social segregation of the city. The practice of 'visiting the poor' was pioneered by the church and increased steadily after the 1851 religious census had shown that the christianization of the working class would only be accomplished by active missionary work. In the years that followed, the mission hall became a familiar feature of the slum landscape and evangelical crusades were directed at every sector of the 'friendless and fallen.' [. . .] Under the aegis of the local church, household management classes, coal and blanket clubs and penny savings banks were started, teetotal working men's clubs promoted, ragged school unions fostered, railway excursions organized and wholesome athletic sports encouraged. By the end of the 1860s, the idea of inter-class contact was being employed in purely secular missionary enterprises. [. . .]

This belief that missionaries from civilization would dispel the 'shades' and 'shadows' in which the poor dwelt, reached its apotheosis in the settlement houses of the 1880s. [. . .]

The cumulative external effect of this middle-class onslaught in the Victorian period was considerable. Old haunts of crime, vice and disease were demolished and their inhabitants scattered. [. . .] The sites [. . .] were now occupied by acres of model dwellings. By 1891, these blocks housed 189,108 people and by the end of the century the numbers had increased by a further substantial amount.[20]

By the end of Victoria's reign, gin palaces had virtually disappeared. The social and economic functions of the pub had been reduced; drinking hours had been restricted and children had been excluded from the bar. Cock-fighting, bearbaiting and ratting had all but died out. Gambling had been driven off the streets. 'Waits,' 'vales' and other traditional forms of 'indiscriminate charity' had been increasingly resisted by large sections of the middle class. Evangelical disapproval had hastened the disappearance of tea gardens, free-and-easies and judge-and-jury clubs. Public executions at Newgate had ceased in 1868. Southwark, St. Bartholomew and the other great London fairs had been abolished. Craft drinking rituals had declined and St. Monday had disappeared in most trades. In place of these traditional carnivals and holidays, four regular bank holidays had been instituted in 1871 and a growing number of parks, museums, exhibitions, public libraries and mechanics' institutes promoted a more improving or innocuous use of leisure time.

The church's ambition to bring the working class into contact with its ideology had also benefited from legislative assistance. From the time of the 1870 Education Act, all children were subjected to religious education and initiated into the rituals of established Christianity through a daily routine of morning prayer. Legislative attempts to change the unsabbatarian habits of adults had not been so successful. Lord Robert Grosvenor's Sunday Trading Bill provoked serious riots in Hyde Park in 1855 and had to be hastily withdrawn. Even in 1880, R.A. Cross, the Conservative Home Secretary, said that if Sunday closing were introduced he would not be responsible for the peace of London.[21] Nevertheless, at an unofficial level, the scale of missionary activity had increased enormously and by the 1890s efforts to establish inter-class contact in working-class areas had in some cases reached saturation point. [. . .] Salvationists paraded up and down the main streets, while armies of religious volunteers visited the poor in their homes. At the turn of the century, these visible symbols of religious and charitable intervention could be found in every poor borough of London.

How far had this middle-class onslaught changed or influenced working-class attitudes and behaviour? Certainly not in the way it had been intended. By the Edwardian period, it had become inescapably clear that middle-class evangelism had failed to recreate a working class in its own image. The great majority of London workers were not Christian, provident, chaste or temperate.

The results of fifty years of Christian missionary activity had been insignificant. [. . .] 'The churches,' according to Booth, 'have come to be regarded as the resorts of the well-to-do, and of those who are willing to accept the charity and patronage of people better off than themselves.'[22] Where the poor did attend church, it was generally for material reasons. Church attendance was rewarded by church charity. When charity was withdrawn, the congregation disappeared.[23] It was a pleasant irony that the poor should adopt a thoroughly utilitarian attitude in the one realm in which the middle class considered it to be inappropriate. The consequence of this association between church and charity was that religion became a symbol of servile status. Church attendance signified abject poverty and the loss of self-respect. As Booth noted of the Clapham-Nine Elms district, 'the poor are regularly visited, but others are above visitation, and apt to slam the door, and say, "I am a respectable person." '[24] Even among the poor themselves however, clergymen complained that they were unable to make contact with the men. Dealing with middle-class intruders, like paying the rent and all other activities pertaining to family expenditure and the upkeep of the home, was the province of the wife. [. . .]

If efforts to christianize the working class were largely a failure, efforts to induce temperance appear to have made even less impact. [. . .] At the end of the century, Booth reported that drunkenness had decreased but that drinking was more widespread than before. The pub remained a focal point of local working-class life. But its role had changed. It had been shorn of many of its former economic functions and was now more narrowly associated with leisure and relaxation. Women used pubs more frequently, and so apparently did courting couples. Straightforward heavy drinking had become less widespread, as was testified by the virtual disappearance of the gin palace. But there had been no dramatic shift. Frequent and heavy bouts of drinking remained common in traditional London trades and jobs requiring great physical exertion. In the long term, the moderation of drinking habits depended upon the increase of mechanization and the decrease of over-crowding. Neither of these tendencies was characteristic of London in the period before 1914.[25]

The results of the pressures exerted by poor law officials, charity organizers and self-help advocates to induce thrift among the working class were similarly disappointing. The bulk of the working class did not adopt middle-class savings habits. What saving there was among the casual workers, the unskilled and the poorer artisans was not for the purpose of accumulating a sum of capital, but for the purchase of artic-les of display or for the correct observance of ritual occasions. Thus the 'goose club' run by the publican to ensure a good Christmas dinner, or the clothing clubs providing factory girls with fashionably cut dresses were much more prevalent and characteristic forms of saving than mem-bership of a friendly society which was confined to the better paid and regularly employed.[26] The one form of insurance common among the poor, death insurance, was typical of their general attitude towards thrift. The money was intended, not for the subsequent maintenance of dependants, but to pay for the costs of the funeral. If one thought obsessed the minds of those in poverty, it was to escape a pauper's funeral, and to be buried according to due custom. [. . .]

More generally, evidence about patterns of spending among the London poor suggests that a concern to demonstrate self-respect was infinitely more important than any forms of saving based upon calcula-tions of utility. When money was available which did not have to be spent on necessities, it was used to purchase articles for display rather than articles of use. [. . .] This concern for display and for keeping up appearances was not confined to the poor, it was predominant through-out the working class. Even the well paid artisan who could afford to

rent a terrace house in Battersea or Woolwich reserved the front room
for occasions when he dressed in his best clothes, for Sunday high teas
with family relations, to entertain a prospective son-in-law or as a place
to lay out the coffin when a death occurred. The room generally
remained unused during the week.[27]

For the poor, this effort to keep up appearances, to demonstrate
'respectability' entailed as careful a management of the weekly family
budget as any charity organizer could have envisaged. But its priorities
were quite different. 'Respectability' did not mean church attendance,
teetotalism or the possession of a post office savings account. It meant
the possession of a presentable Sunday suit, and the ability to be seen
wearing it. [. . .] But if Sunday was the occasion to demonstrate self-
respect and to shut out for a day the pressures of poverty, Monday
meant an abrupt return to reality. For Monday meant, not only the
return to work, but also the day when the rent had to be paid. According to Alexander Patterson:

> On Monday morning a group of women, with bundles tied in old
> newspapers, will be seen outside the pawnshop, waiting for the doors
> to open at 9 am; for this is a common weekly practice, and not the
> urgent measure of exceptional distress. It is true that on next Satur-
> day night the suit will in all probability be redeemed, but the suit by
> then will have cost a guinea, instead of a pound, and every time it is
> pawned in future will add a shilling to the price.[28]

It is clear from these and other accounts that the priorities of expenditure among the poor bore little relation to the ambitions set before
them by advocates of thrift and self-help. Joining a friendly society to
insure against sickness, medical expenses, unemployment or old age,
apart from being enormously expensive for those whose incomes were
low or irregular, was too abstract and intangible an ambition for families whose whole efforts were concentrated on getting through the week
ahead without being beset by disaster.[. . .]

Finally, it is clear that although the popular use of leisure time had
changed dramatically in the course of the century, the direction of
change had not been of a kind to give much encouragement to religious and moral reformers. Certainly, the cruel animal sports of the
eighteenth century had declined substantially. [. . .] It is also true
that Saturday half holidays established in most trades in the late 1860s
and early 1870s had led to an enormous increase in the number of
railway excursions to the country and the seaside. But bank holidays,
according to clergymen in the 1890s, were a great 'curse.'[29] The old
association of holidays with betting, drinking and extravagant expenditure, remained strong. Derby day was the major festive event in the

calendar of the London poor. [. . .] Two hundred thousand people were said to congregate on Hampstead Heath on a fine Easter or a Whitsun, while similarly vast numbers made for Crystal Palace or the Welsh Harp on August bank holidays.[30]

One of the main reasons why fairs and races provoked middle-class disapproval was their association with betting and gambling. Far from decreasing in the second half of the nineteenth century, these pastimes increased enormously. The trend was already apparent at the end of the 1860s. [. . .]

The prevalence of these 'unimproving' recreations in the daytime was matched by the enormous popularity of the music hall at night. Despite the repeated claims made for its educational value by its promoters, the music hall like the fairs and the races, was subject to constant evangelical disapproval.[31] Music halls began as extensions to public houses and the sale of drink remained the mainstay of their profits.[32] Added to this there were frequent allegations — often well-founded — that the halls were used by prostitues to pick up clients. Yet, despite the efforts of campaigners for temperance, moral purity or a more intelligent use of leisure time, not to mention determined attempts by theatre managers to crush a dangerous rival, the number of music halls increased dramatically between 1850 and 1900.[33] [. . .]

Although music hall entertainment spread to the provinces, it began and remained a characteristically London creation. According to a Parliamentary Commission in 1892, 'the large collection of theatres and music halls gathered together, the amount of capital used in the enterprise, the great number of persons, directly and indirectly provided with employment, the multitudes of all classes of the people who attend theatres and music halls of London, find no other parallel in any other part of the country.'[34] Apart from the central palaces which particularly from the 1880s onwards began to attract sporting aristocrats, military officers, students, clerks and tourists, the music hall was predominantly working-class, both in the character of its audience, the origins of its performers and the content of its songs and sketches. [. . .] There were countless small halls [. . .] in working-class suburbs between the 1860s and the 1890s. In general the music hall appealed to all sectors of the working class from the casual labourer to the highly paid artisan. Its importance as a social and cultural institution in proletarian districts was second only to that of the pub. As one working man told the 1892 Committee, 'The music halls in the East End and South East of London are considered the great entertainment of the working man and his family.'[35] Of its enormous popularity there can be no doubt. Even in 1924, thirty years after the music hall's heyday, 100,000 people turned out to attend the funeral of Marie Lloyd.

From this preliminary discussion of working-class spending habits and leisure time activity, it is clear that by the beginning of the twentieth century a new working-class culture had emerged in London. Many of its institutions dated back to the middle of the century, but its general shape had first become visible in the 1870s, and dominant in the 1890s. By the time Booth conducted his survey of 'religious influences' its general components had already set in a distinctive mould. This culture was clearly distinguished from the culture of the middle class and had remained largely impervious to middle-class attempts to dictate its character or direction. Its dominant cultural institutions were not the school, the evening class, the library, the friendly society, the church or the chapel, but the pub, the sporting paper, the race course and the music hall. Booth's 'religious influences' series were compiled from information provided by clergymen, school board and poor law officials, vestrymen, policemen and charity organizers. It could be read as one interminable confession of impotence and defeat. But, significantly, Booth did not draw a pessimistic conclusion from his enquiries. There is an inescapable tone of assurance, even of complacency, running through his final volumes — in marked contrast to the anxiety which coloured his first investigations. This difference in tone could not and was not attributed by him to any substantial decrease in poverty and overcrowding. What principally impressed him was the growing stability and orderliness of London working-class society. [. . .] Describing the local music halls, he admitted their vulgarity and unimproving tone, but observed, 'the audiences are prevailingly youthful. They seek amusement and are easily pleased. No encouragement to vice can be attributed to these local music halls.'[36] The general working-class objection to church going, as Booth described it, stemmed from the class associations of religion. But secularism had sharply declined since the 1880s and the prevailing attitude had changed from hostility to good-natured indifference. In Woolwich it was apparently still 'bad form . . . even to nod to a parson in the street.'[37] But this was exceptional. In London as a whole the working class were 'more friendly, more tolerant perhaps of religious pretensions.' The final impression conveyed by the Booth survey was of a working-class culture which was both impermeable to outsiders, and yet predominantly conservative in character: a culture in which the central focus was not 'trade unions and friendly societies, cooperative efforts, temperance propaganda and politics (including socialism)' but 'pleasure, amusement, hospitality and sport.'[38] [. . .]

So far I have argued that from the 1850s a working-class culture gradually established itself, which proved virtually impervious to evangelical or utilitarian attempts to determine its character or direction. But it has also be shown that in the latter part of the century, this impermeability no longer reflected any widespread class combativity. For the most prominent developments in working-class life in late

Victorian and Edwardian London were the decay of artisan radicalism, the marginal impact of socialism, the largely passive acceptance of imperialism and the throne, and the growing usurpation of political and educational interests by a way of life centred round the pub, the race course and the music hall. In sum its impermeability to the classes above it was no longer threatening or subversive, but conservative and defensive. Two questions remain to be asked: firstly, what factors had combined to produce a culture of this kind? And secondly, what were the central assumptions and attitudes embedded within this culture?

Undoubtedly, the primary cause was the undermining of the distinctiveness and cohesion of the old artisan culture in London. In the period between 1790 and 1850 it was this artisan class which had provided political leadership to the unskilled and the poor. But in the second half of the century, it became increasingly defensive and concerned to protect itself from below as much as from above. In 1889, far from welcoming the opportunity to organize the unskilled, its most prominent spokesmen and its Trades Council offered no constructive assistance and reacted more often with alarm than with enthusiasm to the upsurge of new unionism.

In the course of the nineteenth century, this artisan culture based upon traditional London trades was undermined by a variety of disintegrating tendencies. [. . .] The larger trades either declined in the face of provincial competition or else were broken up through the subdivision of the work process into separate semi-skilled tasks. [. . .] The conditions which had sustained a strong political culture no longer existed. The skilled workshop in which the trade society controlled the work process and in which artisans had taken turns in reading aloud from Paine or Owen, had been replaced either by home work or else by the warehouse where the skilled operative was surrounded by semi-skilled 'greeners' and unskilled slop-hands.

The traditional culture of all London artisans had been work-centred. [. . .] Even if some artisans discussed politics with their wives, women were *de facto* excluded from the focal institutions of this culture.

In the second half of the century, this work-centred culture began to yield to a culture oriented towards the family and the home. By the mid-1870s, weekly hours of work had been substantially reduced in most skilled trades. A 54-56½ hour week, or a nine-hour day and a Saturday half holiday became general. The growth of sporting interests, seaside excursions, working men's clubs and music halls from about this time is therefore not accidental. In London however, this increase in leisure time should be seen in connection with another tendency – the growing geographical separation between home and work place.[. . .] By the time of the Booth survey, the majority of workers commanding skilled wage rates commuted to work on a tram, a workman's train or on foot.[39]

This combination of increased leisure time and suburban migration would alone have eroded the strength of the work-centred culture. But it was combined with a number of other factors which further reinforced this process. The fall of prices in the Great Depression period produced a rise in real wages spread over the whole employed population. This increased spending power again strengthened the importance of home and family. In the eighteenth and early nineteenth century, all wives were expected to work in some capacity.[40] By the 1890s however, Booth found that the wives of workers in skilled trades did not normally work.[41] Increased earnings were not generally spent in trade drinking customs, but were handed over to the wife who became the decision maker in all aspects of household expenditure. In many households the husband was only entrusted with pocket money to be spent on fares, beer, tobacco and a trade union or club subscription.[42] The effect of this division of labour could be seen in the growing institutionalization of the Sunday suit and the elaborately furnished front parlour.[43] [...]

This stricter division of roles between man and wife was to an increasing extent generalized throughout the working class by the 1870 Education Act. Once children, particularly girl children, were forced into school, it became more difficult for the wife to go out to work and leave household cleaning and the care of infants to the older children.[44] Among all sectors of the working class, the association of mother with home became increasingly axiomatic. Even the poorest women in the riverside districts, once encumbered with children, generally took in home work, garment marking, matchbox making, envelope making, etc. Furthermore, as the home increasingly became the wife's sole domain, her control over it appears to have become increasingly absolute. [...]

Since wives had generally had little contact with the traditional centres of political discussion, the workshop, the house of call, the coffee shop, and since in the second half of the century wives increasingly retreated from productive employment itself except in the form of home work, home and family life tended to become a depoliticized haven. With the shortening of the working week and the separation of living quarters from work place, home and the family occupied a larger place in the working man's life. Yet, despite its growing ideological significance the home remained a crowded and unrelaxing environment. After the evening meal therefore, men and to some extent women continued to pass a high proportion of their evenings in the pub. If the man commuted to work, however, the regular pub visited would no longer be the trade pub near the work place, but the 'local'. At the 'local' they would mingle with men of different trades and occupations.

Conversation was less likely to concern trade matters, more likely to reflect common interests, politics to a certain extent, but more often, sport and entertainment. [. . .] The elementary education provided by the 1870 Act appears to have acted as yet another solvent of artisan traditions of self-education. [. . .]

The combination of declining industries, the breakdown of skilled crafts into a mass of semi-skilled processes, the prevalence of home work, the decline of a work-centred culture, the growth of commuting and the deadening effects of elementary education made a politically demobilizing impact in London. Some of these tendencies were of course present elsewhere in Britain. But they did not generally produce such demoralizing results. What intensified the purely negative aspect of these developments in London was the continuation of small-scale production combined with chronic unemployment. The problem of unemployment, as Paul de Rousiers wrote in the 1890s, was largely a problem of London.[45] In the years before 1914, London was stranded between a small workshop system which refused to die and a system of factory production which had scarcely begun to develop. Its workforce was divided between a highly skilled but technically conservative elite and a vast mass of semi-skilled and unskilled workers subject to varying degrees of under-employment. In the 1920s and 1930s, London was to be transformed by the development of light industry on its peripheries. But few would have prophesied this transformation before 1914. In the late Victorian and Edwardian period, rents and prices rose, wages remained stagnant and unemployment a permanent feature of the landscape. Yet London continued to grow at a phenomenal rate. The new suburbs were flooded with rural immigrants from the depressed and conservative home counties. With the exception of a few outlying areas like Woolwich or Stratford, London working-class districts were shifting and unstable. The eviction of the poor from the central area continued and everywhere 'shooting the moon' (moving furniture from an apartment after dark before the landlord collected the rent) was a familiar feature of London working-class life — one need only think of perhaps the best known of all music hall songs — *My Old Man said follow the Van*. The family as a working-class institution may have grown in importance, but in London there was nothing very settled about the home.

Co-op and professional football, two of the most prominent features of the new working-class culture of the north, were still of minor importance in London. Like trade unionism and friendly societies, their strength was greatest in more stable and homogeneous industrial areas. If we wish to find a peculiarly metropolitan form of the new working-class culture, it is to the music hall that we must look.

Once the evidence is sifted critically, the music hall can give us a crucial insight into the attitudes of working-class London. But this can only be done if working-class music hall is disentangled from its West End variant with which it is generally confused.

Music hall was both a reflection and a reinforcement of the major trends in London working-class life from the 1870s to the 1900s. 'Music halls and other entertainments,' wrote T.H. Escott in 1891, 'are as popular among the working men of London as they are the reverse with the better stamp of working men out of it.'[46] Music hall was a participatory form of leisure activity, but not a demanding one. The audience joined in the chorus, but if they didn't like the song or the sentiments expressed, they 'gave it the bird,' and it was unlikely to be heard again. [. . .]

In working-class districts, where the multiplicity of occupations, the separation of home from workplace and the overcrowding and impermanence of apartments made any stable community life very difficult, the local hall with its blaze of light and sham opulence, its laughter and its chorus singing, fulfilled, if only in an anonymous way, a craving for solidarity in facing the daily problems of poverty and family life. Music hall stood for the small pleasures of working-class life — a glass of 'glorious English beer,' a hearty meal of 'boiled beef and carrots,' a day by the seaside, Derby Day and the excitements and tribulations of betting, a bank holiday spent on Hampstead Heath or in Epping Forest, the pleasures of courtship and the joys of friendship.[47] Its attitude was *a little bit of what you fancy does you good*. Music hall was perhaps the most unequivocal response of the London working class to middle-class evangelism. As Marie Lloyd told her critics in 1897,

> You take the pit on a Saturday night or a Bank Holiday. You don't suppose they want Sunday school stuff do you? They want lively stuff with music they can learn quickly. Why, if I was to try and sing highly moral songs they would fire ginger beer bottles and beer mugs at me. They don't pay their sixpences and shillings at a Music Hall to hear the Salvation Army.[48]

Or, as the *Era* had put it in 1872,

> The artisan tired with his day's labour, wants something to laugh at. He neither wants to be preached to, nor is he anxious to listen to the lugubrious effusions of Dr. Watts or the poets of the United Kingdom Alliance.[49]

Music hall appealed to the London working class because it was both escapist *and yet* strongly rooted in the realities of working-class life. This was particularly true of its treatment of the relations between the sexes. While its attitude towards courtship could be rhapsodic, there were few illusions about marriage. Writing about marriage among the London poor in the 1870s, Greenwood remarked of the couples he saw entering and leaving the church, 'they are as a rule, cool and business like, as though, having paid a deposit on the purchase of a donkey or a handsome barrow, they were just going in with their witnesses to settle the bargain.'[50] Paterson observed a similar attitude in 1911:

> A funeral demands special clothes and carriages, very considerable expense, and to attend such an event, second cousins will take a day off work, and think it but dutifully spent. Yet a marriage is, by comparison, almost unnoticed . . . It occurs most frequently on a saturday or sunday, as it is hardly worthwhile to lose a day's work . . . few attend it outside a small circle of lady friends.[51]

Among the poor, marriage was normally the result of pregnancy, but among all sectors of the working class, marriage meant children and the constant drudgery of work on a declining standard of living until they were old enough to bring money into the home. Marriage as a 'comic disaster' is an endless refrain of music hall songs. The titles of the best known male songs are self-explanatory: Tom Costello's *At Trinity Church I met my doom*, Charles Coburn's *Oh what an Alteration*, Gus Elen's *It's a great big shame* or George Beauchamp's *She was one of the early birds and I was one of the worms*. The lead in translating courtship into marriage was normally taken by the woman. For working-class women, marriage was an economic necessity and unlikely to happen after the age of 25. Booth stated that among the poor, marriage banns were almost invariably put up by the woman.[52] The anxiety of girls to get married was the theme of many female songs like Lily Morris's *Why am I always the bridesmaid, never the blushing bride*? or Vesta Victoria's *Waiting at the Church*. According to Dan Leno, in his sketch of the lodger entitled *Young Men taken in and Done for*

> I'll tell you how the misfortune happened. One morning Lucy Jagg's mother came upstairs to my room, knocked at the door and said, 'Mr. Skilley are you up?' I said, 'No, what for?' Mrs. Jaggs said, 'Come along get up, you're going to be married.' I said, 'No, I don't know anything about it.' She said, 'Yes you do, you spoke about it last night, when you'd had a little drink.' Well, I thought, if I did say so, I suppose I did, so I came downstairs half asleep (in fact I think every man's half asleep when he's going to be married).[53]

But despite their determination to achieve wedlock, the attitude of women to marriage was no more romantic than that of men. The pros and cons were summed up by Marie Loftus in *Girls, we would never stand it*

> When first they come courting,
>   how nice they behave,
> For a smile or a kiss,
>   how humbly they crave
> But when once a girl's wed,
>   she's a drudge and a slave.

Nevertheless, she concludes,

> I think we would all prefer
>   marriage with strife
> Than be on the shelf
>   and be nobody's wife.[54]

The same comic realism dominated the depiction of relations between husband and wife. Husbands make themselves out to be dominated by the tyranny of their wives. They escape to the pub, go off to the races and lose money on horses or are cheated out of it by 'welshers,' they get drunk and return home to face the consequences. Males are generally represented as incompetent at spending money and are endlessly getting 'done.' But if a wife is incompetent at managing the household, the results are much more serious. In the end the wife who 'jaws' is preferable to the wife who drinks. The problems of the lodger, the landlord and the pawnbroker shop are also constantly discussed. Finally, the threat of destitution in old age, once children no longer contribute to the family income and the man is too old to work, is not evaded. [. . .]

In music hall, work is an evil to be avoided when possible. But the only real escape suggested in the songs is the surprise inheritance or the lucky windfall. It is the same sort of phantasy escape from poverty that could be detected in the passionate interest with which poor Londoners followed the case of Arthur Orton, the Tichbourne claimant between the 1870s and the 1890s. Nevertheless, when such an escape is made in the songs, the result is consternation; the former friend begins 'to put on airs,' as Gus Elen sang, *'E don't know where 'e are*. Class is a life sentence, as final as any caste system. The pretensions of those who feigned escape aroused particular scorn, as did those who suggested that education would change this state of affairs. According to a *Daily Telegraph* report of Mrs. Lane's Britannia Theatre in Hoxton in 1883:

Here is a large audience mainly composed of the industrious classes, determined to enjoy itself to the utmost . . . Mrs. Lane's friends feel the disgrace which attaches to a fulfilling of the requirements of the School Board so that when one of the characters upon the stage pertinently asks, 'if every kid's brought up to be a clerk, what about labour? Who's to do the work?' there rises a mighty outburst of applause.[55]

There was no political solution to the class system. It was simply a fact of life. They certainly did not consider it to be just, for as Billy Bennett sang, 'it's the rich what gets the pleasure, It's the poor what gets the blame.' But socialism was just a lot of hot air. As little Tich put it, in his sketch of the gas-meter collector, 'My brother's in the gas trade too, you know. In fact he travels on gas. He's a socialist orator.' Music hall never gave class a political definition. Trade unionism was accepted as an intrinsic part of working-class life and the music hall songs of 1889 supported the 'Docker's tanner.'[56] But music hall didn't generally sing about the relationship between workers and employers, and the capitalist is completely absent as a music hall stereotype. The general music hall attitude was that if a worker could get a fair day's wage for a fair day's work, that was a good thing, but if the worker could get a fair day's wage without doing a fair day's work, that was even better. The attitude towards the rich was similarly indulgent. The general depiction of the upper class was, as MacInnes has remarked, not hostile but comic.[57] Upper-class figures like Champagne Charlie, Burlington Bertie, the 'toff' and the galloping major were incompetent and absurd, but there was no reference to the source of their income.

Music hall has often been associated with a mood of bombastic jingoism, associated with MacDermott's 1878 song, *We don't want to fight but by jingo if we do* or *Soldiers of the Queen* sung at the time of the Boer war.[58] The audiences of Piccadilly and Leicester Square sang these songs with undoubted gusto, and, judging by the innumerable song sheets on these themes, could never get enough of them. But the predominant mood of the working-class halls was anti-heroic. Workers were prepared to admire and sing about the bravery of the common soldier or the open-handed generosity of the sailor, but they did not forget the realities of military life. Men joined the army usually to escape unemployment, and if they survived their years of service, it was to unemployment that they would return. According to one song of the 1890s which recounts a conversation between Podger and his lodger, a soldier on leave:

Said he, now Podger,Why don't you enlist,
    you'll get cheap beer
The glories too, of war in view

> Come be a soldier bold
> Said I, not me. No not me,
> I'm not having any don't you see
> Might lose my legs, come home on pegs.
> Then when I'm O-L-D
> Not wanted more.
> Workhouse door
> Not, not, not, not me.[59]

In a song which was enormously popular in the 1890s, Charles Godfrey's *On Guard*, an old Crimean veteran asks for a night's shelter in the workhouse casual ward. 'Be off you tramps,' exclaims the harsh janitor. 'You are not wanted here.' 'No,' thunders the tattered veteran, 'I am *not* wanted *here*, but at Balaclava, I *was* wanted *there*.' This scene, which was a working-class favourite, was apparently curtailed in the West End because officers from the household brigade complained that it was bad for recruiting.[60]

Working-class music hall was conservative in the sense that it accepted class divisions and the distribution of wealth as part of the natural order of things. By the 1890s, the class resentment expressed in Godfrey's sketch was as near as it came to political criticism. But the music hall industry was not merely a passive barometer of working-class opinion. And here lies the difficulty of using it simply as an index of working-class attitudes. For in the period between 1870 and 1900 it became actively and self consciously Tory. There were two major reasons for this development.

The first reason was the growth of a second audience for music hall entertainment, alongside that of the working class. This new audience consisted of sporting aristocrats, from the Prince of Wales downwards, guards officers from St. James's, military and civil officials on leave from imperial outposts, clerks and white-collar workers, university, law and medical students and the growing number of tourists from the white Dominions. This audience can be dated back to the 1860s, but it first reached boom proportions in the 1880s, as witnessed by the opening of the new Pavilion in 1884, rapidly followed by the Empire, the Trocadero, the Tivoli and the Palace.[61] The Empire was the most famous centre of this new audience. It provided a natural focus for jingoism, upper-class rowdyism and high-class prostitution. The most popular event in its annual calendar was boat race night, a drunken saturnalia in which all breakable objects had to be removed from the reach of tipsy 'swells.'[62] There was little in common between these imperial playgrounds and the working-class halls, except for the important fact that these new palaces drew upon the working-class halls for many of their performers. Furthermore, as the entertainment business became more organized and monopolistic, and combines began to take over the proletarian halls, the turns offered in Hackney or Piccadilly to some extent converged.[63]

In the 1860s many of the songs sung in the working-class halls were still anti-aristocratic and populist in tone. They were still at a halfway stage between the old street ballad and the mature music hall song.[64] Even Frederick Stanley, defending music hall interests before a Parliamentary enquiry in 1866, conceded as the one valid objection to the music-hall 'the immense difficulty of improving the comic element.' 'I believe,' he stated, 'it is impossible to get a comic song written worthy of the present age.'[65] But the atmosphere changed in the 1870s with the appearance of stars like Leybourne, Vance and MacDermott. The anti-aristocratic element in the songs disappeared, the intellectual level fell and a jingoist tone became prominent. The effects of the new audience were clearly evident by the late 1880s when Vesta Tilley stated:

> Nowadays, nothing goes down better than a good patriotic song, for politics are played out as they are far too common. Talking of that suggests the oddity of the music hall audience in their political bent. Every such allusion must be Conservative.[66]

This first reason for music hall Toryism, the growth of an aristocratic and jingoist clientele, had little to do with any marked shift in working-class opinion. But the second reason affected slum and West End music halls alike. This was the increasing association between Toryism and the drink trade. In the first half of the nineteenth century, as Brian Harrison has shown, the pub was not the exclusive property of any particular political interest and in fact London brewing magnates tended to be Whig or Liberal rather than Conservative. But the rise of the teetotal movement and its growing tendency to operate as a pressure group on the flank of the Liberal party began to push publicans and music hall proprietors towards Toryism. This tendency became increasingly apparent after the 1871 Liberal Licensing Act.[67] In the 1880s, liberals, teetotallers and radical temperance advocates attacked both the central pleasure palaces and the working-class halls with equal vigour, for both were associated, although in unequal proportions, with drinking, gambling, prostitution, crude chauvinism and the absence of educational content. In the early 1880s, temperance crusaders were active: F.N. Charrington launched his attack on Lusby's Music Hall on the Mile End Road and the Salvation Army made an unsuccessful attempt to close down the Eagle in the City Road.[68] But reformers did not confine their assaults to the working-class halls. In 1894, Mrs. Ormiston Chant of the Social Purity League challenged the licence of the Empire in the name of 'the calm steady voice of righteous public opinion, the non-conformist conscience.'[69] Supported by the Progressive party and the Labour bench on the London County Council, Mrs. Chant was successful in getting a screen erected between the auditorium and the bars, thus fencing off the audience from the provision of drink and the solicitation of prostitutes. But the young 'swells' and 'toffs' of the period who regarded the Empire as their spiritual home, violently resisted this restriction of their prerogatives. On the Saturday following the erection of the screen, 200-300 aristocratic rowdies smashed it down again with their walking sticks and paraded in triumph around Leicester Square, waving its fragments at the passers-by. The ringleader of this group then made a speech to the assembled crowd: 'You have seen us tear down these barricades tonight; see that you pull down those who are responsible for them at the coming election.'[70] The speaker was the young Sandhurst cadet, Winston Churchill.

Music hall proprietors, swells, cabmen and bizarrely, George Shipton, the Secretary of the London Trades Council (he also ran a pub off Leicester Square), enrolled in defence of the Empire's rights. A 'Sporting League' was formed. According to one of its spokesmen:

> They were now approaching the County Council Elections, and it would be the duty of every true lover of sport to see that no 'wrong'uns' got on the council again . . . These faddists came upon them in all shapes and kinds, either as members of the Humanitarian League, or the anti-Gambling League, or Anti-Vaccination. They were all acting on the same principle, trying to interfere with the enjoyment and pleasures of the people.[71]

This incident was no doubt the origin of the myth, assiduously cultivated by the upper class after the war, of an affinity of outlook between the 'top and bottom drawer' against the 'kill-joys' in between. It is true however that for different reasons, both the proletarian halls and the West End pleasure strip were devitalized in the succeeding twenty years. The West End became more decorous after the Wilde scandal, while the working-class halls were bought up by the Moss-Stoll syndicate whose policy was to replace the 'coarseness and vulgarity' of the halls, by the gentility and decorum of the Palace of Variety. Music hall entertainment was given its final kiss of death with the achievement of a Royal Command Performance in 1912. Music hall artistes removed from their acts any allusions that could be considered offensive or coarse and vainly tried to win the approval of King George V — 'a lover of true Bohemianism,' according to Conan Doyle's unctuous description of the proceedings.[72]

If these had been the only tendencies at work in music hall since the

1870s, it would be difficult to explain its prominent position in London working-class culture. But it was the mid-eighties which also witnessed the emergence of the greatest and best loved music-hall performers — Dan Leno, Marie Lloyd, Gus Elen, Little Tich, Kate Karney and others. These artistes, who all sprang from poor London backgrounds, articulated with much greater accuracy than their predecessors the mood and attitudes of the London masses. Although they were popular both in the West and the East End, they sang or spoke not about the Empire or the Conservative party, but about the occupations, food, drink, holidays, romances, marriages and misfortunes of the back streets. It is from their songs that the specificity of London working-class culture can best be assessed.

Unlike the ballad, the songs of these performers expressed neither deep tragedy nor real anger. They could express wholehearted enjoyment of simple pleasures or unbounded sentimentality in relation to objects of affection. But when confronted with the daily oppressions of the life of the poor, their reactions were fatalistic. In the middle of the century, Mayhew had written,

> Where the means of sustenance and comfort are fixed, the human being becomes conscious of what he has to depend upon.
>
> If, however his means be uncertain — abundant at one time, and deficient at another — a spirit of speculation or gambling with the future will be induced, and the individual gets to believe in 'luck' and 'fate' as the arbiters of his happiness rather than to look upon himself as 'the architect of his fortunes' — trusting to 'chance' rather than his own powers and foresight to relieve him at the hour of necessity.[73]

This was precisely the attitude to life projected by the London music hall. The two greatest products of that culture, Dan Leno and Charlie Chaplin, play little men, perpetually 'put upon'; they have no great ideals or ambitions; the characters they play are undoubtedly very poor, but not obviously or unmistakably proletarian; they are unmistakably products of city life, but their place within it is indeterminate; their exploits are funny but also pathetic; they are forever being chased by men or women, physically larger than themselves, angry foremen, outraged husbands, domineering landladies or burly wives; but it is usually chance circumstances, unfortunate misunderstandings, not of their own making which have landed them in these situations; and it is luck more than their own efforts which finally comes to the rescue.

The art of Leno and Chaplin brings us back again to the situation of the poor and the working class in late Victorian and Edwardian

London, to that vast limbo of semi-employed labourers, casualized semi-skilled artisans, sweated home workers, despised foreigners, tramps and beggars.

In this paper, I have attempted to put into relationship two themes which traditionally have been kept apart: on the one hand, the history of the labour movement, on the other, the investigations of working-class culture. It is only a preliminary analysis, based upon the study of one city, and any conclusions that might be drawn from it can only be provisional. Nevertheless, the mere conjunction of these two themes points towards the necessity of questioning some of the traditional assumptions of English labour history.

Music hall highlighted the peculiarities of the working-class situation in London. But it also reflected the general development of the English working class after 1870. Fatalism, political scepticism, the evasion of tragedy or anger and a stance of comic stoicism were pre-eminently cockney attitudes because the decline of artisan traditions, the tardiness of factory development, the prevalence of casual work and the shifting amorphous character of the new proletarian suburbs were particularly marked features of London life. But it would be a mistake to overemphasize the purely local significance of these themes. In industrial areas more homogeneous than London, trade unionism tended to occupy a much more commanding place in working-class culture. In such communities, co-ops, friendly societies, choral clubs and football teams were also more likely to flourish. But these were differences of degree, not of kind. There are good historical reasons why after 1870 London pioneered music hall, while coal, cotton and ship-building areas in the north generated the most solid advances in trade unionism.[74]

Trapped in the twilight world of small workshop production, London was not well-placed to sustain the defensive corporate forms of solidarity upon which working-class politics was increasingly to be based. The strength of its own political tradition had not been founded on the factory. It therefore registered the new situation in predominantly cultural forms. But music hall did spread to the provinces and trade unions were slowly able to secure important pockets of strength in certain areas of London. There was great diversity of local experience, but no unbridgeable gulf. What is finally most striking is the basic consistency of outlook reflected in the new working-class culture which spread over England after 1870.

If the 'making of the English working class' took place in the 1790-1830 period, something akin to a remaking of the working class took place in the years between 1870 and 1900. For much of the cluster of 'traditional' working-class attitudes analyzed by contemporary sociologists and literary critics dates, not from the first third, but from the last third of the nineteenth century. This remaking process did not obliterate the legacy of that first formative phase of working-class history, so well described by Edward Thompson. But it did transform its meaning. In the realm of working-class ideology, a second formative layer of historical experience was superimposed upon the first, thereby colouring the first in the light of its own changed horizons of possibility. The struggles of the first half of the century were not forgotten, but they were recalled selectively and re-interpreted. The solidarity and organizational strength achieved in social struggles were channelled into trade union activity and eventually into a political party based upon that activity and its goals. The distinctiveness of a working-class way of life was enormously accentuated. Its separateness and imperme-ability were now reflected in a dense and inward-looking culture, whose effect was both to emphasize the distance of the working class from the classes above it and to articulate its position within an apparently permanent social hierarchy.

The growth of trade unionism on the one hand and the new working-class culture on the other were not contradictory but inter-related phenomena. Both signified a major shift in the predominant forms of working-class activity. What above all differentiated the Chartist period from the post-1870 period was the general belief that the economic and political order brought into being by the industrial revolution was a temporary aberration, soon to be brought to an end. This belief sustained the activities of moderate Chartists like Lovett and Vincent no less than Harney and O'Connor. It was this half articulated conviction that had made Chartism into a mass force.

Once the defeat of Chartism was finally accepted, this conviction disappeared. Working people ceased to believe that they could shape society in their own image. Capitalism had become an immovable horizon. Demands produced by the movements of the pre-1850 period — republicanism, secularism, popular self-education, co-operation, land reform, internationalism etc. — now shorn of the conviction which had given them point, eventually expired from sheer inanition, or else in a diluted form, were appropriated by the left flank of Gladstonian liberal-ism. The main impetus of working-class activity now lay elsewhere. It was concentrated into trade unions, co-ops, friendly societies, all indicating a *de facto* recognition of the existing social order as the inevitable framework of action. The same could be said of music hall. It was a culture of consolation.

The rise of new unionism, the foundation of the Labour party, even the emergence of socialist groups marked not a breach but a culmina-tion of this defensive culture. One of the more striking features of the social movements between 1790 and 1850 had been the clarity and concreteness of their conception of the state. There had been no hypostasisation of the state into a neutral or impersonal agency. It had been seen as a flesh and blood machine of coercion, exploitation and corruption. The monarchy, the legislature, the church, the bureaucracy, the army and the police had all been occupied by 'bloodsuckers,' 'hypocrites,' 'placemen,' etc. The aim of popular politics had been to change the form of state. The triumph of the people would replace it by a popular democracy of a Leveller or Jacobin sort — an egalitarian society of independent artisans and small-holders — a society built upon petty commodity exchange on the basis of labour time expended (the Chartist land plan and the Owenite labour bazaar formed part of a single problematic). The Charter, a purely political programme, was to be its means of realization.

Late Victorian and Edwardian labour leaders had no such concrete conception of politics or the state. The emphasis had shifted from power to welfare. Socialism, as Tom Mann defined it, meant the abolition of poverty. The founding moment of the Labour party was not revolution abroad or political unheaval at home, but a defensive solution to the employers' counter-offensive of the 1890s. The ending of Britain's industrial monopoly did recreate an independent labour politics, as Engels had prophesied, but not in the way he had intended. The Labour Representation Committee was the generalisation of the structural role of the trade union into the form of a political party. It was not accountable directly to its constituency, but indirectly, via the trade unions upon which its real power was based. Its mode of organisation presumed mass passivity punctuated by occasional mobilisation for the ballot box. As a form of political association, it was not so much a challenge to the new working-class culture that had grown up since 1870 as an extension of it. If it sang *Jerusalem* it was not as a battle-cry but as a hymn. *De facto*, it accepted not only capitalism, but monarchy, Empire, aristocracy and established religion as well. With the foundation of the Labour party, the now enclosed and defensive world of working-class culture had in effect achieved its apotheosis.

Notes

1. *The Heart of the Empire* (London, 1901), p. 3.
2. *Times*, 21 May 1900.
3. *Heart of the Empire*, pp. 7-8.
4. Richard Price, *An Imperial War and the British Working Class* (London, 1972), Ch. IV.
5. Price, *Imperial War*, Ch. III; Henry Pelling, *Social Geography of British Elections 1885-1910* (London, 1967), pp. 45, 47, 52, 57; Pelling, *Popular Politics and Society in Late Victorian Britain* (London, 1968), p. 94.
6. Price, *Imperial War*, Ch. V.

7. Richard Hoggart, *The Uses of Literacy* (London, 1957). A pioneer historical exploration of the origins of this culture has been made by Eric Hobsbawm. See *Industry and Empire* (London, 1968), pp. 135-7.

8. C. Booth, *Life and Labour of the People in London*, Religious Influences Series 3 (London, 1902), vol. 2. p. 97.

9. H. Mayhew, *London Labour and the London Poor* (London, 1861), vol. 1, pp. 1-2.

10. For a selection of slum-life literature employing this imagery, see Gareth Stedman Jones, *Outcast London* (London, 1971), pp. 398-407.

11. See George Rudé, *Hanoverian London 1714-1808* (London, 1971), pp. 183-227; E.P. Thompson, *The Making of the English Working Class* (London, 1963), pp. 69-73.

12. Mary Thale (ed.), *The Autobiography of Francis Place* (London, 1972); William B. Boulton, *Amusements of Old London*, 2 vols. (London, 1901); Sybil Rosenfeld, *The Theatre of the London Fairs in the Eighteenth Century* (London, 1960).

13. M. Dorothy George, *London Life in the XVIIIth Century* (London, 1930), pp. 95-6.

14. Brian Harrison, *Drink and the Victorians* (London, 1971), pp. 45-6.

15. For an exploration of some of these themes, see Dickens's *Little Dorrit*.

16. Booth, *Life and Labour*, Series 2, vol. 5. p. 36; Series 1, vol. 4, pp. 295-7.

17. Humphrey House, *The Dickens World*, 2nd edn (London, 1942), pp. 46-52.

18. For a discussion of these themes, see Stedman Jones, *Outcast London*, part III; and E.P. Thompson, 'Henry Mayhew and the Morning Chronicle' in E.P. Thompson and Eileen Yeo, *The Unknown Mayhew* (London, 1971), pp. 11-50.

19. George Howell, 'The Dwellings of the Poor', *Nineteenth Century* (June 1883), p. 1004.

20. Henry Jephson, *The Sanitary Evolution of London* (London, 1907), p. 368.

21. See Harrison, *Drink and the Victorians*, pp. 244-5.

22. Booth, *Life and Labour*, Series 3, vol. 7, p. 426.

23. A missionary in Hackney told Booth, 'You can buy a congregation, but it melts away as soon as the payments cease,' Booth, *Life and Labour* Series 3, vol. 1, p. 82.

24. Ibid., Series 3, vol. 5, p. 190.

25. Ibid., Final Volume, Notes on Social Influences, pp. 59-74; and see also Harrison, *Drink and the Victorians*, Ch. 14.

26. See Charles Manby Smith, *Curiosities of London Life* (London, 1853), pp. 310-19; Booth, *Life and Labour*, Series 1, vol. 1, pp. 106-12; J. Franklyn, *The Cockney* (London, 1953), pp. 183-4.

27. For the attitude of class 'E' — Booth's typical London artisan, see Booth, *Life and Labour*, Series 2, vol. 5, pp. 329-30; for the atmosphere of the parlour, see Fred Willis, *101, Jubilee Road, London, S.E.* (London, 1948), pp. 102-3.

28. Alexander Paterson, *Across the Bridges* (London, 1911), p. 41.

29. Booth, *Life and Labour*, Final Volume, p. 51.

30. James Greenwood, *Low Life Deeps* (London, 1876), p. 176.

31. For contemporary defences of music hall, see the deposition handed in by Frederick Stanley, on behalf of the London Music Hall Proprietors Association to the Select Committee on Theatrical Licenses and Regulations, PP, 1866, XVI, Appendix 3; see also John Hollingshead, *Miscellanies, Stories and Essays*, 3 vols. (London, 1874), vol. III, p. 254; and the dramatic critic Clement Scott's tribute to Charles Morton, 'the father of the halls' on his eightieth birthday, Harold Scott, *The Early Doors* (London, 1946), pp. 136-7.

32. Ewing Ritchie, *Days and Nights in London* (London, 1880), pp. 44-5;

33. For the early development of music hall in London see Appendix to

1866 Select Committee; Scott, *The Early Doors*; C.D. Stuart and A.J. Park, *The Variety Stage* (London, 1895).

34. Select Committee on Theatre and Place of Entertainment, PP, 1892, XVIII, iv.

35. Ibid., q. 5171.

36. Booth, *Life and Labour*, Final Volume, p. 53.

37. Ibid., Series 3, vol. 5, p. 121.

38. Ibid., Series 3, vol. 7, p. 425.

39. See ibid., Series 2 (industry series) *passim*, for commuting habits of skilled workers in various trades, and see Series 2, vol. 5, Ch. III, for summary. In the last quarter of the nineteenth century, working-class use of commuter transport increased sharply, but even in the 1890s a high proportion of workers travelled long distances to work on foot. See T.C. Barker and Michael Robbins, *A History of London Transport* (London, 1963), vol. 1, pp. xxvi-xxx.

40. George, *London Life*, p. 168.

41. Booth, *Life and Labour*, Series 1, vol. 1, pp. 50-1.

42. Paterson, *Across the Bridges*, p. 32; M.E. Loane, *An Englishman's Castle* (London, 1909), p. 183.

43. See Booth, *Life and Labour*, Series 3, vol. 5, p. 330; M.E. Loane, *The Next Street but One* (London, 1907), p. 20.

44. The care of the house and of babies fell particularly on girl children. See Greenwood, *Low Life Deeps*, p. 140.

45. P. de Rousiers, *The Labour Question in Britain* (London, 1896), pp. 280, 357.

46. T.H.S. Escott, *England, Its People, Polity and Pursuits* (London, 1891), p. 161.

47. See Colin MacInnes, *Sweet Saturday Night* (London, 1967), pp. 106-23.

48. Quoted in Daniel Farson, *Marie Lloyd and Music Hall* (London, 1972), p. 57.

49. A.E. Wilson, *East End Entertainment* (London, 1954), p. 215.

50. Greenwood, *Low Life Deeps*, p. 140.

51. Paterson, *Across the Bridges*, p. 130.

52. Booth, *Life and Labour*, Final Volume, p. 45.

53. *McGlennon's Star Song Book* (1888), no. 10, p. 4.

54. Ibid., no. 4, p. 3.

55. Wilson, *East End Entertainment*, p. 183.

56. See 'The Dock Labourers' Strike' and the 'Dock Labourer' in *New and Popular Songs* (1889).

57. MacInnes, *Sweet Saturday Night*, p. 108.

58. According to one report, Disraeli used to send his secretary, Monty Corry, to the music hall to listen in on MacDermott's song to assess the extent of support for his foreign policy. See J.B. Booth (ed.), *Seventy Years of Song* (London, 1943), p. 38.

59. *MacGlennon's Song Book* (1896-7), no. 105.

60. Scott, *The Early Doors*, p. 215.

61. See Stuart and Park, *The Variety Stage*, pp. 191 *et seq*.

62. Farson, *Marie Lloyd*, p. 60.

63. Real convergence was more possible in Variety than in Music Hall. Even Marie Lloyd found herself booed in the East End music hall, when she attempted to sing some of her more risqué West End numbers. See Farson, *Marie Lloyd*, p. 75.

64. See for instance the songs of J.A. Hardwick in *Comic and Sentimental Music Hall Song Book* (n.d. [1862]).

65. SC 1866, Appendix 3, p. 307.

66. *McGlennon's Star Song Book*, no. 8, p. 2.

67. Harrison, *Drink and the Victorians*, pp. 319-48.

68. On Charrington, see Guy Thorne, *The Great Acceptance – the Life Story of F.N. Charrington* (London, 1912), Ch. v; on the attempt to close down the Eagle, see H. Begbie, *Life of William Booth* (London, 1920), vol. 2, pp. 10-13.

69. Mrs. Ormiston Chant, *Why We Attacked the Empire* (London, 1895), p. 5.

70. Winston Churchill, *My Early Life* (London, 1930), p. 71.

71. Chant, *Why We Attacked the Empire*, p. 30.

72. See Farson, *Marie Lloyd*, pp. 88-97.

73. Mayhew, *London Labour*, vol. 2, p. 325.

74. See S. and B. Webb, *History of Trade Unionism* (London, 1920), pp. 299-325.

5 WELLS AS THE TURNING POINT OF THE SF TRADITION

Darko Suvin

Source: *Metamorphoses of Science Fiction* (Yale University Press, New Haven, Conn., 1979), Ch. 9. © D. Suvin.

H.G. Wells's first and most significant SF cycle (roughly to 1904) is based on the vision of a horrible novum as the evolutionary sociobiological prospect of mankind. His basic situation is that of a destructive newness encroaching upon the tranquillity of the Victorian environment. Often this is managed as a contrast between an outer framework and a story within the story. The framework is set in surroundings as staid and familiarly Dickensian as possible, such as the cozy study of *The Time Machine*, the old antiquity shop of 'The Crystal Egg,' or the small towns and villages of southern England in *The War of the Worlds* and *The First Men in the Moon*. With the exception of the protagonist, who also participates in the inner story, the characters in the outer frame, representing the almost invincible inertia and banality of prosperous bourgeois England, are reluctant to credit the strange newness. By contrast, the inner story details the observation of the gradual, hesitant coming to grips with an alien superindividual force that menaces such life and its certainties by behaving exactly as the bourgeois progress did in world history — as a quite ruthless but technologically superior mode of life. This Wellsian inversion exploits the uneasy conscience of an imperial civilization that did not wipe out only the bison and the dodo: 'The Tasmanians, in spite of their human likeness, were entirely swept out of existence in a war of extermination waged by European immigrants. Are we such apostles of mercy as to complain if the Martians warred in the same spirit?' (*The War of the Worlds*, Book 1, Ch. 1).

As Wells observed, the 'fantastic element' or novum is 'the strange property or the strange world.'[1] The strange property can be the invention that renders Griffin invisible, or, obversely, a new way of seeing — literally, as in 'The Crystal Egg,' 'The Remarkable Case of Davidson's Eyes,' and 'The New Accelerator,' or indirectly, as the Time Machine or the Cavorite sphere. It is always cloaked in a pseudo-scientific explanation, the possibility of which turns out, upon closer inspection, to be no more than a conjuring trick by the deft writer, with 'precision in the unessential and vagueness in the essential'[2] — the best example

122

being the Time Machine itself. The strange world is elsewhen or else-where. It is reached by means of a strange invention or it irrupts directly into the Victorian world in the guise of the invading Martians or the Invisible Man. But even when Wells's own bourgeois world is not so explicitly assaulted, the strange novelty always reflects back on its illusions; an SF story by Wells is intended to be 'the valid realization of some disregarded possibility in such a way as to comment on the false securities and fatuous self-satisfaction of everyday life.'[3]

The strange is menacing because it looms in the future of man. Wells masterfully translates some of man's oldest terrors — the fear of dark-ness, monstrous beasts, giants and ogres, creepy crawly insects, and Things outside the light of his campfire, outside tamed nature — into an evolutionary perspective that is supposed to be validated by Darwinian biology, evolutionary cosmology, and the fin-de-siêcle sense of a historical epoch ending. Wells, a student of T.H. Huxley, eagerly used alien and powerful biological species as a rod to chastize Victorian man, thus setting up the model for all the Bug-Eyed Monsters of later chauvinistic SF. But the most memorable of those aliens, the octopus-like Martians and the antlike Selenites, are identical to 'The Man of the Year Million' in one of Wells's early articles (alluded to in *The War of the Worlds*): they are emotionless higher products of evolution judging us as we would judge insects. In the final analysis, since the aliens are a scary, alternative human future, Wellsian space travel is an optical illu-sion, a variation on his seminal model of *The Time Machine*. The func-tion of his interplanetary contacts is quite different from Verne's liberal interest in the mechanics of locomotion within a safely homogeneous space. Wells is interested exclusively in the opposition between the bourgeois reader's expectations and the strange relationships found at the other end: that is why his men do land on the Moon and his Mar-tians on Earth.

Science is the true, demonic master of all the sorcerer's apprentices in Wells, who have — like Frankenstein or certain folktale characters — revealed and brought about destructive powers and monsters. [. . .] The prime character of his SF is the scientist-adventurer as searcher for the New, disregarding common sense and received opinion. Though powerful, since it brings about the future, science is a hard master. Like Moreau, it is indifferent to human suffering; like the Martians, it explodes the nineteenth-century optimistic pretentions, liberal or socialist, of lording it over the universe:

Science is a match that man has just got alight. He thought he was in a room — in moments of devotion, a temple — and that his light would be reflected from and display walls inscribed with wonderful secrets and pillars carved with philosophical systems wrought into harmony. It is a curious sensation, now that the preliminary splutter is over and the flame burns up clear, to see his hands and just a glimpse of himself and the patch he stands on visible, and around him, in place of all that human comfort and beauty he anticipated — darkness still.[4]

This science is no longer, as it was for Verne, the bright noonday certainty of Newtonian physics. Verne protested after *The First Men in the Moon:* 'I make use of physics. He invents . . . he constructs . . . a metal which does away with the law of gravitation . . . but show me this metal.' For Wells human evolution is an open question with two possible answers, bright and dark; and in his first cycle darkness is the basic tonality. The cognitive 'match' by whose small light he determines his stance is Darwinian evolution, a flame which fitfully illumines man, his hands (by interaction of which with the brain and the eye he evolved from ape), and the 'patch he stands on.'[5] Therefore Wells could much later even the score by talking about 'the anticipatory inventions of the great Frenchman' who 'told that this and that thing could be done, which was not at that time done' — in fact, by defining Verne as a short-term technological popularizer.[6] From the point of view of a votary of physics, Wells 'invents' in the sense of inventing objective untruths. From the point of view of the evolutionist, who does not believe in objects but in processes — which we have only begun to elucidate — Verne is the one who 'invents' in the sense of inventing banal gadgets. For the evolutionist, Nemo's submarine is in itself of no importance; what matters is whether intelligent life exists on the ocean floor (as in 'In the Abyss' and 'The Sea Raiders'). Accordingly, Wells's physical and technical motivations can and do remain quite superficial where not faked. Reacting against a mechanical view of the world, he is ready to approach again the imaginative, analogic veracity of Lucian's* and Swift's story-telling centred on strange creatures, and to call his works 'romances.' Cavorite or the Invisible Man partake more of the flying carpet and the magic invisibility hood than of metallurgy or optics. The various aliens represent a vigorous refashioning of the talking and symbolic animals of folktale, bestiary, and fable lore into Swiftian grotesque mirrors to man, but with the crowning collocation within an evolutionary prospect. Since this prospect is temporal rather than spatial, it is also much more urgent and immediate than Swift's controlled disgust, and a note of fairly malicious hysteria is not absent from the ever-present violence — fires, explosions, fights, killings, and large-scale devastations — in Wells's SF.

The Time Machine (1895), Wells's programmatic and (but for the

---

*[The Greek satirist (*c.* AD115-*c* AD200) whose *The History* narrated imaginary travels.]

mawkish character of Weena) most consistent work, shows his way of proceeding and his ultimate horizon. The horizon of sociobiological regression leading to cosmic extinction, simplified from Darwinism into a series of vivid pictures in the Eloi, the giant crabs, and the eclipse episodes, is established by the Time Traveller's narration as a stark contrast to the Victorian after-dinner discussions in his comfortable residence. The Time Machine itself is validated by an efficient forestalling of possible objections, put into the mouth of schematic, none too bright, and reluctantly persuaded listeners, rather than by the bogus theory of the fourth dimension or any explanation of the gleaming bars glimpsed in the machine. Similarly, the sequence of narrated episodes gains much of its impact from the careful foreshortening of ever larger perspectives in an ever more breathless rhythm. [. . .] Also, the narrator-observer's gradually deepening involvement in the Eloi episode is marked by cognitive hypotheses that run the whole logical gamut of sociological SF. From a parodied Morrisite* model ('Communism,' says the Time Traveller at first sight) through the discovery of degeneration and of persistence of class divisions, he arrives at the anti-utopian form most horrifying to the Victorians – a run-down class society ruled by a grotesque equivalent of the nineteenth-century industrial proletariat. Characteristically, the sociological perspective then blends into biology. The labouring and upper classes are envisioned as having developed into different races or indeed species, with the Morlocks raising the Eloi as cattle to be eaten. In spite of a certain contempt for their effeteness, the Time Traveller quickly identifies with the butterfly-like upper-class Eloi and so far forsakes his position as neutral observer as to engage in bloody and fiery carnage of the repugnant spider-monkey-like Morlocks, on the model of the most sensationalist exotic adventure stories. His commitment is never logically argued, and there is a strong suggestion that it flows from the social consciousness of Wells himself, who came from the lower middle class, which lives on the edge of the 'proletarian abyss' and thus 'looks upon the proletariat as being something disgusting and evil and dangerous.'[7] Instead, the Time Traveller's attitude is powerfully supported by the prevailing imagery – both by animal parallels, and by the pervasive open-air green and bright colours of the almost Edenic garden (associated with the Eloi) opposed to the subterranean blackness and the dim reddish glow (associated with the Morlocks and the struggle against them). Later in the story these menacing, untamed colours lead to the reddish-black eclipse, symbolizing the end of the Earth and of the solar system. The bright pastoral of the Eloi is gradually submerged by the encroaching night of the Morlocks, and the Time Traveller's matches sputter out in their

---

*[William Morris (1834-96), author of the utopian *News from Nowhere* (1891).]

oppressive abyss. At the end, the unforgettable picture of the dead world is validated by the disappearance of the Time Traveller in the opaque depths of time.

Many of these devices reappear in Wells's other major works. The technique of domesticating the improbable by previews on a smaller scale, employed in the vivid vanishing of the model machine, is repeated in the introduction to the Grand Lunar through a series of other Selenites up to Phi-oo, or to Moreau's* bestial people through the brutal struggles in the boat and through the ship captain, or to the Cavorite sphere's flight through the experimental explosion raising the roof. The loss of the narrator's vehicle and the ensuing panic of being a castaway under alien rule (in *The War of the Worlds* this is inverted as hiding in a trap with dwindling supplies) recurs time and again as an effective cliff-hanger. Above all, [. . .] Wells's whole first cycle is a reversal of the popular concept by which the lower social and biological classes were considered as 'natural' prey in the struggle for survival. In their turn they become the predators: as labourers turn into Morlocks, so insects, arthropods, or colonial peoples turn into Martians, Selenites, and the like. This exalting of the humble into horrible masters supplies a subversive shock to the bourgeois believer in Social Darwinism: at the same time, Wells vividly testifies that a predatory state of affairs is the only even fantastically imaginable alternative. The world upside-down — where strange animals hunt Man, and the subterranean lower class devours the upper class — recurs in Wells, as in Thomas More.** But whereas More's sheep were rendered unnatural by political economics, Wells's Morlocks, Beast People, and so forth, are the result of a 'natural' evolution from the author's present. Nature has become not only malleable — it was already becoming such in More and particularly in Swift — but also a practically value-free category, as in bourgeois scientism. At the end, the bourgeois framework is shaken, but neither destroyed nor replaced by any livable alternative. What remains is a very ambiguous attack on liberalism from the position of 'the petty bourgeois which will either turn towards socialism or towards fascism.'[8]

The human/animal inversion comes openly to the fore in *The Island of Dr. Moreau* (1896) with admirable Swiftian stringency. Dr. Moreau's fashioning of humans out of beasts is clearly analogous to the pitiless procedures of Nature and its evolutionary creation. He is not only a latter-day Dr. Frankenstein but also a demonically inverted God of Genesis, and his surgically humanized Beast Folk are a counterpart

*[See below *The First Men in the Moon* and *The Island of Dr. Moreau*.]

**[Sir Thomas More (1478-1535), author of *Utopia* (1516).]

of ourselves, semibestial humans. Wells's calling their attempts to mimic the Decalogue* in the litanies of 'The Saying of the Law' and their collapse back into bestiality a 'theological grotesque' indicates that this view of mankind's future reversed Christian as well as socialist millennialism into the bleak vistas of an evolution liable to regression. *The Island of Dr. Moreau* turns the imperial order of Kipling's *Jungle Book* into a degenerative slaughterhouse, where the law loses out to bestiality.

Wells's next two famous SF novels, though full of vivid local colour, seem today less felicitous. Both have problems of focusing. In *The Invisible Man* (1897) the delineation of Griffin hesitates between a man in advance of his time within an indifferent society and the symbol of a humanity that does not know how to use science. This makes of him almost an old-fashioned 'mad scientist,' and yet he is too important and too sinned against to be comic relief. The vigour of the narration, which unfolds in the form of a hunt, and the strengths of an inverted fairy tale cannot compensate for the failure of the supposedly omniscient author to explain why Griffin had got into the position of being his own Frankenstein and Monster at the same time. In this context, the dubious scientific premises (an invisible eye cannot see, and so forth) become distressing and tend to deprive the story of the needed suspension of disbelief. *The War of the Worlds* (1898), which extrapolates into xenobiology the catastrophic stories of the 'future wars' subgenre, [. . .] descends in places to a gleeful sensationalism difficult to stomach, especially in its horror-fantasy portraiture of the Martians. The immediate serialization in the US yellow press, which simply suppressed the parts without action, made this portraiture the most influential model for countless later Things from Outer Space, extendable to any foreign group that the public was at that moment supposed to hate, and a prototype of mass-media use of SF for mindless scaremongering (inaugurated by Orson Welles's famous 1938 broadcast). [. . .] Of course, *The War of the Worlds* also contains striking and indeed prophetic insights such as the picture of modern total warfare, with its panics, refugees, quislings, underground hidings, and an envisaged Resistance movement, as well as race-theory justifications, poison gas, and a 'spontaneous' bacteriological weapon. (In other tales, Wells — a lifelong lover of war games — added air warfare, tanks, atom bombing of a major city, and other bellicose devices.)

Except for the superb late parable 'The Country of the Blind' (bp. 1911), Wells's sociobiological and cosmological SF cycle culminated in *The First Men in the Moon* (1901). It has the merit of summarizing and explicating openly his main motifs and devices. The usual two narrators have grown into the contrasting characters of Bedford, the Social-

*[I.e. the Ten Commandments.]

Darwinist speculator-adventurer, and Cavor, the selfless scientist in whom Wells manages for once to fuse the cliché of absent-mindedness with open-mindedness and a final suffering rendered irremediable by the cosmic vistas involved. The sharply focused lens of spatial pin-pointing and temporal acceleration through which the travellers perceive the miraculous growth of Lunar vegetation is the most striking rendering of the precise yet wondering scientific regard often associated with the observatories and observation posts of Wells's stories. The Selenites not only possess the Aesopian fable background and an endearing grotesqueness worthy of Edward Lear's creatures, they are also a profound image of sociopolitical functional overspecialization and of an absolute caste or race State, readily translatable from insect biology back into some of the most menacing tendencies of modern power concentration. Most Swiftian among Wells's aliens, they serve a double-edged satire, in the authentic tone of savage and cognitive indignation:

> . . . I came upon a number of young Selenites, confined in jars from which only the fore limbs protruded, who were being compressed to become machine-minders of a special sort . . . these glimpses of the educational methods of these beings have affected me disagreeably. I hope, however, that may pass off and I may be able to see more of this aspect of this wonderful social order. That wretched-looking hand sticking out of its jar seemed to appeal for lost possibilities; it haunts me still, although, of course, it is really in the end a far more humane proceeding than our earthly method of leaving children to grow into human beings, and then making machines of them. (Chap. 23)

The usual final estrangement fuses biological and social disgust into Bedford's schizophrenic cosmic vision of himself 'not only as an ass, but as the son of many generations of asses' (Ch. 19). Parallel to that, Cavor formulates most clearly the uselessness of cosmic as well as earthly imperialism, and articulates a refusal to let science go on serving them (had this been heeded, we would have been spared the Galactic Empire politics and swashbuckling of later SF). Finally, Bedford's narration in guise of a literary manuscript with pretences to scientific veracity, combined with Cavor's narration in guise of interplanetary telegraphic reports, exhibit openly Wells's ubiquitous mimicry of the journalistic style from that heyday of early 'mass communications' — the style of 'an Associated Press dispatch, describing a universal nightmare.'[9]

Yet such virtuosity cannot mask the fundamental ambiguity that constitutes both the richness and the weakness of Wells. Is he horrified or grimly elated by the high price of evolution (*The Island of Dr. Moreau*)? Does he condemn class divisions or simply the existence of a menacing lower class (*The Time Machine*)? Does he condemn imperialism (*The First Men in the Moon*) or only dislike being at the receiving end of it (*The War of the Worlds*)? In brief, are his preoccupations with violence and alienation those of a diagnostician or of a fan? Both of these stances coexist in his works in a shifting and often unclear balance. For example, – to translate such alternatives into an immediate determinant of narration – Wells's central morphological dilemma in the years of his first and best SF cycle was: which is the privileged way of understanding the world, the scientifically systematic one or the artistically vivid one? [. . .]

Wells's SF makes thus an aesthetic form of hesitations, intimations, and glimpses of an ambiguously disquieting strangeness. The strange novum is gleefully wielded as a sensational scare thrown into the bourgeois reader, but its values are finally held at arm's length. In admitting and using their possibility he went decisively beyond Verne, in identifying them as horrible he decisively opposed Morris. Wells's SF works are clearly 'ideological fables,'[10] yet he is a virtuoso in having it ideologically both ways. His satisfaction at the destruction of the false bourgeois idyll is matched by his horror at the alien forces destroying it. He resolutely clung to his insight that such forces must be portrayed, but he portrayed them within a sensationalism that neutralizes most of the genuine newness. Except in his maturest moments, the conflicts in his SF are therefore transferred – following the Social-Darwinist model – from society to biology. This is a risky proceeding which can lead to some striking analogies but [. . .] as a rule indicates a return to quasi-religious eschatology and fatal absolutes. Wells expressed this, no doubt, in sincerely Darwinist terms, but his approach is in fact marked by a contamination of echoes from a culturally sunken medieval bestiary and a Miltonic or Bunyanesque colour scheme (dark and red, for example, as satanic) with the new possibilities of scientific dooms. [. . .] The annihilation of this world is the only future alternative to its present state; the present bourgeois way of life is with scientific certainty leading the Individualist *homme moyen sensuel* toward the hell of physical indignity and psychic terror, yet this *is* still the only way of life he can return to and rely on, the best of all the bad possible worlds. Thus Wells's central anxious question about the future in store for his Everyman – who is, characteristically, a bright, aggressive, white, middle-class male – cannot be resolved as posed. His early SF can present the future only as a highly menacing yet finally inoperative novum, the connection with its bearers (Time Traveller, Moreau, Griffin, Martians, Selenites, or Cavor) being always broken off. Formally, this impasse explains his troubles with works of novel length: his most successful form is either the short story or the novelette, which lend themselves to ingenious balancings on the razor's edge between shock and cognitive development. In them he set the pace for the commercial norms of most later SF (which adds insult to injury by calling such works novels).

Wells's later SF abandoned such fragile but rich ambiguity in favour of short-range extrapolations. His first attempt in that direction, *When the Sleeper Wakes* (1899), was the most interesting. Its picture of a futuristic megalopolis with mass social struggles led by demagogic leaders was 'a nightmare of Capitalism triumphant'[11] and an explicit polemic against Bellamy's* complacent optimism about taming the organizing urge and the jungle of the cities. In Wells's complex corporate capitalism 'everything was bigger, quicker and more crowded; there was more and more flying and the wildest financial speculation.'[12] Since Wells's sketch of the future was full of brilliant and detailed insights (as, for example, those about competing police forces and stultifying mass media) that turned out to be close to actual developments in the twentieth century, this novel became the model for anti-utopian anticipation from Zamyatin and von Harbou to Heinlein and Pohl. But Wells's imaginative energy flagged here at the crucial narrative level: the observer-hero waking after two centuries behaves alternatively like a saviour (suffering his final passion on an airplane instead of a cross) and vacillating liberal intellectual. The jerky plot concerns itself primarily with the adventure of a beautiful soul in the future, and is thus coresponsible for a spate of similar inferior SF with more rugged heroes who are given wonderful powers and who experience sentimental entanglements. 'A Story of Days To Come' (1899) and 'A Dream of Armageddon' (1903), told wholly from inside the same future, are not much more than an exploitation of that interesting locale for sentimental tales seen from the bottom, respectively the top, of society. Wells's later SF novels — though even at their worst never lacking flashes of genuine insight or redeeming provocation — do not attain the imaginative consistency of his first cycle. In *The Food of the Gods* (1904) the fundamental equation of material and moral greatness is never worked out. His series of programmatic utopias, from *A Modern Utopia* (1905) to *The Holy Terror* (1939), has interesting moments, especially when he is describing a new psychology of power and responsibility such as that of the 'Samurai' or the 'holy terror' dictator. However, its central search for a caste of technocratic managers as 'competent receivers'[13] for a bankrupt capitalist society oscillates wildly from enlightened monarchs or dictators, through Fabian-like artists and engineers, to airmen and Keynesians (in *The Shape of Things to Come*, 1933): millen-

*[Edward Bellamy (1850-98), author of the utopian romance *Looking Backward* (1888).]

nium has always been the most colourless part of Christian apocalypse. What is worst, Wells's fascinated sensitivity to the uncertain horizons of humanity gives only too often way to impatient discursive scolding, often correct but rarely memorable. A visit to young Soviet Russia (where his meeting with Lenin provided an almost textbook example of contrasts between abstract and concrete utopianism) resulted in the perhaps most interesting work in that series, *Men Like Gods* (1923), where Wells gave a transient and somewhat etiolated glimpse of a Morris-like brightness. But his work after the first World War vacillated, not illogically for an apocalyptic writer, between equally superficial optimism and despair. His position in the middle, wishing a plague on both the upper and the working classes, proved singularly fruitless in creative terms – though extremely influential and bearing strange fruit in subsequent SF, the writers and readers of which mostly come from precisely those 'new middle classes' that Wells advanced as the hope of the future.

With all his strengths and weaknesses Wells remains the central writer in the tradition of SF. His ideological impasses are fought out as memorable and rich contradictions tied to an inexorably developing future. He collected, as it were, all the main influences of earlier writers – from Lucian and Swift to Kepler and Verne, [. . .] from Plato and Morris to Mary Shelley, Poe, Bulwer,* and the subliterature of planetary and subterranean voyages, future wars, and the like – and transformed them in his own image, whence they entered the treasury of subsequent SF. He invented a new thing under the sun in the time-travel story made plausible or verisimilar by physics. He codified, for better or worse, the notions of invasion from space and cosmic catastrophe (as in his story 'The Star,' 1899), of social and biological degeneration, of fourth dimension, of future megalopolis, of biological plasticity. Together with Verne's *roman scientifique*, Wells's 'scientific romances' and short stories became the privileged form in which SF was admitted into an official culture that rejected socialist utopianism. True, of his twenty-odd books that can be considered SF, only perhaps eight or nine are still of living interest, but those contain unforgettable visions (all in the five 'romances' and the short stories of the early socio-biological-cum-cosmic cycle): the solar eclipse at the end of time, the faded flowers from the future, the invincible obtuseness of southern England and the Country of the Blind confronted with the New, the Saying of the Law on Moreau's island, the wildfire spread of the red Martian weed and invasion panic toward London, the last Martian's lugubrious ululations in Regent's Park, the frozen world of 'The New Accelerator,' the springing to life of the Moon vegetation, the lunar society. These summits of Wells's are a demonstration of what is

*[Sir Edward Bulwer-Lytton (1803-73), novelist, author of the scientific romance *The Coming Race* (1871).]

possible in SF, of the cognitive shudder peculiar to it. Their poetry is based on a shocking transmutation of scientific into aesthetic cognition, and poets from Eliot to Borges have paid tribute to it. More harrowing than in the socialist utopians, more sustained than in Twain, embracing a whole dimension of radical doubt and questioning that makes Verne look bland, it is a grim caricature of bestial bondage and an explosive liberation achieved by means of knowledge. Wells was the first signifi-cant writer who started to write SF from within the world of science, and not merely facing it. Though his catastrophes are a retraction of Bellamy's and Morris's utopian optimism, even in the spatial disguises of a parallel present on Moreau's island or in southern England it is always a possible future evolving from the neglected horrors of today that is analyzed in its (as a rule) maleficent consequences, and his hero has 'an epic and public . . . mission' intimately bound up with 'the major cognitive challenge of the Darwinist age.'[14] For all his vacilla-tions, Wells's basic historical lesson is that the stifling bourgeois society is but a short moment in an impredictable, menacing, but at least theoretically open-ended human evolution under the stars. He endowed later SF with a basically materialist look back at human life and a rebelliousness against its entropic closure. For such reasons, all subse-quent significant SF can be said to have sprung from Wells's *Time Machine*. [. . .]

Notes

1. H.G. Wells, 'Preface' to *Seven Famous Novels* (New York, 1934), p. vii.

2. Patrick Parrinder (ed.), *H.G. Wells: the Critical Heritage* (London, 1972), pp. 57, 101-2, 69.

3. Geoffrey West, *H.G. Wells* (Pennsylvania, 1973), p. 112.

4. Robert M. Philmus and David Y. Hughes (eds.), *Early Writings in Science and Science Fiction by H.G. Wells* (Berkeley, 1975), pp. 30-1.

5. Parrinder, *H.G. Wells: the Critical Heritage*.

6. Wells, 'Preface' to *Seven Famous Novels*.

7. Christopher Caudwell, *Studies and Further Studies in a Dying Culture* (New York, 1971), pp. 76 and 93.

8. V.S. Pritchett, *The Living Novel* (London, 1976), p. 128.

9. Parrinder, *H.G. Wells: the Critical Heritage*.

10. Patrick Parrinder, *H.G. Wells* (New York, 1977), pp. 69, 273.

11. H.G. Wells, 'Author's Preface', *The Sleeper Wakes* (London, 1921).

12. H.G. Wells, *Experiment in Autobiography* (New York, 1934), pp. 551, 206.

13. Ibid.

14. Parrinder, *H.G. Wells*.

6 RESIDENTIAL AMENITY, RESPECTABLE MORALITY AND THE RISE OF THE ENTERTAINMENT INDUSTRY: THE CASE OF BLACKPOOL, 1860-1914

John Walton

Source: *Literature and History*, vol. I (1975). © Thames Polytechnic, London, England.

The early nineteenth-century seaside resort was directly descended from the spa, and this ancestry showed in its clientèle and daily régime. A leisured class of aristocrats, gentry, merchants and prosperous tradesmen, their ranks swelled by lawyers and half-pay officers, supported the nascent holiday industry. They alone could afford the high cost of travel, accommodation and time away from work. The season in most resorts ran from May to October, with a few favoured places attaining the prestige of a winter season. The emphasis lay, ostensibly at least, on cure rather than amusement, and pastimes were generally decorous and sedate: bathing in the morning, promenading at lunchtime and in the evening, cards, subscription concerts, novels, botany and geology. Brighton retained some of its raffish reputation almost throughout the nineteenth century, but most resorts aimed at the patronage of respectable families, and paid the resulting penalty of dullness.

The reformation of manners in the higher strata of society, with its impact in emulation and social controls on those lower down the scale, confirmed this tendency. The extension of the moral values of the puritanical, dissenting section of the middle classes to achieve great influence on the aristocracy and within the Church of England had far reaching effects on the nation's social life. Traditional customs and amusements deemed cruel, indecent, immoral or potentially disorderly under the new orthodoxy were suppressed or fell under heavy weight of disapproval; urbanisation and the spread of industrial discipline were anyway eroding or changing them. The theatre was almost suppressed in some areas, and even cards and frivolous reading were frowned upon by strict evangelicals. A pall of gloom descended upon the English Sunday.

The seaside resorts conformed to the new morality, in general, by the 1830s; not only did landowners and tradesmen themselves share the evangelical orthodoxy, but they were also obliged to look to the tastes of their visitors. Even Brighton succumbed, at least on the surface. [. . .]

Moreover, in many resorts the dominance of health over pleasure, and the preoccupation with morality and 'rationality' in entertainment, survived until the 1900s. [. . .]

During the nineteenth century the hegemony of these middle-class values in the resorts was threatened on two fronts: by working-class excursionists, not all of whom were thrifty and deferential and, later in the century, by the spread of an increasingly open, secular attitude to leisure activities, an apostasy from the strict controls on behaviour imposed by 'respectable' society at the mid-century. Conflict in the resorts was inevitable, especially where the pressures for change were strongest, for the moral issues were entangled with the bread-and-butter question of what sort of visitor it would be best to attract. The speed and degree of change varied from resort to resort, influenced by such factors as the extent of local authority powers, the pattern of land-ownership, the accessibility of the resort to excursionists, and the attitudes of local tradesmen. Blackpool provides an interesting case-study in that, although open to all the forces of change at their strongest, it yet managed to preserve a quiet middle-class coastal enclave. In showing how Blackpool embraced and reacted to the pressures of the late nineteenth century, I shall begin by examining the emergence of a system of social zoning for both visitors and residents. I shall then discuss the impact of excursionists on the town centre, and show how, while the northern part of the town retained a higher status, the southern coastal strip was invaded by the excursionist.

II

Working-class excursionists are as old as steam railways, for the earliest companies soon realised the potential profitability of conveying vast numbers in some discomfort at very cheap fares. [. . .] Most resorts frowned on [excursions], despite the opportunities for health and 'rational entertainment' they offered to the serious-minded, thrifty artisan. Unfortunately, less deferential sectors of the working classes could also afford the fares, and disrupted the cosy gentility of the established resorts. They sought to enjoy their limited leisure to the full, arriving early and departing late. They cleaved to the holiday traditions of their home towns, being uninhibited in shouting, singing, drinking and dancing, and bringing with them all the trappings of a fair at home, street vendors, showmen and quacks, to block the streets. They offended against middle-class notions of hygiene, [. . .] privacy and decency (the taboo on nudity in bathing and athletics was also a creation of the early nineteenth century). Moreover, until the mid-1850s they usually came on Sundays. In short, they were offensive to the resorts' established customers, and their numbers increased as the century wore on, especially during the great price fall after 1873. All resorts within easy day-trip range of a populous industrial area were obliged to find ways of excluding or coming to terms with the excursionist. Exclusion was rarely practicable. The advantages of railways for the middle-class trade were such that no resort could remain competitive without one. [. . .] A few resorts contrived to discourage excursion trains or trippers. Cheltenham, Malvern and Lytham, for example, with influential residents or Lords of the Manor, were able to lobby the railway directors against Sunday excursions, and resorts largely controlled by a single landowner could discourage the tripper by excluding the stall and fairground amusements he craved.

Blackpool did not fall into these favoured categories. It had no resident Lord of the Manor with an interest in self development, and [. . .] was divided into a multitude of small properties. [. . .] This was especially the case in the key areas close to the sea front. [. . .]

As Blackpool was wide open to the speculative builder and entertainment promoter, from stalls and sideshows upwards, it was necessary to find a way to separate the 'respectable' middle-class visitors from the excursionists, and to regulate the latter's behaviour, to prevent a catastrophic loss of 'better-class' patronage. We shall deal with regulation by by-laws in the next section; we are here concerned with separation.

The ideal solution, to which most resorts aspired, was that achieved by Brighton: separation by time, or 'different seasons for different classes'. By the 1870s Southport, with its planned layout and reputation for mildness, had pre-empted the fashionable autumn and winter season market for those who stayed in Lancashire, and Blackpool found its season becoming steadily shorter and more hectic until a concerted effort by Corporation and entertainment companies in the early twentieth century brought about an improvement.

The growing excursionist ascendancy in Blackpool after 1870 brought conflicting reactions in the town. Caterers for the older private middle-class family holiday often had deferential values and preferred to deal with sedate, decorous visitors whose respectability enhanced their own status and self-esteem. They were unwilling to make the transition to catering for trippers, arguing that prosperity based on working-class custom was uneasy and possibly transitory, and advocating a policy of season extension based on respectable entertainment and Sunday observance. The working-class sector of the holiday industry, rapidly increasing in numbers and influence, was for concentration on quantity rather than quality, and saw season extension and respectability as at best secondary objectives, at worst dangerous irrelevancies.

This power-struggle came to be reflected in municipal advertising policy. In 1879 Blackpool obtained the power to levy a two penny rate to advertise its attractions. Local government in other resorts was denied this power until the eve of the First World War, and it proved an invaluable asset to Blackpool, enabling her to present a unified profile rather than relying on the fragmented efforts of competing entertainment companies, or the uncertain bounty of railway companies or ad hoc committees. At first, an existing policy of fêtes to extend the season at either end was continued, supported by an alliance of professional men and retired residents of independent means; but in 1881 the emphasis shifted to the attraction of a mainly working-class clientèle by the use of picture posters. Supported largely by publicans and directors of the entertainment companies, this policy was pursued with energy and success, but its effects were confined to the established working-class season between mid-July and early September. Apart from Whitsuntide and, increasingly, Easter, Blackpool was relatively quiet for the rest of the year.

Determined attempts to revive a 'better-class' spring or autumn season were delayed until after 1900, when the influence of respectable shopkeepers and the retired on the borough council was in the ascendant. Rapidly increasing rateable value — the product of the success of the 'popular policy' — meant that the cost of newspaper advertising and autumn attractions did not involve the diversion of funds from the poster campaign, and a varied programme each September and October from 1906 was supported by the entertainment companies and the railways, who had previously been unwilling to accept short-term losses in the hope of long-term gains. The September and October season was stimulated by such novelties as motor-racing and an aviation meeting, and its success was assured by the discovery of the popularity of electrical illuminations in 1912. By this time a significant new market for Blackpool's attractions had at last been created. Press comments suggest that the autumn visitors were largely middle-class and white-collar, from clerks with a spare week's holiday upwards, and the importance of a Musical Festival among the annual autumn attractions indicates the probable significance of cultural pretensions or at least deferential values. We shall see that such tastes were not completely neglected even at the height of the season, but there is a clear difference in emphasis and tone. Further evidence that 'respectable' visitors were overcoming prejudices against Blackpool's proletarian reputation, at least outside the most crowded months, is provided by the development of a limited but valuable winter season, with the more prestigious hotels having to turn away visitors at Christmas and on fine week-ends. Social zoning by time was thus beginning to emerge in Blackpool by the early twentieth century, but it was belated and limited in scope, especially when set against the enormous growth of the popular season.

To avoid the danger of becoming completely a one-class resort during the late nineteenth century, Blackpool thus had to adopt an informal system of physical separation. This depended entirely on market forces, on an investment decision to consolidate properties and build a select estate large enough to impose its character on an area or, more difficult, on a series of individual decisions with the same result.

During the 1860s, both types of social zoning developed on Blackpool's sea front. On the cliffs north of the original settlement, an estate company began a relatively select and tightly controlled development on land purchased from several owners, commencing operations in 1864. Estate companies had the advantage of being able to impose a common building policy on their land, removing the danger of adjacent low-class property which encouraged mediocrity where small landowners predominated. [. . .] Blackpool's North Shore (north of Talbot Road) was already the resort's highest-status area even in 1861, thanks mainly to the imposition of minimum values and high building standards by Dickson's Trustees in Queen Street and along the coast. [. . .]

The Blackpool Land, Building and Hotel Company's estate confirmed and safeguarded this trend. Most of its capital came from Manchester, and building began with a crescent facing the sea, the first such development in Blackpool. [. . .] Claremont Park, as it was called, [. . .] offered quiet and relative privacy to commuters and patrons of its 'better-class' lodging and boarding-houses, at a safe distance from the trippers in the town centre.

Until the 1890s South Shore also offered a quiet retreat for the middle-class visitor. Although built up in small plots with little residential differentiation beyond the usual tendency for the sea-front to attract the best houses, the area south of the Manchester Hotel, at the junction between Lytham Road and the Promenade, was out of reach of all but the more curious and energetic of the trippers. By 1871 a colony of the leisured and retired had collected in Dean Street, Church (now Bond) Street and along the sea front, and during the next two decades the population of the borough's two southern wards increased eightfold to more than 8,400, with new villas and terraces of respectable lodging-houses radiating from the new promenade, although much of the increase was inland cottage property. South Shore prided itself on the patronage of fashionable Lancashire families, and aspired to the title of 'the premier residential suburb'; publicity of the kind it sought was provided by a Preston paper which remarked in 1883 that passing from Blackpool to South Shore was like the transition from Fleet Street to Temple Gardens, or Carfax to New College.

In the late nineteenth century Blackpool was thus able to retain a certain amount of middle-class patronage, both visitor and resident, at either end of the town. Entertainments, shops and other amenities were concentrated in the town centre, however, where 'respectable' visitors and rowdy excursionists had to rub shoulders. In this area, the social controls operated by the local authority were important.

III

Blackpool's shopping and entertainment centres became concentrated between the railway stations in the original core of the town, an unplanned area of haphazard, narrow streets. In 1861 the central shopping area consisted of two streets, both of which retained vestigial residential functions; by 1901 almost all of the 1861 built-up area, including the promenade between North and Central Piers, had become commercialised, and the business district was surrounded by a belt of lodging-houses, many of them purpose-built since the 1870s. The great entertainment centres of the late nineteenth century, with the single exception of the Raikes Hall pleasure gardens, were all sited in this area, which attracted the full weight of excursionist demand for amusement of all kinds.

Blackpool's permanent large-scale entertainment facilities were provided entirely by private enterprise, although we have seen that the local authority was increasingly active in promoting stunts aimed at publicity or season extension. There was no municipal investment or entrepreneurial activity as such in providing or maintaining the capital for a permanent entertainment industry, nor was there any such activity by individual large landowners anxious to hasten estate development. Like its neighbour Morecambe, Blackpool owed its large-scale attractions to the efforts of public companies drawing investment from a wide geographical and social spectrum. This may have made for an unusual sensitivity to changes in popular taste.

Entertainment facilities remained rudimentary [. . .] until the early 1860s. Then, growing awareness of competition for a 'better-class' visitor galvanised a group of local residents into promoting a pier company which aimed at providing a 'select lounge' where the tone could be maintained by the imposition of a toll. This, the present North Pier, was opened in 1862, but its initial failure to discourage the excursionist soon led to the creation of the South Jetty, the present Central Pier, by a splinter group of shareholders. Opened in 1868, the South Jetty aimed expressly at the working-class market, offering open-air dancing from 5 a.m. and cheap steamers with a view to keeping the North Pier for the 'better classes' and thereby safeguarding the investments of its shareholders without loss of tone; although many investors also had a shrewd eye to the growing potential of the excursionist sector itself.

The entertainment centres of the 1870s grew up between the piers and, at least in their early stages, reflected similar attitudes to social segregation. The Royal Palace Gardens, Raikes Hall, half a mile inland, concentrated from its first full season in 1872 on dancing and popular spectacular, specialising in acrobats, fireworks and novelties rather than the educational and 'improving' attractions advocated by its critics. The excursionists' custom brought healthy dividends, and it is significant that as early as 1875 the conservatory, one of the few concessions to respectability, was the 'worst paying portion of the grounds'.

The Winter Gardens, the other major speculation of the decade, began by concentrating on the 'better-class' market, hoping to encourage a genteel winter season by providing sheltered walks, conservatories and concerts. Admission charges were not high enough to exclude trippers, although programmes were not at first popular enough to encourage them, and for the first decade of its existence the Winter Gardens fell uncomfortably between two stools.

These early companies were dominated by local men, although investment was attracted from a wide area of Lancashire and the West Riding. When the excursionist avalanche of the late nineteenth century stimulated the development of entertainment complexes on a still grander scale in the 1890s, London and Manchester became the main centres for entrepreneurial activity, but local investment and management remained important. The Tower and the Alhambra were heavily-capitalised sea-front enterprises on adjacent central sites, aiming primarily at the trippers' sixpences; the Gigantic Wheel in the grounds of the Winter Gardens was embarrassingly dependent on the arrival of excursionists from an ever wider catchment area in order to sustain its novelty value. Both Tower and Alhambra offered circuses, music-hall, novelty acts and the inevitable dancing in opulent surroundings, and were successful dividend-earners in the excursionist market after early problems of over-capitalisation.

In 1887, the Winter Gardens also began to concentrate on the excursionist market under a new manager, William Holland, who had made his name at such London resorts as North Woolwich Gardens, where he introduced such novelties as a postman's race, a barmaid show and a beard and moustache show. At Blackpool he brought in 'ballets' and variety shows with such popular themes as 'Our Empire', despite resistance from some of the directors to this 'departure from our usual serene concert scene'. The innovations were commercially successful, but opposition remained among those who preferred prestige to profit.

The 'better-class' market was still not entirely neglected in central Blackpool, however. The Winter Gardens' Opera House, opened in 1889, offered Gilbert and Sullivan and West End comedies, often with the original cast, as well as concerts and occasional visits from artistes of the calibre of Caruso or Melba. Thomas Sergenson's Grand Theatre, which opened in 1894, also catered for the whole range of playgoers. The main bastion of the 'better classes', however, remained the North Pier, which was, as we have seen, at the 'respectable' end of the town. A shilling was the minimum charge for orchestral concerts at the end of the pier, and comedians were advertised as 'without one trace of vulgarity'; on Sundays promenading facilities only were offered, and the main attraction was the millinery on show in the 'church parade' after morning service.

Despite the existence from 1893 of another pier offering restrained, decorous entertainment at South Shore, there remained a problem of social control in the town centre. Entertainments as well as shops continued to be patronised by the 'better classes', but the relative importance and obtrusiveness of the excursionist economy was rapidly increasing and corporate intervention was necessary to keep the custom of the middle classes, which was still important to the town's prestige and to the well-being of many of its traders.

The behaviour of the trippers themselves posed few legal problems; they could be dealt with under the common law if they became drunken, threatening or obstructive, and the main difficulty was the obvious one of enforcement, for policemen were always in short supply at the height of the season. Annoyance and offence were caused more by those who catered for the trippers: street traders, entertainers and the like, parasitic on the crowds drawn by the larger concerns. These were regulated increasingly by the local authority, which steadily built up its power to restrain noise and obstruction in the streets, using Improvement Acts and by-laws.

There was, of course, no overall strategy for dealing with problems of public order; issues were dealt with as they arose. Blackpool was relatively late among existing resorts in acquiring local authority controls, but in 1853 the need to regulate such services as cabs and donkeys, to promote Sunday observance and to prevent promiscuous nude bathing led to the obtaining of an Improvement Act extending the existing Local Board's powers already acquired under the Public Health Act. Donkeys, bathing-machines, boats and cabs were licensed, and the restoration of order to the streets and beach apparently encouraged the return of 'a class of visitors much superior to that of late years'. Blackpool was still a compact resort, and the lack of residential differentiation made such powers all the more necessary. When a misunderstanding in 1861 led to fears of their being withdrawn by the Local Government Act Office, the Local Board threatened to resist such a decision to the utmost, as 'utter confusion' would ensue.

The 1853 Act and by-laws met Blackpool's needs until the changes which began in the 1870s, when rising real wages coincided with extensions of the Lancashire Wakes holidays to bring a rapid increase in the number of working-class visitors and in their length of stay, and a shift in the balance between middle-class visitors and trippers as elements in the town's economy. The result was the spread in the town centre and on the beach of the rough-and-ready amusements associated with the Lancashire Wakes inland: bawling street sellers of everything from hot peas to cheap walking sticks, quack doctors, games of chance, even swingboats and 'whirly-go-rounds'. Front gardens and vacant lots were pressed into service for stalls and fairgrounds by scores and later hundreds of small proprietors. Competition for the patronage of excursionists led to the appearance in the street of touts for lodging and eating-houses and for entertainments of all kinds, including such vast new pleasure palaces as the Winter Gardens, Raikes Hall and later the Tower and Alhambra. Passers-by were accosted, and the streets were blocked and noisy; the beach between the piers was 'like a Knott Mill fair'. To keep the patronage of its more decorous, 'respectable' visitors, the Corporation (as it had become in 1876) was obliged to extend its powers.

The rise of the popular season also had an effect on the social structure of the holiday industry, however, as the number of those catering for excursionists in various ways increased, and their influence on the town's government grew. For the most part, the town was run by established shopkeepers and directors of the entertainment companies, with an interest in attracting the excursionist but keeping down the competition from stalls and outdoor amusements. The interests of the latter, however, were defended by Parliament and the Local Government Board, both unwilling to allow Draconian restraints on free trade at this level, and in some cases by public opinion and the fear of losing excursionist custom.

Some of those whom the Corporation sought to regulate had very little support in the town. Itinerant hawkers for example, detested both by shopkeepers and by advocates of the maintenance of the 'better-class' season, found defenders only at the level where powers were granted. During Whit-week and the July and August Wakes season the local street vendors were augmented by an increasing number of itinerants, who blocked the narrow central streets and repelled visitors by their appearance and manner. The Town Clerk described them in 1886 as 'rough, dirty, drunken and noisy', and passage along the main shopping streets was likened to 'running the gauntlet'. In 1879, the Corporation obtained licensing powers, awarding licences only to ratepayers, but itinerants evaded this by taking out national pedlars' licenses, and others regarded prosecution and fines as an occupational hazard. The Local Government Board forbade the Corporation to exclude all hawkers without local licences and their numbers stood at over 350 in the late 1880s, although annoyance may have been reduced by by-laws against the use of noisy instruments, excessive shouting and 'persistent importuning to buy'. The Corporation was able to keep the nuisance within bounds, but without much sympathy from a central government lacking in local knowledge.

Touts and stall-holders had vested interests and extreme advocates of an excursionist-based economy to support them, but met with disapproval from those who sought to retain some 'better-class' patronage. Stalls on front land proliferated rapidly during the 1890s, and the stall-owners successfully resisted an attempt to levy a separate rate on them in 1898. Three years later a clause to enable the Corporation to prohibit further stalls was hotly opposed in Parliament by the same people, who accused the Corporation of unfairly restraining free competition and seeking confiscatory powers. The Lords Committee was sufficiently impressed to reduce the applicability of the clause, and refused to allow any penalty to be imposed on offenders, to the annoyance of the local press. Under the circumstances, the measure was surprisingly effective. Touting became a serious problem during the 1870s, being difficult to prove and substantiate (witnesses were often elusive). It was a necessary form of free advertisement for many as competition intensified and the season shortened, and there was some sympathy for such hard-pressed exponents as back-street lodging-house keepers. A series of by-laws, beginning in 1879, had little effect on noisy, obtrusive touting from private land until an Appeal Court ruling in 1911, but even after this a certain amount of quiet touting was tolerated, the Corporation admitting that without it 'the whole business of the town would be stopped'.

In both these cases, the need to maintain order and decorum had to be balanced against the growing necessity of providing the services and atmosphere the excursionists appreciated. This conflict was particularly apparent in the regulation of the beach. Stalls on the beach between the present North and Central Piers seem to have appeared in the late 1850s, but did not become a nuisance until the end of the next decade. In 1869 the Local Board decided to clear the beach after complaints about refuse and 'the rabble of the town' congregating around shooting galleries, but it was found that its jurisdiction extended only as far as high water mark. Beach trading and shows increased rapidly with the expansion of the popular season, and by 1873 it could be claimed that the character of 'the whole district as a watering-place for the better class of visitors' was at risk. Two further attempts at clearance in the 1870s were abortive, and 'better-class' visitors began to take their custom elsewhere. The Corporation purchased the foreshore rights, extended its by-law powers, and in 1896 adopted a licensing policy, confining pitches to ratepayers and reducing the number of stalls from 350 to 140. When this failed, an attempt was made in 1897 to clear the sands altogether, but by this time the beach fairground had become an essential element in the town's popularity, and an outcry in the inland press, predicting loss of trade through this 'curious freak of exotically delicate sentiment', helped to persuade the Corporation to return to a policy of regulation and licensing.

This retreat was symptomatic of changing attitudes to the working-class holidaymakers. By the 1890s they dominated the town's economy, and their wishes carried increasing weight towards the end of the century. Moreover, class attitudes to recreation were becoming less divergent, with the beginnings of a decline in the early Victorian cult of outward 'respectability' and decorum beginning to show itself. Theatres and music-halls became increasingly socially acceptable on the one side, and on the other drunkenness was decreasing and the mid-century threat of social revolution had receded. There is some evidence of increasing mutual toleration at Blackpool in this period. This was accompanied by a relaxation of some of the moral and religious sanctions which had interfered with amusement. In particular, Sunday trading, for many years passively tolerated by Blackpool's authorities, was given moral support in 1896, when the Corporation tramways began Sunday working, and Blackpool was among the pioneers of Sunday concerts and cinemas. Despite non-conformist and low Church protests, it is clear that residents and visitors alike preferred a 'Continental Sunday', and even forebodings that the 'better-classes' would be frightened away found only brief expression. In this respect, Blackpool's success as a popular resort was largely due to its keeping pace with changing, if unarticulated, public attitudes.

The regulation of the town centre was successful in that it prevented excursionists and those catering for them from getting out of control, allowing 'better-class' visitors to use the town centre amenities without undue discomfort, while giving sufficient latitude to satisfy the working-class demand for outdoor, informal amusement. The balance between the middle- and working-class norms shifted towards the end of the century, as the latter became more important to the town's economy and the former became less intolerant, but Blackpool was able to retain some of its 'better-class' visitors only because part of the coastline, the Claremont Park estate at North Shore, resisted the pressure to commercialise. We must now analyze the forces involved and how they were resisted.

IV

During the 1890s the spread of the entertainment industry along the coastline threatened the residential amenities which continued to attract the 'better-class' to Claremont Park and South Shore. The

opening of the promenade tramway in 1885, with its subsequent extensions, made the whole coastline more accessible to the tripper, and
changes in user and status appeared likely.

They actually took place on part of the South Shore sea-front. [. . .]
The lack of a large estate to set the tone was sorely felt after the tramway arrived, as a series of fairgrounds appeared on vacant land, to the
chagrin of their respectable neighbours. The largest of these grew up at
the tram terminus opposite the South Pier in the early 1890s, causing
so many complaints that the Corporation bought the land at an exorbi-
tant price in 1896, evicting the showmen. The fair was by now so well-
established, however, that it migrated first to the beach, and later to
the adjoining Watson's Estate, a low-lying area disadvantaged for building until the promenade could be extended to it. Here it grew rapidly
in the early twentieth century, organised by an amusement syndicate,
to become the permanent Pleasure Beach amusement park.

South Shore residents put heavy pressure on the Corporation to suppress the fairground, alleging that it was driving away 'better-class' visitors and residents; they were supported by the general entertainment
interests. A sustained campaign during 1906-7 failed, however, the
Corporation stressing that the extent of its legal powers was uncertain.
In fact, the Pleasure Beach was already too great an asset to be lightly
suppressed, and many local property-owners were finding that excursionists at eighteenpence per night actually increased property values,
although South Shore's shopping centre suffered from the change. By
1907 excursionist domination was a recognised fact at the south end
of the promenade. [. . .]

North Shore was more successful in retaining its distinctive character. The Land, Building and Hotel Company resisted all innovations
and the desirability of protecting the area's amenities was recognised
by the Corporation. The area was opened out during the 1890s, when
the Corporation took over the cliffs from the Land Company, which
had refused to bear the cost of maintaining them. Special by-laws were
provided to suppress noise, disturbance and itinerant showmen, and
waggonettes and hired vehicles were prohibited. Despite these precau-
tions, the Company and the frontagers united to resist the Corporation's plans to run a tramway along the new promenade and abolish
the toll. They were unsuccessful, and a major source of annoyance to
the majority of the town's visitors was removed. But the by-laws
proved sufficient, strictly enforced as they were, to maintain the
character of the area, and the Corporation was willing to assist the Land
Company against further encroachments. A pier proposal was beaten
off, and in 1903 the Corporation decisively suppressed a fairground near
the estate's northern boundary (in sharp contrast to its attitude to the
Pleasure Beach). Moreover, the Corporation fortuitously acquired

twenty-six acres of key coastal building land to the north of the estate in 1894, and ensured that it was developed to a high standard, with all amusements excluded. The value of the North Shore as a haven for the 'better-class' visitors who, as the restaurateur T.P. Taylor pointed out, did more shopping and put more money into the town than any others, was fully appreciated in Blackpool. The combined efforts of the Land Company and Corporation thus ensured continuing social diversity in the town's visiting population in spite of the pressures exerted by excursionist amusements.

V

Despite the changing social structure of its visitors during the latter half of the nineteenth century, and the pressure for change exerted by those who catered for the tripper, Blackpool was able to reconcile quantity with quality and please the working-class visitor while retaining a share of the 'better-class' market. [. . .] The conflicting forces of an expanding working-class holiday season on a scale unmatched elsewhere, with its attendant commercialization and the spread of popular amusement, and an established middle-class season based on quietness and sedate, 'improving' recreations, were reconciled in Blackpool. The rise of two relatively select social areas, and their subsequent resistance to the spread of the tripper along the coastline, was coupled with the adoption of a policy (if that is not too positive a word) of moderate regulation in the town centre, and an apparent reduction of class tensions with regard to leisure activities as the century wore on. [. . .]

7 THE GREAT BRITISH PICTURE SHOW: BOOMTIME AND SLUMPTIME

George Perry

Source: *The Great British Picture Show* (Paladin, London, 1975), Chs. 7 and 8. © George Perry.

In November 1931 a young Hungarian who had been a critic and film producer in his native country, and more recently in Paris, arrived in England with a contract to direct two films for Paramount. The first, a comedy called *Service For Ladies*, reintroduced Leslie Howard, and the other was *Women Who Play*. In early 1932 Alexander Korda founded his own company, reviving the disused name of Dr Ralph Tennyson Jupp's Company of 1913, London Films, and was soon joined by his younger brothers, Vincent and Zoltan. The company set to and began producing 'quota quickies', cheap, speedily produced films to meet the demands of the Renters' Quota. The first was *Wedding Rehearsal* which, in spite of its low budget, was well-received. The brothers continued making these films, swapping the direction around between them. Merle Oberon, Robert Donat and Emlyn Williams were among the new performers who found their faces on the screen as a result of Korda's London Films.

In a few short months, with a handful of low-budget pictures, Korda had demonstrated a taste and a capacity for serving entertaining material. It was inevitable that sooner or later he would attempt something more ambitious. He is alleged to have heard a cockney cab-driver singing 'I'm 'Enery the Eighth', although the weight of apocryphal stories about Korda is phenomenal. Nevertheless he was the driving force behind the setting up of *The Private Life of Henry VIII*, a costume biography of the famous monarch which enabled Charles Laughton to deliver one of his earliest virtuoso performances in the cinema, with a supporting cast that included Merle Oberon, Robert Donat, Binnie Barnes and Elsa Lanchester. The cameraman was the lugubrious Georges Perinal, imported from France in his first association with Korda. Money was somehow raised from the City; when it was exhausted Ludovico de Grand Ry, an Italian financier, bailed the company out. Korda held a world première at the Radio City Music Hall in New York, the largest cinema in the world, which had been opened by the legendary showman S.K. ('Roxy') Rothafel in the previous year. With immensely flattering American press notices behind it, the film opened in

London two weeks later on 24 October 1933 at the Leicester Square Theatre. The British press went wild in a fury of patriotic excitement. There was an immense attraction in the subject of a lusty, wenching, foul-mouthed, virile English king. Contrary to popular belief, it had not been a wildly expensive picture; its cost was probably less than £60,000, which was small beer by American standards. Its first release grossed a respectable half a million pounds, a valuable figure to be displayed on Korda's balance sheet the next time he approached the City bankers. What is more, the international prestige gained for the British industry for this one film was staggering. Korda was acclaimed as the new genius who could save British films.

And now the vast Prudential Assurance Company was induced to open its coffers. Grandiose plans were set in hand for building an enormous complex of studios at Denham in Buckinghamshire for London Films, which were to cost more than a million pounds. Korda, meanwhile, continued to make films on rented sound stages. His next starred the German actress Elisabeth Bergner, and was directed by her husband, Dr Paul Czinner. It was *Catherine the Great*, and included in the cast Douglas Fairbanks Jr and Flora Robson, as well as Gerald du Maurier and Irene Vanbrugh. In spite of such powerful casting the film failed to achieve anything approaching the same success as *Henry VIII*. In a way it was a direct challenge to Hollywood, for Joseph von Sternberg had just made *Scarlet Empress* with Marlene Dietrich. Although the public failed to take to the Korda film, its taste and worthiness only enhanced his prestige with critics and backers. But this evaporated when his next film, *The Private Life of Don Juan*, appeared. The title part was played by the paunchy, muscle-bound Douglas Fairbanks Sr, his last film, with his best swashbuckling days by now well behind him. The film was a failure, and Korda's persuasive charm was called to good account to keep the Prudential happy. His luck returned with the next film, *The Scarlet Pimpernel*, a romantic costume drama from the Baroness Orczy novel which made nearly half a million pounds on its first run. The director was Harold Young and the cast included Leslie Howard, Merle Oberon and Raymond Massey. Faith was completely restored, and the foundations were laid down on the site at Denham.

Meanwhile in other studios London Films went on producing pictures. Zoltan Korda directed *Sanders of the River*, a chauvinistic tribute to the paternalism of the British colonizers in Africa. The American director, William Cameron Menzies, was called in to direct a screenplay by H.G. Wells, *Things to Come*, which dealt in a prophetic way with a world that almost destroyed itself in a nuclear holocaust, and sought salvation through the opening up of space travel. With its strident Arthur Bliss score and ambitiously designed sets, its intriguing theme and Wellsian propaganda that humanity's hopes lay with the scientists, it was the sensation of the year. Both this film and *The Ghost Goes West*, a whimsical comedy with Robert Donat, directed by René Clair, had their exteriors shot in the grounds of the unfinished Denham Studios, as did the second H.G. Wells subject, *The Man Who Could Work Miracles*. The day before the studios were to be opened, a fire occurred causing £45,000 worth of damage. The Prudential as well as meeting the building costs in the first place had also insured it with themselves and so had to pay out for the repairs.

The first film to be made completely at Denham was one of the highwater marks of Korda's career, a careful, tender, devoted reconstruction of the life of a great painter, *Rembrandt*, who was played with dignity and compassion by Charles Laughton, with Elsa Lanchester as Hendrijke. Korda did not expect the film to be a commercial success but he wanted the first product of the new head-quarters of London Films to be worthy of the industry he had in such a short time managed to transform. Korda was at the summit of his career; he had shown himself to be the foremost producer in Britain, his confidence, ambition, charm and sensitivity attracting attention for British films all over the world. Korda films were made with an intelligent and careful eye on public taste and he was not afraid to run ahead of it. Regrettably *Rembrandt*, an excellent picture, was far ahead of its time and languished in half-empty houses.

But Korda was not the only producer to force the pace between 1933 and 1936. Another remarkable figure was Michael Balcon, who as head of production at Gaumont-British and Gainsborough had already set things rolling with *Rome Express*. In 1933, the year of *The Private Life of Henry VIII*, he was responsible for several interesting films, three of them directed by Victor Saville: *Friday the Thirteenth*, with Sonnie Hale, Jessie Matthews and Gordon Harker; *I Was a Spy*, an accomplished essay into First World War romanticism with Madeleine Carroll, Conrad Veidt and Herbert Marshall; and the best of the trio, *The Good Companions*, with Edmund Gwenn, Jessie Matthews and John Gielgud, an adaptation of J.B. Priestley's novel about a travelling concert party in the north of England. It was the first sound film to receive a Royal Gala Performance. In the following year Balcon capital-ized on the enormous and unique talent of Jessie Matthews and put her into musicals where her magnificent legs and high, throbby voice were exploited to great effect. The first was Victor Saville's superb *Ever-green*, an evocation of the Edwardian musical theatre as well as high life in the thirties, with a Rodgers and Hart score. This was followed by *First a Girl, It's Love Again, Head over Heels* and others, the first two again directed by the prolific Victor Saville. Balcon also lured Alfred Hitchcock away from John Maxwell at BIP and set him to work at directing the kind of films he could do better than anybody else. The first of the Gaumont-British thrillers was *The Man Who Knew Too Much*; it followed an unsuccessful and dismal attempt at a light musical comedy costume picture, *Waltzes from Vienna*, which was one of Hitchcock's worst mistakes, and an area into which he would never venture again. The new thriller, from its shock opening to a thinly disguised version of the Sidney Street siege at its climax, was an exciting work. It starred Leslie Banks, Nova Pilbeam as a kidnapped small girl, and introduced Peter Lorre, the villain of Fritz Lang's *M* and now a refugee from Nazi Germany, to British cinema. Hitchcock followed this film with his even more celebrated version of John Buchan's *The Thirty-Nine Steps*, a far cry from the novel, but a brilliant film with superb counterplaying by Robert Donat and Madeleine Carroll. *The Secret Agent* in 1936 again featured Madeleine Carroll, this time with Peter Lorre and John Gielgud, and was loosely based on Somerset Maugham's *Ashenden*. It was as richly imaginative as the previous two films, but less successful at the box-office. In the same year Hitchcock directed an updated version of Joseph Conrad's novel *The Secret Agent*, and to add to the confusion called it *Sabotage (A Woman Alone* in America). The anarchist, now a London cinema manager, was played by Oscar Homolka, and his wife by the American actress, Sylvia Sidney. A notable sequence involved a small boy carrying a parcel bomb in a crowded bus, marred according to Hitchcock by the subsequent detonation, which killed the innocent carrier. It was the last Hitchcock film produced by Michael Balcon.

His tastes, like Korda's, also embraced the elaborate historical type of film. One of the most successful, made in 1936 with Nova Pilbeam playing Lady Jane Grey, was *Tudor Rose*, directed and written by Robert Stevenson, who in another age was to direct *Mary Poppins*. *Rhodes of Africa*, in the same year, starring Walter Huston, Oscar Homolka and Peggy Ashcroft, was, in comparison with the quiet stylishness and restrained acting of the first film, a ponderous bore in a style which Hollywood could plainly mount a great deal more successfully. The director was Berthold Viertel, who also made *Little Friend* from a novel by the author of *The Constant Nymph*, Margaret Kennedy, in which Nova Pilbeam, one of the liveliest young actresses of the thirties, was given a big publicity build-up. [. . .]

Other producers found mileage in costume films. Herbert Wilcox remade his silent Dorothy Gish picture *Nell Gwyn*, with Anna Neagle playing the King's mistress, and achieved the dubious distinction of having it banned in the United States until the distributors had emasculated it to such a degree that a failure was inevitable. Nevertheless, in Britain, although by no means a lavish spectacle, it achieved a good run for its money. It was followed up by Anna Neagle playing Peg Woffington, the eighteenth-century actress, in the equally successful

Peg of Old Drury .

During this period of the thirties another fruitful and sometimes overlooked genre of British film began to appear in increasing numbers, the broad comedy pictures which featured comedians who had made reputations for hilarious and earthy working-class humour in the music halls. These films were modest in intention — most of them never got near the West End — but they did a great deal to provide a common interest between the producer and the mass audience. Among the comics it is fair to include Gracie Fields, the popular comedienne from Rochdale, who made her film debut in 1931 with *Sally in our Alley*, and through a series of delightful films in the thirties achieved the status of Britain's highest paid star. Typical, for instance, was her 1934 film, *Sing As We Go*, produced and directed by Basil Dean, in which she became a maid in a Blackpool boarding house. Scenes shot in the Lancashire resort, on the 'golden mile' and at the Pleasure Beach, gave a documentary insight into how half the British population lived, while the comedy was rich and human. Also in 1934, another Lancashire comedian, George Formby, made an initial screen appearance — a toothy and gormless young man, son of a famous music-hall star, with a penchant for finding trouble in the most unlikely places. His first film was made in Manchester and was called *Boots, Boots*. He too was to become one of the top box-office draws in Britain. The third great comic to become an established element of the British cinema made his debut in a film about old-time music hall, in 1934, *Those Were the Days*, which was directed by Thomas Bentley. This was Will Hay, who a year later appeared in the famous guise of the seedy, uneducated, crooked schoolmaster, Dr Twist, in *Boys Will Be Boys*. The film was directed by Marcel Varnel, a Frenchman who was to become a prime force in the English comedy film of the thirties. His position as the foremost comedy director was rivalled only by Anthony Kimmins, who made most of the Formby pictures.

In 1936 film output in Britain reached the staggering total of 212 features. Yet in spite of both the quantity and quality of the best British films, earnings from overseas markets were minuscule in comparison with the amounts spent on importing films into the country, mostly from America. The British film-producing business was basking in false sunshine and it was not to do so for very much longer.

However poor the studios' prospects were in the mid-thirties, the exhibitors were in an excellent position. New cinemas mushroomed and attracted new audiences. Hollywood's output of excellent pictures was staggering — it was the age of the superstar, of Clark Gable and Gary Cooper, Joan Crawford and Claudette Colbert, Carol Lombard and Jean Arthur, and of course, Fred Astaire and Ginger Rogers. In the ranks of the exhibitors, however, a new and important name had emerged. Oscar Deutsch, an ex-metal merchant who in the early twenties had been chairman of W. & F. Film Service, formed a company in 1931 called Cinema Service. It initially owned six cinemas. In 1933 the company was reformed as Odeon Theatres with a complement of twenty-six cinemas, making it the eighth largest circuit. Deutsch was one of the first British exhibitors to recognize that brand marketing was applicable to the cinema business. He set out to create a readily recognizable corporate image for Odeon, with distinctive lettering, façades and display units. Deutsch embarked on an ambitious policy of building; his intention was to set up a major circuit of up-to-date houses which would outshine their rivals by the luxuriousness of their fittings and the unity of their design. The newly built Odeons were all separate companies in their own right, an arrangement which enabled each theatre to raise its own capital by selling shares to local interests, which would benefit from a good cinema in the locality. After three years the Odeon circuit had become the fourth largest in the country, with 142 theatres, including twenty-nine under construction. But having good theatres was not enough, for Odeon's booking power was inferior to that of the rival circuits, ABC and Gaumont-British. After much negotiation a deal was completed with one of the major American renters, United Artists. This company, unlike its other big American rivals, did not produce its own films, but distributed the work of independent producers. It had been founded in the twenties by Douglas Fairbanks Sr and Charles Chaplin to combat the stranglehold of the big studios. Consequently, although Odeon could now have the bulk of the UA output, there was still an obligation on their part to let other exhibitors have a slice of the cake as well. But at least UA now had a guaranteed base market in Britain, and Odeon a guaranteed film source. Since one of the United Artists' partners from 1935 was Alexander Korda, Deutsch now had the beginnings of vertical integration in the British cinema. The financial arrangements, however, were complicated and created certain problems for the future.

Gaumont-British had greatly increased in size during the mid-thirties, owning 305 cinemas by 1936. ABC had only a few less, 296. John Maxwell, head of ABPC, then announced that he was joining the GB board and that the two circuits would merge. This would have created a giant unit, controlling thirteen per cent of British cinemas and seventeen per cent of seats. But they were the better theatres, mainly first-run houses. Although Maxwell did indeed join the rival board the proposed merger did not occur, possibly because the American interests carried out adroit financial moves to prevent the growth of the monster. Twentieth-Century Fox, the majority shareholders of Metropolis and Bradford Trust, who in turn were controllers of GB, objected to the scheme and formed a new holding company in association with

Loew's (MGM). In fact Maxwell remained on the board of both companies until he resigned from GB in 1938 after an unsuccessful legal battle with the Ostrer brothers. In spite of this setback Maxwell's ABC circuit continued to expand, its most important acquisition being the Union circuit, with 136 cinemas in 1937 boosting the total of theatres owned to nearly a hundred more than the 345 of the GB group. Consequently, Maxwell was able to ensure that his exhibiting interests outstripped those of his rivals.

There was another figure, who was to have an almost apocalyptic effect on the British film, now beginning to take an interest in the industry. Joseph Arthur Rank came into films from a wealthy background of Yorkshire flour-milling. An ardent Methodist, the first films he produced were religious shorts. His mission was to make films suitable for church audiences, which would be equal in production standards with the day-to-day output of the normal commercial cinema. There was considerable opposition within the Methodist Church to the use of films for sectarian purposes, and Rank had to fight hard. But in 1934, fired with evangelical zeal, he succeeded in forming a new company, British National Films, in partnership with Lady Yule, the remarkable and immensely wealthy widow of a jute millionaire. Rank initially wanted to make a film of *The Pilgrim's Progress* but this project never materialized. Instead, the first film made by his new company was set in a Yorkshire fishing port and concerned the rivalry between two families. Called *The Turn of the Tide*, it was directed by Norman Walker and starred Wilfrid Lawson, Moore Marriott and Geraldine Fitzgerald, a newcomer who later did well in Hollywood. It pleased both the critics and Rank, who had ensured that although the subject was a secular one its morality would be of a high order. In spite of the prestige of a major placing in the Venice Film Festival the film did not get a wide circuit release and so failed to recoup its costs. It was the beginning of Rank's march towards a situation where he became the most influential force in British films. In order to find a way of getting his films a fair showing he became a backer of C.M. Woolf, who in 1935, after a row with the Ostrer brothers, resigned from Gaumont-British and set up General Film Distributors. This company in a short space of time became very successful, buying, for instance, a quarter share of the American producing company, Universal, which reversed the tendency for American companies to buy their way into British ones. Meanwhile, Rank had become chairman of Pinewood Studios, which had been built at Iver in Buckinghamshire, a few miles from Korda's Denham. In many ways it was superior; the stages were linked by covered arcades and the site included some extensive landscaped grounds, once the estate of Heatherden Hall, which were put to frequent use for exterior shooting.

By 1936 Rank was poised for action. But another crisis was to intervene.

Slumptime

Over-confidence had led to over-expansion. British studio space grew at a rapid pace, the number of stages quadrupling in the decade 1928-38, and the amount of floor space multiplying seven-fold. In the year 1937-8 production output achieved a total of 228 films, far more than could reasonably be accommodated on British cinema screens, let alone in overseas markets. One of the bad results of the 1927 Act, as had been forecast, was the predominance of 'quota quickies' in the industry's production record, rather than large, well-made, prestige films. The former were cheap to produce and more likely to yield a profit than quality pictures. In theory they met the obligations of exhibitors and renters to favour the domestic producers, but in practice they contributed to public resentment against British films. It was always hard for a worthy, well-made picture, such as *The Turn of the Tide*, to bulldoze its way on to the screen in the face of Hollywood films and the quickies.

It was not the exhibitors who were to suffer in the crisis. As long as the supply of good American films was maintained, they could not lose. These were the films that the public was eager to see. Consequently, the vertically-integrated companies – the Ostrer's Gaumont-British, Maxwell's ABPC – would survive in spite of the jolt to their production arms.

The extravagant success of Alexander Korda's 1933 picture, *The Private Life of Henry VIII*, had set in train a period of excessive speculation with City firms almost falling over themselves in the rush to get a stake in the new booming business. But there was one factor that had been imperfectly calculated in the eternal optimism of the film-makers. The home market was inadequate and incapable of producing a profit for a reasonably expensive picture – in fact, almost any picture other than a quickie. Access, therefore, to the American market was absolutely essential. And in spite of all efforts this was a target which constantly eluded the British producers. The American companies themselves were not, obviously, interested in the plight of British films, and made little effort to provide any form of reciprocal dealing.

There was another serious aspect to the City's interest in films and that was that the money being poured in was in the form of loans, not capital. In the first ten months of 1936 alone more than £4 million was lent to the British film industry. The only alternative to profitability would be bankruptcy. All the warning signs were present; that they were ignored is a measure of the euphoria of the mid-thirties. Many if not most film companies had made insufficient profit to pay dividends for several years. Waste and inefficiency were legendary and Korda's oft-quoted remark, that when the industry makes money it is in millions, 'and so obviously, when we lose, it must be in millions', was an indication of the unreality and profligacy of this apparently glamorous business.

At the beginning of 1937 a receiver was appointed at Twickenham Studios. Korda ordered salary cuts at London Films. Then came a shock from Gaumont-British — a debit of nearly £100,000 on the previous year's trading. GB would cease to produce its own films, Lime Grove was to shut down, Gaumont-British Distributors was to fold. Henceforth GB News and the Gainsborough films made at Islington would be handled by General Film Distributors. This solemn story continued for many more months, with companies going bankrupt and studios closing. Output for 1938 was considerably less than half that of the previous year and the available studio space was only half-utilized.

The ten-year period of the 1927 Cinematograph Act was nearing its end when the Government in March 1936 appointed a committee under Lord Moyne to investigate and recommend measures to be adopted in a new Parliamentary Bill. After exhaustive evidence-taking and deliberation the Moyne Committee plumped solidly for more protection on a progressively increasing basis. The quota system, the Committee felt, had to a large extent been effective. Mindful of the harm done to the industry by 'quota quickies' it urged the creation of a quality test which a film would have to pass before it could qualify for renters' quota. This test would be administered by a new Government Films Commission. It also wanted to introduce a quota for short films, which had suffered as a result of a loophole in the wording of the 1928 Act. With its recommendations adopted, the Committee felt that in the next ten year period fifty per cent of screen time would be given to British films.

When put to the trade the Report was received with the same mixed feelings that preceded the introduction of the 1927 Cinematograph Act. As agreement was not possible, Parliament proceeded to enact the legislation as it had done ten years earlier, without the voluntary support of the business itself. The new Act accepted the quota recommendations except for the quality test. The long film quota was dropped to 15 per cent for exhibitors, 12½ per cent for renters in the first year, rising in stages eventually to 30 and 25 per cent respectively. The reason for the initial reduction was that instead of a quality test a cost test had been introduced, and it was felt that production would be bound to drop at first. The minima were £7,500 per film, based on labour costs, and a rate of £1 per foot. With an almost indelicate equation of money with artistic results a system of double and triple quotas was also instituted, so that a film costing £3 a foot counted as twice its length for renters' quota and £5 per foot three times. The Films Commission idea, however, was rejected because it was felt that an enlarged Advisory Committee, now called the Cinematograph Films Council, could do the job in an advisory capacity. Another mild proposal advanced in the Moyne Report, for the Government to set up a film-financing agency, was not covered in the Act. In order that working conditions in the industry should be improved a Fair Wages Clause made it mandatory for employers to offer terms and conditions approximating to trade union agreements. In order that the quota system should not seem too chauvinistic, special provision was made for specialist, 'art-house' type foreign films to be exempted from the requirements, providing that their circulation remained on a small scale.

The new Act could not restore lost fortunes or reopen the closed studios, but one beneficial effect was a new interest from American companies towards production in Britain. The first company to set up a British production wing was MGM, and Michael Balcon, now cut off from GB, was signed up to take control of an ambitious programme of Anglo-American films, each of which would justify its expense by being treated in the United States as a normal MGM product. The first film was suitably transatlantic in tone, *A Yank at Oxford*, directed by the American, Jack Conway, and starring Robert Taylor, Maureen O'Sullivan and Lionel Barrymore with the young British actress, Vivien Leigh. The story, concerning the adventures of a brash Middle West athletics student on a scholarship to the ancient cradle of learning, made a mildly satirical poke at the eccentricities of both Anglo-Saxon nations and was an entertaining box-office success. Balcon, unable to achieve compatibility with Louis B. Mayer, left MGM in disgust and Victor Saville stepped into his shoes. King Vidor, an extremely accomplished Hollywood director, was responsible for the second MGM-British film, an adaptation of an A.J. Cronin novel, *The Citadel*, about a doctor who progresses from the mining slums of Wales to the Adam-decorated consulting rooms of Harley Street, only to lose his ideals along the way. Rosalind Russell came from America to play opposite Robert Donat and Ralph Richardson. The last film, made in 1939, just before the start of the Second World War and the suspension of MGM's film-making activities in Britain, was *Goodbye Mr Chips*, an outstanding world success and an acting tour-de-force for Robert Donat, who was required to span almost a lifetime, from youthful vigour to apparent senility. *Goodbye Mr Chips*, an unashamedly sentimental James Hilton story about a beloved master in an English public school, was directed by Sam Wood, a Hollywood veteran, responsible for among other things two of the best Marx Brothers films, *Night at the Opera* and *Day at the Races. Goodbye Mr Chips* also introduced Greer Garson to the screen. Although only seen for a few minutes' running time the impression she made was strong enough to guarantee a lengthy Hollywood career.

What really made the three MGM films stand out from most British films of the time was their technical superiority. They had been made with the gloss and skill of the Hollywood film industry and proved that British technicians under proper guidance could produce work as polished as the Americans. Had the brief MGM period continued, the subsequent story would have been substantially different for all three films had made money, not only in England but in many other countries.

Output in other studios during the two or three years between the beginning of the crisis and the even more drastic upheaval of the war became erratic as the courts filled with bankrupt film men. But by no means were they completely fallow years. Korda, now ensconced in his stately Denham studios, continued extravagantly to hire his directors and stars from abroad (to say nothing of technicians: the standing joke was that the three Union Jacks outside the studios represented the three native Englishmen on the Korda payroll). [. . .] Korda also persuaded Robert Flaherty, a giant of documentary films, to make *Elephant Boy* on location with a young Indian, Sabu. Ultimately the film was finished on the backlot of Denham, with elephants pounding through the Buckinghamshire jungle, and the film is far from vintage Flaherty.

Korda's extravagance, flamboyance and penchant for employing so many foreigners, especially Hungarians, aroused xenophobic passions among certain sections of the public, and articles appeared denouncing him as the cause of the British film crisis. Undoubtedly Korda was a brilliant and magnetic force in the cinema. Like many dynamic men he could not do things by halves, and that included his failures which were inevitably more spectacular and more catastrophic than anyone else's. His genius was persuasive and when he turned on the charm even his bitterest enemies melted. Korda rode out the storm with the skill with which he was to survive many others before the end of his career. It was plain that no man had been so successful in raising the British flag in other countries. Like many other exiles who have settled in Britain he was motivated by a patriotism far more passionate than that of many Englishmen.

Herbert Wilcox, born in County Cork, Ireland, has also throughout his long career vigorously waved the British flag. His exultantly triumphant *Victoria the Great* arose from a request by the Duke of Windsor during the brief period in 1936 when he occupied the throne as King

Edward VIII. Alexander Korda was for once left at the post. The film was shot in five weeks, a remarkably short time for such a subject, with Anna Neagle playing the Queen and Anton Walbrook Prince Albert. Its treatment was episodic, being based on Laurence Housman's *Victoria Regina*, which was more a series of sketches based on Victoria's life than a play. The film was exhibited to the public at a psychologically appropriate time, and Britain, troubled by a worsening European situation, gladly revelled in a frenzy of nostalgic imperialism. Wilcox followed up the film with *Sixty Glorious Years*, which was the same mixture as before, except that the Royal Family granted permission for certain sequences to be shot at Balmoral, and the whole film was made in Technicolour. [. . .]

Michael Powell, a prolific but unnoticed director of the early thirties, shot an impressive film on location on the Scottish island of Foula, *The Edge of the World*, outstanding for its dramatic photography which captured the quality of the northern climate and the beauty and grandeur of rocks and wild seas. Until then Powell's work had been mainly in quickies, but with this film he revealed himself as a front runner in the new British realist school which was to emerge properly in the wartime forties. An important film of 1937, again set in Scotland, but of a rather more amusing nature, was *Storm in a Teacup* with Rex Harrison and Vivien Leigh, directed by Victor Saville and Ian Dalrymple. In spite of the axiom that 'satire is what closes Saturday night' this film was very successful as well as witty, and demonstrated that British film comedy could sometimes work with subtlety.

In the broader vein George Formby and Gracie Fields continued to be at the top of the box-office popularity ratings. George Formby was a comedian who had adapted particularly well to films, most of which were constructed to a prescribed formula — George trying to hold a job down in spite of appalling disasters beyond his control and trying also to win the girl in the face of opposition from a handsome, accomplished rival. There was always room for a song or two with the banjo (always called a ukelele) and a regular number of hurled pies, whitewash buckets and paint cans. A chase or a sequence in which a machine goes out of control, such as the RAF aerobatic plane in *It's in the Air*, was also mandatory. Most of the George Formby films were directed by Anthony Kimmins, later succeeded by Marcel Varnel, who at this time was concentrating on Will Hay and the Crazy Gang. Varnel's 1937 near-masterpiece of comic film-making was *Oh Mr Porter!* in which Will Hay played an appalling country stationmaster, with Moore Marriott and Graham Moffatt as unco-operative platform staff. Will Hay had a particular skill in evoking sympathy even for the incompetent scoundrels he usually played. In the following year he appeared in *Convict 99* and in a parody, *Old Bones of the River*, as a schoolmaster, attempting the Leslie Banks role of the earlier film. Films such as these were not noted for the amounts spent on them but they moved at a crisp pace and demanded little from their audiences beyond the ability to enjoy a good laugh. They were particularly popular in northern England and cinema managers knew that they could pack in bigger audiences than many of the best Hollywood pictures.

Alfred Hitchcock, whose days at Gaumont-British ended with *Sabotage*, made *Young and Innocent (The Girl Was Young* in America), an engaging comedy thriller with Derrick de Marney and Nova Pilbeam, for Gainsborough, which continued in business when GB production was suspended. It was that favourite Hitchcock theme, the double chase, with innocent hero, searching for the real value, pursued by the law. At the climax of the film Hitchcock inserted a phenomenal example of his technical bravura, a long shot of a crowded ballroom with a tracking camera ending in a big close-up of a musician's twitching eye, all in one sweep. Hitchcock's last film that properly belongs in the tradition of the Gaumont-British thrillers, although made by Gainsborough at Islington, was *The Lady Vanishes*. A spy thriller set in a mythical mid-European country, it starred Margaret Lockwood, who was becoming the leading young British heroine, and Michael Redgrave. Because of a distribution deal with MGM this film was given a much wider screening abroad and earned a large amount of foreign currency, ensuring Hitchcock's commanding reputation as the best-known British director. Shortly after this film was made he left GB and Gainsborough altogether with the expiry of his contract, and signed a new one with David O. Selznick to go to Hollywood to make *Rebecca*. [. . .]

One director whose work was now attracting critical attention was Carol Reed, who had managed to make an episodic collection of experiences of English holiday-makers into a warm, amusing and well observed film. *Bank Holiday* was the prototype for many post-war pictures which showed the fabric of life in holiday camps, stations and airports. There had to be a typical working-class couple (Kathleen Harrison gave the first performance of her well-known 'mum' figure in *Bank Holiday*), a girl out for a good time who nearly comes to a sticky end before she realizes the folly of her ways (Margaret Lockwood) and a plausible young man (Hugh Williams). Carol Reed managed to rise above potentially banal material and confirmed the promise he had shown in *Laburnum Grove* in 1937. Another picture which also fitted into the new pattern of sociological observation was Victor Saville's *South Riding*, from the novel by the tragic young author Winifred Holtby dealing with local politics in a Yorkshire country town; this starred Edmund Gwenn, Ralph Richardson and Edna Best. It was con-structed with an eye turned to the realism of the documentary film movement, and its climax was a real event, the Coronation, as seen by the local inhabitants. *This Man Is News*, directed by David MacDonald, with Barry K. Barnes, Alastair Sim and Valerie Hobson, was also an extremely well constructed film with a pace and energy that reflected credit on its writers, Roger MacDougall (who later became a successful playwright) and Alan Mackinnon. A sequel was demanded and the same team went on to make *This Man in Paris*. And as the threat of war became reality Michael Powell recalled the 1914-18 conflict in a well directed picture, *The Spy in Black*, with Conrad Veidt and Valerie Hobson, which dealt with a crisis of conscience in a German U-boat commander.

After Michael Balcon's brief career at MGM had come to an end he became in 1938 a partner with Reginald Baker in a company called Balford, whose purpose was to turn out good programme films at Ealing Studios. On the resignation of Basil Dean, Balcon became head of production at Ealing and started one of the most consistent and worthwhile of all the British film factories. The first picture, *Gaunt Stranger*, had its West End showing as a second feature, but the second, *The Ware Case*, drew more attention. *There Ain't No Justice*, a low-budget boxing exposé, was an incisive examination of the prize-fighting world and marked out the twenty-seven-year-old director, Pen Tennyson, as a most promising socially-minded film-maker. Tennyson's next film for Balcon, *The Proud Valley*, was actually a plea for the nationalization of the coal industry, although it starred the powerful-voiced Negro singer Paul Robeson. It would have been easy for the film to have had a soft centre with such a performer in the lead, yet it retained a trenchant viewpoint. Unfortunately, Tennyson was killed early in the war and made only three films. But on the basis of these, it would be fair to assume that had he lived he would have become one of the most prominent of British directors. *There Ain't No Justice* was greatly under-rated when it was released in 1939 and failed to make money, possibly because it received a very poor distribution.

And so a period not only of British films but a whole way of life came to a close. After September 1939 some changes would be abrupt, some gradual, but hardly anything would remain as it was. It is said that the film industry fell into the same habits as other media of communication and produced little that could be interpreted as comment on the world situation. No films about the Nazi menace were made before the war; British films kept a silence as close-lipped as any of the appeasers, and spared the German government from the embarrassment of criticism. Even documentaries did not look at the menace threatening the entire world; it was left to the American series *The March of Time* to produce a journalistic account of the events inside Germany, which was frowned upon by the British Board of Film Censors. Similarly the

British cinema had nothing to say about the Spanish Civil War, which raged from 1936 onwards. Undoubtedly, commercial pressures prevented a more serious cinema emerging and the feeling that messages were for Western Union was applied as vigorously to British output as to that of Hollywood. The picture palace with its neon façade and gilded auditorium represented for most of the thousands who flocked to it week by week an escape from reality into a fantasy world. The British cinema was a lesser version of Hollywood, with men like Korda, Wilcox, Balcon, Saville, Hitchcock demonstrating that their mastery of it as an entertainment medium was equal to that of the Americans. But with fewer resources, a smaller market and a succession of crises it was impossible for the imitation to come anything more than a very bad second place. If there was an essential British cinema it was an observation of the British people in close-up; the beginnings were there already in *Bank Holiday*, in *South Riding*, in *There Ain't No Justice*, in *Storm in a Teacup*, even in the films of Gracie Fields and George Formby. Here had been found an area in which the British film could develop a uniqueness that borrowed nothing from Hollywood. But bread and butter has always counted in the cinema for more than social consciences, and survival depended on *The Four Feathers* and *Victoria the Great* and *Pygmalion*; it was the box-office subject which could equally well have emerged from the studios of Hollywood that drew audiences and profits.

Possibly the industry was at fault in trying so hard to follow in American footsteps, rather than develop its own indigenous style. But to condemn it on these grounds is to ignore the nature of the problems endured before war. Had the decision been made when the bubble burst to concentrate on small, low-budget films that had an even chance of making a profit, it is possible that in time feature-film production would have collapsed. On the other hand, that might have happened anyway if the war had not, paradoxically, while closing down studios and recruiting its workers for the armed forces, brought an unexpected salvation from the hard time that had undoubtedly been coming since 1937. The conditions of wartime provided the film industry with a proper role to play in the national life, and the challenge was taken up, producing a miraculous transformation in content, style, subject matter and aesthetics. At last British film had matured and could pass into its golden age of the forties.

8 SERVING THE NATION: PUBLIC SERVICE BROADCASTING BEFORE THE WAR

Paddy Scannell and David Cardiff

Source: Specially written for this Reader. Copyright © The Open University.

The history of the foundation of broadcasting in Britain is the history of a single institution — the British Broadcasting Corporation. Its general characteristics are well known. It enjoyed a monopoly of broadcasting until the state permitted commercial television in 1954 and commercial radio in 1972. It had a guaranteed revenue from the licence fee, freeing it from commercial pressure and the exigencies of profits. It was established as a service operating in the public interest, and was animated from the beginning by a high sense of moral purpose which it realised in giving an educational and cultural lead to its listening public. But how and why broadcasting took these specific forms and objectives are questions that this article considers.

Broadcasting and the State

Control of wireless technologies rested with the state. When telegraphy was first invented, the Telegraphy Act (1869) was passed giving the Postmaster General exclusive right to transmit telegrams. Later his powers were extended to the licensing of wireless transmitters and receivers, forcing radio hams to buy a licence from the Post Office (Wedell, 1968, p. 56). In the early 1920s the Post Office was faced with demands from wireless manufacturers, who had begun to see the large-scale possibilities, for permission to broadcast. The Post Office, to avoid a decision between rival interests and anxious to avoid the confusion of the American 'chaos of the ether', persuaded the manufacturers to merge into a single cartel to whom the Postmaster General could grant a licence to broadcast. In the end they did, and formed the British Broadcasting Company, licensed to broadcast in 1922, with a working capital of £60,000 and revenues derived from the ten shilling licence fee for a receiver payable to the Post Office (half of which went to the Company), and from a percentage of the royalties on the receiving sets sold by the manufacturers (*BBC Handbook*, 1928, p. 37). Parliament had decided that only one licence to broadcast should be granted at any one time, so the Company was granted an exclusive licence to broadcast

161

for two years. This was extended for another two years after an official commission of inquiry (the Sykes Commission) had recommended that although the state should regulate broadcasting, it should not itself operate the broadcasting system. In 1925 the Crawford Committee, set up to examine the future of broadcasting, rejected free and uncontrolled broadcasting for profit (the American system) and a service directly controlled and operated by the state (Briggs, 1961, p. 330). It proposed that broadcasting be conducted by a Public Corporation acting as a trustee for the national interest, and consisting of a Board of Governors responsible for seeing that Broadcasting was carried out as a public service (*Sound and TV services*, 1964, pp. 2-3). It further recommended that the British Broadcasting Company was a fit body for such a task, and the Company duly became a Corporation in January 1927. Its Managing Director, John Reith, became the first Director General.

The BBC began to operate under the authority of two documents, each granted for ten years: the Charter, which prescribed the objectives of the Corporation, how it should function, its internal organisation, its financial arrangements; and the Licences and General Agreement between the Corporation and the Postmaster General. This allowed the BBC to establish broadcasting stations subject to the Post Office's technical conditions relating to wavelength and the power of transmitters. It prevented the BBC from broadcasting advertisements or sponsored material, and defined the percentage of the licence fee to be received by the Corporation. The state reserved the right to appoint (and dismiss if necessary) the Board of Governors; it also reserved an ultimate control over the BBC in the right to veto any material to be broadcast by the Corporation. In practice this power has seldom been used, and the BBC has usually been granted autonomy in its day to day programming and policies.

In normal times the state keeps the BBC on its toes not through the threat of direct intervention but in a number of indirect ways. First, the BBC has never had the right to broadcast in perpetuity. Its licence has always been granted for strictly limited periods (usually ten years), and its performance has always been subject to review. Various committees have reported on its progress and made recommendations, and to this date the Charter has always been renewed. The effect has been perpetually to remind the BBC of its dependence upon the state. Second, the state controls the purse strings; only it can increase the licence fee, about which it can of course prevaricate if displeased with the Corporation. Lastly, it controls the governing body of the BBC — the Board of Governors — which it can fill as it chooses.

The BBC was not, however, defined simply by the Conservative Government of the day. When John Reith became manager in 1922 the company became active in its own definition. In *Broadcast over Britain*, written in 1924, Reith laid down unequivocally his concept of the BBC's role in broadcasting, and underlined the implications: 'It would not have been difficult', he declared, 'to make the service a clearing house for sensationalism.' But he and his colleagues had a high conception of the new medium's potential: 'Our responsibility is to carry into the greatest possible number of homes everything that is best in every human department of knowledge, endeavour and achievement, and to avoid the things which are, or may be, hurtful.' Reith was perfectly well aware of the implications of all this. The BBC was not merely a monopoly in a business sense, but a cultural dictatorship with the BBC as arbiter of tastes and definer of standards: 'It is occasionally represented to us that we are apparently setting out to give the public what we think they need, and not what they want, but few know what they want, and very few what they need. There is often no difference . . . Better to overestimate the mentality of the public than to underestimate it' (Reith, 1924, p. 37).

This side of Reith's concept of public service broadcasting as cultural enlightenment is well known. What has largely been forgotten, however, was his equal concern in those days to establish a genuine political independence for radio so that it might effectively realise its potential as an agent of a more informed and enlightened democracy. Through its universal availability, its capacity to relay important political events 'live' and as they happened, all members of society might have access to the processes that ruled their lives. The live coverage of the daily proceedings of the House of Commons was an idea widely canvassed in the BBC between 1924 and 1926. But more than that, by raising the level of knowledge, by presenting informed and balanced debate amongst political leaders, experts and authorities on the political and social issues of the day, radio might make an important contribution to the formation of a more informed and educated public opinion, a more active and participatory democracy:

Broadcasting brings relaxation and interest to many homes where such things are at a premium. It does far more; it carries direct information on a hundred subjects to innumerable people who thereby will be enabled not only to take more interest in events which formerly were outside their ken, but who will after a short time be in a position to make up their own minds on many matters of vital moment, matters which formerly they had either to receive according to the dictated and partial versions and opinions of others, or to ignore altogether. A new and mighty weight of public opinion is being formed, and an intelligent concern on many subjects will be manifested in quarters now overlooked. I have heard it argued that, insofar as broadcasting is awakening interest in these hitherto more or less sheltered or inaccessible regions, it is fraught with danger to the community and to the country generally. In other words, I gather that it is urged that a state of ignorance is to be preferred to one of enlightenment . . . To disregard the spread of knowledge, with the consequent enlargement of opinion, and to be unable to supplement it with reasoned arguments, or to supply satisfactory answers to legitimate and intelligent questions, is not only dangerous but stupid (Reith, 1924, pp. 18-19).

Such arguments, which are to be found a little later in John Grierson's claims for the role of documentary film for instance, were based on a realisation that there was now, and for the first time, since the vast extension of the franchise in 1918, a truly mass electorate, the majority of whom possessed no formal schooling beyond the age of about fourteen.

Reith's efforts to secure the spread of knowledge and the enlargement of opinion were constantly checked and thwarted between 1924 and 1927. He wanted greater freedom for the company in the areas of news, talks and outside broadcasts to give listeners access to the political processes and debates of the day. In all these areas he was hampered and blocked by the powerful vested interests of the press and press agencies, the Post Office and the government, frequently acting in concert.

The General Strike (May 1926) brought all these issues to a head. That the BBC sided with the government in the matter is well known. It had no option. To have done otherwise would have jeopardised the very continuance of the Company and the new charter and licence, now nearing final preparation, which would transform it into the Corporation. Reith had worked energetically to persuade committees of inquiry, the Post Office and his own board of directors of the need to change the status and constitution of broadcasting. He had done so in the belief that it would bring a genuine freedom not only from commercial interests, but also from the restraints imposed till then by the state. He even hoped that by proving the 'responsibility' of broadcasting during the strike he would at last win the right to deal fully with the controversial political and industrial issues of the time. When he read the draft terms of the charter in late 1926 he was filled with anger and dismay. Controversial broadcasting and editorial news comment (the latter enjoyed briefly, in the absence of the daily press, during the strike) were expressly forbidden, and considerable chunks of the revenue from licence fees were to be pocketed by the state. Reith immediately tried to get these terms reversed, but the Postmaster General simply went behind his back and blackmailed Lord Clarendon (chairman-designate of the new Board of Governors) into signing the documents with the simple threat of sign or be sacked. When finally the charter and licence were publicly released as 'agreed documents' Reith's indignation knew no bounds. He felt betrayed both by the government and the Chairman of his new board (cf. Briggs, 1961, pp. 354-60).

Thus it must be recognised that when the form and content of broadcasting took on a more settled and permanent form in the late twenties and across the thirties, what came together then was not in any sense a simple realisation and fulfilment of an initial conception of radio's social and political role in national life. In the process of continuing struggle and negotiation (particularly between 1924 and 1927) initial aspirations and intentions were modified, readjusted or thwarted. It was the government who set the terms for the Corporation, whose subsequent history was in part an accommodation to and acceptance of those terms. The independence of the BBC has always been a strictly *relative* autonomy; for while it has seldom been directly interfered with by governments (though the number of instances is greater than might be supposed), it has had to live constantly with the certain knowledge that if its activities should seriously irritate or anger the state, it can be brought to heel by a variety of direct or indirect pressures.

Towards a National System of Broadcasting

Between 1922 and 1924 19 'main' and 'relay' stations had been set up in strategically populous centres of England, Wales and Scotland. Between them they provided a service for nearly 80 per cent of the population. A network system was introduced, whereby local stations could take, via Post Office trunk lines, 'simultaneous broadcasts' of news and important programmes (a symphony concert, a talk by a national figure) from the London station. Alternatively any one station in the network might 'feed' the rest with one of its own local products. Thus Cardiff's rather successful Christmas panto, *Singbad the Wailer* (1925), was given a repeat performance on the network, 'flu permitting'!

The nine main stations in these early years produced most of their own material, with relay stations, supplied largely by London, producing a much smaller percentage of their own programmes. Their budgets were limited, and they very much depended upon what they could find locally in the way of talent (often amateur) or interest to make up their programmes. Inevitably they developed in themselves and in the areas they served a considerable degree of local pride. Their relations with the audiences they served were cosy and remarkably informal compared with radio a decade later. There were quiz programmes, competitions with cash prizes and even phone-in request programmes. In spite of difficulties in finding enough material to fill the hours each day; in spite of technical hitches (of which there were many); in spite of a growing trend towards duplication, the stations had each in their own way adapted themselves to the areas they served, and offered not only entertainment but a public service to their community of a rather different kind to what was shortly to be installed in the reorganised system of distribution.

When Leeds put on a charity concert for ailing children, when Liverpool ran a series about the city past and present during its Civic Week, or when Sheffield let its university students put on a show in aid of local hospitals during rag week – these were unemphatic instances of a kind of local public service, rooted in the community, performed by radio in its infancy which has scarcely yet been recovered. Something valuable was lost, though it was hardly recognised at the time except by local people, in the growing centralisation of control and production in London, and in the decision to change the system of distribution which began to take shape there in 1925-6.

In Reith's mind *unity* of control (the monopoly) and *centrality* of control (in London) were inextricably linked. Unity of control, the absence of competition, allowed for the rapid, efficient and planned expansion of broadcasting. That was to be effectively secured by the imposition of a set of policies, a concept of public service, upon the whole system by a small nucleus of decision-makers headed by Reith and based in Head Office. The overriding argument in favour of central control was that it was ethically essential in order that 'one general policy may be maintained throughout the country and definite standards promulgated' (Memorandum of Information, 1925). This meant bringing all stations in line. Ultimately it meant their elimination. The regime of control was to replace informality by a studied formality; to replace local variety and differences by a standardised conception of culture and manners; to replace audience participation by a more distanced, authoritative and prescriptive approach to broadcasting; to replace ordinary people and amateur performers in the studios by 'authorities', 'experts' and 'professionals'. The diversity of the individual stations, and the sometimes heterodox activities of their directors, were carefully brought to heel.

By 1930 local radio had vanished. In its place was the National Programme from London and the Regional Programme produced from five centres serving the Midlands, North, South, West and Scotland (later Wales and Northern Ireland were added). This reorganisation, planned from 1925 onwards, was based on a number of factors. For technical and economic reasons it made better sense to concentrate on a smaller number of stations with high-powered transmitters to extend reception to the whole of Great Britain, rather than to go on adding to the number of local stations. Second, to allay the obvious criticism of the monopoly (that it restricted choice) it was necessary to provide listeners with an alternative choice of programmes. But thirdly, and in the end most crucially, this greater unity and centrality of control permitted a more effective organisation of programme output to fit the concept of public service broadcasting.

In essence two different concepts of culture were articulated in the National and Regional programmes. The London service, in line with Matthew Arnold's ideal of 'sweetness and light', would provide the 'best' in music, talks and drama and entertainment. This ideal of cultural enlightenment operated within a larger ideology of nationalism, for the best meant the best of British. This was easily invoked in the domains of literature and drama, less so in the case of music. In this sphere the BBC sought actively to raise Britain from being a 'third class' musical nation to one that would bear comparison with other more evidently 'musical' European nations. The regional service, rooted in provincial centres which could not match (so it was assumed) the quality that London could tap, offered culture, in Williams's phrase, as 'a way of life'. It was intended to reflect the everyday life and variety of the areas it served.

It should not be thought that this system was either intended, or ever worked, as an equitable balance of forces between London and the rest of the country, between metropolitan and provincial interests and needs. The National Programme was, in every sense, the senior service, with the regions very much as juniors. There were frictions and tensions throughout the thirties between the dominant cultural prescriptions of London, and the subordinated (but insubordinate) intentions of the regions. One example must serve to illustrate the point. In the mid-thirties London had scheduled a Sunday concert conducted by Casals and ordered all regional stations to take this 'top quality' programme unless there were very good reasons for not doing so. North Region had already filled this slot with a concert by a Merseyside group of un-employed musicians. They were very reluctant to drop this broadcast, which they believed was of great *social* importance for the region, in spite of strong pressure from London urging the *cultural* importance of Casals. In the end North Region had its way (cf. Briggs, 1965, p. 328), but in this one area of music a host of other incidents – most notably over regional orchestras – might be cited to add substance and detail to the differences and tensions between 'the margins' and 'the centre'.

The unceasing production and reproduction of material for trans-mission was a central problem of programme organisation and planning once the overall character of the channel had been determined. By the end of the 1920s the BBC had settled down to a pattern of broadcasting that remained unchanged until the outbreak of war – a policy of mixed programming both in the national channel and the regional alternative. Mixed programming offered a wide and diverse range of programme materials over the course of each day and week. Typically it included news, drama, sport, religion, music (light to classical), variety or light entertainment. Not only did it cater for different social needs (education, information, entertainment), but for different sectional interests within the listening public (children, women, businessmen, farmers, fishermen, etc.).

The sum of the material transmitted on such a channel may be seen as amounting to a socio-cultural universe (a complete world) because the overall content or repertoire appears *exhaustive*; what lies outside the catchment of the channel (what is *not* broadcast) is not part of the 'normal' range of the social experience and needs of the audience as expressed in the sum of its contents. Thus the various single elements in the channel (the separate programmes) reveal their social significance when considered as a whole. Separately, the programmes point to different social needs and different listening publics; collectively, they reveal how the broadcasters conceived of the audience as a whole.

Any broadcasting channel is based on a set of assumptions about the particular audience for whom its bill of fare is intended; an audience which is constructed and continuously reproduced in the individual programmes and the overall repertoire that makes up the contents of the channel. Wireless reception, from its earliest days, had been naturalised as part of private, not public, life. The radio in the living-room was part of the furniture of domestic everyday existence. It was in this context that the BBC recognised and addressed its audience, not as an aggregated totality (a mass audience) but a constellation of individuals positioned in families. The home was an enclave, a retreat burrowed deeply away from the pressures of work and urban living, with radio as part of that cosy, domestic warmth. The social level of the ordinary English family, as typified in many instances, was within the lower and middle reaches of the middle class: Acacia Avenue or Laburnum Grove, the tree-lined suburbs of Greater London and the Home counties.

Radio, it was felt, enlarged and enriched the sphere of private life, linking it to the public world and its discourses, broadening horizons, extending informally the education of family members and providing them with new topics of conversation (cf. Jennings and Gill, 1939). The 'listener-in' was recognised as carrying a range of social interests and needs, as inhabiting a particular local community, as having domestic and social responsibilities both in the home and in the community; and beyond that as having a role to play – a more public role as 'citizen' – in the larger community of public affairs and national life.

The BBC saw its audience both as a unity and a diversity. It presumed a 'national community' whose general interests the BBC had a duty to serve: moreover it must always be the case that 'the general needs of the community come before the sectional' (*BBC Yearbook*, 1933, p. 37). As for those sectional needs (whether political – as between different legitimated parties; or regional — as between different areas of the country; or cultural — as between high-, middle- or low-brow tastes) the BBC regarded itself as an impartial arbiter between their various claims, assessing their relative importance and catering for them accordingly. These policies were based on the basic principle 'that broadcasting should be operated on a national scale, for national service and by a single national authority' (*Yearbook*, ibid., p. 14).

The Determinations of Programmes

In this brief synoptic account of the social and political formation of broadcasting it is not possible to offer more than a hint of the rich, dense and complex histories of the major categories of programme output in all production centres, regional and national. Each area of production has its own history that must be grasped in its own terms and in relation to what is simultaneously taking place in other areas of output. The histories of talks, or news, or music (to take major instances) register separately and relatedly the continuing and conscious search for new and appropriate methods of production and styles of presentation — a process that is always and necessarily subject to a complex range of determinations; an ever shifting play of forces — external and internal — upon the level of production itself.

External pressures include those exerted by all the apparatuses and departments of the state and by the major political parties; by various lobbies and pressure groups (e.g. the press; entrepreneurs in the entertainment industries; composers, performers and music publishers . . . etc. etc.) defending interests which appear to them to be threatened by the activities of radio; and lastly, by the audience. More particularly they come from different (and antagonistic) 'taste publics' — dance band fans who complain of too much high-brow music, versus the 'serious' musical public who deplore the vulgarity of jazz, crooners etc. who flood the ether. More broadly they are from the general level of social, political and cultural 'tolerance', the normative (consensual) field of values, attitudes, beliefs and tastes to which broadcasting must be ever alert and sensitive as it partly adjusts to correspond with these dispositions and partly seeks to transform them.

Within the BBC economic, technical and staff resources in part constrain the limits of the practicable at any one time, but the major internal determination of production is shaped by the division of labour within the institution. Once established in 1927 as the Corporation, as a national broadcasting institution, the BBC embarked on the consolidation and expansion of its institutional position within the established social and political order. When Reith resigned as Director General in

1938 one newspaper congratulated him for making the BBC into a national institution as thoroughly typical and representative as the Bank of England — i.e. safe, responsible and reliable, a bed-rock guarantor of the nation's 'cultural capital', of the existing order of things. The question is *how*, by what material processes, was this achieved?

It was done through a careful and unceasing attention to all aspects of the organisation of the system of distribution, to the character of the programme channels, and lastly, crucially, to the form, content and presentation of the repertoire of material that filled those channels. Programmes remain the final register and bearers of institutional intentions and assumptions about the scope and purposes of broadcasting and about the audiences to whom they speak. Programmes are the highly determinate end products of broadcasting; they are the point of exchange between the producing institution and society. Judgements of the adequacy or otherwise of broadcasting's efforts are always, and rightly, based on them. So it was through the control of policy in relation to all aspects of programme output that the task of securing acceptance and recognition of the claims and status of broadcasting was performed.

The implementation of a coherent, corporate programme policy began in the days of the company, but was greatly accelerated thereafter. It required the establishment of more authoritative styles and modes of address in the announcing and presentation of programmes; the pursuit of social and cultural prestige in the fields of music and talks especially; the arbitration of the claims of different taste publics in a single national channel; the trimming of the wayward tendencies of individual programme makers or departments; the moulding of each area of output into the bearer of an articulate set of intentions and prescriptions, consonant with the ongoing work of other areas, collectively working together to produce, in a complex unity, the corporate ethos of public service broadcasting in the national interest.

To these ends Reith, in the early thirties, undertook the thorough reorganisation of the running of the BBC. The intention and effects of the changes he introduced were to remove control over programme decisions from the programme makers, and to deliver it into the hands of a small, elite nucleus of senior administrators and planners who now, in consultation with Reith or on their own initiative, determined the overall policy objectives of the BBC. By the mid-thirties the control of programming had slipped from the level of production to the newly installed level of administration. This was not achieved then, or ever after, simply and smoothly. To bring production in line new personnel were brought in from outside to establish orthodoxy; departments were split up, regrouped or dismantled; 'progressives' were eased out of programme making by 'promotion' or sending them elsewhere.

In the mid-thirties the BBC was a troubled, unhappy place in which to work. It was riven by internal feuds and rivalries; by dissatisfactions with conditions and terms of employment, pay and promotion; by the lack of adequate mechanisms for bargaining and negotiating on these matters; by corporate meddling in the private affairs of staff members (to get divorced, or to be cited as co-respondent in divorce proceedings was to court dismissal); by the growing gap between rulers and ruled within the institution. By the end of the decade programme makers had become, in the phrase of one contemporary, 'the creative helots' of broadcasting. They had begun to learn the rules, to recognise 'what goes' and what does not, to accept the limits of the possible, to develop routines and strategies that would protect their flanks and smooth their way to a less troubled life within the institution. 'Referral up' became a standard practice − i.e. seeking 'guidance' and official clearance from senior personnel on potentially 'sensitive' subjects. Greater care was now taken to anticipate in advance the likely impact of programmes on those influential quarters that might take exception to them and kick up a public fuss. Programme proposals from producers were now tempered by an inbuilt sense of what might be acceptable to the rulers of the BBC. In early 1939, for instance, Lawrence Gilliam (in charge of Features, London) floated the idea of a topical series on the lines of the American *March of Time* programmes. He recognised that for policy reasons the major political events of the time would be out of court, but still felt this left a vast field of non-controversial issues which could be worked up into a regular features series. 'If we can prove to the authorities that we can tap a new source of topical features, without running them into a lot of trouble, we can go a long way to filling one of the Corporation's biggest gaps − that is, topicality' (Gilliam to Midland Region Director, 1 March 1939). A them/us mentality, producers trying to steer their way round the authorities by adapting their ideas to what 'they' might accept, had become a reflex way of thinking.

The play of all these forces, upon and within broadcasting, comes to bear on the level of production. They are the real, material determinants that constrain and shape what is finally delivered to audiences. A full and detailed examination of these processes at work in all major areas of programmes cannot here be attempted. Three brief sketches of some of the work of the Talks, News and Variety departments must serve to give substance to the bones of these arguments.

Talks and Controversy

In 1928, after further pressure from Reith, the government agreed to lift the ban on the broadcasting of controversial matter for an experimental period. Though it never subsequently happened, it was made quite clear at the time to the BBC that it was on probation, and that this new freedom might be revoked if it was not discharged with due responsibility. The lifting of this ban brought the Talks Department forward as a crucially sensitive area of programme output, for upon it now devolved the delicate task of finding new ways and means for the balanced presentation of contentious political, economic and social issues. It is not surprising that it dipped its toes into the chilly waters of controversy gingerly at first.

It would begin by the gradual and experimental introduction of political and economic controversy on clearly defined occasions with adequate safeguards for impartiality and equality of treatment. Religion would still remain, by Reith's fiat, outside the pale of strife. Apart from straight talks or lectures by individual speakers two other methods of handling controversy were favoured. The first method was to hold debates in which the topics should be carefully worded so there would be some inherent equality in the contending opinions. The debaters should be well matched and balanced. The other method was 'the discussion', defined as 'challenging and opposing points of view expounded in prepared statements in sequence' (*BBC Handbook*, 1929, p. 41: cf. Cardiff, 1980, pp. 36-40). Gradualism was the watchword. Controversy would not dominate the activities of the talks department. For the most part it would continue to graze in safer pastures, 'to interpret the vast field of interests and knowledge which is happily beyond the frontiers of acute current partisanship' (*Handbook*, ibid.).

By 1931 Britain was in the throes of political and economic crisis, both a result of the catastrophic world-wide slump in trade. As the effects of the recession bit deeper the department took the plunge. Major series on housing, unemployment, trade unions, modern industry (from the employee's point of view) and 'the condition of England' question addressed themselves to the urgent problems of the day. Under the direction of Hilda Matheson (1927-31) and Charles Siepmann (1932-5) the talks department shared a common commitment to radio as a new social form of communication, and a common interest in developing new and effective means of communication via the spoken word. These talks series introduced new and direct methods of social reportage: eye-witness, first-hand accounts by BBC staff 'observers' of slum conditions in Glasgow, Tyneside and the East End; the unemployed themselves at the microphone to describe what it was like living on the dole. Through such programmes radio now began to enter into the very fabric of political life, becoming material evidence — appropriate as ammunition in quite contradictory ways by government, political parties and audiences — for debate and controversy.

For Hilda Matheson they demonstrated and confirmed the social role of broadcasting as a mediating agency between the state and the people; they were a means of bridging the gulf between expert and citizen, and of reducing the awkward time-lag between perceiving a remedy and making it understood. What they more exactly did, through exposing the very urgency of the problems, was to point to the inadequacies of the remedies proposed by the National Government which was far removed from Matheson's idealistic conception of 'the modern state' (she had, like a true progressive of that time, the model of Stalin's Russia in mind) (cf. Matheson, 1933, pp. 95-7). What was not anticipated was the extent to which such series, on housing and unemployment particularly, might affront the ignorance and prejudices of the middle-class listening public or tread on official toes. There was an increasing rumble in the Conservative Party and in the popular press that the talks department was run by a bunch of lefties, a view which Reith increasingly shared (for a full account of these issues cf. Scannell, 1980).

Things came to a head in 1935, a year in which the BBC, its charter and licence up for renewal, was under the scrutiny of a government committee of inquiry (the Ullswater Committee). At such a time Reith did not want trouble in the ranks for there were quite enough complaints and criticisms (particularly on regional and musical policies) floating around in the various submissions, written and verbal, to the committee from lobbies and pressure groups. In the summer a second major reshuffle took place in the BBC which firmly installed a new hierarchy of administrators and planners in charge of programme planning and policy. At the same time the talks department was dismantled and key members of staff were 'promoted' to posts which took them a very long way from Broadcasting House (New York, India or Manchester). Later in the year the BBC was compelled by the Cabinet and the Foreign Office, against the unanimous will of the Board of Governors and the General Advisory Committee, to cancel a major talks series, *The Citizen and His Government*, because it included a Fascist (Oswald Moseley) and a Communist (Harry Pollitt) amongst its speakers. The BBC was forbidden to make it known publicly that the Cabinet had exercised its power in this case. It must appear as a voluntary decision, 'freely' taken by the BBC in the light of the general political climate in Europe (cf. Briggs, 1979, pp. 198-201).

Hilda Matheson, who had resigned from the BBC a few years earlier in an atmosphere of intrigue and bitterness, described the dismembering of the Talks Department as 'a dispersal and disintegration unparalleled in any other department . . . which has not been without consequent loss to the common body of experience, techniques and tradition'. In the autumn of 1935, she saw signs already of 'a widespread arrested development' (cf. Matheson, 1935, pp. 512-14). For the next few years the department, confused and demoralised and lacking any decisive leadership, contented itself with safer, less controversial subjects. In the later thirties the most striking things about the work of talks (and features) in London is an *absence* – the lack of any programmes dealing with the major political and social issues of the time.

In the second half of the decade the focus of politics had shifted from internally divisive domestic issues (the recession, unemployment) to foreign affairs (the rise of Fascism, the threat of war in Europe). In the aftermath of its success in *The Citizen and His Government* affair, Chamberlain and the Foreign Office, by a discreet blend of force and persuasion, effectively prevented the BBC from giving access at the microphone to any voices opposed to the official policy of appeasement. As Hitler marched into Austria (March 1938), the talks department was running a major series called *The Ways of Peace*. By the time Munich arrived (September/October 1938) there was widespread dismay at all levels of the BBC, in the provinces as well as London, at what the ex-head of News (now Director, North Region) called 'a conspiracy of silence' in which the BBC was an increasingly unwilling and reluctant partner.

News, Press Agencies and the State

The development of the BBC's news service is an exemplary instance of the effects of external pressures on the formation of a major area of broadcast output, and of the BBC's continuous efforts to overcome them. In 1922, before the British Broadcasting Company came into being, the Post Office, the press barons and the news agencies had fixed it between them that radio would not develop its own news service in competition with the newspapers, or in any other way threaten their interests. When it began broadcasting the new company was allowed only to deliver news bulletins written and supplied, for a flat annual fee, by Reuters (incorporating material from the other agencies). These could not be broadcast before 7 p.m. to prevent them damaging the market for evening newspapers. Even under such severe restraints the BBC was able by little and little to impose something of its own ideas of 'news values', tempered by its understanding of its listening audience, upon the material supplied by the agencies. There should be no sensational stories of crime, violence or disaster; 'human interest' stories should be avoided; strict balance should be observed in the presentation of political (i.e. party) coverage.

It was the General Strike of 1926 which showed everyone – the public, the government, the opposition, the labour movement as well as the BBC – the critical importance of radio news in a moment of crisis. The BBC learnt many lessons from the strike, which had a lasting impact on its subsequent relations with, and attitudes towards, the British state. In particular it had enjoyed a brief freedom to produce – with the 'help' of the state – its own news and comment. From this moment onwards its long-term objective was to regain that freedom.

By 1930, after protracted and tortuous negotiations with Reuters, the BBC secured the right to edit and write its own news bulletins. Under the terms of a new agreement, the agencies installed their tape machines in the BBC and provided along with these the full supplementary service they offered to the press. From these sources a tiny News Section began to compose the nightly bulletins for broadcasting. Up to 1934 the news section was part of the much larger talks department who seem to have treated it in cavalier fashion as a dumping ground for short talks they could not otherwise fit into their schedules. In 1934 John Coatman was appointed to the new post of Chief News Editor. He had previously been a Professor of Economics at London University, and before that had worked in the Indian police service. His appointment not only acknowledged the increasing importance of news: he was also brought in as a right-wing offset to counterbalance the left-wing tendencies of the talks department (Briggs, 1965, p. 147). A year later, under pressure from Coatman, news became a full department in its own right.

Though Coatman himself had no journalistic experience, under his guidance, and from 1938 under R.T. Clarke (ex *Manchester Guardian*), a more fully professional approach to radio news began to develop. Staff numbers increased from six in 1934 to thirty by 1939. Journalists from the newspapers were recruited to supervise and edit Home, Foreign and Sporting news. Though the bulk of the material used in the bulletins still came from agency tapes, eye-witness reports, recorded actuality and news talks were now regular features in these years (for a useful account of this period cf. Dimbleby, 1975).

Such a brief summary conceals the continuing process of negotiation and struggle behind the scenes with press interests and the state over the nature and scope of the BBC's news service. One concession made by the charter in 1927 had been the recognition in principle of the BBC's right to establish its own news-gathering facilities. Though largely dependent on agency material throughout this period, there was, after 1927, a continuous effort to either supplement or by-pass this material by obtaining information direct from official sources. At this moment the organs of the state were themselves embarking on the systematic management and control of publicity and information for the media. The spearhead of this quite new trend was the Empire Marketing Board under Stephen Tallents (appointed as the BBC's first Public Relations Officer in 1935), though the Foreign Office had long maintained close links with the foreign correspondents of the serious press. By the early 1930s all major state departments had installed Publicity and Press Officers to release information, to organise publicity for departmental campaigns and to promote, via formal and informal channels, the policy objectives of the department (cf. PEP Report, 1938). The BBC worked hard and long to establish and maintain routine and continuous links with state departments, the Prime Minister's office and other authorities (e.g. the GLC, Scotland Yard) on the same footing as the press. Since departmental press releases were usually given in the late afternoon the BBC was advantageously placed to nip in and pick the plums for its evening bulletins ahead of the morning press. But the agencies retaliated by slapping embargoes on such releases, labelling them 'not for Broadcasting' before the following day. Across the whole of the thirties there were continuing efforts by the BBC to negotiate with agencies and the government an agreed code of practice for the classification of official publicity and news releases.

It made little headway. The government's attitudes to radio news had been formed in the General Strike. It saw it as, particularly in moments of crisis, a malleable instrument for the advancement of its own purposes. There is little doubt that in many instances the organs of government and the state, along with other authorities and powers that be, successfully 'used' the bulletins in various ways: to promote their own campaigns and projects, to 'correct' errors in press stories, and in critical moments (such as 1931) to paper over the cracks in the social structure (and official policies) by appealing for calm and national unity. The BBC was guileless in allowing itself to be so used in the early thirties. It hoped, by currying favour with the authorities, to steal a march on the agencies and newspapers. It saw itself as in partnership with the state and civil authorities in upholding the national interest and maintaining 'the settled community'.

Such complaisance must be understood, in part, as symptomatic of the political *naïveté*, compounded by the absence of any journalistic experience, of the handful of people working in news. They were grateful for any crumbs the state supplied, and petulant when it turned to feed the press instead. For if in moments of crisis the state favoured the more reliable medium of radio, in normal times it prudently favoured the senior news medium which it had wooed, cajoled or threatened for centuries. Newspapers were much better placed to kick up a public fuss than the BBC. The Corporation had yet to grasp the extent of the state's power over it, or that it might be being used by the state for purposes and policies that did not square with its own concept of service to the nation.

The loss of innocence came a few years later, over the government's appeasement policy. From mid-1937 the BBC's senior management had been making contingency plans for broadcasting in wartime based on the assumption that a European war was imminent and inevitable. By the summer of 1938 these plans, down to the fine details of wartime salaries, had been accepted by the Cabinet and ratified and agreed by the BBC's management boards. Yet all this time its public stance had been to acquiesce in Chamberlain's foreign policy and to promote the illusion that peace might still be preserved.

The Munich crisis brought this contradiction to a head. For the News Department it finally revealed the complete inadequacy of agency coverage of foreign affairs. The serious press, through its special correspondents, had provided a far fuller and more authoritative coverage of the crisis. From this moment News resolved to develop its own staff correspondents; in the meantime, it despatched what resources it had (Murray, Dimbleby and the recording van) to Czechoslovakia for up-to-the-minute reports on the aftermath of Munich. At the same time its resolve was stiffened to keep on plugging away at the truth, no matter how unpleasant. Night after night, in early 1939, the bulletins contained recorded extracts of the live speeches by Hitler and the Nazi leadership which made plain their bellicose intentions and the imminence of a European conflict. This provoked an extraordinary backlash in the Tory press. For the whole of February 1939 the letter columns of *The Times* were filled with an avalanche of angry letters attacking the tenor of radio news: scaremongering, sensationalism, a left-wing bias against Fascist countries (old charges of a similar nature against news coverage of the Spanish Civil War were frequently dug up), subverting the good efforts of the government to establish friendly relations with Germany and Italy — such were the accusations in a babble of voices as the chorus of protest swelled and became ever more shrill. Other newspapers joined in with the *Daily Mail* as usual squealing loudest. In March the press produced a spate of 'BBC Suicides', of people alleged to have killed themselves in a fit of depression after hearing the news on radio. No similar instances of press suicides were reported.

After the General Strike Reith had tried to rationalise the role of radio in the matter by arguing that 'since the BBC was a national institution, and since the Government in the crisis was acting for the people . . . the BBC was for the Government in the crisis too'. Munich was the first major crisis (Suez was another) which put to the test that syllogism as a definitive precedent for the role of the BBC in a national crisis. In this case the BBC came to see that the government, in spite of its own claims, was manifestly not acting in the national interest. Having grasped that nettle, the BBC saw its final responsibility as resting with and to the audience, not the state. It made strenuous efforts in those final months before war to alert the public to the true implications of Munich by trying to bring the opponents of appeasement (Eden and Churchill above all) to the microphone. It was prevented from so doing by the Conservative Chief Whip, by Chamberlain's Office and by the short-sighted opportunism of the Labour Party. It strove to produce talks series on home and civil defence to prepare the public for the outbreak of hostilities. Again it was largely thwarted. Between the implacable obstinacy of Chamberlain and the crass blindness of the conservative listening public, the BBC was cast in the role of Cassandra – a sooth-sayer of hateful and unpalatable truths which were doomed to go un-heeded.

Variety and Entertainment

'Let there be no idea that this category is one given grudgingly and under pressure from the public or press', wrote Reith in 1928; 'To pro-vide relaxation is no less positive an element of policy than any other' (*BBC Handbook*, 1928, p. 14). The defensive tone of the statement reflected the fact that there had indeed been public demands for an increase in the BBC's provision of entertainment. Newspapers had con-ducted somewhat unreliable polls which showed that variety and dance bands were among the most popular programmes, yet they made up a small proportion of total output. But the scarcity of light entertainment could not be ascribed entirely to the imposition of Reithian standards. It is true that limitations were placed on the amount of dance music broadcast. This could be produced cheaply; in 1934 it accounted for 9.5 per cent of the output of all stations but absorbed only 5.8 per cent of programme costs. (By way of comparison, serious music made up 14.4 per cent of output but costs amounted to nearly 30 per cent of the programme budget.) Variety, on the other hand, was the most ex-pensive category of programme. In the same year, the proportion of time devoted to vaudeville, variety, revue and musical comedy was 4.8 per cent, but the proportion of cost was 15.3 per cent. In spite of this relatively high expenditure per programme, successive Directors of Variety complained of inadequate funds. They could afford to splash out on the occasional star performer but admitted that the bulk of their acts were second-rate. They could seldom afford to commission scripts from successful writers who could command far higher fees working in film or theatre than the BBC was prepared to pay. Overworked staff writers were depended upon for much of the original material in shows.

There were further limitations. Many top variety stars could not switch from the footlights to the microphone; more significantly, they feared that on radio they would quickly exhaust their material. In the old days, the music hall stars could rely on a limited number of routines to last them for almost a lifetime. They toured the provinces giving one-night performances, and the gaps between their appearances in any one place were such that their material always seemed fresh. Radio could not tolerate such a crop rotation of variety acts. Then there were the recurring disagreements with the leading theatrical agencies, Moss Em-pires and the General Theatre Corporation, who periodically banned their contracted artists from the microphone or refused permission for relays from their stages. Even when such relays were permitted, they often made awkward broadcasting; loud applause might overpower the microphone and purely visual acts, like juggling or conjuring, were incomprehensible to listeners unless the clumsy expedient of using a commentator was adopted.

In the face of these difficulties, the BBC became determined to originate more of its own material and, if possible, to nurture its own star performers. But it was not until 1933 that a separate Variety Department was formed. Its first Director, Eric Maschwitz, adopted a number of strategies to improve the quality and range of broadcast entertainment. He moved both upmarket and downmarket in his search for new talent, recruiting stars of musical comedy, like Binnie Hale and Jessie Matthews, and at the same time exploiting the cheaper pool of talent available in Concert Party, a type of variety which had first made its appearance at seaside resorts in the 1890s. The end-of-the-pier shows made do with few props and a minimum of visual spectacle and were easily adaptable to radio. In 1932 the BBC had employed as a producer, Harry S. Pepper, who revived his father's *White Coons Concert Party* for radio. Other troupes such as the *Fol-De-Rols* and the *Air-Do-Wells* brought to the microphone fresh talents like the comedian Cyril Fletcher. There was a need for new blood. Maschwitz recognised that the BBC had come to depend too much upon a small group of radio 'regulars'. Some, like the dance band leaders Henry Hall and Jack Payne, had established a genuine national following through radio, but it was suspected that many of the comedians who had made their reputation in broadcasting were being overexposed. None of these comedians had their own shows. They were heard as individual turns in variety programmes. The true potential of radio comedy was not realised until the regular comedy series, with its stock characters and imaginary settings, began to evolve in the late 1930s.

Nevertheless Maschwitz did introduce a number of regular series which escaped from the stage conventions of the variety theatre and exploited the power of radio to evoke scenes in the listener's imagination. One of the few existing series was *Music Hall*, but the only consistent element in this show was the opening announcement and the signature tune. Each act was introduced without a trace of ballyhoo by an anonymous compère. But in 1934 Maschwitz created *Café Collette*, which featured a gypsy orchestra in the setting of a Parisian café. The 'Chef d'Orchestre' presented the show in broken English against a background of popping champagne corks and Continental chatter. It was claimed that many listeners believed that the café really existed and the format was adopted in other series. Another innovation was *In Town Tonight*, one of the earliest magazine programmes. This too began with imaginary evocation in sound; the roar of London's traffic and the flower girl murmuring 'sweet violets' supplying an appropriate frame for a medley of talks and interviews reflecting the lighter side of metropolitan life. Such programmes not only began to convince the public that radio had an original contribution to make to entertainment; they were also remarkably cheap. Much more costly were the elaborate productions in which Maschwitz indulged his taste for sophisticated revue and radio operettas with a Ruritanian flavour. These met with critical success and some were even transferred to the stage. They helped to enhance the prestige of the BBC within the entertainment profession. But listener research was subsequently to show that these were the least popular categories of light entertainment.

The BBC's output of entertainment doubled between 1933 and 1936. The Variety Department was short-staffed but relatively free from bureaucratic interference. It was based outside Broadcasting House in St George's Hall, the site of the new BBC Theatre. Here staff relations were informal; producers were not kept to office hours, nor were their private lives subjected to administrative scrutiny. They were free to initiate their own ideas for programmes. However, while the administrators had few positive suggestions to make about the content of entertainment programmes, producers were expected to work within prescribed limits.

As long as the BBC was not originating much of its own variety material, there was little it could do to impose strict cultural standards. The susceptibilities of the family audience had to be taken into account and there was constant vigilance against 'vulgarity' and 'dirt' in comedy scripts. There was some tension between London and the regions over the supposed metropolitan bias of much entertainment output. In 1930 London suggested that there was too much dialect comedy in North Region variety. The North Region Director replied fiercely that this was 'really excellent British humour' and returned the attack. 'It is of course possible that London listeners appreciate large slabs of Cockney humour and American sob-stuff. If so it is time that a corrective of some kind were supplied' (Liveing to Wellington, 17 February 1930). Throughout its existence the BBC, in its role as guardian of the national culture, had tried to resist American influences on its programmes. The danger was explicitly recognised in 1929 when the Director of Outside Broadcasting prepared a report on 'the degree to which the BBC may be affected by U.S.A. control of world entertainment'. He warned that the BBC's monopoly would not necessarily protect it from the 'ramifications of the Transatlantic octopus', since American interests were investing in Britain and would attempt to establish monopolies of performers, writers, composers, plays and copyrighted music: 'it is even possible that the national outlook and with it, character, is gradually becoming Americanised' (Cock, Memorandum on American control of the Entertainment Industry, 7 November 1929).

Although the *Radio Times* conducted a propaganda campaign disparaging the style of American commercial radio, the BBC found it difficult to supply alternatives to American popular styles and was often forced to reproduce them in a diluted and de-energised form. It asked singers not to adopt American accents, and tried to ban crooning altogether: but its efforts were hampered by the inability of the Music Department to supply a precise definition of the style to be avoided. While it could not avoid jazz rhythms, it encouraged their adulteration. Henry Hall was congratulated by the *Radio Times*: 'So tactful has he been in the compilation of his programme that he can now include an occasional "hot" number without being accused of betraying 'negroid tendencies".' Though Maschwitz might turn to the Continent for inspiration, America continued to supply the models for new shows. The Canadian Carroll Levis imported the type of amateur discovery show originated by Major Bowes in the USA. The comedy series *Danger Men At Work* was a pastiche of Marx Brothers humour. The first domestic series, *The English Family Robinson*, was inspired by American soap opera, but replaced melodrama with tepid humour and a banality of incident.

In the late 1930s a number of factors led the BBC to take a more whole-hearted approach to the supply of entertainment. Listener Research, which began in 1936, forced producers to take the differentiation of audience needs and tastes more seriously. There was a growing awareness of competition from the commercial stations on the Continent. Reith's departure early in 1938 appears to have facilitated a process of popularisation. Resistance to the routinisation of schedules began to break down. By 1937 there were as many as 40 'fixed points' in weekday output between 6.00 and 10.30 p.m. As early as 1936 the Programme Board had moved towards the 'consecutive programming' of several light items in one evening. One symptom of the change in attitudes was the introduction of audience participation shows on the American model; quizzes, spelling bees, amateur discovery shows and sing-songs. The *BBC Handbook* for 1940 noted that

> rightly or wrongly, it was being urged a year or two ago that the BBC was aloof from its listening millions, offering programmes with a complacent air of 'Take it or leave it'. These various experiments in 'Listener participation' with many others are evidence that the ice if it ever existed, has rapidly melted. New and friendlier contacts have been established on the air (*BBC Handbook*, 1940, p. 83).

The increased routinisation of schedules signalled the development of many new programmes with a serial or series format. In 1937 the Drama

Department successfully serialised *The Count of Monte Cristo*. A year earlier the BBC introduced the first variety series which rested on a repetitive formula. This was *Monday Night At Seven*, referred to at the time as a 'continuity show'. It consisted of a compendium of individual acts and regular features, bound together by a mellow-voiced 'singing commere'. The most enduring regular items were a weekly detective mystery, *Inspector Hornleigh Investigates* and the quiz, *Puzzle Corner*. There were also attempts to include short situation comedies such as *Thompson And Johnson*, a below-stairs farce involving a butler and a cook. Radio comedy came of age in 1938 with the start of a new continuity show, *Band Waggon*. This was also a compendium of items but between the acts, comedy was supplied by the 'resident comedian', Arthur Askey, and his playmate Richard Murdoch. Askey and Murdoch began to script their own material and soon evolved a method of production that could not have been applied outside radio. With a lavish and bizarre use of sound effects, they conjured up their household in the mythical flat above Broadcasting House, complete with their pets, Lewis the goat and the pigeons, Basil and Lucy. When the tenants hoovered the floor, the entire BBC Variety Orchestra, practising in the studio below, were sucked up to the ceiling. The programme was immensely popular and set the pattern for a whole tradition of British radio comedy.

Some Versions of Culture: Talks, Music and the Regions

Entertainment did not rank high on the scale of pre-war BBC values. In the more tranquil pastures of non-controversial talks the educative intentions of radio were carried through by recruiting the intelligentsia of the day to speak at the microphone. They trooped into the studios to pontificate on every subject, from 'The menace of the leisured woman' to the origin of species. Shaw, Wells, Keynes, Beveridge, the Webbs, Chesterton . . . all the great men of the day. There were very few women. They did not have, it was felt, the right microphone voice. The most portentous bid for prestige in this area were *The National Lectures* which began in 1928 and were designed

> to hold the blue ribbon of broadcasting, and to provide, on two or three occasions in the year, for the discussion of issues of major importance and the interpretation of new knowledge by men of distinction in the world of scholarship and affairs.

By 1936 greater efforts were being made to make talks less boring for the ordinary listener. New styles of presentation were developed for 'popular' as distinct from 'serious' talks as the department became more keenly aware of the stratified nature of the audience, and greater consideration was given to the point of view of 'the man in the street' (cf. Cardiff, 1980, on these points).

Dance band music, the cinema organ, musical reviews and operettas were not classified as music and were produced by the Variety Department. The Music Department dealt with serious music (symphonies, chamber music, opera and the *avant-garde*) and light classical and contemporary orchestral music. These two categories accounted, in the mid-thirties, for over 50 per cent of the output of the National Programme. There were two aspects to musical policy: to improve popular taste, and to present systematically to listeners the best music with the highest attainable standards of performance. The Music Department was more concerned with the latter; programme planners and policy makers with the former. The department showed increasing distaste for the notion of trying to popularise serious music, and preferred to address itself to what it regarded as the serious musical public. There was resentment at the ways in which the administration tried to impose 'missionary work' (i.e. reforming public taste) upon the department, which focused on the issue of 'jazzing' the classics. Official policy was prepared to countenance this distressing habit by arguing that a dance band version of a Mozart theme might lead the musically illiterate to a taste for Mozart. But the Music Department declared that jazzed classics were merely proof of the unbridgeable gulf between serious and popular music, and only confirmed the vulgar philistinism of the latter.

The pursuit of new standards of performance led to the establishment of the BBC Symphony Orchestra (1930), the first orchestra in Britain to offer full-time employment to musicians. It creamed off the best instrumentalists in the country, and provoked great hostility at first in the musical world as unfair competition. Sir Thomas Beecham and other conductors and orchestras, music publishers, teachers, entrepreneurs and performers all opposed the musical activities of the BBC as undermining active music-making, concert-going and job opportunities, though there is no evidence for the truth of any of these claims. London had considerable powers of musical patronage which it was unwilling to extend to the regions. It was argued by the regions and by Beecham and others that London's cultural monopoly was eroding the vitality of provincial music. In 1930 the size of the regional orchestras had been severely reduced, and it took considerable pressure from the regions and the musical profession to restore them to an adequate size (for details on music policy cf. Scannell, 1981).

Regional radio took some time to establish its presence, but by the mid-thirties it was showing signs of vigorous life. At its worst provincial radio lapsed into exaggerated insistence on its own identity by over-playing quaint local customs, dialect, etc. At its best it set up a quite different relationship with its audiences, more intimate and equal than the National Programme. Since its major task was the reflection of the region it served, there was a much more conscious effort to get the microphone out of the studio and into real life; and some of the major developments in radio features and documentary took place in North Region, which had the largest regional audience of all. Under the leadership of E.A. Harding, who had been 'banished' to Manchester by Reith in 1933 after making a programme which upset the Polish Ambassador, a group of talented producers and performers began to make 'actuality' feature programmes which reflected back to the audiences for whom they were made aspects of their own life and experience. In this respect the work of D.G. Bridson and Olive Shapley was outstanding. In programmes like *Harry Hopeful, Steel, Cotton, Wool* and *Coal* Bridson found new ways of letting working people express their own opinions in their own words, and of expressing the strength of local community feeling in the people of Yorkshire, Lancashire and Tyneside. Olive Shapley pioneered the use of recorded actuality in programmes about shopping, long-distance lorry drivers, miners' wives, all-night transport cafés and homeless people. Such programmes had no equivalents in London. Some of her best programmes (on Mass Observation, on working-class life in Manchester) were topical and socially relevant in ways that London could not match in the late thirties. Nor was topicality confined to documentary programmes. The regions led the way in public affairs programmes such as *Midland Parliament* from Birmingham and North Region's *Public Enquiry*, while many of the radio plays produced in the regions were more socially engaged and to the point than the drama offerings of London.

In 1935 Charles Siepmann, who had just been unseated as Director of Talks, was sent to tour the regions and write a report. He was much impressed by their work, particularly Manchester, and his report has been described as 'a precise attack on the centralisation of cultural life'. When the activities of the regions are compared with those of London in the late thirties one has a strong impression of caution and stifled initiative at the centre and of experiment and innovation in the margins. The regions were less amenable to the dead hand of policy control. They were more in touch with their audiences, and more in sympathy with them, than London. Since there were only about a dozen staff in each regional station working relations were much more informal, and individuals had much greater freedom to decide on the work they wanted to do and then do it. When Grace Wyndham Goldie retired as radio critic for *The Listener* in 1939 she declared in her last article:

> Let me before I die give one last shout about the importance of regional broadcasting. It is, I assure you, worth shouting about. Its effect on English life is only just beginning to be felt and is already

enormous. It is a side of broadcasting which I never see publicly discussed and the value of which I never see publicly recognised . . . In London the search is for the best possible play, feature, actor, talk or entertainment and to provide it for listeners. But in the regions there is something else. For it is the business of regional broadcasting to be expressive of the region. It is its business to be a channel for regional talent. But there is more than that. For it is also the business of the regions to express the everyday life of the region, its daily work, its past, its attitude of mind, and above all the quality of the people (*The Listener*, March 1939).

Conclusions

The institutional presence of the BBC was massively established and accepted by the end of the thirties. Outwardly its policies, channels and programmes seemed to be permanently enshrined as part of the British way of life. Inwardly there were forces at work to undermine the solid foundations of this edifice.

In particular the contradictions between the attitudes of the BBC to its audiences, and of the audiences to the BBC, were becoming more apparent. The whole concept of public service, of raising the level of knowledge and taste, had rested on a set of expectations invested by the BBC in 'the great audience'. It must help to make the ideal work by attentive listening, by a careful selection from the goods on offer: 'on the other side of the microphone the listener must recognise that a definite obligation rests on him to choose intelligently from the programmes offered to him' (*BBC Yearbook*, 1930, p. 60). The listener must *listen*. 'If you only listen with half an ear, you haven't a quarter of a right to criticise.' Leaving the radio on all the time, as background noise, was frowned on. 'Think of your favourite occupation. Don't you like a change sometimes? Give the wireless a rest now and then.'

Both programme continuity and programme building (i.e. scheduling) were so arranged at first as to inhibit lazy non-stop listening. Properly speaking there was no continuity between programmes in the early thirties, no announcer's chat, previews of what was to come later, to maintain a smooth flow from one item to the next. Instead the spaces between programmes were deliberately left as little oases of silence, save for the tick of a studio clock, to allow people to switch off rather than stay on, or to let them recompose themselves after a particularly stirring play or musical performance. The concept of programme building was remote and alien from the present-day art of television scheduling designed to capture and maintain large audiences in prime time (cf. Wheldon, 1972). Central to the art of programme building was the attempt to cater for all tastes, minority and majority, *over a period of time* (a month was the period sometimes quoted). The balance was not maintained in the daily or weekly bill of fare. One need not expect to find variety or light entertainment on offer every night. Fixed scheduling (i.e. placing programmes at the same time on the same day from week to week) was, with one or two exceptions, avoided. It was not easy to keep track of a talks series or drama serial, for their time and place varied quite markedly from one week to the next. Through such means the BBC aimed to keep the audience awake, to stop it falling into idle habits or taking the output on offer for granted. The monopoly was essential for this ideal. Through it the BBC was not obliged to compete for audiences, but was able to presume them.

But as time went by this set of expectations vested in the audience began to wear thin. The drift to Luxembourg, especially on Sundays, of a large portion of the working-class audience signalled the dubious success of the project in that quarter at least. It is unlikely, though, that any large part of the audience ever behaved itself as ideally it was supposed to do. Against the wishes of the BBC the circumstantial evidence suggests that for most people most of the time, irrespective of class or education, radio was treated as no more than a domestic utility for relaxation and entertainment − a convenience, a commodity, a cheerful noise in the background − which occasionally in moments of national crisis, mourning, celebration or sport became compulsory listening for the whole country.

The signs of creeping doubt begin to appear in the shift to lighter fare in the late thirties. Listener Research, established in 1936 in part under pressure from programme makers who wanted real information about what the audience thought of their products, confirmed the increasing inroads made by European commercial radio stations. There was an increasingly jaundiced attitude to the whole idea of 'coaxing Caliban' (i.e. trying to raise the level of cultural appreciation in the majority audience) in departments such as Drama or Music. The separation out of 'serious' and 'popular' styles of presentation and production implicitly accepted the need to find formats that were suitable for and acceptable to different publics with different levels of taste and education. The beginnings of social and cultural 'streaming' were present before the war. Regional broadcasting again suggested a different relationship between a programme service and its audience. At this time there developed a routinisation of programme schedules, an increasing number of fixed slots in the week, and a growth of series and serials and of continuity programming. These processes, begun in the late thirties, were greatly accelerated during the Second World War.

The war scuttled the hopes and values of the Reithian era by irreversibly changing the channel structures, programme services and audience definitions of the BBC's radio service. When war was declared in September 1939 the Regional Programme was immediately closed down, and the National Programme became the Home Service (to distinguish it from Overseas Programmes). Early in 1940 the Forces Programme was launched for the British Expeditionary Force in France. It reversed at a stroke all the principles of pre-war radio. It was designed as an entertainment service to please the troops, to give them what they wanted to hear — dance music, sport and variety. After Dunkirk it became an alternative 'light' programme to the Home Service. It immediately established itself as the majority channel, winning about 70 per cent of the listening public.

At first these changes were seen, in the BBC, as temporary measures, expedient necessities of the moment, to maintain the nation's morale. But just as the multiple needs and imperatives of a total war compelled the British state to pay far greater attention to public opinion and the collective needs of the people, so too broadcasting found itself adjusting to popular demand. The BBC no longer sought to lead and reform public taste; it now tried to match or to anticipate it. These shifts towards more popular radio were accomplished with enthusiasm in some quarters and with reluctant distaste in others. But they were, in the end, unstoppable.

In 1945 the landslide victory of the Labour Party showed the strength of the collective will that there should be no going back to the economic and social conditions of 1939. No more could radio hope to return to its pre-war ways. With more than a touch of weary resignation the postwar radio service had been redesigned as a three-channel service: the Light, the Home and Third Programmes, each corresponding to low-, middle- and high-brow tastes. Gone was the effort to cater for all these publics in a single channel. This social and cultural streaming marked the end of the attempt to impose a single set of standards and tastes upon the whole of the listening public. Reith himself, by now a rather sad and embittered man, was not deceived:

> The Third Programme, positively and negatively is objectionable. It is a waste of a precious wavelength; much of its matter is too limited in appeal; the rest should have a wider audience. *When overall programme policy and control was abandoned* [our emphasis], the Third Programme was introduced as a sop to moral conscience, a sort of safety valve (Stuart, 1975, p. 474: cf. pp. 462-82).

The ideal of public service broadcasting he had fostered, and the means he had created for its achievement, had been blown away by the winds of wartime change.

Note on Sources: Much of the information on which this article is based has come from the BBC Written Archive, Caversham, Reading. Since this is a general article, detailed references to these sources have not been given.

References

BBC Annuals (1935-7) BBC
BBC Handbooks (1928-9: 1938-40) BBC
BBC Yearbooks (1930-4) BBC
Bridson, D.G. (1971) *Prospero and Ariel*, Gollancz
Briggs, A. (1961) *The Birth of Broadcasting*, The History of Broadcasting in the United Kingdom, vol. 1, Oxford University Press
— (1965) *The Golden Age of Wireless*, The History of Broadcasting in the United Kingdom, vol. 2, Oxford University Press
— (1979) *Governing the BBC*, BBC
Cardiff, D. (1980) 'The Serious and the Popular: Aspects of the Evolution of Style in the Radio Talk, 1928-1939', *Media, Culture and Society*, 2 (1)
Dimbleby, J. (1975) *Richard Dimbleby*, Hodder and Stoughton
Jennings, H., and Gill, W. (1939) *Broadcasting in Everyday Life*, BBC
Matheson, H. (1933) *Broadcasting*, Thornton Butterworth
— (1935) 'The Record of the BBC', *Political Quarterly*, 6 (4), 506-18
PEP Report (1938) *Report on the British Press*, Political and Economic Planning, London
Reith, J. (1924) *Broadcast over Britain*, Werner Laurie
Scannell, P. (1980) 'Broadcasting and the Politics of Unemployment, 1930-1935', *Media, Culture and Society*, 2 (1)
— (1981) 'Musical Chairs: a Policy for Broadcast Music', *Media, Culture and Society*, 3 (3)
Sound and Television Services in Britain (1964) HMSO
Stuart, C. (ed.) (1975) *The Reith Diaries*, Collins
Wedell, E. (1968) *Broadcasting and Public Policy*, Michael Joseph
Wheldon, H. (1972) *The Effects of Competition*, BBC

PART TWO

INTRODUCTION

The readings assembled in this section offer a number of different perspectives on the popular culture of post-war Britain. Though the field has not yet been sufficiently investigated, and no doubt also because we still lack overall historical perspectives that will eventually replace a rough-and-ready periodisation by means of decades, these readings deal with popular forms, recognisably distinct from those of the pre-war period.

In the first piece, Dick Hebdige attempts a 'cartography' of the very difficult area of *taste* in the period 1935-62. He charts the ways in which arguments around this issue have foregrounded and thrown a critical light upon received definitions of 'high' and 'low' culture, 'good' and 'bad' taste. Around the central issues of 'Americanisation' and 'streamlining' the author scans the cultural field from refrigerators to car design to spectacular youth cultures and links these phenomena to substantial changes in patterns of production and consumption. More ambitiously, Hebdige traces connections between the various forms of language — the signifiers — deployed in this period and shows how they form the distinctive features of many of our attitudes to the field of popular culture in general.

In 'Football since the War', Chas Critcher traces the complex changes within a major form of working-class culture which have profoundly affected players, supporters and the economics of the football clubs. The abolition of the maximum wage which freed footballers to bargain directly in the market, selling their skill to maximum advantage, also initiated more far-reaching transformations, socially dislocating the more successful players and encouraging supporters to move from a sense of participating membership with the local club (win or lose) to a distanced consumerism of an entertainment spectacle, preferably mediated through TV. Critcher proposes that such structural changes within the form throw light upon the phenomenon pilloried in the media as 'football hooliganism', which can be seen as a rear-guard action against the process of change within football and the cultural nexus of which it forms a part. 'They look to football, not as an excuse for a punch-up but for the regeneration of football's role within working-class culture.' But football has lost its 'partial autonomy' from dominant economic and cultural trends in post-war Britain, though whether finally or not remains an open question. Critcher ends with suggestions for restructuring the game that depend, however, on first breaking the hold of its present owners, for whom football is a unique opportunity to achieve public power and status.

'Narrative Structure in Fleming' (U.Eco) is one of the earlier structuralist analyses of popular fiction. It undertakes to lay bare the latent
patterning which informs all, or most, of Fleming's novels, by whose
means different stages of the Cold War were 'incorporated' into an
identical narrative structure. Eco identifies to a deep-seated Manichean
ideology which the basic narrative structure reproduces in response to
the changing power balance which characterised relationships in the
1950s and 1960s between Britain, America, Russia and (in more
shadowy form) Third World countries. While particular novels produce
different manifest ideological positions, these 'do not derive so much
from the structural contents as from the method of constructing the
contents into a narrative'. This formal analysis is accompanied by (and
consorts uneasily with) a view of Fleming as a characteristic example of
'mass culture', who first perfected a successful narrative formula and
then adapts it 'with the cynicism of the disillusioned' to shifts in popular perception of the political climate.

It is against such dismissive mass-culture approaches to the forms of
popular culture that A. McRobbie elaborates an account of *Jackie*, a
magazine for teenage girls. This account both locates the social position
of the readership and conducts a formal analysis of the contents,
balance of pictorial and verbal material, and specific visual style of the
comic-strip presentation of romantic narratives. These function
together in the construction of a particular teenage feminine subject,
which excludes all aspects of social life (family, school, work, location)
except those assimilable to the fantasy-romance, and is itself built upon
a contradiction. Woman, or girl, is constructed on the basis of two
identities: that of belonging to a close and intimate sorority where
secrets can be exchanged and useful advice given, but which is simultaneously a claustrophobic world of sexual rivalry, in which the other
woman is always a rival. A girl's life is thus defined in terms of jealousy
and competition towards other girls, and of devoted faithfulness to the
boy/man of her choice with whom effective initiative and control
always rest. A 'code of romance' edits out sexuality, and a favourite
genre of historical romance, which locates narratives in the Victorian or
Edwardian period, displaces issues like class and poverty into 'the past'.
McRobbie concludes with a significant rider: although on sales figures
'*Jackie* is a force to be reckoned with by feminists . . . this does not
mean that its readers swallow its axioms unquestioningly'. We should
not, that is, rule out the possibility of oppositional readings. Nevertheless, one way of beginning the task of confronting the ideological power
of such fiction 'would be for feminist teachers and youth leaders to
involve girls in the task of "deconstructing" this seemingly "natural"
ideology; and in breaking down the apparently timeless qualities of

girls' and women's "mags" '.

Paul Willis's more descriptive account of 'The Motor-bike and Motor-bike Culture' attempts to decipher the symbolic meanings which inform the activities centring on motor-bike clubs. Clothes, personal appearance, hair-style, the rejection of goggles, gloves and helmets are seen as conscious expressions of the basic 'cultural' meaning: the assertion of physical power in a world of direct physical experience. Accidents, if not sought, are prized like victories. Engine noise is exaggerated and actively enjoyed, whether the machine is stationary or in use. Probable death from a motor-bike accident is felt to be appropriate, memorialised in rituals and motor-bike folklore. The machine itself, to the external and ignorant observer the product of a specifically modern technological industrialism, had been incorporated into a set of expressive practices, which are 'increasingly *the form* of cultural life, *everyday* life, for underprivileged groups'.

The next extract, 'Confessions, Concoctions and Conceptions' by Allison James, also draws on structuralism, but in its anthropological version. The subject differs from the others in addressing less a form of popular culture than a widespread, though little-discussed, social practice: children's sweets. Noting the unusual use of the North-East dialectal term 'kets' for such sweets, whose normal meaning is 'rubbish', James proposes that the children's adoption of it for their highly coloured, sticky confections points to a reversal of adult values. What is rubbish to adults is valuable to children. Adults see 'kets' as an interference with the routine of health-giving meals; children see meals as an exasperating interruption to the consumption of unnourishing but exciting 'kets'. 'Kets' thus contribute to the assertion of a specifically children's world of values, constructed against the overriding authority of adults. By re-coding the term, children appear to concede the adult evaluation, but secretly triumph over it.

With T.A. Shippey's account of magazine science fiction in the period 1940-60, there is another exception to the group as a whole. The material is American, not British, an emphasis justified by the predominance of American production in this genre. Shippey's approach to the texts is 'traditional' in its attention to manifest narrative, characterisation and theme, but he also relates the material to the political climate of the Cold War, arguing that in these stories, representing the disregarded *genre* of science fiction, political problems created by the interplay of government and advanced quasi-military technology were foreseen and discussed with remarkable prescience.

9 TOWARDS A CARTOGRAPHY OF TASTE
1935-1962

Dick Hebdige

Source: *Block*, no. 4 (1981). © Dick Hebdige.

To an ever greater degree the work of art reproduced becomes the work of art designed for reproducibility. From a photographic negative, for example, one can make any number of prints; to ask for the 'authentic' print makes no sense. But the instant the criterion of authenticity ceases to be applicable to artistic production, the total function of art is reversed. Instead of being based on ritual, it begins to be based on another practice – politics. (Benjamin, 1977).

[. . .] In this paper I want to consider some of the changes in British social and cultural life during the period 1935-62, to refer these changes back to the emergence of new patterns of consumption and new technological developments, particularly to the qualitative transformations which automation was seen to have effected and to examine some of the conflicting interpretations of these changes offered in contemporary accounts.

What we call 'popular culture' – a set of generally available artefacts: films, records, clothes, TV programmes, modes of transport etc – did not emerge in its recognisably contemporary form until the post War period when new consumer products were designed and manufactured for new consumer markets. In many of the debates about the impact and significance of popular culture, these profound social and economic transformations have been mediated through aesthetic concepts like 'quality' and 'taste'. These words are passionately contested. Different ideologies, different discourses – we would cite at random here the 'sociological', the 'art historical', the 'literary critical', as well as the discourses of marketing and industrial design – cut across these words at different angles producing different meanings at different moments. Underneath the discussion of an issue like 'discrimination', complex moral, social even economic options and strategies are more or less openly examined and the issue of taste – of where to draw the line between good and bad, high and low, the ugly and the beautiful, the ephemeral and the substantial – emerges at certain points as a quite explicitly political one.

From the 30's to the 60's, the debates about popular culture and popular taste tended to revolve, often obsessively, around two key terms: 'Americanisation' and the 'levelling down process'. We shall see how a number of cultural critics and commentators working out of quite different traditions equated the expanded productive potential opened up by the automation of manufacturing processes with the erosion of fundamental 'British' or 'European' values and attitudes and further associated this 'levelling down' of moral and aesthetic standards with the arrival in Britain of consumer goods which were either imported from America or designed and manufactured 'on American lines'. I shall open by mapping out the connections between certain varieties of cultural conservatism focusing on the 'spectre of Americanisation' and indicating some of the ways in which the ideologically weighted separation of the 'serious' from the 'popular' was undertaken. I shall then analyse the formation of those connotational codes which framed the reception given by certain key elites to imported streamlined products and popular American music. Finally, I shall attempt to assess how far the fears concerning the impending 'Americanisation' and 'homogenisation' of British society were borne out by empirical work in the sociological and market research fields. This paper deals, then, with some of the controversies surrounding the emergence from 1935-62 of new cultural forms and patterns of consumption.

The full complexity of the relations between such a heavily loaded series of debates and the larger set of historical transformations to which however indirectly, they refer can hardly be adequately treated in a paper of this length. But by pursuing a limited number of themes and images across a fairly wide range of discourses it may be possible to reconstruct at least some of that complexity [. . .]

It is perhaps only in this way by outlining the connections and breaks between groups of separate but interlocking statements that we can begin to imagine the particular dimensions of a language which is now largely lost to us and to appreciate not only the historical conditions under which that language was originally constructed but also the social conflicts and shifts in power which were registered inside it and which ultimately led to its dispersal and decline. Moreover, it is only through such a process that we can begin, albeit tentatively, to specify the conditions under which a project as elusive and forbidding as a 'cartography of taste' might be developed.

Waugh and the War of Position

In the archaeology of taste, fictional sources can be as 'authorative' (i.e. as revealing) as factual ones, and no one attempting to reconstruct the full range of reactions to qualitative social changes in Britain during the period covered by this paper could afford to overlook the blustering elitism of one major British novelist: Evelyn Waugh. His later work is relevant to this project insofar as it both symptomatises and parodies the complicity between definitions of 'good taste', class origin and political position.

For instance, the *Sword of Honour* trilogy, set in World War II, is an allegory for the decline of the divinely authorised caste-system and its replacement after 1945 by what Waugh no doubt regarded as the 'democratic sham'. One minor character in *Officers and Gentlemen* (1955), the second novel in the trilogy, embodies for Waugh the most offensive modern traits. The name 'Trimmer' is a synecdoche: the short, clipped vowels sum up the man exactly. He is meticulously neat — he has a clipped moustache, wears tightly waisted suits and two-tone shoes. He has worked as a hairdresser (trimmer) on a transatlantic liner but through a certain native cunning by using his knowledge of the social forms, he has managed to insinuate himself into the officer class. Once there, he takes his place alongside the protagonist, Guy Crouchback, the sole surviving male in an old English Catholic family of impeccable lineage (there are connections with Italy, with the most antique of antique traditions). Crouchback, with his fine sense of honour and decorum, represents a doomed elite, and when the 'awful' Trimmer sleeps with Crouchback's estranged wife, Virginia, whom he meets one night in a cocktail bar in Glasgow, the inference is clear: here is a hopeless future, a post-war future in which we are destined to witness the inevitable supercession of the Old Order by the New, of a noble but effete aristocracy by modern man who is quite clearly a vapid imposter.

This example indicates just how closely Waugh regarded the aesthetic, cultural and moral boundaries to be aligned. And for Waugh these boundaries in their turn served to mark out the social domain, separating rule from chaos, 'masters' from 'men', the legitimate from the illegitimate. (The fact that Virginia has a child as a result of her liaison with Trimmer is meant to be especially ominous.) The preservation of the natural order, then, depended for Waugh upon the continual patrolling of these boundaries by a vigilant, incorruptible soldier like himself. In this context, Waugh's depiction of Trimmer as literal detritus — dirt for Mary Douglas is 'matter out of place' (Douglas, 1966) — is peculiarly telling. Although Waugh was distanced from the British upper classes both by his background and his misanthropic disposition, perhaps because both these factors qualified him more clearly for the role of court jester than palace spokesman, his savage revelations can serve as an illuminating counterpoint to the more guarded statements of his peers.

Like all militant reactionaries, Waugh delineates a previously submerged set of values, preferences and assumptions by attempting to
exculpate them at the moment when those values and the interests
they embody are in crisis, on the point of disintegration. In fact, the
growing belligerence of Waugh's prose from 1945, the year in which
Brideshead Revisited was published, onwards dramatically signals the
extent to which the cultural consensus had shifted against him during
these years, transforming the language of power and control, moving
away not only from the kind of caricatured elitism that Waugh himself
represented but also – and more gradually – from the 'gentler' patrician and paternalist ideologies which had found favour during the inter
War period. David Cardiff has demonstrated how these shifts had
already registered at the BBC by the late 30's in the evolution of
characteristic styles of presentation in radio talks, in the demarcation
of the boundary between the 'serious' and the 'popular' and in the
debates about who should speak for the 'common man', in what voice,
how often and in support of whose interests (Cardiff, 1980). The spectacular trajectory of Waugh's later career in which he posed as the obstinate and unrepentant defender of privilege throws into stark relief the
ground on which discussions concerning 'high' and 'low' culture,
'popular' and 'classical' values were initially conducted in the years
immediately after 1945. The iconoclasm which motivated Waugh's
choice of persona here can only be fully appreciated when it is placed
against the emergent orthodoxies of progress, moderation and reform.

In 1945 the Attlee Government had been lifted to power on a wave
of left wing populism and had succeeded in inaugurating the welfare and
nationalisation programmes which made possible the transition to the
corporate post War State. With the institutionalisation in the pledge to
full employment and the provision of secondary schooling, of the rights
to work and to free education, the quasi-feudal structures on which
Waugh's vision of British society rested were [. . .] seriously disfigured.
A social anachronism, Waugh's only possible role was the one to which,
finally, he was most temperamentally suited – that of 'Anastasias
contra mundum' – a kind of cultural Canute, and this eventually led
him to codify the rituals of exclusion through which the power of an
already superceded *ancien régime* had been perpetuated. [. . .]

In his last book, *The Ordeal of Gilbert Pinfold* (1957), written some
9 years before his death, we find locked away in the usual labyrinth of
irony his keenest fear: that together affluence and universal education
will fulfil the promise or rather the threat of democracy by removing
the fact of difference which alone confers value:

His strongest tastes were negative. He abhorred plastics, Picasso, sun-
bathing and jazz – everything in fact that had happened in his own

life-time. The tiny kindling of charity which came to him through his religion sufficed only to temper his disgust and change it to boredom . . . He wished no one ill, but he looked at the world 'sub specie aeternitatis' and he found it flat as a map; except when, rather often, personal arrogance intruded. Then he would come tumbling from his exalted point of observation. Shocked by a bad bottle of wine, an impertinent stranger or a fault in syntax . . .

Waugh's list is revealing: 'plastic' (ie festival of Britain/'inauthentic' mass culture); 'Picasso' (Continental modern art/subversive high culture); 'sun-bathing' (increased leisure/national inertia/a 'soft' obsession with cosmetics/'immoralism, naturism . . . non-conformism' (Hillier, 1971), and jazz (American negro/subversive 'low' culture). Together Waugh suggests, these items and the shifts in taste and value which they embody form part of that process whereby the contours of achievement produced by a tradition based on privilege, have been progressively planed down until the world for Waugh seems as 'flat as a map'.

This provides a starting point. For Waugh merely stood in the vanguard of a widespread backlash against the confident post War rhetoric of reconstruction and equal opportunity — a blacklash which spread across the entire field of cultural criticism during the 1950s.

Hoggart and Orwell: a Negative Consensus

The critical space in which this reaction took place had already been opened up by the literary tradition of dissent and polemic which Raymond Williams describes in *Culture and Society* (1961). Though different political perspectives coexist within that tradition, the 'levelling down process' associated with 'mass culture' provided a radical populist like George Orwell, a self-confessed elitist such as T.S. Eliot and a social democrat like Richard Hoggart with common cause for concern.

Cultural if not political conservatism drew together writers who were prepared to take opposing sides on issues which at the time were more openly contentious (eg the role of education in the State). Though there was never any agreement as to what exactly should be preserved from the pre-War world, there was never any doubt amongst these writers that clearly *something* should. Whereas Eliot and F.R. Leavis were pledged to defend the immutable values of minority culture against the vulgar inroads of the popular arts, to defend in Matthew Arnold's terms 'culture' against 'anarchy', Orwell and Hoggart were interested in preserving the 'texture' of working class life against the bland allure of post War affluence — television, high wages and consumerism. The blanket hostility with which the former set of writers greeted the advent of mass culture requires little explanation or critique. It has become part of the 'commonsense' of cultural studies.

However, the resistance to cultural innovation offered by Hoggart and Orwell was more ambivalent and uncertain. Both these writers castigate the emerging 'consumer culture' on roughly the same grounds. They both equate the classless tone of the glossy advertisements with the erosion paradoxically of meaningful choice.

Both Orwell and Hoggart use the image of the holiday camp as a paradigm for working-class life after the War. Orwell imagines a modern design for Coleridge's Kubla Khan consisting of air-conditioned caverns turned into a series of tea-grottoes in the moorish, Caucasian and Hawaiian styles. The sacred river would be dammed up to make an artificially warmed bathing pool and, playing in the background there would be the constant pulse of muzak 'to prevent the onset of that dreaded thing — thought' (Orwell, 1979).

In the same way, to achieve the same effects, Hoggart sets one of his parodies of the cheap romantic fiction of the 50s in a place called the Kosy Holiday Kamp complete with 'three dance halls, two sun-bathing parades and lots of milk bars' (Hoggart, 1958) in which the imaginary female narrator *drools* over a 'hunk of luscious manhood' who combines the dubious appeal of 'Marlon Brando and Humph. Bogart' (ibid). Strangely enough, then, despite the ideological gulf(s) which separate these two writers from a man like Evelyn Waugh, there are common themes and images linking what they all wrote on developments in the field of popular culture in the post war years. When Waugh saw a decline and fall, a flattening out of social and aesthetic criteria, Hoggart and Orwell see the substitution of an 'authentic', 'vigorous' working class community by the *idea* of a community; the replacement of 'real' values by what Hoggart at his most evocative calls a 'shiny barbarism' '. . . the ceaseless exploitation of a hollow brightness' . . . 'a spiritual dry-rot' . . . a 'Candy Floss World' (ibid.).

Though they spoke from quite different positions, these three writers share a language which is historically determined and determining. They are loosely linked in this particular context through a largely unacknowledged because largely unconscious [. . .] *consensus* of taste even if that consensus is organised around a list of negatives — i.e. round those things that they do *not* like.

The Spectre of Americanisation

Increasingly, as the fifties wore on, this negative consensus uniting cultural critics of all persuasions began to settle around a single term; Americanisation. References to the pernicious influence of American popular culture began to appear whenever the 'levelling down' process was discussed and the concept of 'Americanisation' was swiftly and effortlessly absorbed into the existing vocabulary of the 'Culture and Society' debate. [. . .]

Whenever anything remotely 'American' was sighted, it tended to be read, at least by those working in the context of education or professional cultural criticism, as the beginning of the end whether the imagined apocalypse took the form of Huxley's *Brave New World*, Fyvel's 'subtopia', Spengler's 'megalopolis' or at a more mundane level, Richard Hoggart's Kosy Holiday Kamp where we will all float together, 'A great composite . . . of the unexceptional ordinary folk: minnows in a heated pool.' (ibid.). America was seen by many of these writers as *the* homogenising agent and from the 1930s onwards the United States [. . .] began to serve as the image of industrial barbarism; a country with no past and therefore no real culture, a country ruled by competition, profit and the drive to acquire. It was soon used as a paradigm for the future threatening every advanced industrial democracy in the Western world.

Unfavourable depictions of the 'American way of life' and the American way of business such as these were of course hardly novel [. . .] but during the War and immediately afterwards these depictions broke more decisively into the arena of public, explicitly *populist* discourse and were circulated in a wider number of printed and broadcast contexts. This wider 'official' resistance to American influence can only be understood in the light of particular historical developments – the American military presence in Britain from the early 1940s onwards and Britain's increasing dependence on American economic and military aid. The first *direct* experience of American popular culture for most 'ordinary' Britons occured during the War through informal contact with American servicemen. [. . .] It is difficult to estimate the impact of this dramatic encounter though reactions seem to have been ambivalent: curiosity, envy and resentment are blended in those popular representations of American soldiers which stressed their 'affluence' and their relaxed and 'casual manner' (and by inference their 'easy morals'). [. . .]

The American serviceman with his dollars and chewing gum, listening to jazz on the A.F.N.,* buying favours with candy, stockings, cigarettes and beer became a familiar stereotype – one which was easily assimilated into existing mythologies – superimposed on the stock image of the American tourist in Europe. One US chaplain writing

*The American Forces (radio) Network.

home described the typical GI:

> There he stands in his bulging clothes . . . lonely, a bit wistful, seeing little understanding less — the Conqueror with a chocolate bar in one pocket and a package of cigarettes in the other . . . The chocolate bar and the cigarettes are about all that he, the Conqueror has to give the conquered . . . (Goldman, 1961).

After the War, this covert hostility persisted and was exacerbated by new factors: by Britain's declining status as a world power, the disintegration of the British Empire coupled with the simultaneous rise in America's international prestige and the first indications of American imperial ambitions. In addition the War Debt and the continuing reliance on the American military presence in Europe provided a dual focus for popular resentment.

In magazine articles and newspaper reports, Britain's austerity was frequently contrasted against the booming American economy and the strong dollar. In July 1948 to celebrate the launching of the Queen Elizabeth the *Picture Post* carried a report of a transatlantic crossing entitled prophetically 'The American Invasion' which displayed a thinly veiled contempt for the new 'disposable' culture:

> Deck-sweepers are filling buckets with five inch cigar butts and quarter-smoked cigarettes, unconsidered debris from the land of not-yet-too-much-plenty.

This was followed by an image which was guaranteed to grate with a *Picture Post* readership still subject in 1948 to the rigours of strict rationing:

> In the forward bar two loose-shouldered young men apparently limited to six words an hour, four of which are 'Steward' are spending a morning-long dice-session just for the hell of it.

These themes were elaborated in further *Picture Post* articles throughout the late 40s and early 50s.

American Music and the Threat of Youth

The articulation of these historically localised dissatisfactions in a journal as determinedly 'popular' as the *Picture Post* must have helped to condition the reception given to American cultural imports during the period by the official arbiters of good taste — by the BBC and the literary and artistic establishments. [. . .] According to archive research now in progress, BBC policy statements throughout the late 40s and early 50s laid down detailed guidelines as to how much American material should be presented and in what context. The content and quality of American comedy shows were apparently subjected to particularly intense scrutiny and ideally the image of America received by the British public was to be filtered through the paternalistic framings of professional commentators like Alistair Cooke. At a time when a tremendous upsurge of popular radicalism, a popular demand for change, coincided with severe material shortages, BBC personnel – programmers and policy makers alike – appear to have been perfectly aware of the 'damaging' indeed potentially subversive impact which American cultural artefacts (particularly popular music: swing, crooning and jazz) could have on public 'morale'. By 1956, when the 'threat' of left-wing populism was hardly a significant political factor, and memories of austerity were beginning to recede, these practices had become firmly sedimented and institutionalised.

Despite the relaxation in the tone and style of BBC broadcasting allegedly affected by the advent of commercial television in 1954, rock 'n' roll was deliberately ignored and resisted by the BBC radio networks. British balladeers and cabaret-style singers were systematically favoured and in 1956, the year when Elvis Presley's *Heartbreak Hotel* was released, not one rock 'n' roll record was featured in the annual review of popular songs. [. . .]

Historical 'authenticity' and/or stylistic sophistication served as the criteria for distinguishing the acceptable forms (i.e. the 'natural' blues, folk and Trad; sophisticated swing, balladeering etc.) from the unacceptable (i.e. rock, rhythm and blues). As Iain Chambers remarks, 'What in hindsight appear to be the most arbitrary distinctions were at the time fiercely patrolled aesthetic parameters' and the passion with which those distinctions were defended and maintained indicates once more the extent to which the values they embodied were felt to be at risk in this case from the 'monotony of incoherence' which early rock 'n' roll was seen to represent. When the broadcasting authorities eventually capitulated to popular demand, the music was subject to the same elaborate monitoring and framing procedures laid down in the early post War years. *6.5 Special, Thank Your Lucky Stars* and *Juke Box Jury* on television, *Saturday Club* and *Easy Beat* on the radio were all hosted by already-established 'professional' presenters (e.g. Peter Murray, David Jacobs). *Juke Box Jury* was in fact a study in mediation: new musical product was processed through a panel of 'well-known show business personalities' who submitted it to a brief barrage of witty, barbed but self-consciously lighthearted commentary. Jack Goode's *Oh Boy!* was the only programme in which the more delinquent connotations of the music were permitted to creep through unremarked (and this, perhaps significantly, appeared on the commercial channel).

The gate keeping and policing functions undertaken as a matter of course by the BBC were assumed with equal seriousness elsewhere in the broader currents of cultural and aesthetic criticism. By the early 50s, the very mention of the word 'America' could summon up a cluster of negative associations. It could be used to contaminate other words and concepts by sheer proximity as in 'Americanised sex', 'the false values of the American film' etc. (Orwell). Once more an example from the *Picture Post* indicates just how far the Americanisation thesis had infiltrated the more 'respectable' reaches of popular journalism. In an article entitled 'The Best and Worst of Britain' (19 Dec. 1953), Edward Hulton, the editor, describes the emergence of a new race of 'machine minders and comic-strip readers'. He quotes a Welfare Officer who compares a group of factory girls who 'put pieces of paper into slots for 8 hours a day' to 'chickens pecking corn' and when asked about religion confesses:

> They prefer Victor Mature to God because they can understand Victor — and he relieves the monotony of their lives: as far as they know, God doesn't.

Hulton concludes with references to the 'Growth in juvenile crime', talks ominously about young 'thugs . . . who revel in attacking old men and women, and hitting people when they are down' and the article ends with this solemn warning:

> We are on the brink of that horrible feature of American life where, in many a shady district, thugs go round from shop to shop demanding the payment of 'protection money' or 'else' . . .

Here, the way in which images of crime, disaffected youth, urban crisis and spiritual drift are anchored together around 'popular' American commodities (Victor Mature, comic strips) suggests a more completely structured response than those we have so far encountered — a fixing of a chain of associations (between youth, the future, America and crime) which has since become thoroughly sedimented in British common sense. As we have seen, such typifications emerge only slowly; meanings coalesce around particular configurations of attitudes, values and events and are gradually naturalised as they circulate in different contexts. [. . .]

The Streamlining Controversy: (1) The Blasphemy of 'Jazz Forms'

There's a kind of atmosphere about these places (the new milk bars). Everything slick and shiny and steamlined: mirrors, enamel and chromium plate whichever direction you look in. Everything spent on the decorations and nothing on the food. No real food at all. Just lists of stuff with American names, sort of phantom stuff that you can't taste and can hardly believe in the existence of . . . (George Orwell, *Coming Up For Air*, 1939)

Once they had been defined as signs of the perfidious 'American influence', the mere mention of commodities like comic strips and gangster films or of an 'artificial' environment like Orwell's streamlined milk bar could summon up any combination of the following themes: the rebellion of youth, the 'feminisation' of British culture, the collapse of authority, the loss of the Empire, the breakdown of the family, the growth in crime, the decline in church attendance etc. In this way, a word like 'streamlined' could be used to mobilise a whole set of ideologically charged connotations from a number of different sources. To appreciate the complexity of this process we have to consider the way in which the word 'streamlining' itself came to be applied to industrial products by those working within the professional design milieu and to try to tease out some of the meanings *encoded* into streamlined artefacts at the design and production stages. It thus becomes possible to turn at last to those discourses in which the issues of quality and taste were *overtly* confronted and discussed.

References to 'streamlining' first began appearing on a regular basis within American design discourse in the 1930s (though Harold van Doren cites the submission as early as 1867 of a patent for a 'streamlined train'). To begin with the smooth cigar shapes to which the word 'streamlining' referred were associated exclusively with aviation technology where it was argued that they served a specific function – facilitating speed maximalising air flow etc. However these visual motifs were by the early 30s being carried over into American design. (The 1934 Chrysler Airflow, for instance, was modelled on Douglas aircraft designs.) Streamlining soon constituted in this new context a popular, 'eye catching vocabulary' – one which clashed with the purist architecturally based idioms of classical European modernism, the ideals of which in this particular field were most clearly embodied in the angular designs by Walter Gropius for the German Adler Company. (For example, the 1930 Adler Cabriolet is often quoted in books on design theory as the apotheosis of 'tasteful' car design.)

By the end of the decade streamlining was beginning to be applied to commodities totally outside the transport field in which it had found its initial rationale. [. . .] By 1940 Harold van Doren could write:

> Streamlining has taken the modern world by storm. We live in a
> maelstrom of streamlined trains, refrigerators and furnaces; stream-
> lined bathing beauties, soda crackers and facial massages . . . (Bayley,
> 1979)

The ensuing controversy surrounding these allegedly 'improper' applica-
tions of streamlining lasted for more than two decades and [. . .] it still
remains in effect the decisive, determining 'moment' in the formation
of much current academic discourse on design (eg formalism/anti-
formalism; aesthetic/commercial; 'good' design/'popular' design). [. . .]

By exploring the controversy within design over the streamlining
issue it may be possible to determine how the distinctions between the
'serious' and the 'popular', between 'good' and 'bad' taste, came to be
articulated in a particular discursive field between the years 1935-55,
to examine how far they paralleled similar distinctions produced in
other areas at more or less the same time and to relate these developments back to changes in the modes of industrial production, distribution and consumption.

The response of the European design Establishment to the indiscriminate streamlining of imported American products was immediate
and uniformly hostile. A streamlined refrigerator was interpreted as an
act of provocation in direct defiance of the most fundamental principle
of 'good design' – that 'form follows function'. Such an object was
plainly blasphemous: a hymn to excess. It was 'decorative', 'decadent'
and its offensiveness as far as the European design authorities were concerned hinged on its arbitrariness. The intrusion of an expressive design
vocabulary which bore no *intrinsic* relation to the commodities it
shaped was plainly subversive. It introduced the possibility of an *inter-
textuality* of industrial design – of the unrestricted passage of signifiers
across the surfaces of a whole range of unrelated products without any
reference whatsoever to 'essential' qualities such as 'function' and this
ran absolutely counter to the prevailing 'modern' orthodoxy. [. . .]

The differences between dominant European and American conceptions of the place of 'good taste' in product design stemmed from
the different infrastructural links which had been established on the
two continents between manufacturing industry, design practice and
design theory. American design had been firmly placed on a commercial
free-lance footing and was studio and consultancy-based. [. . .]

In Europe on the other hand, national bodies had been set up at
least in Britain and Germany to promulgate the principles of 'good
design' but, in Britain, there were few integral links with industry, and
when design teams were eventually formed they tended to be

permanently attached to a single company or corporation. This separation of theory and practice had direct consequences on the formation of the dominant European design aesthetic. (In America the very notion of privileging 'aesthetic' principles over considerations of market demand and 'popular' taste tended to be regarded as an expensive indulgence.)

In Britain the Design for Industries Association (DIA) which had been established in 1915, [. . .] pursued a policy rooted in the ideals of William Morris and the Arts and Crafts Movement. DIA statements had a strongly paternalistic flavour [. . .] which reflected how far it was institutionally and ideologically identified with Government rather than industrial interests. Its influence on British design was minimal and by the late 30s the DIA was under siege from an Evangelical group of Modern Movement proponents led by Nikolaus Pevsner and John Bertram. Both wrote influential books — Pevsner's *Pioneers of Modern Design*; Bertram's *Design* — which were published eventually as Pelican Specials and which soon found favour and support amongst the dominant taste-making elites. [. . .]

The manner in which modernist principles were predominantly interpreted *in Britain* by people like Pevsner, the kind of intervention which the early British popularisers of modernism imagined they were making (Pevsner, for instance, refers [. . .] to the 'levelling up of class contrasts, the raising of standards of design' (Bayley, 1979))[. . .] fitted in exactly with the more liberal and progressive ideologies which were then just beginning to find favour amongst certain key elites (e.g. the BBC).*

Both Bertram's and Pevsner's writings contain lengthy polemics against the philistinism of British industry, the vulgarity of popular taste and British reticence in the face of the 'new' and 'well-formed'. [. . .]

The excesses of American streamlining were then hardly likely to be welcomed by this new design oligarchy, and when Pevsner accuses 'modernism in its jazz forms' . . . of spoiling the market . . . 'for more serious modern work' (ibid.) one suspects he is referring specifically to American imports or American-influenced designs (the words 'jazz' and 'American' are virtually interchangeable in this kind of writing throughout the 20s and 30s). The disjunction between British and American traditions — the different relationships with industrial practice and the State formed by the respective design elites provide some explanation for the emergence of discursive polarities between what was defined as 'commercial' and 'responsible' work and for the

---

*This was not necessarily the case elsewhere in Europe: modern movement principles were appropriated at different times in Russia for communism, in Italy and Germany for fascism.

development of quite different criteria in America and Europe for judging what constitute 'good' design. But in order to obtain a more adequate account of these differences and to appreciate their wider historical importance we have to go beneath and beyond the terms in which the debate was originally conducted and to consider changes both in the production process and in the scale of consumption.

The Streamlining Controversy: (2) the Shape of the Future

The emergence of streamlining from 1930 to the late50s as *the* popular style — 'popular' in the sense of being simultaneously 'commercially successful' and 'democratic', 'anti-purist', 'running counter to the classical' etc. can be explained by reference to two major developments: the refinement of pressed steel technology and the creation of new consumer markets. The development of pressing and stamping techniques (whereby sections of a product could be stamped out whole and subsequently welded together) can be seen as an integral part of that process of accelerated automation and rationalisation through which in the years immediately before and after the War, financial and technological resources became concentrated into progressively larger and more efficient units. In other words it was just one of the many technological innovations which enabled monopoly capital to become consolidated in the period.

In this context, the movement away from fabricated, geometric forms to pressed or stamped ones [. . .] signalled a more general shift within industrial production towards a greater output of a more limited range of items for a larger domestic market at a lower unit cost. The fact that stamping technology made it easier to produce curved forms [. . .] meant that this innovation and the increased rationalisation of the production process which went with it could literally *declare itself in form*, could advertise through its very newness those quantitative and qualitative breaks that had been made in the production process, in the scale of production and the size of the potential market to which 'streamlined' products were to be directed.

This is not to return to some crude technological determinism. Commercial pressures remained paramount here. The range of design options available continued to be structured by market as well as productive forces. Designers continued to provide appealing and commercially viable designs which at the same time were intended to maximalise the potential for formal and stylistic change opened up by the new technology. And as the American designer Raymond Loewy put it in 1945, ultimately the only streamline aesthetic which was likely to impress the directors and the shareholders continued 'to consist of a beautiful sales curve shooting upwards' (ibid.). But the potential for stylistic experimentation opened up by a new technological 'advance' such as stamping could be cashed in in the market place precisely through the deliberate exaggeration of stylistic *difference*, through the extent to which the new products could be clearly marked off by their very 'newness' and 'uniqueness' — in this case by their 'curvilinear' qualities — from those already available. It was largely through the vocabulary of style and form then that adaptations in the technical apparatus were mediated to the new mass of consumers.

Advertisements for streamlined products appealed directly to popular conceptions of an irresistible 'scientific progress' and frequently drew their inspiration from contemporary science fiction and science faction genres. [. . .] Streamlining became synonymous with the 'shape of the future', with a romantic exultation in the power of the New and its vocabulary simultaneously influenced and was influenced by what Robin Spencer has called the 'popular imaginative concept of tomorrow's world' (Faulkner, 1976). The significance and appeal of this concept, as Spencer points out 'has nothing to do with established art forms' (ibid.). The futurist manifestoes and the popular imagery of progress shared only 'the bright innocence of technological aesthetics' (Mitchell, 1977) but that aesthetic and the meanings constructed round it were transformed as they passed across from high to low, from the lofty assertions of an artistic avant garde to the context of consumption and use — the domain of the popular. [. . .]

Increasingly, American product design became the art of imaginative projection as the pressure to overcome the law of the declining rate of profit necessitated the constant stimulation of demand through the production of ever 'newer', more fancifully and 'futuristically' styled commodities.

The Streamlining Controversy: (3) From Borax to Pop

By the 1950s the policy of 'planned obsolescence' which was admitted, indeed openly paraded in Detroit as a positive factor both in design and 'consumer-satisfaction' led to what can only be described as the 'creation' of some of the most outlandish and, as it turned out, provocative examples of 'dream' styled artefacts to have yet rolled off a production line. (The 1953 Cadillac El Camino was in fact advertised as everybody's 'Dream Car').

Harvey J. Earl, head of General Motors styling department, was responsible for many of the more outrageous designs. His most controversial innovation involved the transposition in 1949 of the Lockheed Lightning tailfin to the rear bumpers of the Cadillac range — a move which he justified by claiming that it conferred 'visible prestige' on the car owner. In the furore which these 'unwarranted' and 'ostentatious' features caused in European design circles many of the themes of the original streamlining debate of the 30s were recapitulated but with the shift in the post War years from a production to a consumer economy, the issue of impending 'Americanisation' was far more clearly foregrounded:

> Streamlining is the jazz of the drawing board — the analogy is close, both are U.S. phenomena, both are 'popular' in their appeal, both are far removed from their characteristic sources — negro music and aero-dynamics and finally both are highly commercialised and use the star-system (Faulkner, 1976).

British and 'classical' American designers united to protest the arrival of General Motors' short-term, low-rent chromium utopia' (Bayley, 1979). The term 'borax', which had been coined in the American furniture industry to denote 'obviously heavy forms and elaborate ornament' (Faulkner, 1976) was taken over by the dissenters and used to refer to the kind of terminal styling represented by Detroit. (There was even an adjective — 'borageous'.) And as Reyner Banham has pointed out, the very presence of such terms in journals as clearly devoted to Modern Movement principles as *The Architectural Review* implies a simple Cold War logic: 'borax is bad ... elegant is good, stylised is bad, functional is good' (ibid.). Indeed the introduction of tailfins which were subsequently described as the 'Vietnam of product design' (ibid.) was even (apparently) blamed for 'the fact that America lagged behind Russia in the space-race. Whilst the Russians had been developing "Sputnik" ... the Americans had been debauching themselves with tailfins' (ibid.).

Nonetheless by this time (as Banham's confidently satirical voice here indicates) the opposition was growing in strength and articulacy: the modernist consensus was being attacked from within (Banham was a former student of Pevsner). The New York journal *Industrial Design* began to carry arch and generally appreciative reviews of new Detroit products and there were attempts on the part of certain sections of the New York intelligentsia as early as 1951 to have Earl's creations reassessed as art in inverted commas. [. . .] In London the emergence of a similarly ironic sensibility — a sensibility which was eventually to produce both 'Pop Art' and Tom Wolfe's New Journalism — was signalled in the formation of the Independent Group and the mounting in 1956 at the Whitechapel Art Gallery of the *This is Tomorrow* exhibition which revelled in the despised iconography of the new popular culture.

Once again these discursive shifts and breaks within the art and design world(s) reproduced transformations in the intersecting spheres of cultural criticism and popular journalism and these were in turn written out of and against the prevailing ideologies of 'Americanisation', the 'levelling-down process', 'cultural decline' and 'consumer affluence'. And to trace the connections one stage further (and one stage back), all these shifts occurred out of or in response to changes in the composition of the market and the forces of production. The 'borax' controversy which extended and accentuated the resistance on the part of dominant European elites to American 'streamlined' products helped to crystallise with exceptional lucidity within the confined space of a professional 'discipline' the issues which were felt to be at stake; the significance of form in everyday life, the need for a 'responsible' interpretation of popular demand, the place of public taste in design practice. The Cadillac of the 1950s merely acted as a catalyst for a clash of values and interests which had been building up since the development in America in the first two decades of the 20th century of mass production technology. [. . .] It was an object which *invited* strong reactions.

In America of course, the Cadillac was, as the El Camino advertisements acknowledged, the embodiment in chrome of the American Dream. Throughout the 50s and 60s it represented the aspirations precisely of the 'disadvantaged American' (ibid.) and it was the blatant expression of these aspirations in their raw state – untouched by the paternalistic mediations of European 'good taste' – which had proved so divisive. This was of course what made the Cadillac so 'vulgar'. It was the levelling down process in-car-nate. It was the tangible elimination of value and distinction (in the twin senses of 'difference' and 'distinguishing excellence') achieved paradoxically through the 'pretentious' claims made on its behalf to 'social status'. (This was the car for the 'upwardly mobile'.) This was the culmination of the whole pernicious process. Here, in the 1950 Cadillac, it was quite evident that the 'hallmarks of distinction' had been at last replaced by the fetish of stylistic variation.

Nor was this interpretation confined solely to conservative cultural critics though the imagined erosion of class differences which affluence was supposed to have produced was subject to a different inflection on the Left. Marcuse, who in *One Dimensional Man* (1964) describes what amounts to a 'streamlined' workforce cites the example of 'the negro who owns a cadillac' along with 'the typist who is as attractively made up as the daughter of her employer' [sic] (Marcuse, 1964) to demonstrate the extent to which subordinate groups have been assimilated and won over by 'passive consumerism' to dominant modes of thought and action. [. . .]

The image of a class of 'privatised', affluent workers locked into a closed circuit of production and consumption, 'watching the same TV programmes and visiting the same resort places' (ibid.) as their employers, struggling only to purchase the products of their own alienated labour informs much of the critical sociological discourse of the 50s and 60s. [. . .]

The Evidence of Change

Of course between the 30s and the 60s patterns of consumption *did* change radically. Quite apart from a steady rise in the availability of a wider range of consumer goods, there was a particularly dramatic transformation in the scale of working class expenditure on leisure in terms both of time and money. For example, Paul Wild has traced the development of new forms of consumption – principally the spread of cinemas and dance halls – in one provincial town, Rochdale, from 1900 to 1940. During these years leisure provision became increasingly centralised (e.g. by 1929 British Gaumont owned 300 cinemas up and down the country, by 1945 the Rank group had opened a further 500 and owned the Ealing and Shepherds Bush studios (Clarke *et al.*, 1979)) and American and American-influenced products began to dominate the 'popular' market. Wild characterises the following broad trends: the growth of recreation oligopolies (e.g. Rank and after the War, EMI), the removal of leisure provision from popular control, a tendency towards greater specialisation in what had previously been communal or class-based rituals, and a swing on the part of a working class audience dominated by a less gruelling work schedule and 'increasingly lured into a world of novelty and the appearance of glamour towards American style entertainments' (ibid.). [. . .]

But whether or not working class people really were deradicalised by the 'lure' such entertainments were thought to represent is open to question.

The issue was further clouded after the war by the emergence of the youth market and the stereotype which grew up alongside it of the well-paid working class teenager prepared to spend a large part of his or her income on leisure. The 'myth of affluence' and the accompanying ideologies of 'classlessness' and 'incorporation' representing, as they did, attempts to provide coherent explanations for changes in the phenomenal forms of working class life and the formation in particular of the new 'popular culture' ran directly parallel to the 'Americanisation' thesis: the assumed eradication of traditional differences remained largely intact. Mark Abrams for instance claimed that:

Under conditions of general prosperity the social study of society in class terms is less and less illuminating. And its place is taken by differences related to age (Abrams, 1959).

However, there was a good deal of confusion here. Abrams went on to insist that by 1959:

> not far short of 90 per cent of all teenage spending is conditioned by working class taste and value (ibid.).

Most of the more dramatic developments as far as adolescent consumption was concerned – e.g. increased provision of leisure facilities (discotheques, boutiques, Wimpy bars, Ten Pin Bowling Alleys etc.) and magazines aimed at a specifically teenage market did not fully emerge until the early to mid 60s. But even here amongst the young, consumption rituals, far from being classless, continued to take place within a culture sharply divided precisely round the class-related questions of quality and taste.*

Before 1962, teenage consumption where it wasn't organised through church youth clubs, voluntary associations (and involuntary ones – National Service continued until 1958) tended to be a largely subterranean affair occurring, at least for working class males in the interstices of the parent culture, on the street corners, in Arcades, cafes and dance halls. And the most conspicuous evidence of change – the emergence in the early 50s of flamboyant subcultures like the teddy boys – of groups whose tastes were most clearly conditioned by exposure to American imports, to American popular music and American films, [. . .] served to accentuate rather than annul class differences. The teds, after all, were drawn more or less exclusively from the 'submerged tenth' of lower working class youth.

According to one survey conducted by the *Picture Post* at the Tottenham Mecca ballroom in 1954, a teddy boy's wages could range from as little as £4.17. 6d per week (an apprentice) to £12.00 (a skilled cabinet-maker) whilst the made-to-measure drape suit which was compulsory wear (described [. . .] as a 'theatrical outfit . . . un-English . . . simply weird' (Fyvel, 1963)) cost £17.00-£20.00, a 'good poplin shirt' £2.00 and a pair of 'beetlecrusher' shoes £3.00. In other words, becoming a teddy boy was not something which could be undertaken lightly. Far from being a casual response to 'easy money', the extravagant sartorial display of the ted required careful financial planning and was remarkably self-conscious – a going against the grain, as it were, of a

---

*In 1971 the National Board of Prices and Incomes reported that the distribution of earnings remained more or less the same as in 1886: material hardship may have diminished but relative deprivation still persisted.

life which in all other respects was, in all likelihood, relatively cheerless and poorly rewarded.

But these groups were hardly representative. They served for most contemporary observers of the scene as the 'dark vanguard' and were perceived as traitors on the shore of the imagined sea of comics, quiffs and bubble gum which threatened to overwhelm the singularity of British culture unless 'something' (rarely specified) was done. [. . .]

Beyond the Shock of the New

It is now possible to reassess the broader political and cultural implications of the debates on taste, American cultural influence and the 'quality of life' which took up so much critical space from the 30s to the 60s. Discourses evolved in a wide variety of relatively autonomous professional contexts are linked together paradigmatically through recurrent ideological themes, images and issues. Specifically we have seen how a number of ideologically charged connotational codes could be invoked and set in motion by the mere mention of a word like 'America' or 'jazz' or 'streamlining'. Groups and individuals as apparently unrelated as the British Modern Design establishment, BBC staff members, *Picture Post* and music paper journalists, critical sociologists, 'independent' cultural critics like Orwell and Hoggart, a Frankfurt-trained Marxist like Marcuse, even an obsessive isolationist like Evelyn Waugh all had access to these codes. Together they form a language of value which is historically particular. With the appearance of imported popular phenomena like 'streamlining' and 'jazz' this language – not only the terms themselves: 'excellence', 'quality', 'distinction' and so on – but the structure of expectations and assumptions which lay behind them – the desirability of cultural continuity and social stability, the existence of moral and aesthetic absolutes – was thrown into crisis.

The challenge represented by shifts in the organisation of market and productive forces was registered at the level of form in the appearance of new recorded musical genres (rock 'n' roll, r & b etc.) and a new order of commodities differentiated from each other by superficial stylistic features. [. . .] The new consumption economy, in turn, engendered a new language of dissent. Those terms which had been negatively defined by the established cultural elites were inverted and made to carry oppositional meanings as they were appropriated (in the way that Marcuse had recommended) by the (counter-cultural) advocates of change and converted into positive values – hedonism, pleasure, purposelessness, disposability, etc. [. . .]

We have seen how streamlining constituted the explicit declaration in form of technological innovations (e.g. stamping and pressing techniques) which made the production of an increasingly standardised and uniform range of commodities possible. Streamlining came to be used as a metaphor for industrial barbarism, stylistic incontinence and excess. The proliferation of 'jazz forms' was cited by European cultural commentators simultaneously to connote: 'popular taste', the 'look of the future' and 'Americanness' — all of which were negatively defined. On the other hand, for designers and advertisers of streamlined products and for the 'public at large' the vocabulary of streamlining was used to signal a positive improvement in the 'quality of life' which in turn entailed a massive expansion in the productive base and in the scale of 'conspicuous consumption'. Quality and quantity were indistinguishable here — the clash over issues of taste was inextricably linked to conflicting definitions of material progress, and the rhetoric of modernism with its references to 'beautiful machines' and 'well-made objects' served only to obscure the extent to which mass production technology under 'free market' conditions *necessarily* entailed the transformation and displacement of traditional aesthetic criteria and established social distinctions. It was the simultaneous articulation of the fact of *accessibility* and *reproducibility* (a million streamlined Chevrolets, a million streamlined radios) which finally proved disturbing to so many cultural critics. A run of different commodities rendered indistinguishable through the identical lines which enfolded them represented, in Banham's words, 'a chromium horde bearing down on you' for a group of European intellectuals educated in a tradition which placed (and still continues to place) value on the 'authentic', the 'unique' or at the very least the 'honest' and the 'functional'.

It was Walter Benjamin who foresaw most clearly the transformation of aesthetic criteria which mass production would eventually necessitate:

> the technique of reproduction detaches the reproduced object from the dimension of tradition . . . by overcoming the uniqueness of every reality (Benjamin, 1977).

Writing in the same spirit at more or less the same time, Gramsci produced a remarkably cogent critique of the response of the Italian intellectual bourgeoisie to the first tentative signs of 'Americanism'. He predicted that the introduction into Italy of American-style mass production technology ('Fordism') would lead to the intensification of economic exploitation and eventually to the more effective penetration of the State into every aspect of private and public life — to a subtler, more developed ideological and 'moral coercion' of the masses. But he refused to deplore the changes in the *phenomenal* forms which inevitably accompanied such structural adaptations. He pinpointed the source of the resistance to American cultural influence precisely:

In Europe it is the passive residues that resist Americanism (they represent 'quality') because they have the instinctive feeling that the new forms of production and work would sweep them away implacably (Gramsci, 1971).

In the image of a streamlined car, in the snatch of 'hot' jazz or 'ersatz' rock 'n' roll blaring from a streamlined speaker cabinet, the cultural conservatives of 1935 or 1965, irrespective of their overt political affiliations were right to perceive what Benjamin described as 'the destructive, cathartic aspect, that is, the liquidation of the traditional value of the cultural heritage' (1977). They were right to perceive that what was at stake was a future — their future.

Conclusions

It would, finally, be misleading to end a discussion of some of the conceptions of 'popular taste' which prevailed from 1935 to 1962 without making at least some reference to the alternative definitions of America and American influence which were circulating at the time or attempting to assess the actual extent of American cultural penetration during this period.

As we have already seen, where changes in taste and patterns of consumption did occur, they tended to be associated with changes in the *composition* of the market, [. . .] and these changes in turn were linked to objects and environments either imported from America or styled on American models (e.g. film, popular music, streamlined artefacts, milk bars, hair styles and clothes). There can be no doubt that America, particularly in the post War period, began to exert considerable cultural and economic influence on European culture, though those statistics which are readily available tend to fall outside the period covered by this paper (e.g. in 1973 it was estimated that 50 per cent of the world's screen time was taken up with American films, and that American-made programmes accounted for more than 20 per cent of total TV transmission time in Western Europe; that 20-25 per cent of British manufacturing output was American controlled and that eight of the leading advertising agencies were owned by American companies (see Bigsby, 1975)).

But there is little evidence to suggest that the eradication of social and cultural differences imputed to these developments by a generation of cultural critics has taken place at least in the form they predicted. For instance, the sheer plethora of youth cultural options currently available (e.g. the rockabillies, heavy metal enthusiasts, ted revivalists etc.), most of which are refracted however indirectly through a 'mythical America', seems to suggest that the early fears about the homogenising influence of American culture were unfounded. Rather, American popular culture — Hollywood films, advertising images, packaging, clothes and music — offers a rich iconography, a set of symbols, objects and artefacts which can be assembled and re-assembled by different groups in a literally limitless number of combinations. And the meaning of each selection is transformed as individual objects — jeans, rock records, Tony Curtis hair styles, bobby socks etc. — are taken out of their original historical and cultural contexts and juxtaposed against other signs from other sources. From this perspective, the style of the teddy boys can be interpreted less as the dull reflex of a group of what Hoggart called 'tamed and directionless helots' to a predigested set of norms and values than as an *attribution* of meaning, as an attempt at imposition and control, as a symbolic act of self-removal — a step away from a society which could offer little more than the knowledge that 'the fix is in and all that work does is to keep you afloat at the place you were born into' (Wolfe, 1968).

In the same way, positive images of America did persist throughout the period though these were generally constructed and sustained underneath and in spite of the 'official' authorised discourses of school and State. Of course, even in 1935 there existed a positive mythology of the 'New World' — perhaps a remnant of much earlier, romantic myths in which America and Americans were depicted as young, innocent, dynamic and vigorous. In the early 60s the Kennedy brothers were portrayed as personifying these qualities. [. . .] But until the 1960s the romantic affirmation of American culture tended to be left to such unashamedly 'popular' weeklies as *Titbits* and to the undergrowth of literature — the novelettes, comics and Hollywood ephemera — which were aimed at a predominantly working class market. And by 1960, this market — at least significant sections of it, particularly amongst the young — had swung again — away from the exuberant vocabularies of streamlining and rock. In 1962, Len Deighton's *Ipcress File* appeared. It contained the following passages:

I walked down Charlotte Street towards Soho. It was that sort of January morning that has enough sunshine to point up the dirt without raising the temperature. I was probably seeking excuses to delay; I bought two packets of Gauloises, sank a quick grappa with Mario and Franco at the Terraza, bought a Statesman, some Normandy butter and garlic sausage . . . In spite of my dawdling I was still in Lederer's Continental coffee house by 12.55 . . . Jay had seen me of course. He'd priced my coat and measured the pink-haired girl in the flick of an eyelid. I knew that he'd paid sixty guineas for each of his suits except the flannel one, which by some quirk of tailor's reasoning cost fifty eight and a half . . . [Later in a

strip club] . . . Finally he went to the Gents excusing himself with
one of the less imaginative vulgarisms. A cigarette girl clad in a handful of black sequins tried to sell me a souvenir programme. I'd seen
better print jobs on a winkle bag, but then it was only costing twelve
and six, and it was made in England.

'I'll have a packet of Gauloises' I said . . .

What is so remarkable here — unsurprising perhaps in a genre [. . .]
so unremittingly brand and status-symbol conscious as the British
spy novel of the 60s — is the defection of a man like Harry Palmer not
to Russia — still less to America — but to Italy ('Mario', 'Franco',
'grappa'), to the Continent (garlic sausage, 'Normandy butter', all those
'Gauloises'). It is perhaps the final irony that when it did occur the
most startling and spectacular 'revolution' in British 'popular' taste in
the early 60s involved the domestication not of the brash and 'vulgar'
hinterland of American design but of the subtle 'cool' Continental
style which had for so many decades impressed the British champions of the Modern Movement. Fyvel, writing in 1961, had recorded
the switch from the teddy boy style betraying in the process a set of
preferences which should require little explanation:

> Step by step, through various deviations, the clothes and haircuts
> grew less eccentric and extreme, until at the end of the fifties they
> had become unified in the rather attractive 'Italian style', which had
> become normal walking-out wear for the working-class boy; and by
> 1960 this had blended with 'conservative cool', or just very ordinary
> but well-cut clothes (Fyvel, 1963).

It was not to be long before the first 'ordinary' (i.e. working class)
disciples of the Modern Style in their Italian suits on their Italian motor
scooters, moving to black American modern jazz and black American
soul were swarming over Soho. And Harry Palmer with his proletarian
origins, his eye for detail (*his* world is hardly as 'flat as a map'), his
refined and discriminating tastes (a 60 guinea suit . . . a 58½ guinea
suit) and his confident appropriation of Italy (Guy Crouchback's sacred
Italy!) is a fictional extension of mod just as Trimmer — the thoroughly
contemporary master of appearances — bore attenuated traces of the
1950s spiv. What is more, the 'spy masters' Burgess and MacLean
(followed later by Philby) — motivated, or so the story goes, by a profound contempt and loathing for America, for American cultural,
economic and military imperialism, for the 'Americanisation' of the
globe — had flown the roost leaving men like Palmer to take care of
things. Needless to say, Gilbert Pinfold would have been appalled.

References

Abrams, M. (1959) *The Teenage Consumer*, London Press Exchange
Bayley, S. (ed.) (1979) *In Good Shape: Style in Industrial Products, 1900-1960*, Design Council
Benjamin, W. (1977) 'The Work of Art in the Age of Mechanical Reproduction' in Curran *et al.* (eds.), *Mass Communication and Society*, Arnold
Bigsby, C.W.E. (ed.) (1975) *Superculture: American Popular Culture and Europe*, Paul Elek
Cardiff, D. (1980) 'The Serious and the Popular: Aspects of the Evolution of Style in the Radio Talk 1928-39', *Media, Culture and Society, 2*
Clarke, J., Critcher, C., and Johnson, R. (1979) *Working-class Culture*, Hutchinson
Douglas, M. (1966) *Purity and Danger*, Penguin
Faulkner, T. (ed.) (1976) *Design 1900-1960: Studies in Design and Popular Culture of the Twentieth Century*, Newcastle-upon-Tyne Polytechnic
Fyvel, T.B. (1963) *The Insecure Offenders: Rebellious Youth in the Welfare State*, Pelican
Goldman, E. (1961) *The Crucial Decade and After: America 1945-60*, Vintage America Publishing
Gramsci, A. (1971) *Selection from the Prison Notebooks*, ed. and trans. Hoare and Nowell-Smith, Lawrence and Wishart
Hillier, B. (1971) *The World of Art Deco*, Dutton
Hoggart, R. (1958) *The Uses of Literacy*, Pelican
Marcuse, H. (1964) *One-dimensional Man*, Routledge and Kegan Paul
Mitchell, S. (1977) 'Marinetti and Majakovsky: Futurism, Fascism, Communism' in *Screen Reader*, Society for Education in Film and Television, London
Orwell, G. (1979) 'Pleasure Spots' in *Collected Essays – Journalism and Letters of George Orwell, vol. 4, 1945-50*; G. Orwell and I. Angus (eds.), Penguin
Wolfe, T. (1968) 'The Noonday Underground' in *The Pumphouse Gang*, Bantam

10 FOOTBALL SINCE THE WAR

Chas Critcher

Source: *Working Class Culture: Studies in History and Theory*
(Hutchinson, London, 1979), Ch. 7. © J. Clarke, C. Critcher
and R. Johnson

It is the basic premise of this essay that general arguments about
changes in working-class culture since the war will always remain unsatisfactory unless they are specified with reference to particular
aspects of working-class culture. Here it will be argued that professional
football can be taken as one index of tradition and change in working-
class culture, both reflecting and affecting broader changes.

The primary focus here is socio-historical, an attempt to trace significant changes. This requires a sketch, however simplified, of football's
role as an element of working-class culture in pre-war English society. It
was and still is a predominantly working-class activity, the majority of
both players and spectators being recruited from a distinctive social
grouping and a specific cultural tradition. Pre-war football was an
integral part of that corporate working-class culture rooted in the late
nineteenth century. The core values of the game as a professional
sport — masculinity, aggression, physical emphasis and regional identity
meshed, according to one account,[1] with other elements of that (male-
dominated) working-class culture, elements carried within its network
of small-scale organizations and supportive mechanisms (working men's
clubs, mutual insurance schemes, co-operatives, public houses, trade
unions) and in a myriad of smaller leisure-time groupings (pigeon
fanciers, whippet trainers, amateur footballers and the rest). It is easy
to over-estimate the homogeneity of this culture. It reflected some
variations and oppositions within the class, according to region and
internal boundaries, notably that between the rough and the respectable. Nevertheless Hopcraft's emphasis on the centrality of football
to the common working-class experience remains a valid generalization:

> By the 1920s football was an established employer in a community
> where jobs were scarce. The clubs had grown up out of pride in
> athleticism, in local importance, in corporate endeavour. The
> stadiums were planted where the supporters lived, in among the
> industrial mazes of factories and hunched workers' houses. The

Saturday match became more than mere diversion from the daily grind, because there was often no work to be relieved. To go to the match was to escape from the dark of despondency into the light of combat. Here, by association with the home team, positive identity could be claimed by muscle and in goals. To win was personal success, to lose another clout from life. Football was not so much an opiate of the people as a flag run up against the gaffer bolting his gates and the landlord armed with his bailiffs.[2]

However, while this subordinated class culture struggled to maintain a fixed corporate identity, it would be a mistake to confuse continuity with a lack of dynamism. This applies especially to football. Some of those most evident changes in post-war football — an expanded transfer market, declining attendances and defensive football — had their counterparts in inter-war football. There were differences of scale but the presence of these factors is not new. [. . .]

Since here we are concerned with trends and influences rather than moments or personalities, the effort will be to identify significant long-term factors rather than to offer a detailed chronological account. [. . .] I have chosen to structure this essay around [four] particular aspects of football which I take to be both essential to its own self-conception and integral to its status as a central element of working-class culture. These are the player, the supporter, [. . .] the clubs and international influences on tactics.* I begin with an examination of the professional footballer as working-class hero.

The Player

From 1945 to 1963 professional footballers were engaged in a continuous collective struggle to improve their economic situation. The details of that struggle have been adequately recounted elsewhere: the annual bargaining over the maximum wage ceiling, the obdurate behaviour of the Football League, the strike threats, the players' final victory with the abolition of the maximum wage in 1960; then the struggle over contracts, culminating in a High Court judgment against Newcastle United in an action brought by George Eastham in 1963. Here it may suffice to note three main implications of these events. The first is the clear roots of the struggle in working-class activity outside the game. This was neatly noted in a *Times* editorial at the moment of abolition:

---

*[In his original essay, Chas Critcher discusses a fifth aspect of post-war soccer: the impact of the media on the game. We have not included this owing to pressure on space — Eds.]

They ask two freedoms: freedom for a player to negotiate his own contract of employment, and freedom to negotiate his own wages with his employer. These are freedoms which are basic, unarguable, and the right of every working man in Britain.[3]

The second feature is the characteristic attitude adopted by the League, seeing absolute control over players as the only bulwark against the rampant greed of the players and the tyranny of the transfer market. In the event some of their worst fears were proved justified, in so far as higher wages did contribute to the ever-widening gap between rich and poor clubs. But this was due at least as much to a spiralling transfer market, about which the League has done precisely nothing. In any case the massive wage differentials opened up by abolition were in part attributable to the form and intensity of League opposition, which ruled out the possibility of negotiating some alternative form of wage control which would have benefited the average as well as the exceptional professional footballer.

Thirdly, and less often noted, are the implications of economic developments for the cultural situation of the player. The professional footballer was traditionally a kind of working-class folk hero, and knew himself to be such. He came from, and only moved marginally out of, the same economic and cultural background as those who paid to watch him. In such a context, a dramatic change in the economic situation of the player was bound to have severe repercussions on the cultural significance of his role as hero. Put simply, the effect of these changes was that 'for some of the star performers in football the "new deal" has meant an everyday life transformed from the kind led by the previous generation'.[4]

The emphasis here must be on 'everyday life'. It was not just a question of footballers having gained the right to more money and more bargaining power in relation to their employing club. What became gradually clear was that the 'new deal' had fractured the set of social and cultural relationships by which the player's identity had previously been structured. His relationships with management were strained by the constant demands for performance returns on the investment in him; his attitudes towards fellow players became more neurotically competitive and the search for a common footballing code found only an uneasy justification of cynicism in the ethos of 'professionalism'; his relationship with the spectators, increasingly mediated by heightened expectations of the successful and the spectacular, came more and more to resemble that of the highly acclaimed entertainer required to produce the 'goods' for public consumption.

If the economic emancipation of the professional footballer was differentiated in distribution and impact, so were its effects on the cultural identity of the professional footballer. A symptomatic reading of household names which span the post-war period – Stanley Matthews, Jimmy Greaves, Bobby Charlton, George Best, Kevin Keegan – may only reveal differences of personality, economic position and social status. However, equally crucial for our purposes is the relationship between the footballer's behaviour on the field and his bearing off it. Together they form his public presence, what public relations terminology would appropriate as his 'image' and which, following Arthur Hopcraft, we shall describe as his style: 'We are not dealing with the style of play, but also with the style and substance of the man, as affected by the game.'[5] [. . .]

Four styles or typologies will be offered here. The first – *traditional/ located* – represents and draws on the values of a traditional respectable working-class culture in a way which becomes increasingly difficult, though not impossible, after the 'new deal'. Those benefiting from greater economic rewards may be typified as *transitional/mobile*, exploring the possibilities of their new freedom. As even more money becomes available to the chosen few and the game as a whole becomes more respectable, players seek and find acceptance into overtly middle-class life-styles. *Incorporated/embourgeoised*, they become small-scale entrepreneurs, a world away from their predecessors and most of their contemporary supporters. Finally, the combination of apparently limitless remuneration and the publicity machine of the mass media nominate a handful of players as 'superstars' raised to new levels and kinds of public adulation and attention. The correct typification of such players, however, is as *superstars/dislocated* from any available models of style. For a while their behaviour on and off the field is a source of tension to themselves and others before they develop a new identity as superstars/relocated into the world of show-business personalities and public celebrities; taking their places, metaphorically and sometimes literally, alongside film and television stars, members of the *nouveau riche* and the more publicity-conscious of the politicians.

The traditional-located style is relatively easy to identify, and has been caught in Arthur Hopcraft's perceptive analysis of Stanley Matthews:

> We were always afraid for Matthews, the non-athlete; the sadly impassive face, with its high cheekbones, pale lips and hooded eyes, had a lot of pain in it, the deep hurt that came from prolonged effort and the certainty of more blows. It was a worker's face, like a miner's, never really young, tight against a brutal world even in repose . . . The anxiety showed in Matthews too: again like the frail miner's fear of the job which must always be done, not joyfully but in deeper satisfaction, for self-respect . . . In communicating this

frailty and this effort Matthews went to men's hearts, essentially to inconspicuous, mild, working men's. He was the opposite of glamorous: a non-drinker, non-smoker, careful with his money. He had an habitual little cough. He was a representative of his age and class, brought up among thrift and the ever-looming threat of dole and debt.[6] [. . .]

Matthews was symptomatic but not unique. Others of his generation − Lofthouse, Finney, Lawton − continued to dominate the football of the immediate post-war period. [. . .]

Yet change was evident. Duncan Edwards, whose career was tragically cut short by the Munich air disaster, is described by another writer as revealing 'that surging irrepressible determination for self-expression and self-reliance of the post-war teenager', yet remaining identifiably working-class.[7] In less symbolic terms money made the difference. Still drawn from and having affinities with the mainstream working class, the salaries of top players began to take them out of the most skilled worker's economic grouping. Johnny Haynes made one kind of breakthrough to become the first £100-a-week player but for various reasons − an unglamorous club, restricted media access, a reluctance to score goals − Haynes never fitted properly into the heroic mould. The central figure of the transitional style is Bobby Charlton − a working-class gentleman who could live like one:

> He gets the star footballer's profusion of flattery. His name is chanted to raise the spirits of ticket queues in the rain; vivid coarse girls have to be held off by policemen when he gets into and out of the Manchester United coach; small boys write him letters of charming clumsiness and kick footballs with his autograph on them; he has been European footballer of the year and a poll of referees voted him model player. His wife is pretty, so are his two daughters, and he lives in a rich man's house in a rich man's neighbourhood. He is the classic working-class hero who has made it to glamour and Nob Hill.[8]

Charlton's long career, like that of Matthews, tends to disguise real changes. The dominance of the transitional style was over long before his World and European Cup triumphs of 1966 and 1968. It flourished in the early 1960s when the England team contained Charlton, Haynes and Jimmy Greaves, who was to bear witness to the changes in style by having lived through all four states.

By the late 1960s the style of incorporation was becoming dominant, as star footballers became self-conscious participants in the process of their own embourgeoisement. It was this rather than the transitional style that was truly anonymous. This was partly due to the impression of conformity which the description 'incorporated' is meant to convey: the image of the small businessman is hardly laden with heroic qualities. The development of tactics, too, had made playing styles more rigid: over-collective, remorseless and functional, the new demands were for the runner, the 'worker' who could fit into a preconceived pattern. Alan Ball is a symptomatic player here: his total style is defined by the new tactics:

> All the adjectives, the superlatives as well as the clichés which surround the modern game apply to Ball — the 90-minute man, genius clothed in sweat, perpetual motion, the essential team-man, hating to lose, living and breathing the game, awesome opponent and valued colleague, selfless yet still essentially a star . . . these are the terms in which one talks of Ball.[9]

A whole generation of such men played for England in the middle and late 1960s: who will remember them? Those who stand out are hybrids. Bobby Moore, for example, maintained a detachment more typical of the transitional style and was accorded, as a result, as much envy as admiration. Perhaps the real anonymity of the incorporated style fed the search for the unusual, on and off the field. If those interested in footballing skills looked in vain for some variation from the stereotyped football of such teams as Leeds, Arsenal, and England, then those with a vested interest in glamour sought celebrities to populate their portrayal of life at the Top. Their separate desires were fulfilled by the superstar.

The superstar emerged most clearly in the late 1960s and early 1970s, and the central figure has to be George Best. But there had been earlier attempts to collude in the cultural dislocation of footballing heroes. Jimmy Greaves and others who followed the lure of gold to Italy in the early 1960s helped to dislocate themselves: a process further dislocated by the press exploitation of their subsequent discontent. *The Times* made this comment on the Greaves affair as early as 1961, when Greaves was finally transferred back to Spurs:

> There it stands, and may the man and the game be spared any more. Seldom in the history of British football can any man have commanded so much attention in so short a time. [. . .]
> Much of it has been unwelcome . . . Yet the suspicion is that latterly Greaves has been as much sinned against as sinning. His every daily action caught the spotlight and much of it was magnified unduly. The whole affair has become tedious beyond words.[10]

In the same year as the Greaves affair a fifteen-year-old boy from a Belfast housing estate came as an apprentice to Manchester United. Within forty-eight hours he and his travelling companion were back in Belfast. Three years later he was a regular member of Manchester United's championship side at the age of eighteen; in 1968 he was instrumental in United's European Cup victory and was voted Footballer of the Year. In 1971 he was sent off the field during an international match for throwing mud at the referee and, amidst increasing controversy over his private life and business associates, he quit the game in 1972. Returning briefly in 1973, he finally left the game, apparently for good in 1974, only to return with Fulham in 1976, then to leave finally for the USA.

That is the bare outline of the career of George Best. But much more was involved in the 'superstar' treatment he received. For seven years his every move was plotted by journalists and photographers; he was alternatively told — in newspaper columns and to his face — that he was the greatest footballer in the world and a spoilt brat; on the field he was kicked, held, punched, and admonished when he retaliated. All these were forces acting on Best, who in response lived it up with fast cars and beautiful women, while securing his future in a chain of boutiques. He lived out, part by personal choice, part by cultural compulsion, the newspapers' dream version of the superstar's life. As crisis succeeded crisis, he eventually exerted his own will in the only way left open to him, and left the English League, contracting himself out for individual appearances.

Of course it is possible to interpret this odyssey as the biography of a not-very-bright and immature lad, who let success go to his head and listened to the wrong people; or as the due reward for a headstrong, conceited man who wanted fame and reward on his own terms and was not prepared to work for it. The suggestion here is that the saga of George Best should be read in wider cultural terms, as the biography of a dislocated footballing hero, whose talent, personality and background were insufficient to withstand the pressures, both on and off the field, to which the new type of superstar was to be subjected. [. . .]

The crisis in the identity of the superstar was short-lived, though more widespread than a concentration on Best alone might indicate. At least one other England international underwent treatment for a nervous breakdown. [. . .] Eventually, however, the expectations of a superstar became clearer, more rationalized both for the players and those who sought to exploit their newsworthiness or feed off their glamour and money. Not, it should be said, that the mix of personal idiosyncracy and the cultural definition of the superstar wholly ceased to be instructive for particular players (Rodney Marsh, Charlie George, Alan Hudson). Still, the negative example of Best prepared those who were to follow. They avoided London clubs, married and 'settled down', took proper economic advice, learnt how to handle interviews. By the mid 1970s young men like Kevin Keegan and Trevor Francis had learnt to cope with their new identity. [. . .]

The Supporter

What will be described here as the disaffection of the supporter from his traditional relationship to professional football has taken three main forms: firstly, a disinclination to continue following the local team regardless of its achievement; secondly and relatedly, a preference for armchair viewing of weekly televised excerpts: thirdly, a symbolic redefinition of the role of the supporter through the activities of ritualized aggression adopted by younger fans.

The first signal of the spectators' disaffection was the fall in total annual attendance at league matches. By 1955 it was clear that the great post-war boom in attendances was over. The peak had been reached with the record total of 41,250,000 in the 1948-9 season, after which the figure decreased steadily to 34,000,000 in 1954-5. By the early 1960s the total figure had stabilized to around 28,000,000 and after a further peak in 1968 a new low was reached in 1971-2 with only 21,000,000, rather less than half of the 1948 figure. By the middle 1970s, however, a further stabilization had taken place at around 25,000,000. The clubs outside the first division have fared worst: in 1964 they accounted for 56 per cent of all attendances but ten years later they had only 48 per cent.[11] Such numbers are a barometer of success or failure. The common response to declining attendances has been to define football as in competition with other often more attractive leisure opportunities. In 1961, *The Times* noted that the changing social habits − 'H.P., the weekend family car, bingo and the rest' − meant 'mediocrity is harder to sell now'. The conclusion was that football's falling gates reflected changed class aspirations: 'Once football was the opium of the masses. No longer. There is a greater awareness of standards and comfort now. So perhaps the real answer at last is for a complete spring clean.'[12] An opinion poll commissioned by the Football League in 1962 came to similar conclusions. Noting the main factors for staying away as changed attitudes towards family and home, the lack of comfort at grounds − and, in a minor key, defensive football and players' lack of discipline − the report concluded that 'the arrest of the fall in gates can be achieved only by making football matches and their surroundings more attractive than other leisure activities.'[13] The government-sponsored Chester Report of 1968 took a similar line.

The financial deterioration has taken place during a period when the general standard of play has reached a very high level. The explanation therefore lies not there but probably in the radical changes which have taken place in the social pattern and in people's attitudes and leisure activities.[14]

The message, then, was clear. Spectators were not disaffected from the game as such, but from the facilities it offered and its inability to adopt a more modern style of self-presentation. [. . .]

There are many potential objections to such comments which are only the logical extension of the remarks previously quoted. [. . .] The main point to note here is that the major response to real changes in spectators' attitudes to football has not been to examine the cultural changes in the game and its immediate context. Rather it has been to import into discussion of the spectator an image which comes not out of a cultural concern but from the heart of commercial activity: the image of the consumer. Raymond Williams has noted the historical development of three kinds of cultural relationship between an individual or social group and social institutions: member, customer and consumer.[15] The first, however illusorily, thinks of himself as a member, and may recognize an informal set of reciprocal duties and obligations between himself and the institution. The customer, more detached, is seeking satisfaction for specific wants: if they are not met over a certain period of time, he may, somewhat reluctantly, take his patronage elsewhere. But the consumer has no loyalty or habit. He is informed of the choices open to him, and when he wants something will make a rational choice about where he will get the best bargain. Such choices are continually made, and the logic of the market is that those who wish to sell their products will compete with each other for his attention.

If this model is applied to the supporter, we may see how his relationship to the main social institution of football, the club, has been changing. Ian Taylor has convincingly suggested that the traditional supporter was able to think positively about his relationship to the club.[16] He could feel that the club and its players belonged to him and his fellow supporters. The players were 'available subcultural representatives' conscious of their closeness, cultural and economic, to their supporters, who in turn fulfilled that role and provided him with cultural and economic support. Thus 'the rank and file supporter could (however wrongly) see himself as being a member of a collective and democratically structured enterprise'.

With the fall in attendances, it became apparent that this illusion was no longer enough to maintain supporters' loyalty. It had to compete with other more powerful illusions. The response of those who dominated the public discussion and practical administration of football was not to look for a model of membership more culturally relevant and more firmly founded than the traditional illusion. It was rather to assume that the only possible relationship was that dominant in other more commercially minded leisure activities. If there was still much talk of the romance of being a supporter, if managers still claimed theirs were the best supporters in the country, if there was a campaign to improve the poverty of the ground facilities, these were more than counterbalanced by the image, explicit or implicit, of the supporter on which major policy decisions were based. The effects, Taylor has argued, were devastating — football was subject to a process of professionalization:

> Professionalization does not consist simply of entry into the transfer market and the beginnings of large transfer fees. It is also the process whereby clubs began to accommodate themselves to their changing role in a declining entertainments industry. Developmental processes in the wider society were increasing the leisure opportunities of an increasingly differentiated working-class. Football was competing for customers over and above football subculture. In one sense, this was a technical question involving the provision of covered accommodation, increasing the number of seats, and most obviously the fitting of floodlights to enable evening matches to be played. In another sense, however, the process involved a transformation of the stereotype of the football supporter. Where once the stereotypical supporter was a working-class man, living for Saturday and inextricably involved — in his own perception — with the fortunes of the club, now he was of undefined class membership, enjoying an escape from responsibilities, the provision of a spectacle from time to time, and expecting fulfilment of these needs from a team of professional entertainers . . . From the participatory and masculine values of the working-class supporter, and from an exclusive concern with victory, football turned its attention to the provision of spectacle, skill and efficient performance — values understood to be important to the stereotypical i.e. middle-class supporter.[17]

If this is a little overdrawn and smacks too much of class conspiracy, it is nevertheless more convincing than other analyses. It also opens the way to an explanation of the second symptom of the supporters' disaffection; ritualized and occasionally realized aggression. Into the hiatus between traditional supporter and modern consumer stepped the football hooligan.

It is almost impossible to write seriously about the problem of 'football hooliganism'. Not only is the phrase itself a label rather than a descriptive or analytical category, but there are virtually no statistics on its incidence even in terms of arrests in or around football grounds. Further, the label is used indiscriminately: are all the Stretford End 'hooligans', and if not, how do we distinguish those who are from those who are not? Finally, in terms of evidence, the media are an extremely unreliable source, involved as they are not merely in reporting but in sensationalizing and socially constructing the image of the 'football hooligan'.[18]

It needs to be said that those who commit — or at least are arrested for — criminal acts at football matches are an infinitesimal proportion of all supporters. The average number of arrests at Manchester United home games, out of gates of 50,000 to 60,000, is 3.2. In so far as it can be traced historically, the problem of 'hooliganism' seems to stem from the early and middle 1960s; at least, there is little evidence of it before that period. What is important for our present purposes is what new forms of spectator behaviour, especially amongst the young, can reveal about the attitude of football authorities to the spectator, and what the 'hooligans'' own self-perceptions can reveal about their relationship to the game.

The Times response was equivocal: crowd disturbances were both 'mindless thuggery' and a 'social problem'. James Callaghan, then Home Secretary, took it upon himself to define as *non*supporters those involved in such incidents.

I agree that wanton destruction is perpetrated by a relatively small number of people who call themselves football fans. They are nothing of the sort and the clubs will be well rid of them. The authorities who try to stamp this out have the full support not only of myself but of the overwhelming majority of the public.

The press weighed in with its careful, constructive analysis of the situation — savages, animals, thugs, lunatics were included amongst the repertoire.[19] Even the more responsible journalists insisted that the phenomenon had nothing to do with football itself. John Arlott argued that such a 'drunken mob' was attracted to football by the possibility of violence and nothing else.[20] Arthur Hopcraft perceived them as 'louts with pimples and knives' and recommended a strategy of draconian measures which he admitted to have 'fascist overtones'.[21]

According to this definition, troublemakers at football matches are a mob of undisciplined psychopaths with minimal interest in football; the source of their behaviour is seen to be outside the game, as part of the social malaise of our times. This not only allows football authorities to disavow any responsibility towards such supporters, other than those of containment and control; it also denies that such behaviour has any rationale in terms of the development of post-war football.

An alternative thesis has been outlined by Ian Taylor.[22] Extending arguments we have already touched upon, he sees football 'hooliganism' as a distorted attempt to restore some meaning and commitment to the role of the supporter. All the developments we have seen to be characteristic of the 1950s and 1960s — spiralling transfer fees, the economic and cultural dislocation of the top-line players, European competition, the attempts to make the game 'respectable' for a new 'model' spectator — have contributed to the undermining of the traditional role and image of the supporter. Thus those who look to the game for the assertion of traditional values are left behind; they are a 'subcultural rump'. With no former channels available to them to express their loyalty, and informal access to club and players closed, they draw on what few resources they have left. They evolve their own songs and chants, institutionalizing long-established individual obscenity and defiance at a collective level. They try to 'help' their team by booing and jeering the opposition, and extend the violent conflict of the field to the terraces and beyond.

But more than that. In symbolically displaced ways they reassert the traditional values which are being discredited in the organization and ideology of the game. They are not selective consumers but totally committed supporters of their team alone; not individual spectators, but part of a collectively responding crowd; not politely passive in their appreciation, but actively interventionist. They are thus the 'real supporters' in the traditional definition. Their general life-experience is reproduced inside football — that of 'cultural alienation', divorced from those communal activities which previously gave those in their situation some possibilities for identification and commitment. They look to football not as an excuse for a punch-up, but for a regeneration of football's role in working-class culture. [. . .]

The argument is by no means completed. Taylor tends if anything to go too far in one direction. If the mainstream attitude to 'football hooliganism' has been to deny its connections with the game, it may be overreacting to locate it wholly within the game. Rather we need to understand more fully this relationship between the game and more general cultural pressures to which some sections of the working class are being subjected. The fusion of the 'skinhead' phenomenon and 'football hooliganism' may have provided a moment when some of those relationships became clear: how football appeared as an element alongside other cultural experiences like housing redevelopment and the break-up of the traditional neighbourhood, frustrated expectations in education and employment, the commercialization of leisure, the 'threat' posed by immigration. [. . .]

What is happening on the terraces is similar to what is happening on the field. There is occasionally discussion of the relationship between violence among players and that amongst spectators, either as a simple causal one (punch-up on the field equals punch-up on the terraces) or in terms of players setting a 'bad example' for younger impressionable players to follow. The connection seems to me more subtle and more indirect. The traditional player and supporter inhabited a set of cultural definitions of themselves and each other: what I propose to call separate but related codes. Neither the laws of the game nor those of the society governing behaviour on the terraces are sufficient to guarantee order. What there has to be in addition is a set of unwritten rules — a code — as to what is acceptable behaviour. For contemporary working-class youth, such a code is not absent (the Town Boy does become like his father), but it is more fragile and tenuous. Within the specific cultural arena of football an appropriate code cannot be generated by the armchair viewer, the sophisticated TV pundit or the club chairman. Their vision of the selective passive family grouping bears little relationship to the general life experience of working-class youth, to their particular involvement behind the goal. In the absence of a code appropriate to their circumstances, the young supporters generate one. It appears to the outsider to be unrestrained in its commitment, uncontrolled in its participation, uncivilized in its demeanour. But for the young supporter, it restores adolescent male working-class identity. The football ground is the established venue for the exploration and expression of this identity. In the absence of alternatives, it is likely to remain so. [. . .]

The Club

In 1954 a *Times* article, taking the form of a post-mortem on the double international defeat by Hungary, concluded that 'if football's place in the national culture is lost, the game will lose as a business and an entertainment as surely as it will lose as a sport and a game.' This recognizes the essential paradoxes of the professional football club while run as a business, it is generally unable (by law) or unwilling (by inclination) to pay out much interest on investment in it; while catering for a substantially working-class following, its finances and policies are controlled by capitalist entrepreneurs. Ever since the late nineteenth century when clubs began to take gate money, pay players and register as limited liability companies, these have been integral characteristics of the football club. The problem here is how these contradictions have worked themselves through in the post-war period and how such developments affect the role of the game as working-class culture.

The finances of a football club are as complex as those of any medium-size business. It is not easy to unravel them and a national picture would require painstaking research. The main trends, however, were analysed by the Chester Report in this fashion:

> The picture we have described in terms of the current financial situation and of the broader social forces at work, is complex. It is not possible to say simply that English League football is in good or bad condition, that the outlook is rosy or bleak. There are a number of quite different conditions, some apparently very rosy, some rather grey, and some very black. For the various reasons set out earlier in this chapter – the distribution and concentration of population, the abolition of the maximum wage, the inflation of transfer fees, the growth of personal affluence and private transport, the demand for highest quality amenities, the impact of television and the introduction of new European competitions which concern and reward only the top clubs – quite distinct classes have developed within the Football League. The League is only theoretically composed of ninety-two equal clubs. In practice, it has an established plutocracy, a middle class who normally just manage to keep their heads above water, and a large proletariat living in nearly permanent poverty. Admittedly the boundaries between the football middle class and the classes below may be fluid and blurred. Exceptionally good management or quirks of good fortune may also help some of the proletariat to above-average achievements. But in general the pattern of relative success is well established. All of the influences outlined above reinforce them, tending to make the rich richer and the poor poorer. What we are witnessing is a circular process in which success tends to perpetuate success, and membership of a lower division to make continued membership of a lower division more likely.[23]

This account is an uneven one. The recounting of specific costs (wages, ground, travel) is put alongside assumptions of consumer orientation. Indeed the report subsequently decides that, 'The question we must ask is – what will the customer buy?' The assumption of the dominance of a dozen or so top clubs is also questionable if extended beyond the assessment of capital assets. While the gates of some clubs do guarantee a set amount of income, this is dependent upon sustained success on the field. If one measures the extent of dominance by examining the distribution of major league prizes and status, the situation is much more open than the report implies. If one takes some indices of dominance over ten-year periods since 1919 the results are not what common sense would suggest. The number of clubs winning the league championship, finishing in the first four places or appearing in the first division has not declined in the post-war decades. Indeed, there may be an argument that the game has become more open: certainly fewer clubs are able to maintain an 'automatic' position in the first division.

So the presence of what might be described as an oligopoly of new football clubs dominating attendances, transfer fees and league success needs to be qualified. The last does not follow on from the first two and, on occasions, however temporarily, the last may be obtained without any immediate expansion of the first two. A successful team may attract resources to the club both in terms of the income from gate money and those willing to provide private capital. For any club in a city or large town, there is a reservoir of public support and private capital ready to be tapped at the first sign of success. [. . .]

Nevertheless the Chester Report's argument does have validity when applied to the lower divisions. Costs have risen relatively faster than in the first division, while income, especially that of gate money, has declined. A particular cost is that of travel, which leads the committee to recommend reverting to the old system of regionalizing competition in the lower divisions. Further, a very careful analysis of the operations of the transfer system in the mid 1960s demonstrated quite incontrovertibly that the transfer system worked to the disadvantage of the lower divisions all the way down the scale. First division teams paid out less to second division teams than they received and so on.

The response of the Chester Report was not, however, to seek to redress this apparently increasing inequality. Using a 'lame duck' metaphor fashionable at the time, they argued that any form of subsidy to smaller clubs would encourage inefficiency. Clubs which came to rely on such contributions for much of their income would have less incentive to balance their accounts and progressive management would not be encouraged. So other than regionalised competitions and more immunity from tax, the Chester Report only recommended that the smaller clubs should embark on programmes in conjunction with local authorities to establish their grounds as focal community resources. There is, of course, a divergent role for the higher clubs — what the report saw as

> the basic point whether it is not just improvement but a change in the nature of the football club which is under consideration — either towards great entertainment centres or towards smaller community social centres.[24]

What we have here are two very different and yet specific images of the cultural role of the football club. The bigger clubs are to provide facilities for an amorphous group of consumers and their families: squash courts, swimming pools and the rest. The smaller club is to encourage various forms of 'involvement': drinking at a club bar, listening to a 'blue' comic, selling a quota of tote tickets.

The central question omitted here is whether or how the supporter should have any control over the clubs he regards as his. The irony is that the supporter has been almost universally treated with contempt by football clubs. He has been expected to urinate in the open air, queue for ages for a stewed cup of tea, wait his turn for tickets while directors and season ticket holders (and their friends) are served first. He has been crammed into a small space with thousands of others to an extent which has literally put life and limb at risk. Now all this is to change: seats are provided, bars opened, car parks provided – all of course at a price around three times the original. He has been changed from supporter into consumer.

The motives are far from altruistic. At their simplest, these are measures to increase attendance revenue. Thus the conversion of a terrace to seating may halve capacity but it will double revenue. Plush enclosed boxes may be leased – at several thousand pounds a season – to businesses who can entertain their own and other executives, whisky in hand, to a spot of instant entertainment. Meanwhile those too young, too poor, or too traditional to understand or appreciate these improvements will be huddled together behind the goals.

The new consumer then receives more status but has no more power. Further, his role, as defined by the surroundings, is essentially a passive one: no impassioned troublemaker he – no physical involvement, chanting or swearing in these new stands. The drive towards all-seated stadia, motivated by the convenient theories that they increase revenue and decrease the possibilities of hooliganism, involves a redefinition of the club's relationship to the supporter.

It remains an open question of whether professional football really is insolvent, or whether it suffers from increasing inequality. The apparent availability of private capital, money from sponsorship and advertising, revenue from pools and television, hardly seems in short supply. Each club, however, is kept in a state of constant competition for resources and no attempt is made to cushion the club against the possibility of failure. It is, in short, a paradigm of capitalism. The strategies which do exist tend to fit images of the supporter as consumer; measures to reduce inequality, such as transfer levies, are steadfastly rejected. This failure is hardly surprising since the Football League is effectively run by the votes of the directors of first and second division clubs, with the two lower divisions having a token four votes between them. A body so constituted is hardly likely to concern itself with the minions. That a typical third division crowd is, in terms of any other sport, a substantial gathering of people who are expressing, through their attendance, support for a specific cultural institution – the local football club – will find little purchase amongst those whose latest investment – a footballer – will be worth more than all of a third division side put together.

It may not matter to football long term that a few obscure small-town northern clubs drop out of the league, or that others depend on the forbearance of the bank and the generosity of a local builder. But even at the very top, financial instability matters, for it is reflected on the field. Between the directors and the players stands the manager: it is on his ability to produce a successful side that the annual accounts — and the continuity of his job — depend. The end product of financial instability is fear of failure.

The International Influence and Tactics

In 1953 a new queen was crowned, an Englishman was one of the first to climb Everest, and Stanley Matthews at last won the Cup Winners' medal which had so long eluded him. All seemed right with the world. But in the same year England were soundly thrashed 6-3 by Hungary at Wembley, the first national side from the continent to beat England on their home ground. To prove it was no fluke they handed out an even more severe beating, 7-1, in the return some months later in Budapest. This provoked a bout of self-criticism throughout the game. *The Times* was strident in its analysis:

> British footballers have a four-point programme to master if they are to survive. They must become athletes, 100 per cent fit; they must become gymnasts; they must make the ball a slave, answering every command, and they must start thinking intelligently ahead of the pass . . . We must reshape our whole outlook.[25] [. . .]

As Percy Young has observed, this defeat reproduced within the game of football a more general crisis of British imperial philosophy — 'more often felt subconsciously than consciously and born of the realisation that Britain does not stand where she did'.[26]

There was little in the form of the English side in the 1950s and early 1960s to reawaken confidence. Only two of the next nine internationals after Hungary were won. England performed indifferently in the 1958 World Cup and were beaten 1-0 by Russia in a group play-off. A disastrous tour of South America in 1959 included a 1-2 defeat by Mexico and was followed by a second Wembly defeat, this time Sweden being the 3-2 victors. Despite the concession of some power and status to team manager Walter Winterbottom, the string of poor results continued and the 1962 World Cup was an action replay of 1958, the only consolation being that England's quarter-final conquerors, Brazil, went on to win the competition. Winterbottom resigned, his assistant Jimmy

Adamson declined to replace him, and Alf Ramsey was appointed manager with complete responsibility at last for team selection and preparation. A new phase had begun.

If the Football Association were slow to grasp the absolute need for efficient administration, serious preparation and extensive experience to have any success at all in international competition, one or two league clubs were more open to experimentation. Manchester United led the way with a series of friendlies against major European club sides. Thus when the Football League was finally prevailed upon to discontinue its embargo on English clubs participating in European competitions, United were more prepared than most. The first English side to enter the European Cup in the 1956-7 season, they reached the semi-finals before going down to the all-conquering Réal Madrid. In the next year, they again qualified for the semi-finals but the tragedy of the Munich air disaster cut short the progress of a young team, whose members might have introduced a whole new style to English football at both international and club level. They were succeeded in the next two season's competitions by Wolverhampton Wanderers, then by Burnley, neither of whom were able to cope with the sophistication of continental sides. It was left to another exceptional team, Tottenham Hotspurs, to emulate United in the 1961-2 season, going down by the odd goal in seven to Benfica in a two-legged semi-final.

In 1963, Spurs won the European Cup Winners' Cup, beating Athlético Madrid 5-1 in Rotterdam, and West Ham emulated them more narrowly – and on the home ground of Wembley – in 1965. But a year earlier, a run of eight games without defeat by the English national side had resulted in another defeat at home, this time by Austria.

It had become obvious that English football was tactically and organizationally anachronistic in international terms. There had been little innovation since the w/m formation produced by the change in the offside law of 1925. It involved three at the back – two full-backs and a defensive centre-half – two wing halves, who were primarily fetchers and carriers, and five forwards, all of whom were expected to attack, but the two inside forwards had special distributive responsibilities. This formation dominated English football from its institution by Herbert Chapman in the 1920s to the innovation of Alf Ramsey in the early 1960s.

The response to the challenge of the continent – and eventually that of South America – was less to alter the basic orientation to the game than to capitalize on the 'English virtues': discipline, organization and stamina. The first move was to withdraw one of the wing halves into the rear line of the defence and one inside forward into the middle position. This was the 4-2-4 system. It became evident, however, that the midfield was the crucial arena: here the opposition must be cramped for space, the ball won and distributed. This was too much for two men so another forward was withdrawn, generally a winger, regarded in the new system as a luxury since he depended on others for the ball. This gave us 4-3-3. The pattern of innovation was abruptly terminated because a 'system' was perceived to have won the World Cup for England in 1966. Ramsey experimented throughout the tournament but the lesson learnt from his success was that exceptional workrate, team understanding and defensive impenetrability could overcome more skilful but less effective foreign sides. Without Ramsey's successful institutionalization, the subsequent tactical system of English football might not have become quite so rigid or have been so slavishly reproduced through the league. The essential was the attitude that (in Arthur Hopcraft's words) 'success was overridingly important, that positive method was indispensable, that attractiveness was incidental'.[27]

In 1968 Manchester United won the European Cup — though again home advantage was crucial. Theirs was not an example to follow: a team of uniquely skilful players, dependent on Celtic flair — Crerand, Law, Best — not without tactical organization but reliant on a kind of individual talent to which few ordinary league clubs could aspire. In the World Cup of 1970 England were eliminated in late and dramatic fashion by West Germany in the quarter final. The method, it was apparent, had its limitation, though there were those who defended Ramsey's record, pointing to the narrow 0-1 defeat by Brazil as possibly the best game of the tournament.

By the early 1970s the necessity to compete seriously at international level had established a new objective and incontrovertible way of testing the health of English football: the performance of the English national side in international competitions, especially the World Cup. It was to be the elimination of England by Poland in the qualifying competition of the 1974 World Cup which was to cause Ramsey's downfall, just as the failure to score sufficient goals against Luxemburg and Finland was the end of his successor, Don Revie.

The immediate impact of these developments on the domestic game is measurable — the number of goals scored annually in the first division dropped from around 1600 in the early 1960s through 1400 in the middle of the decade to less than 1100 by 1971. Though a slight increase was evident in the middle and late 1970s the average was no more than 1200, a loss of one in four goals over twenty years. Amongst its other legacies, systems football had given us the 0-0 draw. Essentially its emphasis was defensive: if you couldn't score, you made sure the other team didn't. The perilous economic situation of some clubs reinforced the tactics of fear, while the defensive emphasis helped further to drive potential supporters away. The player too was affected by the new tightness of the game; ball players were a luxury, work-rate the norm, one small error could cost a game. In such an atmosphere it was hardly surprising that brutality could become incorporated as a tactic. The professional foul was born.

Its conception was at the international level. A loose framework of laws appropriated by different cultural traditions was bound to bring out differences of emphasis. Even so there seemed to be a virtual incompatibility between English versions of acceptable physical contact and those of south European and South American sides.

> There are now two types of football in the world — the British style and the Continental, Latin-American counterpart. When brought face to face — as in Milan recently — they tend on occasions to provide an unhappy marriage. The foreigner, nourished on a game of infiltration and sly intervention, with the minimum of physical contact, regards the British attitude of hard tackling as quite brutal.
>
> However fair and within the laws, this is considered overseas as ugly, coarse and ruthless. The foreigner, for his part, employs subtle body-checking, shielding of the ball and other tricks that rile the Briton. So the bonfire is ready for burning, unhindered by crowds and referees who penalize the British method because it is against their natures and upbringing.[28]

As English football had to face up to the international unacceptability of its essential roughness, so it tacitly agreed to drop some of the more extreme features, especially shoulder-barging and challenges on the goalkeeper. But the essential toughness remained, and the best that could be achieved was an uneasy form of truce which is still in force. In conjunction with the players' removal from the context of traditional working-class attitudes towards violence, the continental influence encouraged the development of premeditated forms of violence. The worst elements of the traditional English game and the new continental game were merged into a pattern of violence which was at once deliberate and uncontrolled.

The one modern English team to successfully master continental styles has been Liverpool. In their current phase (1976-8) they are undisputed club champions of Europe. This has been achieved frequently with only two specialist forwards, but with a midfield of such flexibility that there are always men up in support. Yet still a question remains about the attractiveness of this form of football. It is an effective and efficient combination of pace and skill, determination and virtuosity — but few can hope to emulate it. Such football is essentially cerebral; the comparison frequently made is with chess. The ball is moved sideways and backwards, carefully retained until an opening becomes apparent. Nothing is attempted which may lose possession and the overall effect is frequently claustrophobic. It depends crucially on some exceptional individual skill — first Keegan, then Dalgleish, supplemented by Heighway — and on a managerial ability to convert average players into exceptional ones. [. . .]

While the ability to create or score the unusual goal is prized more than ever, the system of coaching, of tactics, of defensiveness, ensures that such tendencies will be quickly eliminated amongst younger players. If there is a source of cultural innovation it may be ethnic. Anderson of Nottingham Forest, Regis and Cunningham of Albion, Hazell of Wolves may provide a confidence and freedom of expression lacking in the indigenous game. Orient's fielding of five black players at the beginning of 1978-9 may be a sign of things to come. It remains to be seen whether such influences make any headway against the influences which have dominated the tactics of post-war football; the need to succeed internationally, the financial penalties of failure, the sheer negative and defensive response of tactical thought.

Conclusion

The argument here has been that in the post-war period there have been significant qualitative shifts in the game of football, as it is played on the pitch, [. . .] organized through clubs, understood by the spectators, and experienced by the professional footballer. [. . .]

We may not have a language to describe adequately the continuing transformation of football. If there is a concept which can help to distill the dominant tendencies it may be that of the spectacle. The spectacle is an item produced for consumption. The essential relationship is that between producer and consumer. To this end the event itself — in this case the ninety-minute match — is situated within specific 'demands' universally held by the consumer for adequate car parks, pre-match entertainment, organized response, and fed information. The consumer is provided for; his main activity is to decide whether to come, but beyond that he is expected to exert himself little. As has been argued above, the provision of minimal comfort is long overdue, and the loyalties of the existent footballing sub-culture are not easily turned into the vagaries of consumerism. No Aston Villa supporter goes to Birmingham City except to support the away team.

There is an example of a situation where the idea of the spectacle has dominated football, and that is in the United States of America. Adequate information is hard to come by since the English press has alternated between condescension and sycophancy in its reporting of

American football.[29] A few characteristics still emerge: the ownership
of whole clubs by corporations, the franchise system enabling clubs to
be moved from city to city at will; the pre-match car-park barbecues,
organized cheerleading, continuous commentary, scoreboards which
light up when a foul is committed with the slogan 'Did You See That?'.
The game itself has also been altered: offside restricted to part of the
pitch, the abolition of the draw replaced by 'sudden death' playoffs
of beating the goalkeeper on the run; even extending the size of the
goals has been mooted. The objection is not to any of these individually.
The laws, for example, are subject to continuous reinterpretation and
change and there may be a good case for experimenting with the offside
law. The question is what kinds of consideration govern innovation. In
the American example the direction is consistently towards the spec-
tacularization of football. The event has been surrounded and penetrated by the need to provide instant entertainment to keep the consumer
interested.

It is unlikely that English league football will ever approximate to
this kind of cultural aberration (though Queens Park Rangers, among
others, have installed a declamatory scoreboard). But what has been
happening in the post-war years has been that football has lost its
partial autonomy as a form of popular culture from the economic
and cultural forces dominant in the rest of society. This is not to
suggest that football has ever been in any sense oppositional. It was
rather a symbolic displacement, produced, transmitted and recognized
by working-class men as expressive of their situation. It could be
argued that changes in the relative economic situation of the post-war
working class has rendered irrelevant traditional forms of cultural expression, of which football was one. The redefinition of football has
not, however, primarily been by the supporters. An unholy and un-
witting alliance of the Professional Footballers Association, the Football League and Football Association, the pundits of press and television, underwritten by objective financial considerations (actually
of their own making), have begun the long process of making football
respectable, malleable to the needs of the mass media, aesthetic rather
than exciting, aimed at an audience of consumers rather than a body of
supporters.

There may be some measures which could divert football from its
likely fate as one of a number of uniformly packaged spectacles presented by capitalist business. These might include: a change in the points
system, to encourage attacking play; severer penalties, including reduc-
tions in points, for clubs guilty of persistent foul play; an abolition of
the transfer system to stabilize the game's finances; nationalization of
the pools, and a subsidy to smaller clubs. But in the prevailing climate
such proposals are likely to seem too radical a break for those in charge

of the game's fortunes, whose sense of tradition is actually a habit of authority. Ultimately the problem is that in football, as in many of its corporate cultural activities, the power to control the institution does not rest with those on whose behalf it has been created. [. . .]

Notes

1. Ian Taylor, 'Soccer Consciousness and Soccer Hooliganism' in Stan Cohen (ed.), *Images of Deviance* (Penguin, 1971).

2. Arthur Hopcraft, *The Football Man*, rev. edn (Penguin, 1971), p. 24.

3. *The Times*, 14 December 1961.

4. Hopcraft, *The Football Man*, p. 43.

5. Ibid.

6. Ibid., p. 30.

7. Arthur Walmsley, 'Duncan Edwards' in John Arlott (ed.), *Soccer: the Great Ones* (Pelham, 1968).

8. Hopcraft, *The Football Man*, p. 75.

9. David Miller, 'Alan Ball' in Reg Hayter (ed.), *Soccer Stars of Today* (Pelham, 1970).

10. *The Times*, 20 November 1961.

11. *Rothman's Football Yearbook 1977-78*.

12. *The Times*, 11 November 1961.

13. *The Times*, 12 April 1962.

14. Chester Committee, *Report of the Committee on Football* (HMSO, 1968).

15. Raymond Williams, *The Long Revolution* (Pelican, 1961).

16. Taylor, 'Soccer Consciousness'; also Taylor, 'Football Mad' in Eric Dunning (ed.), *The Sociology of Sport* (Frank Cass, 1971).

17. Taylor, 'Soccer Consciousness', p. 363.

18. Stuart Hall, 'The Treatment of Football Hooliganism in the Press' in Roger Ingham (ed.), *Football Hooliganism* (Inter-Action, 1978).

19. Hall, 'Treatment of Football Hooliganism'.

20. John Arlott, 'Like Running Dogs through Arab Villages', *Guardian*, 5 January 1973.

21. Hopcraft, *The Football Man*, p. 160.

22. Taylor, 'Soccer Consciousness' and 'Football Mad'.

23. *Report of the Committee on Football*.

24. Ibid.

25. *The Times*, 21 November 1953.

26. Percy Young, *A History of British Football* (Stanley Paul, 1968).

27. Hopcraft, *The Football Man*, p. 116.

28. *The Times*, 19 May 1955.

29. 'Football in America', *Guardian*, 4-17 September 1978.

11 THE NARRATIVE STRUCTURE IN FLEMING

Umberto Eco

Source: *The Bond Affair* (Macdonald, London, 1966).
© U. Eco.

In 1953 Ian Fleming published the first novel in the 007 series, *Casino Royale*. Being a first work, it is subject to the then current literary influence, and in the fifties, which had abandoned the traditional detective whodunit trail in favour of violent action, it was impossible to ignore the presence of Spillane.

To Spillane, *Casino Royale* owes, beyond doubt, at least two characteristic elements. First of all the girl Vesper Lynd, who arouses the confident love of Bond, in the end is revealed as an enemy agent. In a novel by Spillane the hero would have killed her, while in Fleming the woman had the grace to commit suicide; but Bond's reaction when it happens has the Spillane characteristic of transforming love into hatred and tenderness to ferocity: 'She's dead, the bitch' Bond telephones to his London office, and so ends his romance.

In the second place Bond is obsessed by an image: that of a Japanese expert in codes whom he had killed in cold blood on the thirty-sixth floor of the R.C.A. Skyscraper at Rockefeller Centre — with a bullet — from a window on the fortieth floor of the skyscraper opposite. By an analogy that is surely not accidental, Mike Hammer seemed to be consistently haunted by the memory of a small Japanese he killed in the jungle during the war, though with greater emotive participation (while Bond's homicide, authorised officially by the double-zero, is more ascetic and bureaucratic). The memory of the Japanese was the beginning of the undoubted nervous disorder of Mike Hammer (of his sadistic masochism, of his arguable impotence); the memory of his first homicide could have been the origin of the neurosis of James Bond, except that, within the ambit of *Casino Royale*, either the character or his author solves the problem by non-therapeutic means: that is by excluding the neurosis from the narrative. This decision was to influence the structure of the following eleven novels by Fleming and presumably forms the basis for their success.

After having helped to dispose of two Bulgarians who had tried to get rid of him, after having suffered torture in the form of a cruel abuse of his testicles, having been present at the elimination of Le Chiffre by the action of a Soviet agent, having received from him a scar on the hand, cold-bloodedly carved while he was conscious, and after having risked the effect on his love life, Bond, enjoying his well-earned convalescence on a hospital bed, confided a chilling doubt to his French colleague, Mathis. Have they been fighting for a just cause? Le Chiffre, who had financed Communist spies among the French workers, was he not 'serving a wonderful purpose, a really vital purpose, perhaps the best and highest purpose of all'? The difference between good and evil, is it really something neat, recognisable, as the hagiography of counter-espionage would like us to believe? At this point Bond is ripe for the crisis, for the salutary recognition of universal ambiguity, and he sets off along the route traversed by the protagonist of le Carré. But in the very moment when he questions himself about the appearance of the devil and, sympathising with the Enemy, is inclined to recognise him as a 'lost brother', James Bond is treated to a salve from Mathis: 'When you get back to London you will find there are other Le Chiffres seeking to destroy you and your friends and your country. M will tell you about them. And now that you have seen a really evil man, you will know how evil they can be and you will go after them to destroy them in order to protect yourself and the people you love. You know what they look like now and what they can do to people ... Surround yourself with human beings, my dear James. They are easier to fight for than principles. But don't let me down and become human yourself. We could lose such a wonderful machine.'

With this lapidary phrase Fleming defines the character of James Bond for the novels to come. From *Casino Royale* there remained the scar on his cheek, the slightly cruel smile, the taste for good food, together with a number of subsidiary characteristics minutely documented in the course of this first volume: but convinced by Mathis's words, Bond was to abandon the treacherous life of moral meditation and of psychological anger, with all the neurotic dangers that they entail. Bond ceased to be a subject of psychiatry and remained at the most a physiological object (except for a return to the subject of the psyche in the last, untypical novel in the series, *The Man with the Golden Gun*), a magnificent machine, as the author and the public, as well as Mathis, had wished. From that moment Bond did not meditate upon truth and upon justice, upon life and death, except in rare moments of boredom, usually in the bar of an airport, but always in the form of a casual daydream, never allowing himself to be infected by doubt (at least in novels – he did indulge in such intimate luxuries in the short stories).

From the psychological point of view a conversion has taken place quite suddenly, on the base of four conventional phrases pronounced by Mathis, but the conversion was not really justified on a psychological level. In the last pages of *Casino Royale* Fleming, in fact, renounces all psychology as the motive of narrative and decides to transfer characters and situations to the level of an objective and conventional structural strategy. Without knowing it, Fleming makes a choice familiar to many contemporary disciplines: he passes from the psychological method to that of the formula.

In *Casino Royale* there are already all the elements for the building of a machine that would function basically as a unit along very simple, straight lines, conforming to the strict rules of combination. This machine, which was to function without deviation of fortune in the novels that followed, lies at the basis of the success of the '007 saga' — a success which, singularly, has been due both to the adulation of the masses and to the appreciation of more sophisticated readers. We intend here to examine in detail this narrating machine in order to identify the reasons for its success. It is our plan to devise a descriptive table of the narrative structure in Ian Fleming while seeking to evaluate for each structural element the probable incidence upon the reader's sensitivity. We shall try, therefore, to distinguish such a narrative structure at five levels:

(1) The juxtaposition of the characters and of values.
(2) Play situations and the plot as a 'game'.
(3) A Manichean ideology.
(4) Literary techniques.
(5) Literature as montage.

Our enquiry covers the range of the following novels listed in order of publication (the date of composition was presumably a year earlier in each case):

Casino Royale, 1953
Live and Let Die, 1954
Moonraker, 1955
Diamonds are Forever, 1956
From Russia with Love, 1957
Dr. No, 1958
Goldfinger, 1959
Thunderball, 1961
On Her Majesty's Secret Service, 1963
You Only Live Twice, 1964

We shall refer also to the stories in *For Your Eyes Only* (1960), and to *The Man with the Golden Gun* published in 1965. But we shall not take into consideration *The Spy who Loved Me* (1962), which seems quite untypical.

1. The Juxtaposition of the Characters and of Values

The novels of Fleming seem to be built on a series of 'oppositions' which allow a limited number of permutation and reactions. These dichotomies constitute a constant feature around which minor couples rotate and they form, from novel to novel, variations on them. We have here singled out fourteen couples, four of which are contrasted to four actual characters, while the others form a conflict of values, variously personified by the four basic characters. The fourteen couples are:

(a) Bond – M
(b) Bond – Villain
(c) Villain – Woman
(d) Woman – Bond
(e) Free World – Soviet Union
(f) Great Britain – Countries not Anglo-Saxon
(g) Duty – Sacrifice
(h) Cupidity – Ideals
(i) Love – Death
(j) Chance – Planning
(k) Luxury – Discomfort
(l) Excess – Moderation
(m) Perversion – Innocence
(n) Loyalty – Disloyalty

These pairs do not represent 'vague' elements but 'simple' ones that are immediate and universal, and if we consider the range of each pair we see that the variants allowed cover a vast field and in fact include all the narrative ideas of Fleming.

In Bond-M there is a dominated-dominant relationship which characterises from the beginning the limits and possibilities of the character of Bond and sets events moving. The interpretation, psychological or psycho-analytical, of Bond's attitude towards M has been discussed in particular by Kingsley Amis (*The James Bond Dossier*, Jonathan Cape, 1965). The fact is that even in terms of pure fictional functions M represents to Bond the one who holds the key to action and to knowledge. Hence his superiority over his employee who depends upon him, and who sets out on his various missions in conditions of inferiority to the omniscience of his chief. Frequently his chief sends Bond into adventures of which he had discounted the upshot from the start. Bond is thus often the victim of a trick, albeit a popular one – and it does not matter that in the event things happen to him beyond the cool calculations of M. The tutelage under which M holds Bond – obliged against his will to visit a doctor, to undergo a nature cure

(*Thunderball*), to change his gun (*Dr. No*) — makes so much the more insidious and imperious his chief's authority. We can, therefore, see that M represents certain other virtues, like the religion of Duty, Country and Order (which contrasts with Bond's own inclination to rely on improvisation). If Bond is the hero and hence possesses exceptional qualities, M represents Moderation, accepted perhaps as a national virtue. In reality Bond is not so exceptional as a hasty reading of the books (or the spectacular interpretation which films give of the books) might make one think. Fleming always affirmed that he had thought of Bond as an absolutely ordinary person, and it is in contrast with M that the real stature of 007 emerges, endowed with physical attribute, with courage and fast reflexes, without possessing any other quality in excess. It is rather a certain moral force, an obstinate fidelity to the job — at the command of M, always present as a warning — that allows him to overcome superhuman ordeals without exercising any superhuman faculty.

The Bond-M relationship indubitably presupposes an affectionate ambivalence, a reciprocal love-hate, and this without need to resort to psychology. At the beginning of *The Man with the Golden Gun*, emerging from a lengthy amnesia and conditioned by the Soviets, he tries a kind of actual parricide by shooting at M with a cyanide pistol: the gesture loosened a long-standing series of tensions (in the narrative) which were aggravated every time that M and Bond found themselves face to face.

Started by M on the road of Duty (at all costs), Bond enters into conflict with the Villain. The opposition brings into play diverse virtues, some of which are only variants of the basic couples previously paired and listed. Bond indubitably represents Beauty and Virility as opposed to the Villain, who appears often monstrous and sexually impotent. The monstrosity of the Villain is a constant point, but to emphasize it we must here introduce an idea of the method which will also apply in examining the other couples. Among the variants we must consider also the existence of secondary characters whose functions are understood only if they are seen as 'variations' of one of the principal personages, some of whose characteristics they 'wear'. The vicarious roles function usually for the Woman and for the Villain; also for M — certain collaborators with Bond represent the M figures; for example Mathis in *Casino Royale*, who preaches Duty in the appropriate M manner (albeit with a cynical and Gallic air). As to the characteristics of the Villain, let us consider them in order. In *Casino Royale* Le Chiffre is pallid and smooth, with a crop of red hair, an almost feminine mouth, false teeth of expensive quality, small ears with large lobes and hairy hands. He did not smile. In *Live and Let Die*, Mr. Big, a Haiti Negro, had a head that resembles a football, twice the normal size, and almost spherical; 'the skin was grey-black, taut and shining like the face of a week-old corpse in the river. It was hairless, except for some grey-brown fluff above the ears. There were no eyebrows and no eyelashes and the eyes were extraordinarily far apart so that one could not focus on them both, but only on one at a time . . . They were animal eyes, not human, and they seemed to blaze.' The gums were pale pink.

In *Diamonds are Forever* the villain appears in three different forms. They are first of all Jack and Seraffino Spang, the first of whom had a humped back and red hair ('Bond did not remember having seen a red-haired hunchback before'), eyes which might have been hired from a taxidermist, big ears with rather exaggerated lobes, dry red lips, and an almost total absence of neck. Seraffino had a face the colour of ivory, black puckered eyebrows, a bush of shaggy hair, jutting, ruthless jaws: if it is added that Seraffino used to pass his days in a Spectreville of the old West dressed in black leather chaps embellished with leather, silver spurs, pistols with ivory butts, a black belt and ammunition – also that he used to drive a train of 1870 vintage furnished with a Victorian carriage in Technicolour – the picture is complete. The third vicarious figure is that of Señor Winter, who travels with a ticket which reads: 'My blood group is F', and who is really a killer in the pay of the Spangs and is a gross and sweating individual with a wart on his hand, a placid visage, and protruding eyes.

In *Moonraker*, Hugo Drax is six feet tall, with 'exceptionally broad' shoulders, has a large and square head, red hair. The right half of his face is shiny and wrinkled from unsuccessful plastic surgery, the right eye different from the left and larger because of a contraction of the skin of the eyelashes ('painfully bloodshot'), has heavy moustaches, whiskers to the lobes of his ears, and patches of hair on his cheekbones: the moustaches concealed with scant success a prognathous upper jaw and a marked protrusion of his upper teeth. The backs of his hands are covered with reddish hair, and altogether he evokes the idea of a ring-master at the circus.

In *From Russia with Love* the villain appears in the shape of three vicarious figures: Red Grant, the professional murderer in the pay of Smersh, with short, sandy-coloured eyelashes, colourless and opaque blue eyes, a small, cruel mouth, innumerable freckles on his milk-white skin, and deep, wide pores; Colonel Grubozaboyschikov, head of Smersh, has a narrow and sharp face, round eyes like two polished marbles, weighed down by two flabby pouches, a broad and grim mouth and a shaven skull; finally Rosa Klebb, with the humid pallid lip stained with nicotine, the raucous voice, flat and devoid of emotion, is five feet four, no curves, dumpy arms, short neck, too sturdy ankles, grey hairs gathered in a tight 'obscene' bun. She has shiny yellow-brown eyes, thick glasses, a sharp nose white with powder and large nostrils.

'The wet trap of a mouth, that went on opening and shutting as if it was operated by wires under the chin' completes the appearance of a sexually neuter person. In *From Russia* there occurs a variant that is discernible only in a few other novels; there enters also upon the scene a strongly drawn being who has many of the moral qualities of the Villain but uses them in the end for good or at least fights on the side of Bond. In *From Russia* an example is Darko Kerim, the Turkish agent. Analogous to him is the head of the Japanese secret service in *You Only Live Twice*, Tiger Tanaka; Draco in *On Her Majesty's Secret Service*, Enrico Colombo in 'Risico' (a story in *For Your Eyes Only*) and — partially — Quarrel in *Dr. No*. These characteristics are at the same time representative of the Villain and of M and we shall call them 'ambiguous representatives'. With these Bond always stands in a kind of competitive alliance, he likes them and hates him at the same time, he uses them, and admires them, he dominates them and is their slave.

In *Dr. No*, the Villain, besides his great height, is characterised by the lack of hands, which are replaced by two metal pincers. His shaven head has the appearance of a reversed raindrop, his skin is clear, without wrinkles, the cheekbones are as smooth as fine ivory, his eyebrows dark as though painted on, his eyes are without eyelashes and look 'like the mouths of two small revolvers', his nose is thin and ends very close to his mouth, which shows only cruelty and authority.

In *Goldfinger* the eponymous character is absolutely a textbook monster; that is to say he is characterised by a lack of proportion: 'He was short, not more than five feet tall, and on top of the thick body and blunt peasant legs was set almost directly into the shoulders a huge and, it seemed, exactly round head. It was as if he had been put together with bits of other people's bodies. Nothing seemed to belong.' His 'representative' figure is that of the Korean, Oddjob, with fingers on his hands like spatulas, with fingertips like solid bone, a man who could smash the wooden balustrade of a staircase with a karate blow.

In *Thunderball* there appears for the first time Ernst Starvo Blofeld, who crops up again in *On Her Majesty's Secret Service* and *You Only Live Twice*, where in the end he dies. As his vicarious incarnations, we have in *Thunderball* Count Lippe and Emilio Largo; both are handsome and personable, however vulgar and cruel, and their monstrosity is purely mental. In *On Her Majesty's Secret Service* there appears Irma Blunt, the soul damned by Blofeld, a distant reincarnation of Rosa Klebb, and a series of villains in outline who perish tragically, killed by an avalanche or by a train. In the third book the primary role is resumed and results in the finish of the monster Blofeld, already described in *Thunderball*: two eyes that resemble two deep pools, surrounded 'like the eyes of Mussolini' by clear whites, of a symmetry which recalls the eyes of a doll, also because of silken black eyelashes of feminine type; two eyes with a child-like gaze, and a mouth like a badly healed wound under a heavy squat nose; altogether an expression of hypocrisy, tyranny and cruelty 'on a Shakespearean level'; twenty stone in weight; as we learn in *On Her Majesty's Secret Service*, Blofeld lacks lobes to his ears. His hair is a wiry black crew-cut. This curious similarity of appearance among all the Villains in turn suggests a certain unity to the Bond-Villain relationship, especially when it is added that as a rule the wicked are distinguished also by certain racial and 'biographical' characteristics.

The Villain is born in an ethnic area that stretches from central Europe to the Slav countries and to the Mediterranean basin: as a rule he is of mixed blood and his origins are complex and obscure; he is asexual or homosexual, or at any rate is not sexually normal: he has exceptional inventive and organisational qualities which help him acquire immense wealth and by means of which he usually works to help Russia: to this end he conceives a plan of fantastic character and dimensions, worked out to the smallest detail, intended to create serious difficulties either for England or the Free World in general. In the figure of the Villain, in fact, there are gathered the negative values which we have distinguished in some pairs of opposites, the Soviet Union and countries which are not Anglo-Saxon (the racial convention blames particularly the Jews, the Germans, the Slavs and the Italians, always depicted as half-breeds), Cupidity elevated to the dignity of paranoia, Planning as technological methodology, satrapic luxury, physical and psychical Excess, physical and moral Perversion, radical Disloyalty.

Le Chiffre, who organises the subversive movement in France, comes from 'a mixture of Mediterranean with Prussian or Polish strains, and has Jewish blood revealed by small ears with large lobes'. A gambler not basically disloyal, he still betrays his own bosses, and tries to recover by criminal means money lost in gambling, is a masochist (at least so the Secret Service dossier proclaims), entirely heterosexual, has bought a great chain of brothels, but has lost his patrimony by his exalted manner of living.

Mr. Big is a Negro enjoying with Solitaire an ambiguous relationship of exploitation (he has not yet acquired her favours), helps the Soviet Union by means of his powerful criminal organisation founded on the voodoo cult, finds and sells in the United States treasure hidden in the seventeenth century, controls various rackets, and is prepared to ruin the American economy by introducing, through the black market, large quantities of rare coins.

Hugo Drax displays indefinite nationality — he is English by adoption — but in fact he is German: he holds control of columbite, a material indispensable to the construction of reactors and gives to the

British Crown the means of building a most powerful rocket; in reality he plans to make the rocket fall, when tested atomically, on London, and to flee then to Russia (equation Communist-Nazi); he frequents clubs of high class, is passionately fond of bridge, but only enjoys cheating; his hysteria does not permit one to suspect any sexual activity worthy of note.

Of the secondary characters in *From Russia* the chief are from the Soviets, and obviously in working for the Communist cause enjoy comforts and power; Rosa Klebb, sexually neuter, 'might enjoy the act physically, but the instrument was of no importance'; as to Red Grant, he is a werewolf and kills for passion; he lives splendidly at the expense of the Soviet government, in a villa with a bathing pool. The science-fiction plot consists in attracting Bond into a complicated trap, using for bait a woman and an instrument for coding and decoding ciphers and then killing and checkmating the English counter-spy.

Dr. No is a Chinese-German halfbreed, works for Russia, shows no definite sexual tendencies (having in his power Honeychile he plans to have her torn to pieces by the crabs of Crab Key), he lives on a flourishing guano industry and plans to cause guided missiles launched by the Americans to deviate from their course. In the past he has built up his fortune by robbing the criminal organisation of which he had been elected cashier. He lives, on his island, in a palace of fabulous pomp. Goldfinger has a probable Baltic origin but has also Jewish blood; he lives splendidly from commerce and from smuggling gold, by means of which he finances Communist movements in Europe; he plans the theft of gold from Fort Knox (not its radioactivation as the film states), and to overcome the final barrier sets up an atomic attack in the neighbourhood of N.A.T.O.: he tries to poison the water of Fort Knox; he does not have sexual relationships with the girl that he dominates, limiting himself to the acquisition of gold. He cheats at cards, using expensive devices, like binoculars and radio; he cheats to make money, even though fabulously rich and always travelling with a stock of gold in his luggage.

As to Blofeld, he is of a Polish father and a Greek mother; he exploits his position as telegraph clerk to start a flourishing trade in Poland in secret information, becomes chief of the most extensive independent organisation for espionage, blackmail, rapine and extortion. Indeed with Blofeld Russia ceased to be the constant enemy — because of the general international relaxation of tension — and the part of the malevolent organisation is assumed by Spectre. Spectre has all the characteristics of Smersh, including the employment of Slav-Latin-German elements, the use of torture and the elimination of traitors, the sworn enmity to all the powers of the Free World. Of the science-fiction plans of Blofeld, that of *Thunderball* consists in stealing from N.A.T.O. two atomic bombs and with these blackmailing England and America. That of *On Her Majesty's Secret Service* envisages the training in a mountain clinic of girls with suitable allergies to condition them to spread a mortal virus intended to ruin the agriculture and live-stock of the United Kingdom. That of *You Only Live Twice*, the last stage in Blofeld's career, starts with a murderous mania but shrinks — upon a greatly reduced political scale — to the preparation of a fantastic suicidal garden near the coast of Japan, which attracts legions of heirs of the Kamikaze, bent on poisoning themselves with exotic, refined and lethal plants, thus doing grave and complex harm to the human patrimony of Japanese democracy. Blofeld's tendency towards satrapic pomp shows itself in the kind of life he leads in the mountain of Piz Gloria, and more particularly on the island of Kyashu, where he lives in medieval tyranny and passes through his *hortus deliciarum* clad in metal armour. Previously Blofeld had shown himself ambitious of honours (he aspired to be known as the Count of Bleuville), as a master of planning, an organising genius, as treacherous as needs be and sexually impotent — he lived in marriage with Irma Blofeld, also asexual and hence repulsive; to quote the words of Tiger Tanaka, Blofeld 'is a devil who has taken human form'.

Only the evil characters of *Diamonds are Forever* have no connections with Russia. In a certain sense the international gangsterism of the Spangs appears to be an earlier version of Spectre. For the rest, Jack and Seraffino possess all the characteristics of the canon.

To the typical qualities of the Villain are opposed the Bond characteristics, in particular Loyalty to the Service, Anglo-Saxon Moderation opposed to the excess of the halfbreeds, the selection of Discomfort and the acceptance of Sacrifice as against the ostentatious luxury of the enemy, the stroke of opportunistic genius (Chance) opposed to the cold Planning which it defeats, the sense of an Ideal opposed to Cupidity (Bond in various cases wins from the Villain in gambling, but as a rule returns the enormous sums won to the Service or to the girl of the moment, as occurred with Jill Masterson; thus even when he has money it is no longer a primary object). For the rest some oppositions function not only in the Bond-Villain relationship, but even internally in the behaviour of Bond himself; thus Bond is as a rule loyal but does not disdain to overcome a cheating enemy by a deceitful trick, and to blackmail him (cf. *Moonraker* or *Goldfinger*). Even Excess and Moderation, Chance and Planning are opposed in the acts and decisions of Bond himself. Duty and Sacrifice appear as elements of internal debate each time that Bond knows he must prevent the plan of the Villain at the risk of his life, and in those cases, the patriotic ideal (Great Britain and the Free World) takes the upper hand. He calls also on the racialist need to show the superiority of the Briton. In Bond there are also opposed Luxury (the choice of good food, care in dressing, preference for sumptuous hotels, love of the gambling table, invention of cocktails etc.) and Discomfort (Bond is always ready to abandon the easy life, even when it appears in the guise of a Woman who offers herself, to face a new aspect of Discomfort, the acutest point of which is torture). We have discussed the Bond-Villain dichotomy at length because in fact it embodies all the characteristics of the opposition between Eros and Thanatos, the beginning of pleasure and the beginning of reality, culminating in the moment of torture (in *Casino Royale* explicitly theorised as a sort of erotic relationship between the torturer and the tortured).

This opposition is perfected in the relationship between the Villain and the Woman; Vesper is tyrannised and blackmailed by the Soviet, and therefore by Le Chiffre; Solitaire is the slave of Mr. Big; Tiffany Case is dominated by the Spangs; Tatiana is the slave of Rosa Klebb and of the Soviet Government in general; Jill and Tilly Masterson are dominated, in different degrees, by Goldfinger, and Pussy Galore works to his orders; Domino Vitali is subservient to the wishes of Blofeld through the physical relationship with the vicarious figure of Emilio Largo; the English girl guests of Piz Gloria are under the hypnotic control of Blofeld and the virginal surveillance of Irma Blunt; while Honeychile has a purely symbolic relationship with the power of Dr. No, wandering pure and untroubled on the shores of his cursed island, except that at the end Dr. No offers her naked body to the crabs (Honeychile has been dominated by the Villain through the vicarious effort of the brutal Mander who had violated her, and had justly punished Mander by causing a scorpion to kill him, anticipating the revenge of No — which had recourse to crabs); and finally Kissy Suzuki lived on her island in the shade of the cursed castle of Blofeld, suffering a domination that was purely allegorical, shared by the whole population of the place. In an intermediate position is Gala Brand, who is an agent of the Service but who became the secretary of Hugo Drax and established a relationship of submission to him. In most of the cases this relationship culminated in the torture which the woman underwent along with Bond. Here the Love-Death pair function, also in the sense of a more intimate erotic union of the two through their common trial.

Dominated by the Villain, however, Fleming's woman has already been previously conditioned to domination, life for her having assumed the role of the villain. The general scheme is (1) the girl is beautiful and good; (2) has been made frigid and unhappy by severe trials suffered in adolescence; (3) this has conditioned her to the service of the Villain; (4) through meeting Bond she appreciates human nature in all its richness; (5) Bond possesses her but in the end loses her.

This curriculum is common to Vesper, Solitaire, Tiffany, Tatiana,

Honeychile, Domino; rather hinted at for Gala, equally shared by the three representative women of Goldfinger (Jill, Tilly and Pussy — the first two have had a sad past, but only the third has been violated by her uncle: Bond possessed the first and the third, the second is killed by the Villain, the first tortured with gold paint, the second and third are Lesbians and Bond redeems only the third; and so forth); more diffuse and uncertain for the group of girls on Piz Gloria — each had had an unhappy past, but Bond in fact possessed only one of them (similarly he marries Tracy whose past was unhappy because of a series of unions, dominated by her father Draco, and was killed in the end by Blofeld, who realises at this point his domination and ends by Death the relationship of Love which she entertained for Bond). Kissy Susuki has been made unhappy by a Hollywoodian experience which has made her chary of life and of men.

In every case Bond loses each of these women, either by her own will or that of another (in the case of Gala it is the woman who marries somebody else, although unwillingly) — either at the end of the novel or at the beginning of the following one (as happened with Tiffany Case). Thus, in the moment in which the Woman solves the opposition to the Villain by entering with Bond into a purificating-purified, saving-saved relationship, she returns to the domination of the negative. In this there is a lengthy combat between the couple Perversion-Purity (sometimes external, as in the relationship of Rosa Klebb and Tatiana) which makes her similar to the persecuted virgin of Richardsonian memory. The bearer of purity, notwithstanding and in spite of the mire, exemplary subject for an alternation of embrace-torture, she would appear likely to resolve the contrast between the chosen race and the non-Anglo-Saxon halfbreed, since she often belongs to an ethnically inferior breed; but when the erotic relationship always ends with a form of death, real or symbolic, Bond resumes willy-nilly the purity of Anglo-Saxon celibacy. The race remains uncontaminated.

2. Play Situations and the Plot as a 'Game'

The various pairs of opposites (of which we have considered only a few possible variants) seem like the elements of an *ars combinatoria* with fairly elementary rules. It is clear that in the engagement of the two poles of each couple there are, in the course of the novel, alternative solutions; the reader does not know at which point of the story the Villain defeats Bond or Bond defeats the Villain, and so on. But towards the end of the book the algebra has to follow a prearranged pattern: as in the Chinese game that 007 and Tanaka play at the beginning of *You Only Live Twice*, hand beats fist, fist beats two fingers, two fingers beat hand. M beats Bond. Bond beats the Villain, the Villain beats Woman, even if at first Bond beats Woman; the Free World beats the Soviet Union, England beats the Impure Countries, Death beats Love, Moderation beats Excess, and so forth.

This interpretation of the plot in terms of a game is not accidental. The books of Fleming are dominated by situations that we call 'play situations'. First of all there are several archetypal situations like the Journey and the Meal; the Journey may be by Machine (and here there occurs a rich symbolism of the automobile, typical of our century), by Train (another archetype, this time of obsolescent type), by Aeroplane, or by Ship. But here it is realised that as a rule a meal, a pursuit by machine or a mad race by train, always take the form of a challenge, a game. Bond decides the choice of foods as though they formed the pieces of a puzzle, prepares for the meal with the same scrupulous attention to method as he prepares for a game of Bridge (see the convergence, in a means-end connection, of the two elements in *Moonraker*) and he intends the meal as a factor in the game. Similarly, train and machine are the elements of a wager against an adversary: before the journey is finished one of the two has finished his moves and given checkmate.

At this point it is useless to record the occurrence of the play situations, in the true and proper sense of conventional games of chance, in each book. Bond always gambles and wins, against the Villain or with some vicarious figure. The detail with which these games are described will be the subject of further consideration in the section which we shall dedicate to literary technique; here it must be said that if these games occupy a prominent space it is because they form a reduced and formalised model of the more general play situation that is the novel. The novel, given the rules of combination of opposing couples, is fixed as a sequence of 'moves' inspired by the code, and constituted according to a perfectly prearranged scheme.

The invariable scheme is the following:

A. M moves and gives a task to Bond.
B. The Villain moves and appears to Bond (perhaps in alternative forms).
C. Bond moves and gives a first check to the Villain or the Villain gives first check to Bond.
D. Woman moves and shows herself to Bond.
E. Bond consumes Woman: possesses her or begins her seduction.
F. The Villain captures Bond (with or without Woman, or at different moments).
G. The Villain tortures Bond (with or without Woman).
H. Bond conquers the Villain (kills him, or kills his representative or

helps at their killing).
I. Bond convalescing enjoys Woman, whom he then loses.

The scheme is invariable in the sense that all the elements are always present in every novel (so that it might be affirmed that the fundamental rules of the game is 'Bond moves and mates in eight moves' — but, due to the ambivalence Love-Death, so to speak, 'The Villain counter-moves and mates in eight moves'). It is not imperative that the moves always be in the same sequence. A minute detailing of the ten novels under consideration would yield several examples of a set scheme which we might call A.B.C.D.E.F.G.H.I (for example *Dr. No*), but often there are inversions and variations. Sometimes Bond meets the Villain at the beginning of the volume and gives him a first check, and only later receives his instructions from M: this is the case with *Goldfinger*, which then presents a different scheme B.C.D.E.A.C.D.F.G.D.H.E.H.I, where it is possible to notice repeated moves. There are two encounters and three games played with the Villain, two seductions and three encounters with women, a first flight of the Villain after his defeat and his ensuing death, etc. In *From Russia* the company of Villains increases, through the presence of the ambiguous Kerim, in conflict with a secondary Villain Krilenku, and the two mortal duels of Bond with Red Grant and with Rosa Klebb, who was arrested only after having grievously wounded Bond, so that the scheme, highly complicated, is B.B.B.B.D.A.(B.B.C.). E.F.G.H.G.H.(I.). There is a long prologue in Russia with the parade of the Villain figures and the first connection between Tatiana and Rosa Klebb, the sending of Bond to Turkey, a long interlude in which Kerim and Krilenku appear and the latter is defeated; the seduction of Tatiana, the flight by train with the torture suffered by the murdered Kerim, the victory over Red Grant, the second round with Rosa Klebb who, while being defeated, inflicts serious injury upon Bond. In the train and during his convalescence, Bond enjoys love interludes with Tatiana before the final separation.

Even the basic concept of torture undergoes variations, and sometimes consists in a direct injustice, sometimes in a kind of succession or course of horrors that Bond must undergo, either by the explicit will of the Villain (*Dr. No*) or accidentally to escape from the Villain, but always as a consequence of the moves of the Villain (e.g., a tragic escape in the snow, pursuit, avalanche, hurried flight through the Swiss countryside in *On Her Majesty's Service*).

Beside the sequence of fundamental moves there are numerous side-issues which enrich the narrative by unforeseen events, without, however, altering the basic scheme. To give a graphic representation of this process we may thus summarise the plot of one novel — *Diamonds are Forever* — by representing on the left the sequence of the fundamental moves, on the right the multiplicity of incidental moves:

Long curious prologue which introduces one to the smuggling of diamonds in South Africa.

Move A. M sends Bond to America as a sham smuggler.

Move B. The Villains (the Spangs) appear indirectly in the description of them given to Bond.

Move D. The Woman (Tiffany Case) meets Bond in the role of go-between.

Detailed journey by air; in the background two Villains. *Play situations*. Imperceptible duel between prey and the hunters.

Move B. First appearance in the plane of secondary Villain Winter (Blood Group F).

Move B. Meeting with Jack Spang.

Meeting with Felix Leiter who brings Bond up-to-date about the Spangs.

Move E. Bond begins the seduction of Tiffany.

Long interval at Saratoga at the races. To help Leiter Bond in fact 'damages' the Spangs.

Move C. Bond gives a first check to the Villain.

Appearance of minor Villains in the mud-bath and punishment of the treacherous jockey, anticipating symbolically the torturing of Bond. The whole Saratoga episode represents a *play situation* in miniature.

Bond decides to go to Las Vegas. Detailed description of the district.

Move B. Appearance of Seraffino Spang.

Another long and detailed *play situation*. Play with Tiffany as croupier gambling at table, indirect amorous skirmish with the woman, indirect gamble with Seraffino. Bond wins money.

Move C. Bond gives a second check to Villain.

Next evening, long shooting match between cars. Association of Bond and Ernie Cureo.

Move F. Spang captures Bond.

Long description of Spectre and the train-playing of Spang.

Move G. Spang has Bond tortured.

With the aid of Tiffany, Bond begins a fantastic flight by railway trolley through the desert followed by the locomotive-plaything driven by Seraffino. *Play situation*.

Move H. Bond defeats Seraffino, who crashes into the mountain on the locomotive.

Rest with his friend Leiter, departure by ship, long amorous convalescence with Tiffany between exchanges of coded telegrams.

Move E. Bond finally possesses Tiffany.

Move B. Villain reappears in the form of Winter.

Play situation on board ship. Mortal gamble played by infinitesimal moves between the two killers and Bond. The play situation becomes symbolised on reduced scale in the lottery on the course of the ship. The two killers capture Tiffany. Acrobatic action by Bond to reach the cabin and kill the killers.

Move H. Bond overcome Villains finally.

Move I. Bond knows he can enjoy well-earned repose
with Tiffany. And yet ...

Move H. Bond defeats for the
third time the Villain in
the person of Jack Spang.

Meditations on death in the
presence of the two corpses.
Return home.

... deviations of the plot in South
Africa where Bond destroys the
last link of the chain.

For each of the ten novels it would be possible to trace a general plan.
The collateral inventions are rich enough to form the muscles of the
separate skeletons of narrative: they constitute indubitably one of the
great attractions of Fleming's work, but they do not testify, at least not
obviously, to his powers of invention. As we shall see later, it is easy to
trace the collateral inventions to definite literary sources, and hence
these act as familiar reference marks to romantic situations acceptable
to readers. The true and original plot remains immutable and suspense
is stabilised curiously on the basis of a sequence of events that are
entirely predetermined. To sum up, the plot of *each* book by Fleming
is, by and large, like this: Bond is sent to a given place to avert a
'science-fiction' plan by a monstrous individual of uncertain origin and
definitely not English who, making use of his organisational or productive activity, not only earns money but helps the cause of the enemies
of the West. In facing this monstrous being Bond meets a woman who
is dominated by him and frees her from her past, establishing with her
an erotic relationship interrupted by capture, on the part of the Villain,
and by torture. But Bond defeats the Villain, who dies horribly, and
rests from his great efforts in the arms of the woman, though he is
destined to lose her. One might wonder how, within such limits, it is
possible for the inventive fiction-writer to function, since he must
respond to a wealth of sensations and unforeseeable surprises. In fact, it
is typical of the detective story, either of investigation or of action;
there is no variation of deeds, but rather the repetition of a habitual
scheme in which the reader can recognise something he has already
seen and of which he has grown fond. Under the guise of a machine
that produces information the detective story, on the contrary, produces redundancy; pretending to rouse the reader, in fact it reconfirms
him in a sort of imaginative laziness, and creates escape not by narrating
the unknown but the already known. In the pre-Fleming detective story
the immutable scheme is formed by the personality of the detective and

of his colleagues, by his method of work and by his police, and within this scheme events are unravelled that are unexpected (and most unexpected of all will be the figure of the culprit). But in the novels of Fleming the scheme follows the same chain of events and has the same characters, and it is always known from the beginning who is the culprit, also his characteristics and his plans. The reader's pleasure consists of finding himself immersed in a game of which he knows the pieces and the rules — and perhaps the outcome — drawing pleasure simply from following the minimal variations by which the victor realises his objective.

We might compare a novel by Fleming to a game of football, in which we know beforehand the place, the number and the personalities of the players, the rules of the game, the fact that everything will take place within the area of the great pitch; except that in a game of football the final information remains unknown till the very end: who will win? It would be more accurate to compare these books to a game of basketball played by the Harlem Globe Trotters against a small local team. We know with absolute confidence that they will win: the pleasure lies in watching the trained virtuosity with which the Globe Trotters defer the final moment, with what ingenious deviations they reconfirm the foregone conclusion, with what trickeries they make rings round their opponents. The novels of Fleming exploit in exemplary measure that element of foregone play which is typical of the escape machine geared for the entertainment of the masses. Perfect in their mechanism, such machines represent the narrative structure which works upon obvious material and does not aspire to describe ideological details. It is true that such structures inevitably indicate ideological positions, but these ideological positions do not derive so much from the structural contents as from the method of constructing the contents into a narrative.

3. A Manichean Ideology

The novels of Fleming have been variously accused of McCarthyism, of Fascism, of the cult of excess and violence, of racialism, and so on. It is difficult, after the analysis we have carried out, to maintain that Fleming is not inclined to consider the British superior to all Oriental or Mediterranean races, or to maintain that Fleming does not profess a heartfelt anti-Communism. Yet, it is significant that he ceased to identify the wicked with Russia as soon as the international situation rendered Russia less menacing *according to the general opinion*; it is significant that, while he is introducing the coloured gang of Mr. Big, Fleming is profuse in his acknowledgement of the new African races and of their contribution to contemporary civilisation (Negro gang-sterism would represent a proof of the cohesion attained in each country by the coloured people); it is significant that the suspect of Jewish blood in comparison with other bad characters should be allowed a note of doubt as to his guilt. (Perhaps to prove by absolving the inferior races that Fleming no longer shares the blind chauvinism of the common man.) Thus suspicion arises that our author does not characterise his creations in such and such a manner as a result of an ideological opinion but purely from reaction to popular demand.

Fleming intends, with the cynicism of the disillusioned, to build an effective narrative apparatus. To do so he decides to rely upon the most secure and universal principles, and puts into play archetypal elements which are precisely those that have proved successful in traditional tales. Let us recall for a moment the pairs of characters that we placed in opposition: M is the King and Bond the Cavalier entrusted with a mission; Bond is the Cavalier and the Villain is the Dragon; the Lady and Villain stand for Beauty and the Beast; Bond restores the Lady to the fullness of spirit and to her senses, he is the Prince who rescues Sleeping Beauty; between the Free World and the Soviet Union, England and the non-Anglo-Saxon countries represent the primitive epic relationship between the Chosen Race and the Lower Race, between Black and White, Good and Bad.

Fleming is a racialist in the sense that any artist is one if, to represent the devil, he depicts him with oblique eyes; in the sense that a nurse is one who, wishing to frighten children with the bogey-man, suggests that he is black.

It is singular that Fleming should be anti-Communist with the same lack of discrimination as he is anti-Nazi and anti-German. It isn't that in one case he is reactionary and in the other democratic. He is simply Manichean for operative reasons: he sees the world as made up of good and evil forces in conflict.

Fleming seeks elementary oppositions: to personify primitive and universal forces he has recourse to popular opinion. In a time of international tensions there are popular notions like that of 'wicked Communism' just as there are of the unpunished Nazi criminal. Fleming uses them both in a sweeping, uncritical manner.

At the most, he tempers his choice with irony, but the irony is completely masked, and reveals itself only by being incredibly exaggerated. In *From Russia* his Soviet men are so monstrous, so improbably evil that it seems impossible to take them seriously. And yet in his brief preface Fleming insists that all the atrocities that he narrates are absolutely true. He has chosen the path of fable, and fable must be taken as truthful if it is not to become a satirical fairy-tale. The author seems almost to write his books for a two-fold reading public, aimed at those who will take them as gospel truth or at those who see their humour. But their tone is authentic, credible, ingenious, plainly aggressive. A man who chooses to write in this way is neither Fascist nor racialist; he is only a cynic, a deviser of tales for general consumption.

If Fleming is a reactionary at all, it is not because he identifies the figure of 'evil' with a Russian or a Jew. He is reactionary because he makes use of stock figures. The user of such figures which personify the Manichean dichotomy sees things in black and white, is always dogmatic and intolerant – in short, reactionary; while he who avoids set figures and recognises nuances, and distinctions, and admits contradictions, is democratic. Fleming is conservative as, basically, the fable, any fable, is conservative: it is the static inherent dogmatic conservatism of fairy-tales and myths, which transmit an elementary wisdom, constructed and communicated by a simple play of light and shade, and they transmit it by indestructible images which do not permit critical distinction. If Fleming is a 'Fascist' it is because the ability to pass from mythology to argument, the tendency to govern by making use of myths and fetishes, are typical of Fascism.

In the mythological background the very names of the protagonists participate, by suggesting in an image or in a pun the fixed character of the person from the start, without any possibility of conversion or change. (Impossible to be called *Snow White* and not to be white as snow, in face and spirit.) The wicked man lives by gambling? He will be called Le Chiffre. He is working for the Reds? He will be called *Red* and *Grant* if he works for money, duly granted. A Korean professional killer by unusual means will be *Oddjob*, one obsessed with gold *Auric Goldfinger*; without insisting on the symbolism of a wicked man who is called *No*, perhaps the half-lacerated face of *Hugo Drax* would be conjured up by the incisive onomatopoeia of his name. Beautiful and transparent, telepathic, *Solitaire* would evoke the coldness of the diamond; chic and interested in diamonds, *Tiffany Case* will recall the leading jewellers in New York, and the beauty case of the mannequin. Ingenuity is suggested by the very name of *Honeychile*, sensual shamelessness by that of *Pussy* (a slang reference to female anatomy) *Galore* (another slang term to indicate 'well endowed'). A pawn in a dark game, such is *Domino*; a tender Japanese lover, quintessence of the Orient, such is Kissy Suzuki (would it be accidental that she recalls the name of the most popular exponent of Zen spirituality?). We pass over women of less interest like *Mary Goodnight* or *Miss Trueblood*. And if the name Bond has been chosen, as Fleming affirms, almost by chance, to give the character an absolutely common appearance, then it would be by chance, but also by guidance, that this model of style and of success evokes the luxuries of Bond Street or Treasury bonds.

By now it is clear how the novels of Fleming have attained such a wide success; they build up a network of elementary associations, achieving a dynamism that is original and profound. And he pleases the sophisticated readers who here distinguish, with a feeling of aesthetic pleasure, the purity of the primitive epic impudently and maliciously translated into current terms; and applaud in Fleming the cultured man, whom they recognise as one of themselves, naturally the most clever and broadminded. [. . .]

12 JACKIE: AN IDEOLOGY OF ADOLESCENT FEMININITY

Angela McRobbie

Source: Stencilled Occasional Paper, Women Series SP No. 53, CCCS, Birmingham. © Centre for Contemporary Cultural Studies, University of Birmingham, and A. McRobbie.

Jackie: Cultural Product and Signifying System

Another useful expression though, is the pathetic appealing look, which brings out a boy's protective instinct and has him desperate to get you another drink/help you on with your coat/give you a lift home. It's best done by opening your eyes wide and dropping the mouth open a little looking (hanging your head slightly) directly into the eyes of the boy you're talking to. Practice this (*Jackie*, 15 February 1975).

One of the major reasons for choosing *Jackie* for analysis is its astounding success. Since its first appearance in 1964 its sales have risen from an initial weekly average of 350,000 (with a drop in 1965 to 250,000) to 451,000 in 1968 and 605,947 in 1976. This means that it has been Britain's longest selling 'teen' magazine for over ten years. *Boyfriend*, first published in 1959, started off with sales figures averaging around 418,000 but had fallen to 199,000 in 1965 when publication ceased. *Mirabelle*, launched in 1956, sold over 540,000 copies each week, a reflection of the 'teenage boom' of the mid 50s, but by 1968 its sales had declined to 175,000.[1]

However my aim here is not to grapple with those factors upon which this success appears to be predicated, instead it will be to mount a rigorous and systematic critique of *Jackie* as a system of messages, a signifying system and a bearer of a certain ideology; an ideology which deals with the construction of teenage 'femininity'.

Jackie is one of a large range of magazines, newspapers and comics published by D.C. Thomson of Dundee. [. . .] With a history of vigorous anti-unionism, D.C. Thomson is not unlike other·large mass communication groups. Like Walt Disney, for example, it produces predominantly for a young market and operates a strict code of censorship on content. But its conservatism is most overtly evident in its newspapers which take a consistently anti-union and 'law and order' line. The *Sunday Post*,

263

with a reputed readership of around 3m. (i.e. 79% of the entire population of Scotland over 15) is comforting, reassuring and parochial in
tone. Comprised, in the main, of anecdotal incidents drawn to the
attention of the reader in 'couthie' language, it serves as a 'Sunday
entertainer' reminding its readers of the pleasure of belonging to a
particular national culture.[2]

One visible result of this success has been, at a time of inflation and
of crisis, in the publishing world, 'enviably' high profit margins of 20%
or more. More than this, D.C. Thomson has expanded into other associated fields, with investments for example in the Clyde Paper Co.
(27.15%) and Southern TV (24.8%).

Two points should be made in this context. First, without necessarily
adhering to the 'traditional' conspiracy plot thesis, it would be naive to
envisage the 'interests' of such a company as being purely the pursuit of
increased profits. D.C. Thomson is not, in *Jackie*, merely 'giving the
girls what they want'. Each magazine, newspaper or comic has its own
conventions and its own style. But within these conventions and through
them a concerted effort is nevertheless made to win and shape the consent of the readers to a set of particular values.

The work of this branch of the media involves 'framing' the world
for its readers, and through a variety of techniques endowing with importance those topics chosen for inclusion. The reader is invited to share
this world with *Jackie*. It is no coincidence that the title is also a girl's
name. This is an unambiguous sign that its concern is with 'the category
of the subject',[3] in particular the individual girl, and the feminine 'persona'. *Jackie* is both the magazine and the ideal girl. The short, snappy
name itself carries a string of connotations: British, fashionable (particularly in the 60s); modern; and cute; with the pet-form 'ie' ending, it
sums up all those desired qualities which the reader is supposedly seeking.

Second, we must see this ideological work as being grounded upon
certain so-called natural, even 'biological' categories. Thus *Jackie* expresses the 'natural' features of adolescence in much the same way as,
say, Disney comics are said to capture the natural essence of childhood.
Each has, as Dorfman and Mattelart writing on Disney point out, a
'virtually biologically captive, predetermined audience'.[4] *Jackie* introduces the girl into adolescence outlining its landmarks and characteristics
in detail and stressing importantly the problematic features as well as
the fun. Of course *Jackie* is not solely responsible for nurturing this
ideology of femininity. Nor would such an ideology cease to exist
should *Jackie* stop publication.

Unlike other fields of mass culture, the magazines of teenage girls
have not as yet been subject to rigorous critical analysis. Yet from
the most cursory of readings it is clear that they, too, like those more

immediately associated with the sociology of the media — press, TV, film, radio, etc. — are powerful ideological forces.

In fact women's and girls' weeklies occupy a privileged position. Addressing themselves solely to a female market, their concern is with promoting a feminine culture for their readers. They define and shape the woman's world, spanning every stage from childhood to old age. From *Mandy*, *Bunty* and *Judy*, to *House and Home*, the exact nature of the woman's role is spelt out in detail, according to her age.

She progresses from adolescent romance where there are no explicitly sexual encounters, to the more sexual world of *19*, *Honey* or *Over 21*, which in turn give way to marriage, childbirth, home-making, child care and the *Woman's Own*. There are no 'male' equivalents to these products. 'Male' magazines tend to be based on particular leisure pursuits or hobbies, motor-cycling, fishing, cars or even pornography. There is no consistent attempt to link 'interests' with age (though readership of many magazines will obviously be higher among younger age groups) nor is there a sense of a natural inevitable progression or evolution attached to their readers' expected 'careers'. There is instead a variety of possibilities with regard to *leisure* [...], many of which involve active participation inside or outside the home.

It will be argued here that the way *Jackie* addresses 'girls' as a monolithic grouping, as do all other women's magazines, serves to obscure differences, of class for example, between women. Instead it asserts a sameness, a kind of *false* sisterhood, which assumes a common definition of womanhood or girlhood. Moreover by isolating out a particular 'phase' or age as the focus of interest, one which coincides roughly with that of its readers, the magazine is in fact creating this 'age-ness' as an ideological construction. 'Adolescence' and here, female adolescence, is itself an ideological 'moment' whose *connotations* are immediately identifiable with those 'topics' included in *Jackie*. And so, by at once defining its readership *vis-à-vis* age, and by describing what is of relevance, to this age group, *Jackie* and women's magazines in general create a 'false totality'. Thus we *all* want to know how to catch a man, lose weight, look our best, or cook well! Having mapped out the feminine 'career' in such all-embracing terms, there is little or no space allowed for alternatives. Should the present stage be unsatisfactory the reader is merely encouraged to look forward to the next. Two things are happening here. 1) The girls are being invited to join a close, intimate sorority where secrets can be exchanged and advice given; and 2) they are also being presented with an ideological bloc of mammoth proportions, one which *imprisons* them in a claustrophobic world of jealousy and competitiveness, the most unsisterly of emotions, to say the least.

Jackie and Popular Culture

There are several ways in which we can think through *Jackie* magazine as part of the media and of mass culture in general. The first of these is the traditionalist thesis. In this, magazines are seen as belonging to popular or mass culture, something which is inherently inferior to 'high' culture, or 'the arts'. Cheap, superficial, exploitative and debasing, it reduces its audience to a mass of mindless morons,

> the open sagging mouths and glazed eyes, the hands mindlessly drumming in time to the music, the broken stiletto heels, the shoddy, stereotyped 'with it' clothes: here apparently, is a collective portrait of a generation enslaved by a commercial machine.[5]

Alderson, writing explicitly on girls' weeklies, takes a similar position. Claiming, correctly, that what they offer their readers is a narrow and restricted view of life, she proposed as an alternative, 'better' literature, citing *Jane Eyre* as an example.[6]

The problems with such an approach are manifest. 'High' culture becomes a cure for all ills. It is, to quote Willis, 'a repository of quintessential human values',[7] playing a humanising role by elevating the emotions and purifying the spirit. What this argument omits to mention are the material requirements necessary to purchase such 'culture'. And underpinning it is an image of the deprived, working class youngster (what Alderson calls the 'Newsom girl') somehow lacking in those qualities which contact with the arts engenders. Mass culture is seen as a manipulative, vulgar, profit-seeking industry offering cheap and inferior versions of the arts to the more impressionable and vulnerable sectors of the population. This concept of culture is inadequate because it is ahistorical, and is based on unquestioned qualitative judgements. It offers no explanations as to how these forms develop and are distributed. Nor does it explain why one form has a particular resonance for one class in society rather than another.

The second interpretation has much in common with this approach, although it is generally associated with more radical critics. This is the conspiracy thesis and it, too, sees mass culture as 'fodder' for the masses; the result of a ruling class plot whose objective it is to keep the working classes docile and subordinate and to divert them into entertainment. [. . .] By this logic, *Jackie* is merely a mouthpiece for ruling class ideology, focused on young adolescent girls. Again, mass culture is seen as worthless and manipulative. Not only is this argument also ahistorical, but it fails to locate the operations of different apparatuses in the social formation (politics, the media, the law, education, the family, to name but some) each of which is relatively autonomous, has its own *level* and its own specific material practices. While private sectors of the economy do *ultimately* work together with the State, there is a necessary separation between them. Each apparatus has its own *uneven* development and one cannot be collapsed with another.

The third argument reverses both of the first two arguments, to the extent that it points to pop music and pop culture as meaningful activities: 'for most young people today . . . pop music and pop culture is their only expressive outlet'.[8]

Such a position does have some relevance to our study of *Jackie*. It hinges on the assumption that this culture expresses and offers, in albeit consumerist terms, those values and ideas held by both working class youth and by sections of middle class youth. Youth, that is, is defined in terms of values held, which are often in opposition to those held by the establishment, by their parents, the school, work, etc. Such a definition does not consider youth's relation to production, but to consumption, and it is this approach which has characterised that huge body of work, the sociology of culture and of youth, subcultural theory, and which includes, too, delinquency theory.

To summarise a familiar argument which finds expression in most of these fields: working class youth, denied access to other 'higher' forms of culture, and in any case associating these with 'authority' and with the middle class, turns to those forms available on the market. Here they can at least exert some power in their choice of commodities. These commodities often come to be a hallmark of the subcultural group in question but not exactly in their original forms. The group *subverts* the original meaning by bestowing additional implied connotations to the object(s) thereby extending the range of its signifying power. These new meanings undermine and can even negate the previous or established meaning(s) so that the object comes to represent an oppositional ideology linked to the subculture or youth grouping in question. It then summarises for the outside observer the group's disaffection from the wider society. This process of re-appropriation can be seen in, for example, the 'style' of the skinheads, the 'mod' suit, the 'rocker' motor bike, or even the 'punk' safety-pin![9]

But this approach, which hinges on explaining the choice of cultural artefacts — clothes, records or motor bikes etc., — is of limited usefulness when applied to teenage girls and their magazines. They play little, if any, role in shaping their own pop culture and their choice in consumption is materially extremely narrow. And indeed the forms made available to them make re-appropriation difficult. *Jackie* offers its readers no active 'presence' in which girls are invited to participate. The uses are, in short, prescribed by the 'map'. Yet [. . .] this does not mean that *Jackie* cannot be used in subversive ways. Clearly girls *do* use it as a means of signalling their boredom and disaffection, in the school, for example. The point *here* is that despite these possible uses, the magazine itself has a powerful ideological presence as a *form*, and as such demands analysis carried out *apart from* these uses or 'readings'. [. . .] While the argument made here will include strands from the positions outlined above, its central thrust will represent a substantial shift away from them. What I want to suggest is that *Jackie* occupies the sphere of the personal or private, what Gramsci calls 'Civil Society' ('the ensemble of organisms that are commonly called Private').[10] Hegemony is sought uncoercively on this terrain, which is relatively free of direct State interference. Consequently it is seen as an arena of 'freedom', of 'free choice' and of 'free time'. This sphere includes:

not only associations and organisations like political parties and the press, but also the family, which combines ideological and economic functions.[11]

[. . .] *Jackie* exists within a large, powerful, privately owned publishing apparatus which produces a vast range of newspapers, magazines and comics. It is on this level of the magazine that teenage girls are subjected to an explicit attempt to win consent to the dominant order — in terms of femininity, leisure and consumption, i.e. at the level of culture. It is worth noting at this point that only three girls in a sample of 56 claimed to read any newspapers regularly. They rarely watched the news on television and their only prolonged contact with the written word was at school and through their own and their mothers' magazines. Occasionally a 'risqué' novel like Richard Allen's *Skingirl* would be passed round at school, but otherwise the girls did not read any literature apart from 'love' comics.

The 'teen' magazine is, therefore, a highly privileged 'site'. Here the girl's consent is sought uncoercively and in her leisure time. [. . .] While there is a strongly coercive element to those other terrains which teenage girls inhabit, the school and the family, in her leisure time the girl is officially 'free' to do as she pleases. And as we have seen, teenage girls show a marked lack of interest in organised leisure activities, showing instead a preference for dancing or merely 'sitting about'. Otherwise the girls in the sample defined their leisure interests in terms of consumer goods — clothes, make-up, magazines, records and cigarettes. It is on the open market then that girls are least constrained by the display of social control. The only qualification here is the ability to buy a ticket, magazine or Bay City Roller T-shirt. Here they remain relatively uninterfered with. [. . .]

Commercial leisure enterprises with their illusion of freedom have, then, an attraction for youth. And this 'freedom' is pursued, metaphorically, inside the covers of *Jackie*. With an average readership age of 10 to 14, *Jackie* pre-figures girls' entry into the labour market as 'free labourers' and its pages are crammed full of the 'goodies' which this later freedom promises. *Jackie* girls are never at school, they are enjoying the fruits of their labour on the open market. They live in large cities, frequently in flats shared with other young wage-earners like themselves.

This image of freedom has a particular resonance for girls when it is located within and intersects with the longer and again ideologically constructed 'phase' they inhabit in the present. Leisure has a special importance in this period of 'brief flowering',[12] that is, in those years prior to marriage and settling down, after which they become dual labourers in the home and in production. Leisure in their 'single' years is especially important because it is here that their future is secured. It is in *this* sphere that they go about finding a husband and thereby sealing their fate. [. . .]

The World of Jackie

What then are the key features which characterise *Jackie*? First there is a 'lightness' of tone, a non-urgency, which holds true right through the magazine, particularly in the use of colour, graphics and advertisements. It asks to be read at a leisurely pace, indicating that its subject matter is not wholly serious, is certainly not 'news'. Since entertainment and leisure goods are designed to arouse feelings of pleasure as well as interest, the appearance of the magazine is inviting, its front cover shows a 'pretty' girl smiling happily. The dominance of the visual level, which is maintained throughout the magazine, reinforces this notion of leisure. It is to be glanced through, looked at and only finally read. Published at weekly intervals, the reader has time to peruse each item at her own speed. She also has time to pass it round her friends or swap it for another magazine.

Rigid adherence to a certain style of lay-out and patterning of features ensures a familiarity with its structure(s). The girl can rely on *Jackie* to *cheer her up, entertain her, or solve her problems each week*. The 'style' of the magazine, once established, facilitates and encourages partial and uneven reading, in much the same way as newspapers also do. The girl can quickly turn to the centre page for the pin-up, glance at the fashion page and leave the problems and picture stories which are the 'meat' of the magazine, till she has more time.

Articles and features are carefully arranged to avoid one 'heavy' feature following another. The black and white picture stories taking up between 2½ and 3 full pages are always broken up by a coloured advert, or beauty feature, and the magazine opens and closes by inviting the reader to participate directly through the letters or the problem pages. This sense of solidness and resistance to change (*Jackie*'s style has not been substantially altered since it began publication) is reflected and paralleled in its thematic content. Each feature (as will be seen later) comprises workings and re-workings of a relatively small repertoire of specific themes or concerns which sum up the girls' world. These topics saturate the magazine. Entering the world of *Jackie* means suspending interest in the 'real' world of school, family or work, and participating in a sphere which is devoid of history and resistant to change.

Jackie deals primarily with the terrain of the personal and it makes a 'turning inwards' to the sphere of the 'soul', the 'heart', or less metaphorically, the emotions. On the one hand, of course, certain features do change — fashion is itself predicated upon change and upon being 'up to date'. But the degree of change even here is qualified — certain features remain the same, e.g. the models' 'looks', poses, the style of drawing and its positioning within the magazine and so on. All that does change is the length of the hem, shade of make-up, style of shoe, etc.

Above all, *Jackie*, like the girl she symbolises, is intended to be 'looked at'. This overriding concern with visuals affects every feature. But its visual appearance and style also reflect the spending power of its readers. There is little of the extravagant or exotic in *Jackie*. The paper on which it is printed is thin without being wafer-thin. The fashion and beauty pages show clothes priced within the girls' range and the adverts are similarly focused at a low budget market featuring, principally, personal toiletries, tampons, shampoos and lipsticks rather than larger consumer goods. [. . .]

The Code of Romance: the Moment of Bliss

> The hero of romance knows how to treat women. Flowers, little gifts, love letters, maybe poems to her eyes and hair, candlelit meals on moon-lit terraces and muted strings. Nothing hasty, physical. Some heavy breathing . . . Mystery, magic, champagne, ceremony . . . women never have enough of it.[13]

Jackie picture stories are similar *in form* to those comic strips, and tales of adventure, time travel, rivalry and intrigue which regularly fill the pages of children's weeklies. Yet there is something distinctive about these stories which indicates immediately their concern with romance. First the titles clearly announce a concern with 'you', 'me', 'love' and 'happiness'. Romantic connotations are conveyed through the relationship between titles and the names of 'pop' songs and ballads. (*Jackie* does not however use the older *Boyfriend* technique of using a well-known pop song and its singer to both inspire the story and give it moral weight!)

The title, then, anchors the story it introduces. In our sample these include:

'The Happiest Xmas Ever', 'Meet Me On The Corner', 'As Long As I've Got You', 'Come Fly With Me', and 'Where Have All The Flowers Gone?'

This concern with romance pervades every story and is built into them through the continued use of certain formal techniques and styles.

For a start, the way the characters look indicates clearly that this is serious, not 'kids' stuff'. They are all older and physically more mature than the intended reader. Each character conforms to a well-established and recognisable standard of beauty or handsomeness and they are all smart, fairly sophisticated young adults, rather than adolescents or 'teenagers'.

The most characteristic feature of 'romance' in *Jackie* is the concern with the narrow and restricted world of the emotions. No attempt is made to fill out social events or backgrounds. The picture story is the realm, *par excellence*, of the individual. Each story revolves round one figure and the tiny web of social relationships surrounding him or, usually, her. Rarely are there more than two or three characters in each plot and where they do exist it is merely as part of the background or scenery — in the cafe, at the disco or in the street.

Unlike comic strips, where the subject is fun, excitement or adventure, these stories purport to deal with the more serious side of life — hence the semi-naturalistic style of the drawings and the use of black and white. This, along with the boldness of the drawings, the starkness of stroke and angularity of the figures, conspires to create an impression of 'realism' and seriousness. The form of the stories alone tells us that romance is important, serious and relevant. Yet simultaneously in the content, we are told that it is fun; the essence and meaning of life; the key to happiness, etc. It is this blend which gives the *Jackie* romance its characteristic flavour. In general terms this is nothing new, these stories owe a great deal to popular cinema romances, and to novelettes. For a start the characters closely resemble the anonymous but distinctive type of the 'film star' — dewy-eyed women and granite-jawed heroes. Their poses are equally soaked in the language of film — the clinch, the rejected lover alone by herself as the sun sets — the moon comes up — to name but a few. But this cinematic resemblance is based on more than just *association*. The very form of the comic strip has close links with the film. Strung together, in a series of *clips*, set out across and down the page, the stories 'rise' to a climax and resolution, graphically illustrated in larger images erupting across the page.

From these clips we can see clearly that the emotional life is defined and lived in terms of *romance* which in turn is equated with *great moments* rather than long-term processes. Hence the centrality and visual impact of the clinch, the proposal, the wedding day. Together these *moments* constitute a kind of orchestration of *time*; through them the feminine career is constructed. The picture stories comprise a set of visual images composed and set within a series of frames laid out across the page to be 'read' like a text. But these frames communicate *visually*, resemble film-clips and tell the story by 'freezing' the action into sets of 'stills'. Unlike other comics (*Bunty* or *Judy*), *Jackie* stories do not conform to the convention of neatly mounted images set uniformly across the page. Instead a whole range of loose frames indicating different kinds of situations or emotions is used. This produces a greater continuity between 'form' and 'content', so that as the pace of the story accelerates, the visuals erupt *with* the breathless emotional feelings, spilling out over the page.

Each separate image which makes up the story is 'anchored' with sets of verbal messages illuminating the action and eliminating ambiguity. [. . .] Thus the moment of reading and looking are collapsed into one, and the reader is spared the boredom of having to read more lengthy descriptions; she merely 'takes it in' and hurries on to the next image. The techniques through which this relay operates are well known; — dialogue is indicated by the use of balloons issuing from the mouths of the speakers and filled with words; — and thoughts are conveyed through a series of small bubbles which drift upwards away from the character's mouth — thinking being associated with a 'higher' level of discourse, an 'intellectual' pursuit.

The central and most dramatic incident in each story is specified by the spilling out of one visual image over the page. This image sums up graphically the fraught nature of the moment; the moment when the timid shy heroine catches sight of her handsome boyfriend fascinated by her irresistible best friend at a party which she stupidly invited her to; or when the girl, let down by her boy, rushes out of the coffee bar across the street to be hit by a passing car . . . and so on.

Each frame represents a selection from the development of the plot, and is credited with an importance which those intervening moments are not. Thus the train, supermarket, and office have meaning, to the extent that they represent potential meeting-places where the girl *could well* bump into the prospective boyfriend, who lurks round every corner. It is this which determines their inclusion in the plot; the possibility that everyday life could be transformed into *social life*.

Within these frames themselves the way the figures look, act, and pose contributes also to the ideology of romance. For a start there is very little variation in types of physical appearance. This homogeneity hinges on a blend of modernity and conservatism which typifies the *Jackie* 'look'. The girls are 'mod' but neat and conventional, rarely are they 'way-out'. Boys may look acceptably scruffy and dishevelled by displaying a kind of managed untidiness.

This appearance is matched by language. Deriving seemingly from the days of the teenage commercial boom it has a particularly 50s ring about it. Bereft of accent, dialect, slang or vulgarity it remains the invention of the media — the language of pop, and of Radio 1 disc jockeys. Distinctly modern it is also quite unthreatening, peppered with phrases like:

'rave', 'yacked', 'zacked', 'scrummy hunk', 'dishy', 'fave', 'come on, let's blow this place', 'I'm the best mover in town',

all of which convey an image of youth 'on the move', of 'a whole scene going' and of 'wowee dig the slick chick in the corner', 'a nice piece of talent', teenagers 'doing their own thing'. But these teenagers are a strangely anonymous and unrecognisable grouping, similar only, perhaps, to the 'Young Generation' seen on TV variety shows or the young people in Coca Cola or Levi Jeans adverts. It is a language of action, of 'good times', of enjoyment and of consumerism. The characters in *Jackie* stories and in Coca Cola TV adverts at least seem to be getting things done. They are constantly seen 'raving it up' at discos, going for trips in boyfriends' cars, or else going on holiday. And yet as we shall see, the female and male characters in *Jackie* are simultaneously doing nothing but pursuing each other, and far from being a pleasure-seeking *group*, in fact these stories consist of isolated individuals, distrusting even their best friends and in search of fulfilment only through a partner. The anonymity of the language then parallels the strangely amorphous *Jackie* girls. Marked by a rootlessness, lack of ties or sense of region, the reader is unable to 'locate' them in any social context. They are devoid of history. Bound together by an invisible 'generational consciousness' they inhabit a world where no disruptive values exist. At the 'heart' of this world is the individual girl looking for romance. But romance is not itself an unproblematic category and what I will be arguing here is that its central contradiction is glaringly clear and unavoidable even to the girl herself who is so devoted to its cause. This contradiction is based round the fact that the *romantic moment*, its central 'core', cannot be reconciled with its promise for *eternity*. To put it another way, the code of romance realises, but cannot accept, that the man can adore, love, 'cherish' and be sexually attracted to his girlfriend and simultaneously be 'aroused' by other girls (in the present or the 'future'). It is the recognition of this fact that sets all girls against each other, and forms the central theme in the picture stories. Hence the girl's constant worries, as she is passionately embraced; 'can it last?' or 'how can I be sure his love is for ever?'

Earlier we asserted that *Jackie* was concerned with 'the category of the subject', with the constitution of the feminine personality. Indeed 'personality' itself forms an important organising category in the magazine. Each week there is some concern with 'your' personality, how to know it, change it or understand those of your friends, boyfriends, families. In the picture stories 'personality' takes on an important role alongside 'looks'. The characters depend for their meaning on well-known stereotypes. That is, to be 'read' correctly the reader must possess previous cultural knowledge of the 'types' of subjects which inhabit his or her social world.

Jackie boys fall into four categories. First, there is the fun-loving, grinning, flirtatious boy who is irresistible to all girls; second, the 'tousled' scatterbrained 'zany' youth who inspires 'maternal' feelings in girls; third, the emotional, shy, sensitive and even 'arty' type; and fourth, the juvenile delinquent usually portrayed on his motor bike looking wild, aggressive but 'sexy' and whom the girl must 'tame'.

In every case the male figure is idealised and romanticised so that there is a real discrepancy between *Jackie* boys and those boys who are discussed on the Cathy and Claire page. The central point here is that *Jackie* boys are as interested in romance as the girls.

'Mm! I wish Santa would bring me that for Christmas . . . so how do we get together?'

and this, as countless sociological studies, novels and studies of sexual behaviour indicate, simply does not ring true. Boys in contemporary capitalist society are socialised to be interested in *sex*, although this does not mean they don't want to find the 'ideal' girl or wife. [. . .]

Female characters, significantly, show even less variation in personality. In fact they can be summarised as three opposite or contrasting types. The 'blonde', quiet, timid, loving and trusting girl who either gets her boy in the end or is tragically abandoned; and the wild, fun-loving 'brunette' (often the blonde's best friend) who will resort to plotting and conniving to get the man she wants. This 'bitch' character is charming and irresistible to men although all women can immediately 'see through' her. Finally, there is the non-character, the friendly, open, fun-loving 'ordinary' girl (who may perhaps be slightly 'scatty' or absent-minded). She is remarkable in being normal and things tend to happen *to* her rather than at her instigation. Frequently she figures in stories focusing round the supernatural.

Most of these characters have changed little since the magazine first appeared in 1964. Their 'style' is still rooted in the 'Swinging London' of the mid-60s. The girls have large, heavily made-up eyes, pale lips and tousled hair, turned up noses and tiny 'party' mouths (*à la* Jean Shrimpton). They wear clothes at least partly reminiscent of the 60s, hipster skirts with large belts, polo neck sweaters and, occasionally, 'flared' trousers. Despite the fact that several of these girls introduce themselves as 'plain', their claims are contradicted by the accompanying image indicating that they are without exception 'beautiful'. Likewise the men (or boys) are ruggedly handsome, young versions of James Bond (to the extent that some even wear 'shorty' raincoats with 'turned-up' collars). They have thick eyebrows, smiling eyes, and 'granite' jaws.

While some of the stories seem to be set in London, the majority give no indication of 'locale'. The characters speak without an accent and are usually without family or community ties. They have all left school, but 'work' hovers invisibly in the background as a necessary time filler between one evening and the next or can sometimes be a pathway to glamour, fame or romance. Recognisable 'social' backgrounds are rare. The small town, equated with boredom, is signified through the use of strangely anachronistic symbols – the coffee bar, and the motor-bike and the narrow street. The country, on the other hand, is where the girl escapes *to*, following a broken romance or an unhappy love affair. But when her problems are resolved, she invariably returns to *the city* where things 'really happen'. But it is a city strangely lacking a population that these teenagers inhabit. There are no foreigners, black teenagers, old people or children. No married couples and rarely any families or siblings. It is a world occupied almost solely by young adults on the brink of pairing-up as couples.

The messages which these images and stories together produce are limited and unambiguous, and are repeated endlessly over the years. These are (1) the girl has to fight to *get* and *keep* her man, (2) she can *never* trust another woman unless she is old and 'hideous' in which case she doesn't appear in the stories anyway and (3) despite this, romance, and being a girl, are 'fun'.

No story ever ends with *two* girls alone together and enjoying each other's company. Occasionally the flat-mate or best friend appears in a role as 'confidante' but these appearances are rare and by implication unimportant. A happy ending means a happy couple, a sad one – a single girl. Having eliminated the possibility of strong supportive relationships between girls themselves, and between people of different ages, *Jackie* stories must elevate to dizzy heights the supremacy of the heterosexual romantic partnership.

This is, it may be argued, unsurprising and predictable. But these stories do more than this. They cancel out completely the possibility of any relationship other than the romantic one between girl and boy. They make it impossible for any girl to talk to, or think about, a boy in terms other than those of romance. (A favourite story in both picture form and as a short story, is the 'platonic' relationship which the girl enjoys. She likes him as a friend – but when she is made jealous by his showing an interest in another girl, she realises that it is *really* love that she feels for him and their romance blossoms.)

Boys and men are, then, not sex objects but romantic objects. The code of romance neatly displaces that of sexuality which hovers somewhere in the background appearing fleetingly in the guise of passion, or the 'clinch'. Romance is about the public and *social* effects of and implications of 'love' relationships. That is, it is concerned with impressing one's friends with a new handsome boyfriend, with being flattered by the attention and compliments lavished by admirers. It is about playing games which 'skirt about' sexuality, and which include sexual innuendo, but which are somehow 'nicer', 'cleaner' and less 'sordid'. Romance is the girls' reply to male sexuality. It stands in opposition to their 'just being after the one thing'; and consequently it *makes* sex seem *dirty*, *sordid*, and *unattractive*. The girl's sexuality is understood and experienced not in terms of a physical need of her own body, but in terms of the romantic attachment. In depicting romantic partnerships, *Jackie* is also therefore constructing male and female roles ensuring that they are separate and as distinct as possible. They are as different as they 'look' different and any interchange between the sexes invariably exudes *romantic* possibilities. What *Jackie* does is to map out all those *differences* which exist between the sexes but to assert that what they do *share* is a common interest, indeed devotion to, 'romance'.

So far, I have outlined in some detail the organising principles around which this discourse (the picture story) is structured. Now, while I would not hold the separation of form and content as being either possible, or necessary for analysis, there are a number of recurring themes which can be identified through a process of extrapolation from both the image and the accompanying text. Thus, temporarily holding constant the formal features of the picture story – the 'balloon' form of dialogue; the action through 'relay'; and the style of illustration – we can go on to deal with the patterns, combinations and permutations of those stock situations which give *Jackie* its characteristic thematic unity.

The stories themselves can be categorised as follows:

(1) the traditional 'love' story;
(2) the romantic/adventure serial;
(3) the 'pop' special (where the story revolves around a famous pop star);

(4) the 'zany' tale; and
(5) the historical romance.

But those story-types are worked through and expounded by the use of certain conventions or devices and it is through these that the thematic structure can be seen most clearly.

The first of these is the convention of *'time'* or of *'the temporal'*. Under this heading four different modes can be categorised, including the *flashback*. Here the opening clips signify 'aloneness' conveyed through images of isolation; a single figure against, say, a rugged, beautiful threatening landscape. Along this same chain of signifieds and following 'aloneness' comes the explanation – that is – 'alone-and-rejected-by-a-loved-one', or 'separated-from-a-loved-one'. Next comes the elucidation; what has caused such a state of unhappiness or misery, and this is classified and expounded upon through the use of the *flashback*. 'I remember only a year ago and it was all so . . .' 'But Dave was different from the others even then.' The reader is transported into the narrator's past and confronted with scenes of love, tenderness, excitement etc. The difference between the past and present state is emphasised by changes of *season*, and particularly by changes of *expression*. Warm weather, for example, goes with smiling, happy faces gazing in mutual pleasure at one another.

From this point onwards different conventions intervene to carry the story along, and it is neatly concluded with a return to the present, and a 'magical' or intentionally un-magical resolution. (The boy reappears, or doesn't, or a new one takes his place –.)

Through this device the reader is invited to interpret her life, past and present, in terms of romantic attachments – her life has meaning through *him*.

The second temporal device is the diary. Again this allows the reader access to the innermost secrets of its writer, sometimes mediated through a plotting, and a guilty best friend reading her friend's outpourings. But it is the third convention, *'History'*, which is without doubt the most popular.

By locating the characters in a specific 'period' the scriptwriter and artist are provided immediately with a whole string of easy, and ideologically constructed, concepts with which they can fill out the plot. History *means* particular *styles of clothing, 'quaint' language, strange customs and rituals*. Thus we have the Victorian heroine connoted through her dress and background dissatisfied with her life and bored by her persistent suitor. When she is transported, magically, into the present she is, however, so horrified by 'liberated' women (policewomen and girls in bikinis) that she is glad to return to her safe and secure environment. Thus, culturally defined notions of the Victorian period are used to glamourise the past and criticise the present which is, by implication, bereft of romance. (Bikinis and uniforms don't connote frailty, passivity and fragility.) *At the same time*, this story is incorporating popularised notions of present phenomena which threaten the established order, and in doing so it is thereby diluting and ridiculing them. [. . .]

Likewise the Edwardian period, again recognisable through costume and this time carrying connotations of more active women, is used to relate a simple story of love, jealousy and reconciliation, with its participants (literally) carrying out their romances on bicycle saddles.

But history is not just novelty, it is also used to demonstrate the intransigence of much-hallowed social values, and 'natural resistance' to change. When a patrician (in the setting of Ancient Rome) falls for a slave girl he can only die for her thereby allowing her to escape with her slave boyfriend; he cannot escape or be paired off with her. Similarly, when a flower girl is attracted by a gentleman her thoughts only become romantic when she discovers that he is not *really* a gentleman but rather a bohemian artist. A nineteenth-century woman and her child arrive at the doorstep one Christmas but are turned away. Two guests help them and it emerges that the woman is the disinherited daughter of a wealthy man . . . The messages are clear; love conquers and simultaneously renders unimportant poverty — which at any rate only 'exists' in the past (and is thus contained and manageable). People marry into their own class and their own race. (When a nurse falls for a wounded German prisoner in wartime Britain she knows her love cannot be fulfilled . . . and the prisoner returns to Germany.) Similarly, social class, too 'controversial' an issue to appear in stories set in the present, can be acknowledged as *having* existed in the past.

History then provides the *Jackie* team with a whole set of issues which are more safely dealt with in the past; social problems, social class, foreigners and war. But history also means unchanging *eras* characterised primarily by splendid costumes (the code of fashion), exoticism (language and customs) and adventure. And yet despite this the reader can derive reassurance which lingers on a recognition of the *sameness* which links past and present. Underpinning all the adventures and historical tableaux is *romance*, the young girl in pursuit of it, or being pursued by it. Love, it is claimed, transcends time and is all-important, and history is, again, denied.

The fourth and final temporal device is that of the '*seasons*'. The importance of weather in reflecting 'moods' and creating atmosphere is a feature throughout the stories. 'Love' takes different forms at different times of the year, and holiday romances give way to autumnal 'blues'.

The second set of conventions we will be looking at are those which relate to the exigencies of plot. Thus we have (1) the 'zany' tale where romance is blended with comedy. Here the drawings are less dramatic and are characterised by softer lines. The plots revolve around unusual, unlikely events and coincidences resulting in romantic meetings. At their centre is the 'zany' boy whose bizarre hobbies lead him through a number of disasters until eventually he finds a steady girl who 'tames' him. ('Now they're crazy about each other.')

'Zany' girls of this type are rare. Girls are not really interested in anything outside the confines of femininity, besides which, no girl would willingly make a public spectacle of herself in this way. Often, perhaps instead, animals, always the subject of sentiment, figure strongly in these stories. A camel escapes from the zoo, is caught by a young girl in the city centre who has to await the arrival of the handsome, young, zookeeper. Another favourite centres around the ritual of walking the dog and taking an evening stroll in the local park where numerous handsome young men are doing the same thing or are willing to be pestered by *her* dog — and so on. 'Hmm, funny names you call your cats.'

Again the message is clear — a 'zany' absent-minded boyfriend is a good bet! He is unlikely to spend his time chasing other girls and is indeed incapable of doing so, he is the lovable 'twit', who needs mothering as well as loving. (Some Mothers Do 'Ave 'Em!)

Second, there is the plot which depends on a recognisable social locale. The hospital appears frequently here and carries rich connotations of romance and drama. A girl, for example, is recovering from a throat operation and discovers her boy is going out with someone else, but she overcomes her disappointment by meeting someone new in the hospital.

In another story a dashing young man catches sight of a pretty girl and follows her to her place of work, a bloodbank. Terrified to sign up to give blood he thinks of ways of getting to know her . . .

But hospitals are not the only places where romance can happen; at the bus-stop, on the bus, in the park, in the flat downstairs, depending on luck, coincidence or 'stars'. 'He must be on day release . . . he's on the train Mondays and Wednesdays but not the rest of the week.' And there is a moral here, if love strikes, or simply happens 'out of the blue' then all the girl needs to do is look out for it, be alert without actively seeking it. In fact this allows her, once again, to remain passive, she certainly can't approach a young man, only a coincidence may bring them together (though she may work on bringing about such a coincidence). At any rate she certainly can't hang about the bus-stop or street corner waiting to be picked up.

This convention of *place* also, by implication, deems leisure facilities for youth unnecessary. There is no need for them, if *your* boy is on the bus or train each morning. There are no stories set in youth clubs, community centres, even libraries or evening classes, and discos only appear as a backdrop where a girl is taken *to* by her boyfriend. Youth means individuals in search of or waiting for a partner and when this occurs all other leisure needs evaporate.

The third convention takes the idea of luck or coincidence one step further by introducing unambiguously *supernatural* devices. This way the reader is invited to share a fantasy, or 'dream come true'. These include magazines, leprechauns, magic lamps and dreams themselves.

But the dream or fantasy occupies a central place in the girls' life anyway — to an extent *all* the picture stories are fantasies, and escapist. Likewise real-life boys are frequently described as 'dreamy'. Day-dreaming is an expected 'normal' activity on the part of girls, an adolescent phase. But dreaming of this sort is synonymous with passivity — and as we have already seen, romance is the language of passivity, *par excellence*. The romantic girl, in contrast to the sexual man, is *taken* in a kiss, or embrace. Writing on the development of female sexuality in little girls, Mitchell describes their retreat into the 'Oedipus complex' where the desire *to be loved* can be fulfilled in the comforting and secure environment of the home.[14] Likewise in *Jackie* stories the girl is *chosen*,

'Hmm, this mightn't be so bad after all — if I can get chatting to that little lady later'

is taken in an embrace,

'Hmm, I could enjoy teaching you, love . . . very, very much.'

And is herself waiting *to be loved*.

'I must be a nut! But I'm really crazy about Jay.
If only I could make him care.'

Finally there is the convention based round personal or domestic life. Here the girl is at odds with her family and siblings (who rarely appear in person) and eventually is *saved* by the appearance of a boyfriend. Thus we have a twin, madly jealous of her pretty sister, who tries to 'steal' the sister's boyfriend when she has to stay in bed with flu.

'Story of my life! Just Patsy's twin. He doèsn't even know my name, I bet. Just knows me as the other one. The quiet one.'

Another common theme (echoed in the problem page) is the girl with the 'brainy' family. In one case such a girl is seen reading Shakespeare in the park, by a handsome young man. When he begins to take her out she insists on going to art galleries and museums, but gives herself away when his 'clever' friend shows that she doesn't know what she's talking about. Breaking down she admits to reading cheap romances inside the covers of highbrow drama! Through this humiliation and admission of inferiority (the daughter of another 'clever' family) she wins the true love of the boy. So much for *Jackie*'s anti-intellectualism. All the girl needs is a good personality, 'looks' and confidence. Besides which boys don't like feeling threatened by a 'brainy' girl.

Jackie asserts the absolute and natural separation of sex roles. Girls can take humiliation and be all the more attractive for it, as long as they are pretty and unassertive. Boys can *be* footballers, pop stars, even juvenile delinquents, but girls can only be feminine. The girl's life is defined through emotions — jealousy, possessiveness and devotion. Pervading the stories is an elemental fear, fear of losing your boy, or of never getting one. Romance as a code or a way of life, precipitates individual neurosis and prohibits collective action as a means of dealing with it.

By displacing all vestiges or traces of adolescent sexuality and replacing it with concepts of love, passion and eternity, romance gets trapped within its own contradictions, and hence we have the 'problem page'.

Once declared and reciprocated this love is meant to be lasting, and is based on fidelity and pre-marital monogamy. But the girl knows that where *she*, in most cases, will submit to these axioms, there is always the possibility that her boy's passion will, and can be, roused by almost any attractive girl at the bus-stop, outside the home, etc.

The way this paradox is handled is to introduce terms like resignation, despair, fatalism — it's 'all in the game'. Love has its losers, it must be admitted, but for the girl who has lost, there is always the chance that it will happen again, this time with a more reliable boy. Girls don't, then, fight back. Female 'flirts' always come to a 'bad end'; they are abandoned by their admirers who quickly turn their attention to the quiet, trusting best friend who had always been content to sit in the background.

Conclusion

What, then, are the central features of *Jackie* in so far as it presents its readers with an ideology of adolescent femininity? First it sets up, defines and focuses exclusively on 'the personal', locating it as the sphere of *prime* importance to the teenage girl. It presents this as a totality — and by implication all else is of secondary interest to the 'modern girl'. Romance problems, fashion, beauty and pop mark out the limits of the girl's concern — other possibilities are ignored or dismissed.

Second, *Jackie* presents 'romantic individualism' as the ethos, *par excellence*, for the teenage girl. The *Jackie* girl is alone in her quest for love; she refers back to her female peers for advice, comfort and re-assurance *only* when she has problems in fulfilling this aim. Female solidarity, or more simply the idea of girls together — in *Jackie* terms — is an unambiguous sign of failure. To achieve self-respect, the girl has to escape the 'bitchy', 'catty' atmosphere of female company and find a boyfriend as fast as possible. But in doing this she has not only to be individualistic in outlook — she has to be prepared to fight ruthlessly — by plotting, intrigue and cunning, to 'trap her man'. Not surprisingly this independent-mindedness is short-lived. As soon as she finds a 'steady', she must renounce it altogether and capitulate to *his* demands, acknow-ledging his domination and resigning herself to her own subordination.

This whole ideological discourse, as it takes shape through the pages of *Jackie*, is immensely powerful. Judging by sales figures alone, *Jackie* is a force to be reckoned with by feminists. Of course this does not mean that its readers swallow its axioms unquestioningly. And indeed until we have a clearer idea of just how girls 'read' *Jackie* and encounter its ideological force, our analysis remains one-sided.

For feminists a related question must be how to go about countering *Jackie* and undermining its ideological power at the level of *cultural* intervention. One way of beginning this task would be for feminist teachers and youth leaders to involve girls in the task of 'deconstructing' this seemingly 'natural' ideology; and in breaking down the apparently timeless qualities of girls' and women's 'mags'.

Another more adventurous possibility would be the joint production of an alternative; a magazine where girls are depicted in situations other than the romantic, and where sexuality is discussed openly and frankly; not just contraception, masturbation and abortion, but the *social relations* of sexuality, especially the sexism of their male peers. Likewise girls would be encouraged to create their own music, learn instruments and listen to music without having to drool over idols. Their clothes would not simply reflect styles created by men to transform them into junior sex-objects, products of male imaginations and fantasies. But most of all, readers would be presented with an *active* image of female adolescence — one which pervades every page and is not just deceptively 'frozen' into a single 'energetic/glamorous' pose as in the fashion pages and Tampax adverts in *Jackie*.

Notes

1. See G.L. White, *Women's Magazines, 1963-1968* (1970), Appendix IV.

2. See G. Rosei, 'The Private Life of Lord Snooty', *Sunday Times Magazine*, 29 July 1973, pp. 8-16.

3. L. Althusser, 'Ideology and Ideological State Apparatuses: Notes Toward an Investigation' in *Lenin and Philosophy, and Other Essays* (New Left Books, London, 1971), p. 163.

4. A. Dorfman and A. Mattelart, *How to Read Donald Duck* (I.G. Editions Inc., New York, 1975), p. 30.

5. P. Johnson, *New Statesman*, 1964.

6. C. Alderson, *The Magazines Teenagers Read* (Pergamon Press, Oxford, 1968), p. 3.

7. P. Willis, 'Symbolism and Practice: a Theory for the Social Meaning of Pop Music', Centre for Contemporary Cultural Studies, stencilled paper No. 2, p. 2.

8. Ibid., p. 1.

9. J. Clarke, S. Hall, T. Jefferson and B. Roberts (eds.), *Resistance Through Rituals* (Hutchinson, London, 1976), p. 55.

10. S. Hall, B. Lumley and G. McLennan, 'Politics and Ideology: Gramsci', *Working Papers in Cultural Studies*, no. 10 (1977), p. 51.

11. Ibid., p. 51.

12. R. Hoggart, *The Uses of Literacy* (Chatto and Windus, London, 1957), p. 51.

13. G. Greer, *The Female Eunuch* (Paladin, London, 1970), p. 173.

14. See J. Mitchell, *Psychoanalysis and Feminism* (Penguin, Harmondsworth, 1974).

13 THE MOTOR-BIKE AND MOTOR-BIKE CULTURE

Paul Willis

Source: *Profane Culture* (Routledge and Kegan Paul, London, 1978), Chs. 2 and 3. © Paul Willis.

I made contact with a motor-bike club in a large English city in 1969, and continued field work and interviews there over a period of nine months. The club is now closed and the members disbanded. During the period of 'the research' the club was very successful, and always full, and had an official membership in the hundreds. The boys were in the typical style of the motor-bike boy, or 'rocker', or 'greaser'. Studded leather jackets and greasy denim jeans were the norm. Large motor-cycle boots or large marching boots were worn on the feet. Hair was normally long and greasy, swept back with a small quiff at the front. The leaders' jackets were frequently adorned with badges and mottoes.

Though this group and style was clearly marked out during the 1960s by the opposition — accomplished partly through the media — to the 'mods', the culture still exists today. The style represents one basic form of working-class culture as it is lived by the young, and contains — often in highly explicit forms — central continuing working-class themes and values.

I spent a few evenings simply 'hanging around' the club and taking in its general atmosphere. Contacts could be made with members through the full-time official. One of these contacts, Mick, a long-standing member and one-time secretary to the club, was sympathetic and introduced me to his particular group of friends. These friends, ranging in age from late teens to middle 20s, were not involved in the formal structure of the club, and strongly resisted its latent functions of social control, although they had attended regularly over a number of years. Over the next few weeks, I developed a kind of relationship with this group and finally suggested that they might like to listen to records, and discuss their reactions and whatever else interested them on tape. They agreed — and certainly out of no obligation or coercion. It was frequently impossible to get them all together at one time, and I often spent the evening just drifting around the club chatting here and there or generally observing things. It should be remembered that my study was of the larger social and cultural whole and not of a specific group or of specific individuals except in so far as they embodied central meanings and values. I was not perturbed by this randomness of contact. *General* exposure to the culture was of the utmost importance.

A typical evening for the motor-bike boys would consist of permutations of the same activities: a coffee in the coffee bar, a drink and a game of darts in the local pub, a game of table-tennis or pin-ball in the coffee bar, general horseplay around the premises, chatting in groups around the club. The social situation was very fluid and Mick's group would not remain a coherent whole, but split up and mixed generally about the club. The composition of the group with which I taped discussions also changed over time and varied in number. It centrally included Mick (a foundry worker), Joe (a scaffolder), Fred (a scaffolder), Tim (a milkman), Percy (a student), Roger (unemployed) and Sue (unemployed, girlfriend of Joe). Percy and Roger were not part of Mick's group of friends, but joined our discussions on a few occasions, and were always around the club and well known to all its members. [. . .]

My concern in this essay is with the symbolic values that clustered around the motor-bike within this group. The motor-bike both reflected and generated many of the central meanings of the bike culture. It must be understood as one of the main elements of its stylistic make-up.

In a general and unspecific way, it was clear that the motor-bike was one of the main interests of the motor-bike boys. Most of their activities were based on this interest. A large part of conversation was devoted to the motor-cycle: discussing new models or comparing performance or describing in detail how repair jobs were done.

The club itself acted as an important clearing-house for spares and accessories, sometimes stolen, sometimes legitimate. The boys regarded the club as a centre of information and supply. On numerous occasions experts were approached by acolytes for detailed descriptions of mechanical repair jobs or for a 'professional' diagnosis of mechanical problems. A strange rattle or banging, sluggish acceleration, or bad handling characteristics, would send the less knowledgeable enthusiasts running to the acknowledged 'experts'. At *first* sight an unofficial hierarchy *appeared* to be based on this knowledge: individuals with extremely fast motor-bikes, or with recognized diagnostic and mechanical skill, seemed to enjoy a position of high status. A common approach would be to offer the 'expert' a drink or a cigarette as a prelude to asking advice.

Mick was awarded a senior position within the unofficial hierarchy. This was interesting and alerted me to what lay behind the possibly merely random, chance or purely functional technical involvement with the motor-bike. The motor-bike had a specific *cultural* role, and it was its *cultural* meaning which was most related to status in their social system. Mick's mechanical skills were not at an extremely high level, and nor was his motor-bike particularly fast. In his case it was more his *length* of experience and his *type* of experience with bikes. He was older than the rest, had been riding a motor-cycle for longer and, more significantly, had had several accidents. He had been in hospital several times, had broken a number of limbs, and had, as a memento of one of his accidents, a piece of metal in one of his legs holding a weakened bone together. He recounted these experiences with nonchalance and seemed to make no special effort to avoid further accidents — rather he seemed to expect further accidents as a matter of course. Status, then, in the light of Mick's case, was accorded less for technical competence with the motor-bike, than for full citizenship within the *world* of the motor-cycle, for understanding at some level, as it were, not the surface technical details, but the real cultural meaning of the motor-bike: the way in which it reflected important cultural values.

The solidity, responsiveness, inevitableness, the *strength* of the motor-bike matched the concrete, secure nature of the bikeboys' world. It underwrote in a dramatic and important way their belief in the commonsense world of tangible things, and the secureness of personal identity. The roughness and intimidation of the motor-bike, the surprise of its fierce acceleration, the aggressive thumping of the un-baffled exhaust, matches and symbolizes the masculine assertiveness, the rough camaraderie, the muscularity of language, of their style of social interaction.

That sheer technical competence alone was not rated highly is clearly shown by the case of Percy, a 'conventional' motor-cyclist who attended the club regularly. He had a very advanced technical knowledge of the motor-bike, but was accorded very little status. He did not ride his machine particularly fast, had never had an accident and did not regard the prospect with equanimity. His clothing was within the letter, rather than the spirit, of the motor-bike world. It was simply *too* functional and *too* meticulous to seem natural in this larger symbolic world.

This observation about Percy was important and led to an understanding of the dialectical role of the motor-bike. It mediated not only essential cultural values, but directly developed them in other elements of expressive style. Its nature resonated through the culture. Other cultural atoms took on the structure of its existence, in turn both expressing and further forming the structure of feeling in the culture. The dress of Joe, Fred, Mick and Tim was not primarily a functional exigency of riding a motor-cycle. It was more crucially an extension of the motor-bike into the human zone: this dress was a cultural transposition and *amplification* of the qualities *inherent* within the motor-bike and of the experience of riding it.

For those who have never ridden a motor-cycle, it may not be clear that high-speed riding is an extremely physical experience. At high speeds, the whole body is blown backwards: it was a common way of communicating speed among the boys to say 'I was nearly blown off'. When even a slight bend is taken at high speed the machine and the driver need to go over at quite an angle in order to compensate the centrifugal force which threatens to throw the rider off, and topple the machine away from the direction of the turn. Novices find this an extremely precarious situation to be in, and can panic. The experienced fast motor-cyclist will not take a complete amateur on the back of the motor-cycle in case a lean in the wrong direction on a fast bend may upset the precise balance, and send them both hurtling towards the tarmac. The experienced driver becomes part of the motor-cycle and intuitively feels the correct balancing at high speeds. If there is anything wrong, it is the fault of the motor-bike.

The dangers and the excitement of bodily wind pressure exist of course for the conventional motor-cyclist, too, but he responds only within a technical (culturally arbitrary) framework. He tries to remove himself from the rawness of the experience. He protects his body, face, eyes and hands from the wind. He tries to close down and minimize the influence within the human of the inherent qualities of the motor-bike. He is, in a sense, contained and sealed by his gear, so that he makes decisions, and controls the motor-cycle, at one remove from the direct experiences which made the control necessary. Thus, he must lean with the machine around corners, and he will feel the force of the wind bodily moving him back, but these senses are both blunted and mediated by protective clothing. The clothing is also pulled in tightly without open flaps, streamlined and smooth to minimize unnecessary drag and wind resistance. Thus, the conventional clothing of Percy consisted of a helmet, goggles, belted waist, tightly closed-in neck, gloves and large woollen socks. The helmet clearly protected against head injury in an accident, the goggles prevented eye irritation from dust or high winds. The belted waist and tightly closed-in neck prevented wind from entering and ballooning the clothes at high speeds. The gloves protected the hands, and, by overlapping the jacket, prevented wind from travelling up the sleeve. Large woollen socks prevented air from pocketing, and kept the feet warm. Thus, in this conventional dress, Percy was tightly packaged in, and given the maximum protection from the inherent dangers and discomforts of the motor-bike. The special characteristics of the motor-bike, its openness to the elements, its instability, its speed, the free rush of air, were minimized as far as possible, so as to render the motor-cycle a neutral form of transport. The whole outfit is a carefully worked out, and carefully put together, attempt to negate the effects and characteristics of the motor-bike: it is the technological answer to the problems technology has created –

uniformity, anonymity and featurelessness encircle the rough, roaring, dangerous qualities of the motor-cycle.

The bikeboys' response to the special characteristics of the moving bike is very different. Although their dress contained some of the same basic elements as that of the conventional motor-cyclist, the bikeboys had transformed its meaning and significance by small though crucial changes. To start with, helmets, and goggles and gloves were never worn.* They knew quite well that helmets were advisable if only because of a national safety campaign: 'You know it makes sense.' The reason was that helmets and goggles would have inhibited the force of cultural mediation: the *experience* and the *image* of motor-cycling would have been muffled or blocked. These accoutrements destroyed the excitement of the wind rushing into the face and of the loud exhaust beat thumping the ears. The absence of gloves, goggles and helmet means that the equivalent of a high gale-force wind is tearing into the living flesh. Eyes are forced into a slit and water profusely, the mouth is dragged back. The bikeboys allow no disjunction whatsoever between the fact and the experience of speed. Physical consequences are minutely articulated with control decisions of the motor-bike. There is no sense in which the rider is protected by a panoply within which there is calm to make protected decisions about events in the world out there. For the bikeboy, he is in the 'world out there' and copes with handling his motor-bike, at the same time as feeling the full brunt of its movement in the natural physical world.

More generally the motor-bike boy makes no attempt to minimize the drag effect of the wind. Jackets are partly open and are not buttoned down around the throat, belts are not worn. There is nothing to keep the jacket close to the skin, trousers are not tucked away in boots and socks, there is nothing to prevent wind tunnelling to the sleeves. Adornments of the jacket and free-flowing neckties add, although fractionally, to the total drag, an unncessary drag that would be avoided by conventional motor-cyclists.

The lack of the helmet allowed long hair to blow freely back in the wind, and this, with the studded and ornamented jackets, and the aggressive style of riding gave the motor-bike boys a fearsome look which amplified the wildness, noise, surprise and intimidation of the motor-bike. The point of fast driving was the experience, the expressive force, the public image — never the fact — of speed.

These were some of the dialectical influences of the bike on the appearance and experience of the boys. In the reverse moment of this relation to the motor-bike, they had made physical changes to their

*The law now prohibits the use of a motor-bike without a helmet. It did not in 1969-70 when this research was undertaken.

machines. They partly changed the objective nature of the bike better to express their own preferred meanings.

Handlebars were often of the large cattle-horn type which required an upright sitting position with hands and arms level with the shoulders. This considerably increases drag, and ironically limits the top speed of the motor-bike. But it improves handling ability and increases the sensation of speed dramatically. The conventional motor-cyclist does exactly the opposite, lowers the handlebars and puts the footrests farther back, so that the body can lie virtually flat along the bike and present the minimum surface for wind resistance. Chromium-plated double exhaust pipes and high exuberant mudguards all helped to give the bikes an exaggerated look of fierce power. It was also common practice to remove the baffles from the silencer box on the exhaust, in order to allow the straight-through thumping of the exhaust gases from the cylinder to carry their explosion directly into the atmosphere. The effect could be startling. The breathy, loud, slightly irregular bang and splutter brought the hardness and power of the metal piston exploding down the metal cylinder, abruptly and inevitably reversing up again, right out into the still air. The minutely engineered turn of the crank-shaft brought a power and impersonal ferocity right out into the vulnerable zone of human sensibilities.

An alleyway led up the side of the church to the coffee bar of the club. Members often parked their bikes along this narrow passageway, and stood by them talking, starting and revving their bikes, discussing technical matters or indeed any matters at all. The noise was often overwhelming: the loud thumping of the motor-bike engines seemed to promise sudden movement and action, but none came. Strangers and neophytes could be unnerved by the continually imagined necessity to take evasive action against some fantasy explosion of movement and aggression.

The ensemble of bike, noise, rider, clothes *on the move* gave a formidable expression of identity to the culture and powerfully developed many of its central values.

Perhaps the most massive general dialectical force of the decked-out, souped-up motor-bike on the bike culture and its forms of consciousness was that of death. Death and its mediations and the forms of its subjective and social appropriation were at the heart of the culture. The possibility of accident was recognized — though not sought out — and past accidents were a major topic of conversation. Death on the motor-bike had come to take on a crucial meaning in the culture. It was the ultimate symbolic summing up of courage, masculinity and exhibition.

Joe: I think it's the best way. I'll have a bike until I'm about 35, you know. I think it's the best way to die . . . I'd like to go quickly, mind you, out like a light, 'bang' . . . fast, like, about 100 miles an hour . . . hit a car . . . smash straight into something.

PW: What are the chances do you think of having a serious accident?

Joe: Oh well, I'm a nut case, you know, on a motor-bike, it might do. I've had some near misses, you know, through crash barriers, and I've had concussion and things like that without a crash helmet.

PW: But did that make you think?

Joe: No, funnily enough it didn't, everybody else said 'I bet that's made you think' . . . You see, that's why I think I may die on a motor-bike.

Fred: I'd like to die on . . . I'd like to die on a bike, that's the way I wanna go, fucking great, I'd hate to get old.

PW: Why?

Tim: The thing is —

Fred: Hang on, you daft cunt.

Tim: I'd like to.

Fred: It would be a great sensation to croak out on a bike . . . I'd like a fucking smash, got to be a good one, or I don't want to go.

Certainly the death rate from motor-bike accidents at the club was appalling. This is from the official reports on the club concerning the period summer 1967:

> This period has brought a number of major disasters to club members, both in terms of personal injuries and death on the roads. Four deaths were recorded in August alone, and each brought with it a major shock to the organization with feelings of hopelessness and despair . . . Funerals were attended by large numbers of members wearing ordinary clothes [motor-cycling gear, etc.] and pall bearers were provided from friends.

Death on the motor-cycle had its effects not only on consciousness, however, but on the material organization of the club, which in its turn, of course, further developed particular kinds of meanings and values within the culture. On the altar table in the church* was a large embossed book lying open all the time with the names and dates of the death of past members of the club who had been killed on the road. The pages were turned daily to record exact anniversaries. It was one of the familiar sights around the club to see, alone, or in groups, past girlfriends, friends, acquaintances or admirers of a particular victim looking at the book in solemn ritual silence.

Normally the motor-bike boys treated the church with complete disregard. Before the discussions Joe, Mick and others would often play with a large medicine ball, throwing it back and forth to each other down the length of the church, crashing it through the chairs and bouncing it up on to the altar. This does not imply sacrilege. They simply treated the church as any other building. However, when a member of the club was killed in a motor-cycle crash, there was always a very well-attended memorial service in the church and a formal entering of his name in the memorial book. In these particular moments of crisis the motor-bike boys turned towards the church not out of a sense of religion, but out of marking what they regarded as an important event with formal recognition. Death on the motor-bike sought out a ritualized, formal expression for itself in the face of countervailing everyday attitudes. The motor-bike boys did not have their own institution for recognizing an event of such extreme importance. The church, its paraphernalia and rituals, were turned to because they offered for creative appropriation and modification ready-made and widely recognized *formal* ways of according significance. It was at the memorial church service that the rider was well and truly recognized as dead, and could stay dead, and was marked as such in the memorial book: a kind of formal root for the dark glory, the collective mythology of the motor-bike culture. It did not matter that the church rituals were not understood — they could not have been understood in the way the church would have wanted them understood and they were anyway filled up from the outside with new meaning. What mattered was the sense of presence, the sense of order, the sense of marking within time of a crucial event. Thus, at these times, there was very special conjunction of a traditional received form and a modern informal form. The motor-bike boys who in so many other circumstances delighted in the outrage of conventional society, at a certain point within the internal expressive life of their culture — at a point which was both crisis and transcendence — turned in an act of cultural fusion to a traditional institution to borrow its solemnity and ritual. This regard for death, the fascination in its rituals, the need to push beyond the normal bounds of their culture for these rituals, attest the degree to which

---

*The club was located in the premises of an old church.

death on the motor-cycle and danger on the motor-cycle were integral
to the whole culture and locked in, expressed and developed many of
its meanings. The apocalyptic death on the motor-bike and promethean inflation
of the victim was registered in another dialectical adoption and adap-
tion of an unlikely form chosen for its inherent power to express significance. It was said that deaths on motor-cycles were always reported
in the local press, whereas deaths on scooters or in motor-cars were not
reported:

Fred: They publish a remembrance in the paper,
                 you can cut it out, like, and put it in a scrap-
                 book. They always do that when you croak
                 out on a bike, they always put it in the
                 paper, you know, no scooters, motor-bikes,
                 Johnny Gibson and all them lot, all fucking
                 in the paper.
Joe: Johnny Gibson, that was my mate, I talked
                 to him, you know.

Again, we see a surprising conjunction with, and use of, conventional
society. An element of conventional society was able to mark or accord
significance to something of importance within the culture, in a form
which was possible in no other way. No internal cultural form could
give the public visibility and substantiality which the motor-bike
required. Newspaper items were cut out and kept, and widely talked
about, both at the time and afterwards. Past figures, and the manner
of their death, were one of the main topics of conversation among the
boys. Individuals, who in their time often had achieved no particular
status, soon become heroic, mythological subjects of the bike culture
folk-lore. The build-up of a pantheon of figures in this way owed much
of its legitimacy and resonance to a creative borrowing and decontext-
ualizing of elements of the conventional news media and established
church.

Essentially, then, the motor-cycle was not limited to a functional
use within the motor-bike culture. It was taken up, not blocked, by
experience. It was allowed to make a full dialectical register on human
culture. Mechanical qualities were recognized, appreciated, extended
and transformed into human qualities which then pushed through for
their own material recognition, instituting yet further circuits of
development. This is not to posit a cybernetic model of the relationship
between experience and technology where machines condition and
over-ride specifically human qualities. It is the opposite. It shows a
form of man's domination of the machine. The motor-cycle has to be

controlled, the direct physical consequences of riding accepted, before the 'spirit' of the motor-bike can be appropriated and anthropomorph- ized. The bike plays its part not in some other constructed, but in a *humanly* constructed, world of meaning.

The motor-bike was not, therefore, simply one object in a random collection of objects and activities that occupy the life-space of an underprivileged group. External notions of 'culture' might attach no more importance to it than the table or chair we sit on – a functional object totally lacking in 'culture'. In fact there can be a tight, dialectical formation of meanings and attitudes around apparently functional objects in the normal course of living. Such a distinctive and meaningful construction, such a developed *expressive* function, based on a form of modern technology, cannot be assumed to be valueless and devoid of *cultural* meaning. It is increasingly *the form* of cultural life, *everyday* life, for underprivileged groups.

14 CONFECTIONS, CONCOCTIONS AND CONCEPTIONS

Allison James

Source: *Journal of the Anthropological Society of Oxford*, vol. X, no. 2, Trinity (1979). © JASO.

This article derives from an incident which took place while I was doing fieldwork in the North East of England, investigating the structure and experience of childhood. An old lady of my acquaintance, remarking on the quality of the paint used by the National Coal Board on their properties, grumbled that it was 'all ket — rubbish' and that it would peel off in a few months. Before this I had only encountered the word 'ket' among children who used it as their term for sweets, especially cheaper ones. This difference in use intrigued me, particularly when I remembered that sweets, from the adult perspective, are literally the rubbish which children eat between meals.

Further close attention to conversations revealed that 'ket', or 'kets', was used by adults as a classificatory noun to mean an assortment of useless articles and also as an adjective, 'ketty' meaning rubbishy or useless. Confirmation of this usage comes from Dobson (1974) who defines the word as rubbish. However, Cecil Geeson cites the original meaning as: something smelly, stinking, unhealthy or diseased' generally applicable to the 'carcasses of animals dying a natural death and dressed for market without being bled' (1969, p. 116). The Opies (1959) suggested that many old dialect words which have died out in adult language are stored in the child's repertoire but the example of 'kets' casts doubt on an image of passive retention. In this case the semantic content is not stored, but instead undergoes a significant shift. A word which, in the adult world, refers to despised and inedible substances has been transformed; in the world of the child it refers to a revered sweet. In this article I shall explore the seemingly unrelated uses of the term 'kets' in the worlds of adults and children and shall attempt to reveal and explain an inherent and consistent logic in such uses.

To talk about sweets and rubbish inevitably involved discussing the relationship between the worlds of adults and children. I have argued elsewhere (James, 1979) that the social world of children, whilst being separate in relation to the adult world, is nevertheless dependent on it. This dependence is not passive, however. Instead there is a creative process of interdependence: children construct their own ordered system of rules by reinterpreting the social models given to them by adults. [. . .] Hence, the true nature of the culture of childhood frequently remains hidden from adults, for the semantic cues which permit social recognition have been manipulated and disguised by children in terms of their alternative society.

By confusing the adult order children create for themselves considerable room for movement within the limits imposed upon them by adult society. This deflection of adult perception is crucial for both the maintenance and continuation of the child's culture and for the growth of the concept of the self for the individual child. The process of becoming social involves a conceptual separation between 'self' and 'other'. This process is often described in terms of 'socialization', a model which stresses the passive mimicry of others. I would suggest, however, that this process is better seen in terms of an active experience of contradiction, often with the adult world. It is thus of great significance that something which is despised and regarded as diseased and inedible by the adult world should be given great prestige as a particularly desirable form of food by the child. The transformation of 'kets' from rubbish into food is both logical and consistent with the child's culture.

The notion that food might be a subject worthy of discussion in its own right has long been ignored by social anthropologists. Past ethnographers have either made only fleeting references to what people eat or have submerged the topic under more general headings such as agricultural production, economics and ritual.

However, with the publication of *Le Totemisme Aujourd'hui* (1962) and Lévi-Strauss's provocative suggestion that animals are 'good to think with', the subject of food in relation to the social body has become increasingly central in the discipline (see Leach, 1964; Douglas, 1966; Bulmer, 1967; and Tambiah, 1969). In all these analyses it is argued that ideas people hold concerning the edibility of certain types of food are linked logically to other conceptual domains and that, by examining a people's food categories, a more penetrating and incisive explanation of other aspects of the social system can be achieved. Tambiah argues that 'cultures and social systems are, after all, not only thought but also lived' so that particular attention should be given to exactly what people let inside their bodies (1969, p. 165).

More recently Mary Douglas (1975) has directly confronted the subject of food in her analysis of the major food categories in Britain. She identifies the two main categories as meals and drinks. Of the two, meals are more highly ranked and ordered, being internally structured into 'first, second, main [and] sweet' courses, whereas drinks possess no such structuring (1975, p. 255). Meals are also externally structured by a temporal order — breakfast followed by dinner and tea — which parallels the weekly cycle, climaxing in Sunday dinner, a pattern repeated in the annual sequence of ceremonial meals. Drinks, in contrast, are 'not invested with any necessity in their ordering' (ibid., p. 255).

Douglas further suggests that, besides these major categories of food, some 'food can be taken for private nourishment' but it is likely to be condemned if considered 'to interfere with the next meal' (ibid., p. 254). It is here that she locates sweets, but hers is an adult perspective. Sweets, for adults, are regarded as an adjunct to 'real' food and should not usurp the place of meals. For the child, as I hope to show, the reverse is true: it is *meals* which disrupt the eating of sweets.

Sweets — as in 'Ye Olde Sweete Shoppe' — are an entirely British phenomenon. There is no equivalent abroad and the British sweet industry, in its production of a very extensive range of confectionary, seems to be unique. The concept of the sweetmeat is the nearest parallel to the kinds of confections available in other countries, but it is absent from the supermarket shelves and non-specialist sweet shops in this country.

The European sweetmeat dates back to the seventeenth century with the discovery of sugar. During this period sweetmeats were an integral part of the rich man's menu, forming part of the meal, as is often the case in other countries. Today, in Britain, the sweetmeat is best visualized as a home-made confection to be found on Women's Institute stalls or delicately displayed in tiny baking cases in a traditional confectioner's shop. Mass production techniques have replaced the sweetmeat with similar, but not identical, pre-packed products. However, although the sweetmeat has largely disappeared and the traditional sweet shop must now compete with cinemas, newsagents and slot-machines, the sweetmeat's successor strikingly resembles its forerunner in many aspects. In this sense the sweet, for adults, may be closer to the major food categories than Douglas (1975) supposes. 'Kets', the child's sweets, are an entirely different matter.

Kets and Sweets

'Kets' and sweets must not be confused. Although the distinction may seem to be purely linguistic, other more substantive issues indicate that 'kets' are a very distinctive kind of confectionery, belonging exclusively to the world of children.

The analysis presented below is based on observations made whilst working in a youth club in a small North Eastern village. The children referred to range in age from 11 to 17 but age group distinctions are relatively fluid due to the tight-knit nature of the community. A main focus of activity, for children of all ages in the youth club, is the buying and selling of sweets, primarily of the 'ketty' variety, although older children tend more towards other kinds of sweets. However, children almost always use the word 'kets', whilst adults prefer the word 'sweets'; occasionally, adults may jokingly refer to 'kets', especially if they are confections bought for children, but would never use this word for sweets they themselves are going to consume.

It would seem, therefore, that the term 'kets' usually is used for those sweets at the lower end of the price range and it is these sweets which children most often buy. It could be argued therefore that the distinction between 'kets' and other kinds of confectionery rests solely on economic factors. However, before assuming that children buy 'kets' because they are cheap and that children, in general, have less money to spend than adults, certain problems should be considered. Why don't adults buy 'kets'? For 10p, the price of a chocolate bar, they could buy ten pieces of bubble gum. Furthermore, although it is certainly true that children tend to buy the cheaper sweets, it is apparent from field data that the total amount of money spent by a child on sweets *at any one time* may be quite considerable. A typical purchase might be: four 'Fizz Bombs' at 1p each; three 'Liquorice Novelties' at 2p each and two 'Bubble gums' at 1p each. The total outlay, 12p, could buy two small chocolate bars, which are also available at the club. This may be an example of getting more for one's money, but another factor should be taken into account. The spending power of children is obviously an important consideration for manufacturers, but if this were the sole criterion influencing production, why would manufacturers not produce miniature versions of the kinds of confections available in the higher price range? Some years ago it was possible to purchase slim bars of Cadbury's chocolate for one old penny and a slightly larger version for twopence. The equivalent products today are tiny 'Milky Ways' and 'Mars Bars' sold in bags as 'Family Packs'. Why do manufacturers not sell them singly? The answer seems to be that there is no demand for them.

Children, then, do not buy 'kets' simply because they are cheaper or have a lower unit price. 'Kets' have other properties, besides their cheapness, which make them important for the child. Manufacturers may not be exploiting the power of the child's purse directly, but more insidiously, the power inherent in the conceptual gulf between the worlds of the adult and the child.

Junk Food

In order to resolve such problematic issues concerning the attractions of 'kets' I carried out a statistical survey, dividing the range of confectionery into three groups. The term 'kets' was given to all those sweets costing less than 5p. An intermediate group was established for sweets costing between 6p and 10p and a third group contained all sweets costing 11p or more, including the more expensive boxes of chocolates. By isolating 'kets' as a distinct group according to price it was possible to examine further more elusive contrasts between 'kets' and other sweets, an investigation which suggested that the alternative adult meaning of the word 'kets' — rubbish — was indeed a powerful and persuasive metaphor. Much of the attraction of 'kets' seems to lie precisely in the way they stand in contrast to conventional adult sweets and adult eating patterns generally. This is apparent in their names, their colours, the sensations they induce, their presentation and the descriptions of their contents, as well as in the timing and manner of their consumption.

If adults regard 'kets' as rubbish, low in nutritive value and essentially 'junk food', then it is quite logical that manufacturers should label their products in an appropriate manner. 'Kets' are often given names which emphasize their inedibility and rubbishy content in adult terms. Many have names usually reserved for mechanical and utilitarian objects which adults would never dream of eating. Children, however, will gleefully consume them. There are, for example, Syco Discs, Fizzy Bullets, Supersonic Flyers, Robots, Traffic Lights, Coconut Bongos, Diddy Bags, Telephones, Catherine Wheels, Golf Balls, Pipes, Jelly Wellies, Star Ships and Car Parks. Other kinds of sweets rarely have such names.

Not only do children consume what is inedible, they also ingest many 'animals' whose consumption normally is abhorred by adults and which are surrounded by dietary taboos. Cannibalism, too, ranks highly. Thus children find themselves eating Mr. Marble, Mickey Mouse, Yogi Bear, Mighty Monkey, Snakes, Kangaroos, Spooks, Jelly Footballers, Dinosaurs, Lucky Black Cats, Dormice, Bright Babies, Jelly Gorillas and Fun Faces.

This rubbishy attribute of 'kets' is highlighted when the above names are compared to the names given to other more expensive kinds of sweets. These often describe the actual composition of the confectionery and frequently yield precise and detailed information for the consumer. Adults, it seems, like to know what they are eating. In this range there are names such as Munchie Mints, Butterscotch, Assorted Nut Toffee, Nut Brittle, Coconut Whirls, Rum and Butter Toffee, Caramel, Peppermint Lumps, Toffimallow, Royal Butter Mints, Liquorice Bon Bons and Chocolate Coconut Ice.

Although a few 'kets' possess descriptive names the unfamiliar eater should beware of assuming that the description refers to the taste. The names 'Seafood', 'Shrimps' and 'Jelly Eels' may lead to the expectation of a savoury sweet; they are, however, sweet and sickly. 'Rhubarb and Custard' and 'Fruit Salad' are hard, chewy 'kets' presenting a marked contrast to the sloppy puddings implied by the names. Such inversions and contradictions of the accepted adult order are an essential facet of the child's world so that 'Silly Toffee Banana' and 'Orozo Hard Juice' could only be 'kets'.[1]

'Kets' are mostly brightly coloured, as in the luminous blues and fluorescent oranges of the 'Fizz Bomb' and the vivid yellows and reds of many jellied 'kets'. Some have contrasting stripes, with clashing colours as in the 'Liquorice Novelty'. Here, black strips of liquorice are festooned with shocking greens, reds and blues. All these harsh, saturated colours are absent from the 'real' food of the adult world. Blue, especially, is banned; bright blue belongs to the realm of iced cakes and such concoctions are a highly ceremonial form of food, divorced from the everyday menu.[2] Many sweets, also aimed at the child's market but not classed here as 'kets', are similarly coloured: for example, 'Smarties', 'Jelly Tots', 'Jelly Babies' and 'Liquorice Allsorts'. Such bright and stimulating colours are not normally associated with the dinner plate.

In contrast, the sweets which are aimed primarily at an adult market have a more uniform and duller appearance. Most are coated in chocolate, presenting exteriors of shades of brown, significantly known today as 'natural' — i.e. healthy — colours. In the more expensive boxes of chocolates the highly saturated colours of the 'kets' are present, but they are masked by a coating of chocolate and hidden from sight. Where chocolate is not used, the colours of these sweets tend towards pastel shades, soft, delicate colours inoffensive to the eye, as in 'Sugared Almonds' or 'Mints'. The 'Humbug', with its sedate black and white stripes, is a poor relation of the 'Gob Stopper' and lacks its coat of many colours. For sweets to be suitable for adult consumption, highly saturated colours must be avoided, for such colours are not present in 'real' food, and adults, unlike children, are conservative about what they class as edible.

The eating of this metaphoric rubbish by children is a serious business and adults should be wary of tackling 'kets' for, unlike other sweets, 'kets' are a unique digestive experience. Many of the names given to 'kets' hint at this: 'Fizzy Bullets', 'Fizz Bombs', 'Fizz Balls', 'Festoon Fizzle Sticks', 'Fizzy Lizzies' and 'Fruit Fizzles' all stress the tingling sensation to be gained from eating them. Many 'kets' contain sherbert and 'Sherbits', 'Refreshers', 'Sherbo Dabs', 'Dip Dabs', 'Sherbert Fountains', 'Double Dip Sherbert' and even 'Love Hearts' all make the mouth smart while eating them.

In contrast other sweets provide little in the way of exciting consumption. The nearest rival among these sweets to the explosive taste of many 'kets' is the 'Extra Strong Mint' — a poor rival to the 'Knock Out Lolly'. The stress on citrus fruit flavours and the tangy, often acrid, taste of many 'kets' contrasts radically with the preponderance of sugary or nutty flavours in adult confections. The ferocious taste of a 'Fizz Bomb' is quite distinctive and lingers in the mouth for a long time, temporarily putting the other taste buds out of action.

Chocolate, which is a favoured ingredient in sweets aimed at the adult consumer, is rare among 'kets' but may appear as chocolate flavour. There is a range of 'kets' styled in the shapes of hammers, saws and chisels which, although appearing to be chocolate, are in fact made from a substitute. Similarly, 'Cheroots' look like long sticks of chocolate, but have a gritty texture and are dry and tasteless. They lack the rich, creamy taste and smooth texture so beloved by the advertisers of real chocolate.

This marked difference in taste and texture between 'kets' and other sweets lies naturally in the ingredients used in their manufacture. 'Kets' are frequently unwrapped so that a list of ingredients is difficult to obtain but common substances inc.ude: sugar, glucose, edible gum, edible vegetable oil, citric acid and assorted flavourings. Other sweets, in contrast, proudly list their ingredients, frequently stressing their 'natural goodness'. For example a message on the wrapper of a 'Picnic' chocolate bar states in large letters that the bar contains: 'Milk chocolate with peanuts, wafer, toffee and raisin centre'. In much smaller print it admits that the chocolate contains vegetable fat — thus lessening its nutritive properties and desirability — but stresses that there is a minimum of 20 per cent milk solids which must not be overlooked.

It would seem, therefore, that sweets, as opposed to 'kets', are to be valued as a form of food. The 'Picnic', as its name suggests, is to be regarded as a source of nourishment. These kinds of sweets are, like the sweetmeat, closely associated with our major food categories and many can be concocted at home from common household ingredients. Cookery books include recipes for sweets such as truffles, peppermint creams, coconut ice and toffee. 'Kets', on the other hand, are impossible to reproduce in the kitchen.

Thus sweets belong to the realm of 'real' food, to the private world of the kitchen, and are bound to the concept of the meal. They have names indicative of their wholesomeness; their flavours echo the patterns of taste normally associated with the dessert — the sweet course — of the meal. Mary Douglas suggests that it is 'the capacity to recall the whole by the structure of the parts' which has insured the survival of the British biscuit in our diet and similarly it is this mimetic quality of the sweet which has kept it bound to the realm of 'real' food (1975, p. 747). 'Kets', in contrast, are, by their very nature, removed from the adult domestic sphere and belong to the public, social world of children. In name, taste and consumptive experience, 'kets' belong to the disorderly and inverted world of children, for in this alternative world a new order exists which makes the 'ket' an eminently desirable product.

Lévi-Strauss (1975) suggests that the differing culinary modes to be found in a particular culture may reflect its conceptual categories and it is in this light that the adult meaning of the word 'kets' becomes highly significant. If sweets belong to the adult world, the human cultural world of cooked foods as opposed to the natural, raw food of the animal kingdom, then 'kets' belong in a third category. Neither raw nor cooked, according to the adult perspective, 'kets' are a kind of rotten food. These rubbishy, decaying and diseased sweets are the peculiar property of children who are, from the adult perspective, a tainted group. Children are, from the adult point of view, pre-social, in need of training and correction through the process of socialization and thus it is quite consistent that it should be 'kets' which children regard as their most social form of food. Mary Douglas has argued that 'consuming is finding consistent meanings' and that goods are purchased and needed 'for making visible and stable the categories of culture' (1977, pp. 292-3). In this sense the literal consumption of different kinds of confectionery by adults and children reflects the inherent contradiction between their separate worlds.

Metaphoric Meals

Mary Douglas (1975) argues that the eating of meals involves a whole series of rituals concerning both the presentation and consumption of food. Food is served on different kinds of plates according to the kind of meal. It is eaten with cutlery of assorted shapes and sizes, which transfers food from plate to mouth. The use of the fingers for this act is frowned upon by adults and rarely should food enter the mouth by hand. Chicken legs become embarrassing to eat in the company of others and the eating of lobsters entails a battery of dissecting instruments. Finger bowls and serviettes are provided for the eaters of such foods to remove any particles adhering to the hands or lips. As Goffman suggests, 'greasy foods that are not considered to contaminate the mouth can yet be felt to contaminate the hands should contact have to be made without insulation by utensils' (1971, p. 73). The more ceremonial the meal the more crockery and cutlery necessary to facilitate the eating of it.

Those sweets which are to be regarded as belonging to the realm of 'real' food must be similarly distanced from the body, unlike the non-food 'kets'. 'Kets' are usually unwrapped, whereas other sweets tend to be heavily packaged, for the layers of paper provide the necessary separation between the inner and outer body. The phrase 'a hand to mouth existence' — a poor and despised condition — emphasises the necessity for maintaining this purity. As with the eating of meals, the more packaging provided, the more ceremonial the sweet and the further it is removed from the 'ketty' sphere. The ultimate example is the box of chocolates, which is shrouded in paper. Like the eating of meals, these sweets must be insulated against contamination from external sources.

The 'After Eight Mint' is superlative in this respect. The clock face printed on the box is repeated on each tiny envelope which encases the sweet and it registered the time at which this confection should ideally be consumed. Its other name — the 'After Dinner Mint' — secures the place of this chocolate as a highly ordered kind of confection inextricably bound to the concept of the meal. Douglas (1975) suggests that meals are externally ordered by time and that it is the temporal sequence of meals which is used to divide up the day. The 'After Eight Mint' confirms the suspicion that the eating of sweets by adults should be similarly structured.

After the meal has been eaten, the sweets may be passed round. Their tray shaped box and insulating containers recall the crockery and cutlery of the meal and the hand is allowed minimum contact with the sweet. The most criminal of acts, frequently indulged in by children, is to finger the sweets for, as with the meal, food must scarcely be handled. To nibble a sweet and then to replace it in the box, again common practice among children, is never allowed amongst adults for that which has been in the mouth must ideally remain there.

Just as ceremonial meals have a yearly temporal cycle, so do the purchase and consumption of sweets. Boxes of chocolates are bought at Christmas, birthdays and other ritual occasions, as is apparent from television advertising: in the week before Christmas many of the usual sweet adverts are replaced by ones for the more luxurious boxes of chocolates.

One major ceremonial sweet, heavily packed and adorned, is not, however, aimed at adults directly. This is the Easter Egg, given by adults to children. The Easter Egg bears all the characteristics of an acceptable adult sweet and encapsulates the whole ethos of the adult's conception of food. Firstly, it marks a ritual season. The silver-paper covered egg sits resplendent in a highly decorated cardboard box, frequently adorned with ribbon. Under the outer layers the chocolate egg can be found, already separated into two, to avoid much contact with the hand. It is easily pulled apart to reveal a packet of highly-coloured sweets, such as 'Smarties' or 'Jelly Tots', which although

ostensibly similar to 'kets' are in fact much less 'ketty'. It is significant
that Easter Eggs are never stuffed with 1p 'Bubble Gums'. The Easter
Egg is strictly ordered in both its construction and its consumption and
is ultimately representative of the adult's rather than the child's,
conception of acceptable food.[3]

'Kets', however, are never subject to such constraints. Most 'kets'
can be found piled high in a cardboard box on the shop counter, with
no respect for variety or flavour, into which children's hands delve and
rummage. Few 'kets' are individually wrapped and, if they are, the
packaging is minimal. Children do not heed the purity rules of adults.
They frequently share their sweets, offering each other bites or sucks of
a 'ket'. The absence of wrappers leaves the fingers sticky; dirty hands
break off pieces to offer to friends. 'Kets' are fished out of pockets
along with other articles and 'Bubble Gum' is stuck to the underside
of tables to be reserved for later use.

'Kets' are not distanced from the body. Indeed, many are specifically designed to conflict with the adult's abhorrence of food entering
the mouth by hand: 'Gob Stoppers' are removed from the mouth for
comparison of colour changes and strings of chewing gum continually
pulled out of the mouth. Hands become covered in 'ket' and the normal eating conventions, instilled by parents during early childhood, are
flagrantly disregarded.

Indeed some 'kets' seem not to be designed for eating at all: 'Gob
Stoppers' fill the mouth totally, not allowing any of the normal digestive processes to begin. 'Chews' produce an aching jaw — reminiscent
of eating tough meat — and 'Fizz Bombs' simply have to be endured.
'Bubble Gum' is chewed vigorously but is never swallowed; instead it
is expelled from the mouth in a bubble and held at the point of entry
until it bursts, spattering the face with particles of sticky gum to be
picked off piecemeal later. 'Lollipops' are pulled in and out of the
mouth and 'Jelly Footballers' first decapitated. 'Space Dust', perhaps
the ultimate 'ket', has no rival. The powder is placed on the tongue
where it begins to explode while the mouth remains open and the ears
and throat buzz and smart.

The frequent examination of each other's tongues during the process
of eating 'kets', together with the other eating techniques required to
consume them, manifest a rejection of the mannered and ordered
conventions of adult society. The joy with which a dirty finger probes
the mouth to extract a wine gum contrasts strongly with the need for
a tooth pick to perform a comparable operation at table.

'Kets', therefore, are the antithesis of the adult conception of 'real'
food while, for adults, sweets are metonymic meals.[4] 'Kets' involve a
rejection of the series of rituals and symbols surrounding the concept of
the meal and are regarded as rubbish by adults. Because they are

despised by the adult world, they are prized by the child's and become the metaphoric meals of childhood. Although children will consume sweets of any kind, it is 'kets' which the child will most often buy. Adults never buy them. The child's private funds, which are not controlled by adults, are appropriately spent on those sweets symbolic of his world. 'Kets' deemed by the adult world to be rubbish, are under the child's control. [...]

The importance of these metaphoric meals for children cannot be overstated. 'Ket' times are in-between meal times and the eating of 'kets' begins almost as soon as the adult meal is over, lasting until the structure of adult society again disrupts their consumption. In our society such continual eating of sweets by adults would be classed as a medical disorder requiring a cure.

Not surprisingly, given the coherent and persistent structure of the child's culture, children have an immense knowledge of the varieties of 'kets' available and are always careful to distinguish between them. 'Chewing Gum' is 'chut' or 'chewy' as opposed to 'Bubble Gum' which is 'bubbly'. A lollipop is rarely simply called a 'lolly', but instead a 'Kojak' or a 'Traffic Light'. Planning one's meal is a serious business.

Conclusion

'Kets', therefore, are the child's food, the food over which he has maximum control. By eating 'kets' rather than other sweets children force confrontations with the adult order, for 'kets' have been despised by adults. The esteem which is attached to 'kets' is emphasised by the ridicule and disgust expressed by the child towards adult food, which is food over which children have little control.

Children are highly articulate in their views on food and school lunches come in for high contempt. The authoritarian structure of the school frequently denies any self-expression by the child so it is significant that it is school dinners which are most abused. Mashed potatoes are known as 'Mashy Arty' or 'shit' when too salty. Mushy peas are likened to 'snot' and school rice pudding looks as if someone has 'hockled' (spat) into it. Semolina is like 'frogspawn'. Thus the foods which children are forced to put inside their bodies by adults are given the status of the excretions which pass out. The most graphic statement of all goes as follows:

> Yellow belly custard, green snot pie,
> Mix them up with a dead dog's eye.
> Mix it thin, mix it thick,
> Swallow it down with a hot cup of sick.

As Charlotte Hardman comments, children perceive the adults' 'weaknesses and responsibilities in connection with food and drink' and much time is spent in reducing 'adult order to humorous disorder' (1974, p. 6). Food is used as weapons by children, but more vehement than the physical attacks with food are the verbal onslaughts directed by children against adults and their control of food:

Old Mrs. Riley had a fat cow,
She milked it, she milked it
She didn't know how.
She pulled its tail instead of its tit
Poor Mrs. Riley covered in shit.

The implied sympathy contained in the last line of this rhyme is not genuine, for gales of laughter always accompany the relating of this event.

Finally, if food is equated with harmfulness by the child, it is logical that non-food should be esteemed. 'Kets' are regarded by children as being particularly beneficial but other substances are also considered to be worth investigating. Children frequently dare each other to eat the literally inedible. Sawdust, plant leaves and other natural substances are often consumed, but a particular favourite is the game called 'Fag-Chewing'. A cigarette is passed round with each child taking a draw until all the tobacco is gone. The unfortunate person left with the filter is then made to eat it or, at the very least, to chew it. Such activity is reminiscent of Jimmy Boyle's (1977) memories of a Glasgow childhood, where one child was ostracised until the others discovered that he could eat worms.

This ability to consume metaphoric rubbish is an integral part of the child's culture. Children, by the very nature of their position as a group outside adult society, have sought out an alternative system of meanings through which they can establish their own integrity. Adult order is manipulated so that what adults esteem is made to appear ridiculous; what adults despise is invested with prestige. [. . .]

For children 'kets' are an important vehicle for defining the self. As I have suggested elsewhere (James, 1979) regarding names, adult labels for children are destroyed and a new name – a nickname – is created by children out of the remnants. Similarly the adult, ordered conception of food is thrown into disarray by the child. Adults continually urge their offspring to eat up their food and lament that they are 'fussy eaters', but children are only pernickety in adult terms. Indeed children stuff into their mouths a wide variety of substances; it is just that these are abhorred by adults.

The eating of 'kets' thus represents a metaphoric chewing up of adult order. Food belongs to the adult world and is symbolic of the adult's control over children. By disordering and confusing the conceptual categories of the adult world children erect a new boundary over which adults have no authority. Mary Douglas (1966) has argued that a corollary of the image of dirt as disordering and anomalous is that it can be associated with power. The eating of dirty, decaying 'kets' is condemned by adults and it is this very condemnation which allows the child to assume control over at least one of his orifices. By eating that which is ambiguous in adult terms the child establishes an alternative system of meanings which adults cannot perceive. It is this which allows the culture of childhood to flourish largely unnoticed by adults and, at the same time, to exist largely beyond their control.

Notes

1. The eating of such disordered food is consistent with the child's culture, but adults abhor such anomalies. On sweet wrappers and other foodstuffs there is a guarantee issued which states that: 'This product should reach you in perfect condition. If it does not, please return it' ('Twix' wrapper). 'Kets', on the other hand, offer no such guarantee.
2. It is important to note that bright, artificial colours do appear in 'real' food but such foods are also classed as 'junk'. Many instant products – e.g. Angel Delight and cake mixes – have extremely bright colours. Bright colours appear often in food at children's parties – e.g. jellies, blancmange and cakes. Such food, like 'kets', is also regarded as being detrimental and essentially rubbishy.
3. There is a smaller, less ceremonial Easter Egg on the market which seems to be aimed at the child market. It has some 'ketty' qualities, for the cream filled egg, although appearing to contain albumen and yolk, is extremely sweet to eat, and far removed from the taste associated with fried eggs, which it closely resembles.
4. Adverts for sweets for adults fully substantiate this idea and the eating of sweets for adults is portrayed as (1) helping to achieve a desired end – e.g. a 'Flake' gives a girl the world of motor boats and a 'Bounty' provides 'the taste of paradise'; (2) substitute food – e.g. 'A Mars a Day helps you work rest and play'; or (3) an additional, nourishing extra which will not affect normal food intake – e.g. 'A Milky Way is the sweet you can eat between meals without ruining your appetite.' 'Kets' are rarely advertised but one advert for a 'Fizz Bomb' shows cartoon children, with their eyeballs whizzing round in opposite directions. Far from stressing the utilitarian aspects of eating sweets – whether as a source of physical or mental strength – 'kets' are to be recommended as an unforgettable gastronomic experience.

References

Boyle, J. (1977) *A Sense of Freedom*, Pan, London
Bulmer, R. (1967) 'Why the Cassowary is Not a Bird', *Man*, n.s., *2* (1), 5-25.
Dobson, S. (1974) *A Geordie Dictionary*, Frank Graham, Newcastle
Douglas, M. (1966) *Purity and Danger*, Routledge and Kegan Paul, London

—— (1975) *Implicit Meanings*, Routledge and Kegan Paul, London
—— (1977) 'Beans' Means 'Thinks', *The Listener*, 8 September pp. 292-3
Douglas M., and Nicod, M. (1974) 'Taking the Biscuit', *New Society*, 19
    December, pp. 744-7
Geeson, C. (1969) *A Northumberland and Durham Word Book*, Harold Hill
    and Sons, Newcastle
Goffman, E. (1971) *Relations in Public*, Penguin, London
Hardman, C. (1974) 'Fact and Fantasy in the Playground', *New Society*,
    19 September
James A. (1979) 'When is a Child Not a Child? Nicknames: a Test Case for a
    Mode of Thought' in A. James and M. Young, Durham University Working
    Papers in Social Anthropology, No. 3
Leach, E. (1964) 'Anthropological Aspects of Language: Animal Categories and
    Verbal Abuse' in E. Lenneberg (ed.), *New Directions in the Study of
    Language*, MIT Press, Cambridge, Mass.
Lévi-Strauss, C. (1962) *Totemism* (trans. R. Needham 1963), Penguin, London
—— (1975) *The Raw and the Cooked*, Harper and Row, New York
Opie, I and P. (1959) *The Lore and Language of School Children*, Oxford
Tambiah, S.J. (1969) 'Animals are Good to Think and Good to Prohibit',
    Ethnology, 8 (4), 424-59

15 THE COLD WAR IN SCIENCE FICTION, 1940-1960

T. Shippey

Source: *Science Fiction: a Critical Guide* (Longman, London, 1979). © Patrick Parrinder.

The literary critic, sociologist, or other outsider venturing to cast his eye over science fiction is likely to be struck almost immediately by two facts. One is the intensely participatory nature of the readership's inner core, something which reveals itself in passionate correspondence in the magazines, in a high proportion of amateur writing, and in the ritual of massive and enthusiastic conventions. The other is that all science fiction incontestably contains some datum known not to be true to the-world-as-it-is. The easiest conclusion to jump to is that the two facts are related: the charge that 'fans' get from science fiction is one of irresponsibility, freedom from restrictions. 'The trouble with these here neurotics is that they all the time got to fight reality. Show in the next twitch', to quote the psychologist from C.M. Kornbluth's 'The Marching Morons' (*Galaxy*, 1951). This is an irritating thesis, and one which does no justice to the often intense self-scrutiny of many science-fiction writers and readers. Nevertheless, it does pay *some* attention to observable facts; and this cannot be said of a style of criticism common enough, and easily forgivable, among the fans themselves, but too often reflected back at them by fan-spokesmen venturing into criticism, and by professional critics who should know better.

It is the distinguishing mark of this second critical style to confuse chronology with history and personalities with explanations. Thus, it is certainly true that the first commercial magazine designed to publish nothing but science fiction was *Amazing Stories*, edited from April 1926 till early 1929 by Hugo Gernsback. Gernsback, then, in many accounts becomes the 'father (or founder) of modern science fiction'. All histories of the genre contain some reference to him; the 'Hugo Awards' for the year's best novel, short story, magazine, etc. are called after him; comment on him approaches the hagiographical. Yet in one sense Gernsbackian priority was an accident. He himself might easily have started a science-fiction magazine earlier than 1926, and it is inconceivable that someone else would not have spotted the market opportunities at most a few years later. To see science fiction as led by Hugo Gernsback is therefore a theory of complete naivety. One might say the same even of John W. Campbell Jr, the editor of *Astounding*

Science Fiction from 1938 to 1971, and a much more familiar and dominant personality, whose stimulation many authors even now remember and acknowledge.[1] Surely if anyone 'shaped' modern science fiction, it was him! Yet, though it is an unanswerable question, one might consider for a moment what would have happened if he had opted for a different career. Many novels and stories would no doubt have come out different. Still, they would have come out. In the face of the millions of words published by scores of magazines and thousands of authors between 1926 and now, one is forced to conclude that even individuals at the centre of the field cannot have exerted more than a certain gravitational influence. Listing dates, titles, anecdotes, and conversations is, in short, an established mode of 'fanzine' chatter. But the real question is not who led science fiction on, but what force generated so many willing followers? Allied to that is the question of whether the compulsive element in science fiction is at all reducible by the conventions of ordinary literary criticism. These are the questions which the essay that follows tries to answer. [. . .]

[Amongst other fictional techniques] the elementary strategy of extrapolation [from real historical events] was tried, and not without success. The United States might find itself in an atomic war: Judith Merril's *Shadow on the Hearth* (1951) combined incongruity with probability by relating the event to an American commuter suburb full of housewives. 'But the war's *over*', says the heroine at the end, as she finally realizes that her little girl's illness comes from her deadly cuddly toy, left out overnight in the radioactive rain. The new phenomenon of 'half-life' is integrated with the new indivisibility of war and peace. Of course the United States could engage in such a war and *lose* (or just not win): this prospect was explored best by Wilson Tucker's *The Long Loud Silence* (1952). Least thinkable of all, the United States, for all its 'minuteman' traditions, could in the new conditions of mass destruction be forced to surrender and face occupation: this was outlined in C.M. Kornbluth's *Not This August* (1955, retitled *Christmas Eve* in the UK). But Kornbluth's novel incidentally demonstrated why all these varieties of 'hot war' might be missing something out. For one of his accepted data − of course Hiroshima-derived − is that if one side gains a sufficient technological lead (e.g. by launching an A-bomb-armed satellite) the other side's fleets and bombs and armoured divisions are all immediately reduced to a value zero. This realization leads to a further point: if technological lead is so important, the drama lies in achieving it, not exploiting it. Wars are now information wars, they are fought in filing cabinets. Or, to quote a character from Eric Frank Russell's *With a Strange Device* (1964), 'In this highly technological age, the deadliest strike one can make against a foe is to deprive him of his brains, whether or not one acquires them oneself.'

By an interesting semantic shift, 'brains' in that quotation has become a count-noun, its singular being 'a brain', and meaning 'a scientist capable of furthering weapons research'. The last clause of the quotation further indicates a long-standing popular phobia, especially in America (though Russell is British); for one could hardly fail to notice either the part played in the development of nuclear fission by German émigrés (Einstein, Frisch, and in rocketry von Braun), or the belief of many that the Russian A-bomb of 1949 came from the same source, with a fillip from Western traitors (such as Fuchs, Nunn May, Greenglass). 'Brains', then, were valuable but treacherous. Russell actually does not develop these notions in this book; the 'strange device' of its title is simply a gimmick, a means of 'automated brain-washing' which makes scientists think they have committed murder and must flee from their jobs, the police, their friends in Military Intelligence. Still, the clashes between state and individual, security agent and scientist, are there in potential in a single sentence. If one combined them with the all-politics-is-science belief and the technological-leads-are-total theory, one had a basic plot of intense importance and even human interest. All of it, furthermore, could be felt, like Heinlein's 'foreign policy' statement and Russell's sentence just quoted, to be fictional but also in essence *true*. These hints and implications were best exploited by Algis Budrys's' famous novel *Who?* (1958, expanded from a short story in *Fantastic Universe*, Apr. 1955).

Its central character is Lucas Martino, a scientist working on something called 'the K-88' — Budry's firm rejection of the 'gimmick' strategy is shown by the fact that we never find out what this might be. It is enough to know that (like anything else from the laboratories) it might turn out to be the one vital thing, the thing that decides all human futures. But Martino's lab in West Germany near the border — this was before the Berlin Wall — blows up, and a Soviet medical team obligingly whisks him off to hospital. What they return is unrecognizable, a man half-metal. Is it Martino, or a Soviet agent trained to impersonate him? If the latter, then Martino is the other side of the wire, and the K-88 may turn out Soviet. One of these days, muses the American Security Chief at the start, his opposite number is going to outwit him critically, 'and everybody's kids'll talk Chinese'. One 'brain' (in this scenario) can outweigh the efforts of the rest of the world. But ever since Korea it had been accepted that everybody cracked, that 'brainwashing' was as certain as a surgical operation — see the *Oxford English Dictionary* entry under 'brainwash' in the *Supplement* of 1972, and further Frederik Pohl and C.M. Kornbluth's story 'The Quaker Cannon' from *ASF* (Dec. 1961 (B.)). Finding out who the metal man is thus becomes very much a fulcrum of destiny. But of course he himself does not see things this way. While *Who?* is in one way a story about technological leads, it is also about the discrepancy between subjective and objective knowledge, about the incapacity of states and security systems to control, predict, or even understand the intelligences on whom their existence depends.

So the FBI dog Martino's every step, try furthermore to find out every detail from his past, to check the one set of actions against the other and determine the presence or absence of a consistent pattern. Their massive filing-cabinet thoroughness is almost a parody of the way scientists are supposed to work, inductively, accumulating facts and waiting for the right truth to emerge. But of course induction by itself never pays off. Though Martino is inductive – he 'couldn't ignore a fact. He judged no fact; he only filed it away' – he also works largely by hypothesis, a habit which often leads him directly to the right conclusion via the traditional 'flash of genius', but which also leads him, in youth, to scores of blind alleys and false structures. These are never discarded entirely: 'Another part of his mind was a storehouse of interesting ideas that hadn't worked, but were interesting – theories that were wild, but had seemed to hold together. To a certain extent, these phantom heresies stayed behind to colour his thinking.' They mean that when it comes to the K-88, he cannot be replaced. They also mean that, in personal terms, the actions of Martino before or after his accident may be perfectly logical to him (and to the reader who shares his mind); to the watchers and investigators, though, they are random, inexplicable.

This thesis keeps *Who?* from dating, even though many of its assumptions have been overtaken by events. It also shifts the story in the direction of fable or parable, stressing the element of general truth contained in the setting of particular fantasy. The central scene of the book is the one in which the metal Martino returns to visit one of the two girl-acquaintances of his youth, Edith, now a widow with one son. All through his adolescence the peculiar logic of his mind has made it hard for him to form ordinary relationships. Now his half-metal body reflects and magnifies his inner strangeness. Can he get back to one of the few people he ever understood? The FBI men on their microphones wait with baited breath. But the answer never comes, for though Martino and Edith seem for a moment to recognize and understand each other, her little son, waking up, sees only a nightmare monster. Pursued by his screaming, Martino leaves, collides with a girl, sees in her (momentarily and erroneously) his *other* girl-acquaintance, tries to introduce himself – and terrifies her, too, into panic. Driven by his mechanical heart, he rushes away down the street, the FBI trailing behind him in an ineffectual and (for one of them) fatal attempt to keep up. Their exhaustive enquiries afterwards never reveal what happened, nor (since naturally they cannot see the girl's resemblance to the now-forgotten Barbara) what triggered Martino's reaction. His phrase of self-introduction — '*Barbara — e io — il tedeschino*' — becomes a personal analogue of the K-88, forever beyond explanation except in Martino's mind.

The interpretation of this 'Frankenstein's monster' scene is evident enough. Martino is an image of the scientist post-1945. Both are figures of enormous and world-changing power; yet both remain mortal, isolated, vulnerable. Both would like to be loved, and yet both terrify people through no fault of their own; they are bitterly hurt by ordinary reactions. Martino's clumsily powerful rush down the street, one might think, is a kind of image of the 'arms race' itself. Meanwhile the security men who watch with increasing bafflement and impotence, who are always trying to catch up and never to head off (because they never know where Martino is going), *they* represent the attempts of average men and normal politics to come to terms with the technology they have sponsored, though not created. Naturally, putting it all in these allegorical terms seems over-complicated and may not have been 'designed in' by the author. Still, it is in general there, in essence understood. [. . .] The moral of *Who?* is that in scientific matters security systems are counter-productive (as useless as the descent of Military Intelligence on *Astounding* back in 1944). Admittedly, the fear that generates them is entirely explicable too, so there may be no cure. Still, the G-man and the genius are now yin and yang, growing out of each other but fundamentally opposed. In a sense the most daring theme to which science-fiction authors were attracted during the 1950s was that of inner treason: the obligation to resist at once the Federal government and constitutional processes.

For there had been more than one 'Cold War' going on within the United States. The true date of hell's birthday — according to a character in Wilson Tucker's *The Time Masters* (1953, also published in abridged form in *Startling Stories*, 1954) — was neither 6 August 1945 (Hiroshima) nor 16 July 1945 (Alamogordo), but 8 March 1940. On or about that date 'the President set up the National Defense Research Committee; both the Manhattan District and our organization grew out of that'. What 'our organization' is never appears clearly, but Tucker is thinking of such events as the creation of the CIA in July 1947, the Bill for FBI investigation of Atomic Energy Commission applicants in August 1949, the ban on sending technical publications to the Soviet bloc in March the same year, and a series of other moves in the direction of tight control over atomic power. All this was highly illiberal. But the complaint voiced by Tucker and other science-fiction writers was that it was unrealistic, too. They knew that whatever its etymology 'science' was not the same as 'knowledge'; the 'Deadline' affair had shown there was no need of a security leak to tell people about U-235 and critical mass. So you could not keep 'secrets' this side of the Iron Curtain just by restricting the passage of information. To quote Tucker again: 'There are only two kinds of men in all the world who still believe there are keepable secrets in modern science! One of those men is the blind, awkward and fumbling politician . . . The other man is a jealous researcher . . . Realistic secrecy in modern science is a farce.' The new exemplar of the clown, one might add, is the security agent trying to censor references to data which can be revealed by experiment.

There is no doubt here that science fiction was correct, nor that it was opposing a powerful orthodoxy. J. Robert Oppenheimer ('the father of the atomic bomb') had said 'you cannot keep the nature of the world a secret', and Eisenhower in 1945 had agreed with him, suggesting that the USA should make a virtue of necessity and share nuclear information, so aborting the arms race. But both were readily outvoted. By November 1945 the US had decided not to share nuclear technology with Britain and Canada, who had helped to develop it. Because it was thought that this decision settled matters many politicians were horrified by the Russian nuclear explosion of 1949. An easy explanation was treason. Loyalty investigations got fiercer, and the Rosenbergs were sentenced to death in March 1951. Meanwhile the real secret of the hydrogen bomb had been revealed on television by a US senator trying to educate the nation in security! By a final irony Oppenheimer himself (who appeared in 'Murray Leinster's' *The Brain Stealers* (1947) as the head of a security system dedicated to keeping nuclear technology safe) had been tried and convicted in a case seen by many as a trial of the United States. The phobia over nuclear security was there before Senator McCarthy, and went straight back to the unpredictability-trauma of 1945. Its development showed once more the split between those who felt science was still a human endeavour and those who saw it as a djinn to be stuffed back in the bottle. As McCarthyism advanced, science fiction became increasingly angry and sarcastic.

One can, for instance, turn over the pages of *Astounding* during the worst of the arms-race years and see one story after another about security: 'Security Risk', by Poul Anderson (May 1957 (B.)), 'Security', by Ernest M. Kenyon (Mar. 1956 (B.)), 'A Matter of Security', by W.T. Haggert (July 1957 (B.)). Others present the theme under less obvious titles. In Poul Anderson's 'Sam Hall' (Aug. 1953), the Major in charge of Central Records in a near-future state broods over the 'Europeanization of America: government control, a military caste . . . censors, secret police, nationalism and racism'. All this has been created by a Third World War the US lost, with a consequent *revanche* in the Fourth

World War leading to world domination. The Major himself has a relation arrested by Security. To protect himself he rubs him out of the
records, then creates a fictitious rebel 'Sam Hall' as a kind of therapy.
The fiction comes to life (not in any supernatural sense) and cannot be
caught because Security itself breeds rebels and traitors — as it has done
with the Major. The point of the story is again the self-fulfilment of
fear. Analogous or complementary points are made by the other stories
listed. They insist that the United States has no moral or natural right
to its technological leads, and that attempts to impose the contrary
opinion will lead only to stagnation and totalitarianism. Security systems are the delusions of people who had not understood the nature of
scientific discovery before 1945, and had learnt nothing since. Science
is a tool, not a (dammable) reservoir of knowledge.

Following on this, or overlapping with it, came a further point about
the nature of discovery: if science is not the same as knowledge, it is
also not to be identified with truth. To put it another way, science does
not progress additively any more than discovery works by induction.
To advance, one has to discard. The true obstacle to development may
then be that what needs discarding is deeply integrated in personalities
and academic systems, too familiar to be challenged. In this view, the
intellectual equivalents to security chiefs may well be senior research-
ers — both groups are committed to the *status quo* which has brought
them eminence. A basic plot along these lines is given in Raymond F.
Jones's novelette 'Noise Level' (*ASF*, Dec. 1952).

This begins, conventionally enough, with Dr Nagle, the expert in
electronics, sitting in the anteroom of the Office of National Research
while his colleagues try to get him security clearance to attend the vital
conference to which he has been summoned [. . .] by the Office of
National Research to inform senior physicists that antigravity has been
discovered and demonstrated; there are films, tapes, and eye-witness
accounts to prove it. Unfortunately, an accident has killed the inventor
and mangled his apparatus before the secret could be disclosed. The
physicists' job is to make the rediscovery. But there is a distracting
factor: the original inventor was close to madness, with a compulsive
belief in levitation, mysticism, astrology, etc. and a reluctance to accept
convention of any kind. Clues to his invention may lie in one of the
'mad' areas rather than one of the 'sane' ones.

'This was a project in psychology, not physics', observes its control-
ler at the end. His physicists have in fact polarized. One faction, represented by Nagle, has accepted the real-life data offered and concluded
that, since antigravity is ruled out by the state of scientific knowledge,
something in that knowledge must be wrong: they identify Einstein's
'postulate of equivalence' as the root error, and by rewriting it manage
to produce a feeble, clumsy, hundred-ton antigravity device (their films

had shown a one-man flying harness). At the other extreme Dr Dykstra of MIT insists that the whole thing — and especially the stuff about levitation! — cannot be true, eventually retreating into madness himself when his premises become untenable. The irony is that Dr Dykstra is in a practical sense right. The whole thing *has* been a fraud, concocted by the Office of National Research, its mainspring being the notion that invention is checked not by ignorance but by prior assumptions. To give the analogy of the psychologist-director: (1) all information can be expressed in a series of pulses, and is therefore contained in 'pure noise'; (2) 'there must be in the human mind a mechanism which is nothing but a pure noise generator, a producer of random impulses, pure omniscient noise'; (3) and somewhere else in the human mind there is a filtering mechanism set by education to reject 'all but a bare minimum of data presented by the external universe, and [by] our internal creativeness as well'. Nagle has managed to override the filter; Dykstra has had in the end to shut out all the noise. [. . .]

Just as Algis Budrys in some ways paralleled the ideas of Karl Popper, so 'Noise Level' anticipated the central thesis of Thomas Kuhn's later much-admired book *The Structure of Scientific Revolutions* (1962), offering a proto-structuralist view of science as an activity in practice culture-bound, though in potential (science fiction's fundamental loyalty) infinite. In one form or another, discrepancy between this potential and this practice became a staple of science-fiction plotting: the characters embodying one side tended to be government officials, senior professors, security agents, and politicians, those on the other crackpots, engineers, social misfits, and businessmen — anyone, in short, more interested in results than explanations. The theme is a good one: it relates to reality as well as to wish-fulfilment; perhaps the main criticism one can make of it is that, in the 'participatory' world of science-fiction magazines, it leads easily to a kind of paranoia, in which the underlying statements about the world and those who run it turn sour and strident. [. . .] Readers of *Astounding* were evidently encouraged to see themselves as the leaven and the rest of America as the lump. [. . .] The 'ghettoizing' of science fiction was not entirely imposed from without. If general readers, even after the A-bomb, kept on thinking of science-fiction fans as 'escapist' or 'unrealistic', many writers and readers inside the genre responded equally thoughtlessly by regarding the bulk of their own society as mistaken, ill-informed, and probably ineducable. They had a point, in the 1950s. But they took it too far.

A better-judged example of the same reaction can be seen in James Blish's in retrospect highly courageous book *Year 2018!* (British title *They Shall Have Stars*, published first in 1956, in Britain, but going back in outline to two more *Astounding* novelettes, 'Bridge' (Feb. 1952) and 'At Death's End' (May 1954).) The audacity of this is shown by the fact that even the earlier version contained a perfectly recognizable caricature of Senator McCarthy in the guise of 'Senator Francis Xavier MacHinery, hereditary head of the FBI.' The expanded version began, furthermore, with two Americans deliberately plotting treason: one, Senator Wagoner, the other, Dr Corsi, senior member of the American Association for the Advancement of Science, 'usually referred to in Washington', remarks Blish in evident allusion to the Oppenheimer affair, 'as "the left-wing triple-A-S" '. The speakers' discussion dovetails neatly into a joint politico-scientific opinion: the USSR has *won* the Cold War (this is Wagoner, by the end of the book), and it has done so because 'scientific method doesn't work any more' (Corsi, at the start). As another quasi-true statement this aphorism is particularly provocative: scientific *method* is supposed to work everywhere. But it's not a natural law, argues Blish/Corsi, only 'a way of sifting evidence', a new kind of syllogism. The reasons it need not work in the twenty-first century are, first the control of technical information, and second the low quality of those drawn to government research (familiar notions in science fiction, as has been said), but third, the nature of the facts eventually under investigation – increasingly subtle ones, to be proved only by experiments of increasingly fantastic cost. This view (not entirely without prophetic force, as one can see from the NASA experience) means that Manhattan District Projects will have to stop. It is the crackpot ideas that must be winnowed now, the rejected hypotheses, the notions that are not senseless but out of style. The rebellions that Wagoner and Corsi lead are against scientific method and the 'McCarthyite' US. Behind them lie deeper loyalties to empiricism and to Western tradition, labelled though these may be (in 2018 or 1957) as treason and folly.

The projects set up finally eventuate as the 'gravitron polarity generator' or 'spindizzy' and the 'anti-agathic drugs' which halt old age; the two between them make interstellar flight a possibility. They also lead to disaster within the world of the novel. The impact of anti-agathics will destroy the West, and the Soviets only marginally later. The fact that such initiatives have been concealed will give power to MacHinery and his associates, whose suspicions (like Dr Dykstra's) will for once turn out to be true. Both originators of the new initiative will die by torture, Dr Corsi without knowing what he has brought to life, and Wagoner by the standard treason-penalty of immersion in the waste-dump of a radioactive pile. 'It's a phony terror', says Wagoner. 'Pile wastes are quick chemical poisons; you don't last long enough to notice that they're also hot.' Still, the macabre vindictiveness of the notion offers a final opinion on the 'decline of the West' that Blish foresees, on the long-term effects of victory at Hiroshima, on the way the Cold War could be fought and lost. It took courage to offer such a picture of America in the mid-1950s, when the Korean War was over, the Vietnamese one not yet on, and when the Strategic Air Command still held more than the balance of power. Even more daring, though, was the rejection of 'scientific method' and official physics so soon after their most apparent triumph. Science-fiction authors have often been accused of letting themselves be mesmerized by mere technology. *Year 2018!*, however, shows one of them shaking off the glamour of nuclear power and the Manhattan Project while the rest of America was still trying to adjust to it. The rejection is as creditable, as implausible, as Heinlein's equally unnoticed predictions only a decade and a half before.

All the stories discussed so far have their roots in a critique of the relationship between science and society. The latter either cannot control the former (as in 'Solution Unsatisfactory'), or else breaks it in the attempt at control (as in *Who?*), or else provokes it into rebellion (as in *Year 2018!*). Failure of comprehension is embodied in the two emasculating theses of science as a body of information (some of it 'classified'), and of science as revealed truth to be dispensed through the educational system by the proper authorities. And yet in spite of all these antagonisms science was much more deeply integrated with society than the latter liked to admit. In science fiction this last notion is expressed by the aphorism 'steam-engine time'. 'When a culture has reached the point when it's time for the steam-engine to be invented', lectures a character from Raymond F. Jones's 'The School' (*ASF*, May 1955 (B.)), 'the steam-engine is going to be invented. It doesn't matter who's alive to do the inventing, whether it's Hero of Greece, or Tim Watt of England, or Joe Doakus of Pulaski — the steam-engine is going to get invented by somebody. Conversely, if it's not steam-engine time nobody under the sun is going to invent it no matter how smart he is.'

This opinion contradicts a popular stereotype of the Great Inventor, promoted in the movies about Young Tom Edison which attract Budrys's scorn, and in the 'rituals of mass entertainment' pilloried in one of the epigraphs to *Year 2018!* — the 'hero-scientist . . . discovered in a lonely laboratory crying "Eureka" at a murky test-tube'. But the *raison d'être* of that stereotype is that it makes it easy to fix responsibility on single men or single events. 'It is steamboat time', says someone at the end of Harry Harrison's *In Our Hands, the Stars* (*ASF* serial, Dec. 1969-Feb. 1970); but he says it sadly, because the deadly and plausible image of science as one man's secret has led the security agents of many nations (the US and Israel prominent among them) to join in a multiple fatal hijacking of the new spaceliner built by

Denmark and employing the 'Daleth Effect'. The irony is that the secret was no secret all along. The discoverer's data were freely available. Once other scientists had the clues of knowing what had been done and who had done it, they could duplicate his work and even make his 'Effect' commercial; they were about to do the latter just as the hijack started. 'Steamboat time' means that the deaths were all pointless. And this is not just a fantasy, Harrison insists (via his character). The Japanese independently re-invented radar, magnetron and all, in this way during the Second World War; and as Wilson Tucker had said much earlier, Russian production of the A-bomb followed exactly the same pattern. 'Stimulus diffusion' is a fact of the modern world, not merely an anthropologist's curiosity. But people prefer to think of science as a kind of magic controllable only by individual adepts, because it gives them idols/scapegoats – Einstein, or Oppenheimer.

So what *is* the mutual responsibility of the individual innovator and the society that makes his innovation possible? Several approaches to this question are visible in 1950s science fiction. [. . .] The many social satires or 'dystopias' published during the period tend to share one opinion, which is that the self-images of society are so powerful and so delusive that they channel rebellion just as much as they channel innovation. The heroes of Frederik Pohl and C.M. Kornbluth's *The Space Merchants* (1953, originally serialized in *Galaxy* as 'Gravy Planet', 1952) and of Kurt Vonnegut's *Player Piano* (1952) both start as agents of the system, and have to be virtually excommunicated from it before they can think of going into opposition. Deep in the core of the former book's assumptions, too, is the argument that just as the 'Consies' or Conservationists are necessary scapegoats of the consumer society, so the 'Commies', or forever-rumoured, forever-invisible American Communist traitors of the McCarthy era, are figments of the capitalist imagination, part of a drama which American society has written for itself, and into whose villain-roles weak characters are drawn or thrust. However, full consideration of that issue would lead us away from weapon-makers and towards weapon-users. It is a point that the two are related: the A-bomb was publicly accountable, even if secretly produced. But *next* time that something like the A-bomb came up, where would a future Einstein's duty lie? It is this narrower question which underlies the Harry Harrison novel just mentioned; and also, more surprisingly, many of the 'telepathy' stories published during this period in *Astounding* and elsewhere.

Signs of it can be seen even in such an apparently low-level story as Eric Frank Russell's *Three to Conquer* (1956, serialized in *ASF* as *Call Him Dead*, Aug.-Oct. 1955). This opens with a man, a telepath, 'hearing' in his mind the dying call of a shot policeman. He goes to help, tracks down evidence of what seems to be an interrupted kidnapping, and then, when he comes on the 'kidnapped' girl, shoots her dead. Her mind was projecting alien gabble; her body had been taken over by a parasite-organism from space. The rest of the story is devoted, very naturally, to fighting off the invasion. Yet it is, queerly, almost comic in tone, marked by the habitual irreverence of its hero, Wade Harper. He never obeys orders, always answers back, takes deliberate pleasure in waving at generals when he should salute them. Childish behaviour, especially for a telepath? The story itself insists that it is not. During the first few pages, for instance, we keep hearing, over the radio, of the apparently unrelated battle going on between the US government and the 'Lunar Development Company'. 'According to the latter the government was trying to use its Earth-Moon transport monopoly to bludgeon the L.D.C. into handing itself over complete with fat profits. The L.D.C. was fighting back. It was the decades-old struggle of private enterprise against bureaucratic interference.' One might note, again, the characteristic switch from definite fiction to hypothetical fact. What has this to do with Harper? Nothing immediate: but he sees himself analogously as a man under threat, one who will (from his job as a microforger) become 'federal property the moment war breaks out'; and will become it even sooner if they know he can read minds! The Venusian emergency makes him declare himself, but nothing less would have. And his continuous irreverence is a form of protest against government infringements of liberty.

There is something slightly crazy about this, even (much worse in science-fiction criminology) contra-survival. After all it is sheer chance that the one telepath in the US crosses the invaders' trail right at the outset. The odds were against it, they were even more against Harper as private citizen being able to undo the effects of (say) Soviet telepathic espionage managed by their more autocratic government. Surely Harper should know his public duty, indeed his duty to science. But Russell suppresses this obvious line of argument in favour of appeal to anti-government sentiment, and — traditional *Astounding* train of thought — to a continuing equation of government with social repression, conservatism, scientific orthodoxy. Harper's conversations with scientists are punctuated by their cries of 'Impossible!' 'Unthinkable!', while the FBI repeatedly let him down through their rigid obedience to orders. Both groups, though, are only manifesting an attitude which Harper (and Russell) see as essentially human — fear of the unknown, a wish to shut it out or deny its existence rather than make it a part of one's world. [. . .] Harper is 'in hiding'. That's where innovators ought to stay.

The 'in hiding' theme relates closely to the 'noise level' one and that of 'stimulus diffusion', as well as to the stories about the failure of Security. They all assume that education is essentially education in acceptability, that society acts as a governor on human minds to prevent them realizing their full potential, and that some similar mechanism triggers hate-and-fear reactions in those who detect novelty. 'In Hiding' itself is a story by Wilmar H. Shiras, published in *ASF* (Nov. 1948), and one of the many examples of amateur authors articulating one classic theme and never succeeding – or trying – again. It deals with the discovery of a super-intelligent child by a sympathetic psychologist, rather like Olaf Stapledon's *Odd John* thirteen years before. [. . .] However, the most thorough development of the theme – the book is dedicated to 'Paul Breen, wherever he may be hiding' – comes in Wilson Tucker's *Wild Talent*, serialized in *New Worlds* (Aug.-Oct. 1954): Superman versus the government.

The central irony of this book is that Paul Breen, the telepath, the 'new man', is by nature a loyalist. Like Russell's Wade Harper, he first displays his telepathic talent by hearing the call of a dying man – in this case an FBI agent or G-man (symbolic figure!) shot by the villains he is pursuing. But Breen, unlike Harper, is still only a boy, still 'in hiding'. With complete confidence, however, he writes down what he knows and posts the letter, covered in fingerprints, to:

The President,
The White House,
Washington, D.C.

Eleven years later, in 1945, they get him. Drafted into the army, he has his fingerprints checked against the FBI's files with the massive, routine thoroughness then (as in *Who?*) ascribed to this organization. His secret penetrated, he too becomes 'federal property'. But they don't like him. If 'brains' are valuable but potentially treacherous, 'brain-readers' are bound to be a good deal worse.[. . .]

The mixture of exploitation and anxiety mirrors reactions to the A-bomb itself. Its compulsive nature provides a sort of excuse for society; but then one is needed, for in an obvious way *Wild Talent* is a story of disillusionment. Its hero begins as a normal go-getting teenager riding the rails to the 1934 Century of Progress Exhibition in Chicago. By the end he has chosen exile, alienated by the collapse of all his early father-figures (the President, the FBI), and even more by his government's disregard of his own rights, the continuous 'bugging' by no means compensated by occasional pandering. And yet in a sense the American ideal remains intact. Mutant and superman himself, Breen nevertheless retains a respect for some of his associates, and a deeper, undervalued feeling for the *mores* of his youth – thrift, work, privacy, 'dating', and so on. 'We can't come here again', he says regretfully to his telepath fiancée at the end, as they wait for the escape boat. But she disagrees, and has the final word. To translate back into real-life terms, Tucker seems to be arguing that though contemporary societies are not fit to be trusted with new powers (whether nuclear or tele-pathic), this may nevertheless be a temporary phenomenon sprung from fear and militarization, not a universal law. Hate-and-fear reactions should not be provoked — and that is why Superman goes 'into hiding' — but may be overridden. [. . .] What should have emerged from this essay is that the fantastic elements of the stories were a cover, or a frame, for discussion of many real issues which were hardly open to serious consideration in any other popular medium: issues such as the nature of science, the conflict of business and government, the limits of loyalty, the power of social norms to affect individual perception. It is this which science-fiction fans felt they could not get anywhere else; this which accounts for the horde of 'willing followers' shoving writers and editors on. Of course a great quantity of science fiction was *not* about these themes, but dealt with robots, mutants, aliens, starships, asteroids, time-travellers, or any one of twenty other plot motifs. It would be a mistake, though, to think that even these did not contain a high proportion of serious thought, with a reference to real life not beyond recovery. Even more than most literature, science fiction shows a strong conventional quality which makes its signs and symbols interpretable only through familiarity; to instance only matters touched on above, it was a provocative act to polarize *Odd John* into 'Crazy Joey', while after so many novels (*The Space Merchants, Wild Talent, Year 2018!*) had ended with innovators escaping from govern-ments, it was a striking move by Harry Harrison to make *In Our Hands, the Stars* start with the same scene — and with the innovator's know-ledge that his government was going to come after him. It is this con-ventional quality which makes literary criticism difficult, and fore-dooms to failure the search for isolated fictional pearls. But the same stylization makes it possible to see much science fiction of the 1940s and 1950s, and later, as a 'thinking machine' for the convenience of people largely without academic support or intellectual patronage. This view further explains and excuses the attitude of the thousands of fans to whom the genre appears to be Bible, King's Regulations, and Consti-tution all in one. Does it allow science fiction to qualify as 'literature'? Possibly not. Nevertheless, it does ask questions as to what one means by literature, and as to whether the conventional categories of criticism can afford to leave out so much material uniting such vitality with such serious enquiry. To these considerations professional educators have not yet framed an adequate or accepted reply.

Note

1. *Astounding Science Fiction* changed its name to *Analog: Science Fact/ Science Fiction* in Jan. 1960, an interesting fact in itself. References to either title are abbreviated in this essay as *ASF*. A further difficulty is caused by the fact that up to Sept. 1963 the American edition of this magazine was followed a few months later by a slightly different British one. References are given to the American edition where possible: those to the British edition are marked (B.).

INDEX

This book covers popular culture in
Britain since the early nineteenth century.
Popular Culture is a term of wide application,
varying according to social perspective, and
in this book it is seen as a shifting region
within a historical and cultural totality where
cultural domination, negotiation and
exchange take place. The approach is inter-
disciplinary, tracing the history of and
attitudes towards all kinds of leisure
activities up until the present day.

The book is divided into two sections.
The first brings together a number of
contributions illustrating the historical
development of popular culture in Britain
between the early nineteenth century and
the Second World War. These concern both
societal, cultural phenomena – such as
literacy and class consciousness – and more
specific and concrete popular cultural forms
– such as the music hall and late nineteenth-
century science fiction. The second section
brings together a number of 'readings' of
contemporary popular cultural phenomena
as diverse as motor-cycle gangs, *Jackie*
magazine and children's confectionary, and
here the intention is to illustrate modes of
cultural analysis in concrete and accessible
ways.

Although primarily designed to support
the Open University inter-disciplinary course
on Popular Culture (U203), this book will
appeal to all those interested in such associated
topics as the history and sociology of
leisure and media and communication
studies.

Bernard Waites is a Research Fellow in
the Department of History at the Open
University, Milton Keynes.

Tony Bennett is Chairman of the Open
University 'Popular Culture' Course Team.

Graham Martin is Professor of Literature
in the Faculty of Arts at the Open University.

Jacket illustration by Dave Henderson.

Routledge
11 New Fetter Lane
London EC4P 4EE

29 West 35th Street
New York NY 10001

ISBN 0-415-04033-1

9 780415 040334